Cultures of Resistance in the Hellenistic East

Cultures of Resistance in the Hellenistic East

Edited by
PAUL J. KOSMIN AND IAN S. MOYER

OXFORD
UNIVERSITY PRESS

Great Clarendon Street, Oxford, OX2 6DP,
United Kingdom

Oxford University Press is a department of the University of Oxford.
It furthers the University's objective of excellence in research, scholarship,
and education by publishing worldwide. Oxford is a registered trade mark of
Oxford University Press in the UK and in certain other countries

© Oxford University Press 2022

The moral rights of the authors have been asserted

First Edition published in 2022

Impression: 2

All rights reserved. No part of this publication may be reproduced, stored in
a retrieval system, or transmitted, in any form or by any means, without the
prior permission in writing of Oxford University Press, or as expressly permitted
by law, by licence or under terms agreed with the appropriate reprographics
rights organization. Enquiries concerning reproduction outside the scope of the
above should be sent to the Rights Department, Oxford University Press, at the
address above

You must not circulate this work in any other form
and you must impose this same condition on any acquirer

Published in the United States of America by Oxford University Press
198 Madison Avenue, New York, NY 10016, United States of America

British Library Cataloguing in Publication Data

Data available

Library of Congress Control Number: 2022931931

ISBN 978-0-19-286347-8

DOI:10.1093/oso/9780192863478.001.0001

Printed and bound in the UK by
TJ Books Limited

Links to third party websites are provided by Oxford in good faith and
for information only. Oxford disclaims any responsibility for the materials
contained in any third party website referenced in this work.

Preface

This volume represents the final results of 'The Maccabean Moment' conference held 18–20 January 2016 at the Center for Hellenic Studies in Washington DC. At this gathering, a range of specialists in the history, literature, and archaeology of the Hellenistic Near East and North Africa undertook a collaborative and dialogical examination of resistance to the major Hellenistic kingdoms, with a particular focus on the well-known and roughly contemporary crises of the second century BCE. The conference had two primary goals: (1) to re-assess the role of local cultural norms in the dynamics of resistance and re-integrate that dimension into the predominantly sociological analyses of recent decades, and (2) to discuss the extent to which a globalizing framework – both comparative and connective – could produce integrated accounts of resistance that emerge not only out of the cosmopolitan 'internationalism' of the large Hellenistic territorial states, but also from the positions and perspectives taken by the indigenous subjects of these states. Presenting papers at the original conference were: Andrea Berlin, Laurent Capdetrey, Matthew Canepa, Erich S. Gruen, Johannes Haubold, Sharon Herbert, Sylvie Honigman, Paul J. Kosmin, Rachel Mairs, Ian S. Moyer, Kathryn Stevens, Daniel Tober, and Anne-Emmanuelle Veïsse. Clifford Ando offered stimulating and thoughtful responses to these presentations. Charles Bartlett, Alexandra Creola, Anna Leah Kincaid, Monica Park, and Elliot Wilson introduced and moderated the panels. As organizers and editors, we would like to thank all those who came to Washington and took up our challenging questions with such energy, insight, and generosity. These efforts, together with all the subsequent work of revision and refinement, have succeeded in tracing out subtle contours in the cultural landscape of resistance, creating a varied picture of both connections and disjunctures within and beyond the original 'moment' of the conference.

The success of the conference would not have been possible without the support of Gregory Nagy and the Center for Hellenic Studies and the organizational virtuosity of Sarah Banse, Lanah Koelle, and the other staff from the Center for Hellenic Studies. We are also grateful for the support of Harvard's Weatherhead Center for International Affairs and the Lasky-Barajas Dean's Innovation Fund for Digital Arts and Humanities. Technical wizardry and collaboration allowed the remote attendance of undergraduate and graduate students from the University of Michigan and we would like to thank the staff of the Center for Hellenic Studies and of the University of Michigan College of Literature, Science, and the Arts Instructional Support Services. We would also like to thank Charles Bartlett for his work in transcribing the conference question-and-answer sessions.

Finally, we are grateful to the anonymous reviewers for Oxford University Press who provided incisive and productive comments on the manuscript, Charlotte Loveridge, our editor, who provided unfailing professional guidance to us throughout this process, and, above all, all the contributors for their hard work and commitment to seeing this project through to its conclusion.

Contents

Contributors   ix
Abbreviations   xiii

   Introduction   1
   Paul J. Kosmin and Ian S. Moyer

I. THE BIG EVENTS: PATTERN AND CRISIS

1. The Maccabean Model: Resistance or Adjustment?   33
   Erich S. Gruen

2. The 'Great Theban Revolt', 206–186 BCE   57
   Anne-Emmanuelle Veïsse

II. THE GROUNDS FOR RESISTANCE

3. Memory and Resistance in the Seleucid World: The Case of Babylon   77
   Johannes Haubold

4. 'After Him a King Will Arise': Framing Resistance in Seleucid Babylonia   95
   Kathryn Stevens

5. Diverging Memories, Not Resistance Literature: The Maccabean Crisis in the Animal Apocalypse and 1 and 2 Maccabees   125
   Sylvie Honigman

6. Revolts, Resistance, and the Materiality of the Moral Order in Ptolemaic Egypt   148
   Ian S. Moyer

III. THE EDGES OF RESISTANCE

7. An Impossible Resistance? Anatolian Populations, Ethnicity, and Greek Powers in Asia Minor during the Second Century BCE 177
   Laurent Capdetrey

8. 'Herakles is stronger, Seleucus': Local History and Local Resistance in Pontic Herakleia 203
   Daniel Tober

9. Central Asian Challenges to Seleucid Authority: Synchronism, Correlation, and Causation as Historiographical Devices in Justin's *Epitome* of Trogus 231
   Rachel Mairs

Bibliography 247
Index 295

Contributors

Laurent Capdetrey is professor of Greek history at the University of Bordeaux Montaigne. His work focuses mainly on the Hellenistic world, in particular on the history and organisation of the kingdoms in Asia Minor and in the eastern regions. He is especially interested in the question of the construction of powers and territories, and is the author of *Le pouvoir séleucide. Territoire, administration, finances d'un royaume hellénistique (312-129 av. J-C.)* (2007), and *L'Asie Mineure après Alexandre (vers 323—vers 270 a.C.). L'invention du monde hellénistique* (2021).

Erich S. Gruen is Gladys Rehard Wood Professor of History and Classics, Emeritus, at the University of California, Berkeley. He works in Greek, Roman, and Jewish history. His books include *Diaspora: Jews Amidst Greeks and Romans* (2002), *Rethinking the Other in Antiquity* (2011), *Constructs of Identity in Hellenistic Judaism* (2018), and *Ethnicity in the Ancient World: Did it Matter?* (2020). Current articles in press include 'Nationhood: Was There Such a Thing in Antiquity?' 'Religious Pluralism in the Roman Empire', and 'The Origins of the Jewish War Against Rome'.

Johannes Haubold is Professor of Classics at Princeton University. He has published extensively on the literature and culture of Hellenistic Babylon: his publications include *Greece and Mesopotamia: Dialogues in Literature* (2013), *The World of Berossos* (edited with Giovanni-Battista Lanfranchi, Robert Rollinger, and John Steele, 2013), and *Keeping Watch in Babylon: The Astronomical Diaries in Context* (ed. with John Steele and Kathryn Stevens, 2019).

Sylvie Honigman is Professor of ancient history at Tel Aviv University and specializes in the history and literature of the Hellenistic world. She has published numerous studies on Judea and Judean literature in their transregional context and on Judeans in Egypt and their literary production in context. She is the author of *The Septuagint and Homeric Scholarship in Alexandria: Study in the Narrative of the 'Letter of Aristeas'* (2003) and *Tales of High Priests and Taxes: The Books of the Maccabees and the Judean Rebellion Against Antiochus IV* (2014).

Paul J. Kosmin is Philip J. King Professor of Ancient History at Harvard University. The core of his work to date has focused on the political, cultural, and intellectual history of the east Mediterranean and west Asia in the Hellenistic period. He is the author of *The Land of the Elephant Kings: Space, Territory, and Ideology in the Seleucid Empire* (2014), *Time and Its Adversaries in the Seleucid Empire* (2018), and co-editor, with Andrea Berlin, of *Spear-Won Land: Sardis from the King's Peace to the Peace of Apamea* (2020) and *The Middle Maccabees: Archaeology, History, and the Rise of the Hasmonean Kingdom* (2021).

Rachel Mairs is Professor of Classics and Middle Eastern Studies at the University of Reading. Her research centres on the interaction between Greeks and other ethno-linguistic groups in the Hellenistic world, with a particular emphasis on Egypt and on Central Asia. As well as the ancient world, she also has research interests in the nineteenth-century Middle East. She is the author of *The Hellenistic Far East* (2014), *The Dragoman Solomon Negima and his Clients* (2016) and editor of *The Graeco-Bactrian and Indo-Greek World* (2020).

Ian S. Moyer is Associate Professor in the Department of History at the University of Michigan, Ann Arbor. His work ranges across the fields of history, classics, Egyptology, and the history of religions, and addresses questions of culture, identity, and agency in cross-cultural interactions. He is the author of *Egypt and the Limits of Hellenism* (2011) and editor (with Adam Lecznar and Heidi Morse) of *Classicisms in the Black Atlantic* (2020). In his current research, he is examining the gates and forecourt areas of Ptolemaic Egyptian temples as public sites of political and cultural interaction.

Kathryn Stevens is Associate Professor in Greek History at Corpus Christi College, Oxford. She specialises in Greek and Babylonian cultural and intellectual history, with a particular focus on the Hellenistic period. Her monograph, *Between Greece and Babylonia: Hellenistic Intellectual History in Cross-Cultural Perspective* (2019) examines connections between Hellenistic Greek and Babylonian scholarship and argues for a cross-cultural approach to Hellenistic intellectual history. She has also published on libraries, Seleucid kingship, and ancient celestial scholarship, including an edited volume on the Babylonian Astronomical Diaries with Johannes Haubold and John Steele (*Keeping Watch in Babylon: The Astronomical Diaries in Context*, 2019).

Daniel Tober is Assistant Professor of the Classics at Colgate University. He specializes in Hellenistic history and historiography, with a focus on Greek local histories. He has published a number of articles and book chapters on this topic, including '*Politeiai* and Spartan Local History' (*Historia*, 2010), 'Greek Local Historiography and its Audiences' (*Classical Quarterly* 2017), and 'Greek Local History and the Shape of the Past' in W. Pohl and V. Wieser (eds.), *Ancient and*

Early Christian Narratives of Community (2019). He is currently finishing work on a monograph, *The Autobiographical Polis: Community and History in Classical and Hellenistic Greece.*

Anne-Emmanuelle Veïsse is Professor of Ancient History at the Gustave Eiffel University, Paris. Her research focuses on the political and social history of Hellenistic Egypt. She is the author of *Les "révoltes égyptiennes". Recherches sur les troubles intérieurs en Égypte du règne de Ptolémée III à la conquête romaine* (2004). Her most recent publications include articles on political violence in Alexandria, the foreign policy of the Ptolemies, and relations between the Ptolemies and Egyptian priests.

Abbreviations

ADART   A. Sachs and H. Hunger, *Astronomical Diaries and Related Texts from Babylonia* (6 vols). Vienna, 1988–1996.
BCHP   I. Finkel and R. J. van der Spek, *Babylonian Chronicles of the Hellenistic Period* (preliminary online editions at www.livius.org/cg-cm/chronicles/chron00.html).
BNJ   I. Worthington (ed.), *Brill's New Jacoby*. Leiden: Brill.
CAD   *The Assyrian Dictionary of the Oriental Institute of the University of Chicago* (21 vols). Chicago, 1986–2010.
FGrHist   F. Jacoby, *Fragmente der Griechischen Historiker*. Leiden: Brill.
RE   G. Wissowa, *Paulys Real-Encyclopädie der classischen Altertumswissenschaft*. Neue Bearbeitung. Stuttgar: Metzler.

Abbreviations for classical textual sources follow the conventions of the *Oxford Classical Dictionary*. For biblical texts, standard abbreviations are used (for which see the *Chicago Manual of Style*). Papyrus documents are cited according to the standard abbreviations, which may be found in the *Checklist of Editions of Greek, Latin, Demotic, and Coptic Papyri, Ostraca, and Tablets* (https://papyri.info/docs/checklist). For the standard abbreviations of Greek inscriptions see the *Supplementum Epigraphicum Graecum*.

Introduction

Paul J. Kosmin and Ian S. Moyer

1. Contexts

The Maccabean Revolt against Seleucid rule in the 160s BCE has served both as an exceptional and a maximal case in scholarship on indigenous resistance in the cultural and political history of the Hellenistic era; it has been treated as a singularity, and as the tip of an iceberg of much broader resistance to Hellenistic rule. At the strong end of a spectrum of moments and forms of resistance, the Maccabean Revolt remains the best documented and most extensively studied of those few violent revolts that resulted in secession and a durable state. On the other hand, it can also be seen as an exceptional moment in its own context: an outbreak of violent conflict in a relationship between Judeans and Seleucids that was otherwise characterized by accommodation and a *modus vivendi* acceptable to both.[1] In part, this range of approaches to the Maccabean Revolt – its singularity, exemplarity, and comparability – reflects a long history of disciplinary and regional fragmentation in the study of the Hellenistic world, a fragmentation that contemporary scholars have only recently begun to address anew. The last sustained

---

[1] Earlier surveys of Hellenistic history tended to follow contemporary scholarship and assume a fundamental clash of religion and culture. Préaux 1978: 566–586, for example, treated Jewish relations to Hellenism as distinct from other relations between Greeks and non-Greeks, and took the Maccabean revolt as emblematic of a clash between Hellenism and Judaism. At the same time, Préaux 1978: 586 suggested that there may have been a literature of resistance in Egypt that was as 'abundant and virulent' as Jewish literature, but that it had not survived since it was not translated into Greek. Tarn and Griffith 1952: 210, referred to the Jews as 'the one race strong enough to resist the impact of [Hellenism's] victorious culture', although they downplayed the religious aspect of the Maccabean confrontation (p. 216). For this tendency to see a clash of civilizations in the Maccabean revolt, and a refutation of the presumptions on which it is based, see Gruen 1998: 1–40, who provides numerous citations to the prior literature, which need not be restated here.

comparative monographic treatment of revolts and resistance in the Hellenistic world was published almost sixty years ago: Samuel K. Eddy's *The King is Dead: Studies in the Near Eastern Resistance to Hellenism, 334-31 BC*. This work, owing to its contributions, its limitations, and the contemporary intellectual and political context in which it was written, provides a benchmark for surveying the current scholarly landscape and how we got here – what has happened and what has not, the roads taken and not taken – in order to propose a re-orientation to the Maccabean Revolt, and to related instances of revolt and resistance in the Hellenistic Eastern Mediterranean and Near East.

Eddy's book first took form as a dissertation, written at the University of Michigan under the supervision of Arthur Boak.[2] The book was published in 1961 by the University of Nebraska Press and reviewed in a number of major journals. The reception was mixed: some reviewed the work favourably while others summarily dismissed it as 'unconvincing'.[3] Nevertheless, about ten years after its publication, a young historian of religion, Jonathan Z. Smith, would recognize that, despite the work's problems, it developed an important argument that linked a range of non-Greek responses to the political and cultural conditions of the Hellenistic period:[4] namely, that in addition to economic and social factors emphasized by W. W. Tarn and M. Rostovtzeff, there were two other important causes of resistance to the Hellenistic kingdoms: the

---

[2] Eddy 1958. The style and cross-cultural scope of the dissertation can perhaps be explained by Eddy's place in the History Department and the interdisciplinary nature of his PhD advisory committee. In addition to Boak, the committee included archaeologist Clark Hopkins, director of the French-American excavations at Dura Europos and Seleucia on the Tigris and member of Classics Department at Michigan; the Arab and Islamic historian George Hourani (Department of Near Eastern Studies); and the biblical scholar George Mendenhall (also of the Department of Near Eastern Studies).

[3] The review of Moses Hadas 1964 was generally favourable, but others, such as Marks 1963 were less charitable. Other reviews were a mixture of praise and some implicit blame for Eddy's wide ambitions along with critiques of detail and method (especially the comparisons to more recent colonial history). Several reviewers explicitly saw Eddy's work as a counterpoint to the social and economic emphasis that Tarn and Rostovtzeff put on their explanations of revolt and resistance (Rees 1964; Pouilloux 1965; Hadot 1970), a parallel to some of the concerns animating the current collection of essays. For other reviews and notices, see Aalders 1965; Lieberman 1962; Kraeling 1964; Schuler 1966; Wartelle 1965.

[4] Smith 1971: 236–237. Though Smith would go on to develop a much more sophisticated approach to the displacement of native kingship and its implications for religion in the Hellenistic period, he continued to acknowledge that despite its limitations, Eddy's work had raised significant issues. See Smith 1978: 186 n. 61; Smith 1982: 158 n. 25; Smith 2003: 33 n. 37.

displacement of indigenous kingship traditions and threats to religious traditions. The response to both was what Eddy termed 'religious resistance'. Under this category he analysed not only violent revolts, but also what we would now call 'discursive' forms of resistance (historiography, oracles, and apocalyptic texts), and located their origins squarely in the old military and priestly classes of the Near Eastern societies ruled by the successors to Alexander. In some cases, he traced the genealogies of his 'anti-Hellenic' phenomena to prior moments of resistance to the Achaemenid Persian Empire. This was a bold argument that ran counter to much contemporary scholarship, and it came at a time when anti-colonial movements had been breaking out in various corners of a crumbling European imperial world.[5] The book never quite 'took off' to become a foundational work, and its impact varied immensely across the academic landscape. Although it made a relatively slight impression in ancient history and classical studies, it has had a significant impact in religious studies and the history of religions. Perhaps its patchy reception was down to its sweeping argument, to various scholarly faults identified by specialists, or Eddy's unsystematic comparisons with the modern world, which invited the hostility of some scholars.[6] Whatever the cause, there has not been a similar large-scale comparative treatment of resistance in the Hellenistic world in the decades since Eddy's book, even if there have been some important studies of apocalyptic texts as resistance literature,[7] and essays arguing for the usefulness of comparativism in analysing indigenous responses to Hellenistic rule.[8]

Despite the lack of a comparative treatment of resistance in the Hellenistic world, there have been numerous studies on particular moments or forms of revolt since Eddy's work. A comprehensive review

---

[5] Eddy was aware of this, as several comments and brief comparisons suggest (see, e.g., Eddy 1961: 272, 296, 309, 334, 340). Such observations were also in the original dissertation (see, e.g., Eddy 1958: 416, 430–431).

[6] See especially Rees 1964: 197.

[7] Note the study of Müller (1973), inspired by Eddy. In general, see also the brief overview of Collins 2015: 289–291, who has himself contributed an enormous amount to the study of apocalyptic. See further below (pp. 4 and 8).

[8] Édouard Will's call for a 'colonial anthropology' of the Hellenistic world, for example, outlined comparative categories of active and passive acceptance and resistance (1985). This work and its general proposal of comparison with contemporary colonialism has come under significant criticism and revision. See Bagnall 1997.

of this literature is beyond the scope of this introduction, but it will be useful to point to some broad trends and patterns. In the first case, historical studies of resistance or revolt have primarily focused on either the Ptolemaic or the Seleucid Empires. This is part of a larger pattern of specialization in the study of the Hellenistic world, and perfectly comprehensible owing to the skills and competencies required – especially as more and more scholars have made concerted efforts to integrate material evidence and non-Greek textual evidence into their work. On the Ptolemaic side, Werner Huss's study of relations between Egyptian priests and the Macedonian king outlined evidence of collaboration and opposition (1994); and, of course, Anne-Emmanuel Veïsse published her excellent study of the whole series of Egyptian revolts some eighteen years ago (2004). There have also been examinations of Egyptian and Graeco-Egyptian texts for signs that the indigenous elite were producing a literature of resistance, in which prophetic texts such as the *Demotic Chronicle* and the *Oracle of the Potter* have been particularly prominent.[9] On the Seleucid side, the Maccabean Revolt itself has dominated the picture as the subject of an extensive and significant body of literature, especially since Elias Bickerman's *Der Gott der Makkabäer* (1937) showed that it was essential to study the revolt in its Seleucid context.[10] Jewish literary texts, moreover, have also been analysed extensively for their position in regard to the Seleucid kingdom and Greek culture, including studies that explore elements of critique and opposition.[11] Studies of other forms of revolt and resistance in the eastern parts of the Seleucid Empire have been pursued: for example, the analysis of break-away Persian dynasts and their adoption of Achaemenid imagery

---

[9] Eddy 1961: 290–292, 297, 326, along with the original editor (Spiegelberg 1914: 5) and others understood the *Demotic Chronicle* as Egyptian nationalist literature, but Johnson 1984 has questioned whether it was anti-Greek, arguing that it was in fact anti-Persian. Felber 2002 has even argued (not very convincingly) that the prophesied ruler from Herakleopolis was Ptolemy I Soter. In a series of studies, L. Koenen explored the anti-Greek *Oracle of the Potter* and connected it with an episode of revolt in 131/130 BCE (see Koenen 1959, 1968, 1970; Koenen and Blasius 2002). An important examination of Egyptian apocalyptic texts and their context is found in Blasius and Schipper 2002; see especially the discussions in that work by A. Blasius of the connections between apocalyptic and resistance (pp. 41–62, 294–298).

[10] For an overview of the broad historiographic trends since Bickerman, see Honigman 2014a: 11–42.

[11] See, for example, Collins 1977, 2002; Nickelsburg 2001; Portier-Young 2011; Kosmin 2018: 137–171.

and the title *frataraka*, but again these are understandably localized in focus.[12] Despite these tendencies, there has been a recent revival of efforts to examine resistance to the Hellenistic states in ways that link or compare the Seleucid and Ptolemaic kingdoms,[13] and the present volume is part of that effort.

Another trend over the last half century or so has been the development of much more sophisticated and nuanced explorations of ethnic and cultural identities and affiliations, and the extent to which they play a role in forming the social solidarities behind moments of revolt and resistance. Studies like Eddy's or those of a range of other scholars from the 1960s up to the 1990s would frequently use the term 'nationalism' as a convenient shorthand for describing conflicts in which the lines appeared to them drawn along ethnic or cultural divides, or even more broadly for acts or discourses that appeared to be ethno-cultural self-assertions in the context of a hegemonic Greek culture. This terminology of nationalism has been criticized in the Ptolemaic context by Joe Manning and Anne-Emmanuelle Veïsse,[14] for example, as an anachronistic and unhelpful imposition of modern conceptions tied to the emergence of the modern nation-state in the nineteenth century Euro-American world, and unsuited to the analysis of pre-modern states. On the other hand, some scholars such as Brian McGing have pushed back against the abandonment of the category, particularly in Ptolemaic Egypt,[15] and scholars working in Jewish studies, such as David Goodblatt in his book, *Elements of Ancient Jewish Nationalism*, have argued for continuities between ancient and modern 'nationalism' – a position that has, of course, also been challenged.[16]

---

[12] For the *frataraka*, see Kosmin 2018: 203–212; Plischke 2014: 298–312; the chronology of the *frataraka* and the interpretation of their self-presentation as resistant to or in conflict with Seleucid rule has been challenged by Engels 2013, 2017: 247–306. The latter argues that the *frataraka* appeared earlier than previously dated, and that although they asserted a local identity, were in a basically cooperative relationship with the Seleucids. This interpretation has found some acceptance – see, e.g., Strootman 2017: 194–197, 2018: 140 – but remains a matter of debate.
[13] Gorre and Honigman 2013; Fischer-Bovet 2015b. See also Collins and Manning 2016, a collection of essays on revolt and resistance that takes a broader comparative perspective from the Neo-Assyrian Empire to the Roman Empire.
[14] Manning 2003b: 164–165; Veïsse 2004: 151, 245.   [15] McGing 2006, 2012, 2016.
[16] Goodblatt 2006; for a response, see, e.g., Weitzman 2008.

These debates on the nature of resistance and rebellion against the Hellenistic kingdoms have taken place in a much broader context of scholarship in the field of ancient history and in the academy at large on ethnicity, and especially on the social processes through which ethnic identities are constructed. Such scholarly challenges to primordialist or essentializing notions of ethnicity, especially since the 1990s, have in part been stimulated by the extreme and all-too-real consequences of revived ethnic solidarities and antipathies that played out in sites from the Balkans to the Congo basin, and are as present as ever today.[17] The question of cultural affiliations (as opposed to ethnic identities), whether or not they are entailed in the adoption of Greek language and other practices, and whether they were at issue in episodes of resistance and rebellion in the Hellenistic world, has been an even more complex debate, and likewise tied to contemporary histories. This is a question that has been pursued in part through much wider conversations in anthropology, history, literary studies, and other fields about the culture concept itself and about various terminologies of syncretism and hybridity, especially in scholarship on colonial and post-colonial worlds.[18] This is a vast area, and it is only possible to point out the intersections of these concerns and studies of local dissent in the Hellenistic world that are relevant to the present discussions.

To put it briefly, scholarly treatments of the available evidence and methodological reconsiderations have generally downgraded the explanatory relevance of ethnic or cultural antagonism to 'Hellenism' or to 'the Greeks' in our best-documented revolts: the uprising of the Maccabees and the 'Egyptian' revolts against the Ptolemies.[19] There are

---

[17] Already in the early 1980s, Anthony D. Smith wrote of the confounded and disappointed hopes of rationalists and (neo)liberals who thought ethnicity and nationalism would go away once their version of reason triumphed. Smith 1981: 1. The use of social-constructivist approaches in the study of ethnicity in the ancient world has long been informed by the ground-breaking work of F. Barth 1969. This is true, for example, of works such as Goudriaan 1988; Hall 1997, 2002, and others.

[18] Broadly speaking, historians of the Hellenistic period writing in the 1960s and 1970s reacted against the thesis of cultural fusion and syncretism propounded by Droysen 1877–1878. This reaction was most forcefully articulated by Préaux 1978. For an overview of these scholarly trends, see Moyer 2011b, 11–36.

[19] In addition to the objections to 'nationalism' in the Ptolemaic case noted above, arguments have been raised that ethnic, cultural and religious factors have been overstressed in analyses of the Maccabean revolt, on which see Gruen 1998: 1–40; Honigman 2014a: 26–28.

two parts to this revised picture. In the first place, whereas Eddy saw displaced or threatened elites of Near Eastern societies as key players in his 'religious resistance' to Hellenism, and, conversely, earlier formulations of the ruling stratum in Hellenistic states emphasized its Greek ethnic cohesiveness,[20] studies over the last two or three decades have revised this picture to take account of evidence for the integration of indigenous elites into the administrative structures of Hellenistic states, and the crucial roles they could play in mediating its power in local and regional contexts. Individuals with double names such as Anu-uballiṭ/Nicarchus and Anu-uballiṭ/Cephalon, governors at Uruk, and the Ptolemaic *dioiketes* Harchebis-Archibios, and many others have become representatives of this integrated class.[21] Accordingly, indigenous elites and the Macedonian courts are described as engaged in a politics of alliance and mutual self-interest, and this cooperation is less and less likely to be characterized by loaded terms such as 'collaboration', with its connotations of a betrayal of presumed 'natural' affiliations. Coexistence, accommodation, and pragmatism are much more likely to be invoked than a 'clash of civilizations'. Second, in the face of this complex picture – in which ethnic and culture affiliation and the lines of conflict do not match very neatly – the motivations and solidarities of interest that explain revolt or resistance are more likely to be found in economic, institutional, and political grievances: those who revolt, it is argued, were primarily seeking redress for economic inequalities and exploitation, or for encroachment on traditional prerogatives that resulted from state intervention in institutions such as temples. Alternatively, some indigenous elites (like Greek elites) were simply seeking advantage within the

---

[20] This strong formulation of an ethnically cohesive *herrschende Gesellschaft* was articulated most clearly by Habicht 1958. Dreyer 2011: 46 re-asserts the validity of this model, but also shows that practical considerations led to the integration of non-Greeks into the Seleucid court (such as Hannibal).

[21] On the Uruk figures, and Babylonia more generally, see Sherwin-White 1987; Sherwin-White and Kuhrt 1993: 150–153; on Harchebis-Archibios, see Klotz 2009: 300–305. Mehl 2003 provides more nuanced reflection on Habicht's 'herrschende Gesellschaft' in light of studies of the presence of Iranians and Babylonians in official and court positions. On the ethnic and cultural intersections of the Ptolemaic court and government more generally, see Gorre 2009b; Moyer 2011a; Fischer-Bovet 2016b. For a comparative perspective on Seleucid and Ptolemaic ethnic integration and its relationship to social unrest, see also Fischer-Bovet 2015b.

terms of the dominant economic and political system, rather than attempting to overthrow it.[22]

This is not to say that cultural, ethnic, or religious dimensions of resistance have been neglected in all scholarly fields. In the history of religions, as noted earlier, there has been a different trajectory: J. Z. Smith's scholarship long focused on the comparison of theoretical and ritual texts in order to understand religious responses to the displacement of native kingship, and the implications that displacement had for temple-based traditions. He explored motifs of resistance and rebellion as well as smaller-scale micro-adjustments in the logic of ritual practice. There has also been a long-standing interest in genres such as apocalyptic eschatology across cultures in the ancient Near East and Mediterranean, particularly in the long Hellenistic period. Much of this has been formal or theological in orientation, but examining critiques of temporal powers has also been an ever-present theme. Anathea Portier-Young, for example, has brought resistance to the surface in apocalyptic works such as the *Book of Daniel* through an explicitly theoretical framework that draws on A. Gramsci and J. Scott.[23] Drawing on postcolonial theory, auto-ethnographical works written in Greek by non-Greeks, such as Berossos and Manetho, have also at times been considered more subtle 'counter-discursive' forms of resistance in their use of indigenous knowledge to contest Greek knowledge and representations, even if these works were produced by figures connected with Hellenistic courts.[24]

Such scholarship has been attentive to local political, religious, and moral frameworks as lenses through which to interpret and explain critiques of Hellenistic rule, as well as the motives and justifications for resistance. But, too often, they are part of scholarly conversations in

---

[22] For arguments emphasizing social and economic causes, see Manning 2003b: 164–165; Veïsse 2004: 151, 245; Gorre and Honigman 2013; Honigman 2014a.

[23] Portier-Young 2011.

[24] The link between a subtle anti-Hellenism and this kind of historiography was made already by Eddy 1961: 125, 272, 295. Gregory Sterling set Manetho and Berossos at the origins of 'apologetic historiography', which he understood as both identifying with Hellenism and challenging it (see especially Sterling 1992: 103). See Moyer 2011b: 84–141 for the deployment of post-colonial theories and 'counter-discourse' in the analysis of the form and content of Manetho. Manetho and Berossos are treated together by Dillery 2015.

cultural, literary, or religious studies that stand apart from the more materialist, socio-political, and economic orientation of much current work in ancient history. One of the aspirations of the current volume is to bring together these perspectives into a more integrated account of the culture and politics of resistance, without succumbing to the pitfalls of our currently existing categories of analysis. We have already mentioned a number of important critiques of the presumption that such modern concepts as 'nationality' or other related notions of ethnicity and cultural identity have explanatory value in the analysis of pre-modern societies.[25] Our renewed investigation of cultures of resistance in the Hellenistic world is not a return to anachronistic, essentializing, or primordialist categories of analysis. Few would now disagree that cultures and ethnicities are immanent, historical phenomena, made and remade at the nexus of social and political relations. Yet they are also significant elements of the imagined and enacted worlds within which historical figures made decisions, did things, and justified their actions. There is a danger of overwriting discursive resistance and justifications of open revolt that appeal to religious ideas or traditional cultural norms as secondary elaborations of 'real' – which is to say, social and economic – motives. The consequence: either dismissing the expressed rationales of the historical agents or explaining them away as elite ideology or legitimation.

The latter accounts are variants of the functionalist explanation of culture, and are open to critique for converting the particularities of recent Western historical experience into universals.[26] Ideology and legitimation both imply the representation of things as other than they really are – the masking of realities of power and the disposition of material resources by referring to social ideals and norms or supernatural propositions, whether this masking is perpetrated by those with control or the leaders of those contesting it. Drawing on Marxist or Weberian traditions, these concepts imply the attempt to make some phenomenon (political or economic) appear to conform to a set of norms when it may

[25] See also Pollock 2006a: 505–511; Pollock 2006b: 282–283.
[26] Sheldon Pollock's observations in his work on culture and power in pre-modern South Asia and the broader Sanskrit cosmopolis have been particularly valuable in formulating these observations. Pollock 2006b: 282–286; 2006a: 511–524.

not do so.[27] Invoking 'legitimation' begs a set of questions about whether the addressee of such messages can be presumed modern until proven otherwise. Is the subject of a Hellenistic kingdom engaged in any kind of meaningful rational choice about the form of government or its office-holders? Is the revolting subject the dupe of elite class that has knowledge not available to others? Or, as some critics of legitimation theory in the modern context have suggested, are these messages really aimed at consensus-building among elites?[28] And the complementary question: were subaltern classes not as susceptible to this kind of consensual politics as sometimes imagined? In short, what do the concepts of legitimation and ideology explain about the relationship between culture and power (social, economic, political) in pre-modern as opposed to modern societies? Were the crises, the moments of decision and judgement involved in resistance and revolt, ontological, or were they adjustments that could be contained within existing local social knowledge and practice? We have to be clear about all these relationships, so that we do not allow 'legitimation' and 'ideology' to become nothing more than convenient containers for the residues – the undigested by-products – left behind by the process of translating ancient history into modern terms.

Dipesh Chakrabarty has famously provided one guide to finding a place for historical difference in the way he advocates 'provincializing Europe' while dealing with the continuing importance of European social-scientific thought for subaltern studies and post-colonial historical writing. In a close reading of Marx on the history of Capital, Chakrabarty distinguishes two kinds of history that are retrospectively posited by Capital as antecedent to itself. Chakrabarty calls them History 1 and History 2. History 1 is the 'backbone' of all histories of transition to the capitalist mode of production: the past posited by Capital itself as its own precondition. History 2 is something of a remainder: the past that is not part of Capital's coming into being and that does not lend itself to the reproduction of the logic of Capital. Taking a broader view, History 1 can

---

[27] For example, in Marxist analysis, ideology masks capital's extraction of surplus labour through hegemonic illusion that workers are 'free' to sell their labour in the market. See Pollock 2006a: 519–520.
[28] See Pollock 2006a: 523, citing Giddens 1981: 67; Scott 1990; Abercrombie et al. 1980; 1990.

be seen as history in a universalizing social-scientific mode, while History 2 is a history of human diversity, of the life worlds that are not wholly or necessarily assimilable to the categories of History 1. Chakrabarty is not, however, simply claiming cultural relativism or incommensurability. His approach is to sustain simultaneously two histories based on two different modes of translating the past, two different modes of commensuration: History 1 is translation as commodity exchange – translation that assumes universal, homogenizing middle terms, like money or labour; it is a translation that embraces both sides in a single system that can be replicated in other times and places. History 2, on the other hand, is translation as barter exchange – a transaction between two worlds that functions without assuming a mediating third term, and thus disturbs the universal assumptions of History 1 and interrupts its narratives. Chakrabarty proposes historical translation in both modes in order to 'read our secular universals in such a way as to keep them open to their own finitude, so that the scandalous aspects of our unavoidable translations, instead of being made inaudible, actually reverberate through what we write'.[29]

In attempting to sustain this parallax view of the social, political, and economic forces that motivate discontent while also addressing in their own terms ancient representations and actions that reject or critique established power, our hope is to set the stage for an enlarged and integrative view of revolt and resistance in the Hellenistic world. To focus this view and to offer a number of perspectives, the contributions to this volume provide a series of local or regional studies that investigate both historical agents' articulations of their political situation and their resistance to it and also the causes of conflict as understood from modern social and economic perspectives.

In seeking to address these issues, we have adopted two methodological stances: attention to the wide spectrum of dissent, and a global perspective. In the first case, our contributors investigate not only the large, organized, and prolonged military activity in the 'classic' cases of the Great Theban Revolt and the Maccabean Revolt (discussed in Part I), but also the full gamut of indigenous self-assertion and resistant action,

[29] Chakrabarty 2008: 90.

ranging from the differently oriented theologies of monarchic inadequacy, patterns of historical periodization and textual exegesis, and manipulation of authority-spaces (explored in Part II), to the more ambiguous instantiations of local autonomy and identity that emerge in the frontier regions that slipped in and out of the grasp of the Hellenistic big kings (see Part III). Everywhere, we will see that the resistance in question is complicated, ambivalent, highly specific in its targets and ambitions, and fully entwined with imperial power and agendas. And even as an indigenous 'buy-in' or 'mimicry' of Graeco-Macedonian hegemonic forms is recognizable, we must ourselves take care not to reproduce the perspective and interests of the Hellenistic kingdoms in framing resistance or complicity, rejection or acceptance of empire, as binary choices. Power and struggle were – as they still obviously are – implicated rather than autonomous phenomena, coexisting and shaping one another.[30] As we shall see, contestatory behaviours may be incoherent, heterogeneous, derivative, and even contradictory. Furthermore, moving away from the supposedly motivating anti-Hellenism so characteristic of earlier accounts (see above, pp. 1–7), we have incorporated discussion of the subject Greek communities of these empires, so long walled-off from accounts of Hellenistic indigeneity; here, at least provisionally, indigeneity is taken as a universal subject position.

Second, this book is deliberately 'global' (in the limited sense of the Hellenistic world system)[31] and comparative in orientation and purpose. To explain what we mean, it may be helpful to follow Samuel Moyn's and Andrew Sartori's distinction between three kinds of global history – first, the global as a meta-analytical category of the historian, a comparative mode of study that resides entirely in the space of analysis; second, the

---

[30] See, e.g., Haynes and Prakash 1991.

[31] For the application of 'globalization' to ancient societies, see Jennings 2011, who analyses moments of globalization not in literal geographical terms, but as recurrent historical processes of qualitative and quantitative change involving significant leaps in interregional interaction, and social changes correlating with the creation of global cultures (pp. 13–14). The hallmarks of globalization include time-space compression, deterritorialization, standardization, homogenization, cultural heterogenization (the creation of new hybrid forms), the re-embedding of local culture, and vulnerability to systemic shocks (pp. 19–34). These can be applied to the Hellenistic world as well as to the very early periods Jennings considers (e.g. Uruk culture and Cahokia).

global as a substantive scale of historical process, a property of the historian's subject matter; and, finally, the global as an emic, native category, used by the historical agents who are the object of study.[32]

The first type of analysis has been employed, with great success, in a number of important studies of Hellenistic indigenous resistance and imperial response, such as Christelle Fischer-Bovet's recent exploration of ethnic-based social unrest in the Ptolemaic and Seleucid realms[33] or John Ma's and Robert Doran's respective comparison of Antiochus IV's actions in Jerusalem with epigraphically attested institutional changes in western Asia Minor and the historiographically reported treatment of Sparta by the Achaean League.[34] In scholarship of this kind, global comparison is possible without historical connection because of the historian's second-order categories: the comparative operation is entirely that of the modern historian, gazing down upon the ancient world and, like a pearl fisher, picking from different regions the data that most effectively aligns. All contributions to this volume to some degree participate in this etic comparative mode.

But we are also concerned to explore the second and third categories of Moyn's and Sartori's global history – that is, investigating commonalities and differences in local responses to the Hellenistic world system and the rule of Hellenistic states, and asking how historical actors articulated, in emic terms, their identities, conditions, and prospects, whether in globalizing or nativist-indigenizing modes. One of the more widely celebrated features of Hellenistic politics, economies, and cultural and intellectual life are the heroic stories of convergence and integration that ultimately take their shape from Polybius' contemporary model of *symplokē*: the political unification of the Middle Sea, the weaving of a mercantile Eurasia in the linking of the Mediterranean world to the Indian Ocean and central Asia, the complicated meetings, interactions, and hybridizations of cultural and linguistic forms, the intellectual encompassment of the known world or all history in the geographic and chronographic endeavours of library scholarship, and so forth. If such identifications of the Hellenistic 'global' have, for the most part,

[32] Moyn and Sartori 2013: 4–20. [33] Fischer-Bovet 2015b.
[34] Ma 2012, 2013b; Doran 2011: 427.

addressed centralized state power and Hellenic cultural forms, this volume asks: Were there comparable indigenous responses, in this case hostile reactions, to Hellenistic empire? Can we usefully place alongside the Maccabean Revolt and the Great Theban Revolt the assertions of civic identity and political autonomy by Greek city states and their local historians, or the new forms of political communion among the populations of western Asia Minor, or the breakaways of Bactria and Parthia from the Seleucid Empire, or the army mutinies of a Diodotus Tryphon or Dionysius Petosarapis and the street riots of Alexandria and Antioch-by-Daphne, or the coded criticisms of Babylonian temple scribes, or the new textual genres and modes of exegesis that appear across the political landscape, despite all their bottomless and undeniable differences?

Moreover, if there were common phenomena how are we to explain them? Were they the results of shared categorical causes or contingent alignments? How did these operate? Let us briefly offer three different kinds of response. It has been suggested by a number of scholars, including Sylvie Honigman, Gilles Gorre, Philippe Clancier, Julien Monerie, and Anne-Emmanuelle Veïsse, that the late third and first half of the second centuries BCE witnessed, in both the Ptolemaic and Seleucid kingdoms, an intensification of state intervention and fiscal demands in formerly protected spaces in Judea, Babylon, and the Thebaïd,[35] a function of both colonization and revenue needs. It is argued that these constituted, at least from the local perspective, a break with the traditional privileges of indigenous elites and so with the moral script that permitted legitimate foreign kingship. A more recent proposal has been the exciting suggestion of Joseph Manning and Francis Ludlow that considerable levels of volcanic activity in the third and especially second centuries BCE produced the hydrological shocks of Nile flood failure that may have triggered or contributed to revolts in Egypt.[36] The impact of such volcanically triggered 'Ten Plagues'-like climatic stress on the more diverse territories of the Seleucid Empire, remains almost entirely unexplored, though,

---

[35] Gorre and Honigman 2013; Honigman 2014a; Clancier and Monerie 2014, Veïsse, this volume, Chapter 2, though also see the doubts of Gruen, also in this volume, Chapter 1.
[36] Ludlow and Manning 2016.

presumably, correlations between climatic and historical events could be investigated. Finally, we would submit that Rome's defeat and political eradication of the Antigonid kingdom at the conclusion of the Third Macedonian War and in the immediate lead-up to the Maccabean Revolt may have provoked a region-wide awareness of Hellenistic imperial vulnerability. It would be impossible to pin down precisely such an atmospheric disturbance, yet its impact may have been considerable, as with the fall of Neo-Assyrian Nineveh in the late seventh century. Did this contribute to those reflections on the transitoriness of earthly kingdoms and the summons to alternative dispensations of which we catch glimpses in second-century apocalyptic eschatology and Polybius' histories? At odds with this approach is the tendency to treat political relations within the Hellenistic Empires as a set of bilateral interactions between Graeco-Macedonian kings and their various subject communities. This is both a particular consequence of the still dominant 'personal kingship' paradigm of the Successor monarchies and a more general effect of the modern academy's language-based disciplinary boundaries. This often has resulted in structuring indigenous responses as a false dichotomy between Hellenistic cosmopolitanism and indigenous localism. But, we must ask, can we identify alternative, non-Graeco-Macedonian global perspectives? Did the subject communities generate alternative cosmopolitan visions that could challenge the parochialisms of imperial universalities?

On the basis of these two methodologies – an understanding of resistance as a capacious and entangled category, and a 'global' perspective that is both etic and emic – this book seeks to ask how, and why, certain members among the Hellenistic Empires' subject populations worked to assert themselves, their histories, and their worldviews against their Graeco-Macedonian masters. This is, in short, a methodological globalism rather than a comprehensive treatment of all the relevant phenomena.[37] Within the scope of this volume it would be impossible to address all regions from all possible positions within the constellation

---

[37] There are several areas that do not get a full treatment in this volume, but which have been areas of recent scholarly and debate. These include the question of whether the *frataraka* in Persis were cooperative with or resistant to the Seleucids, as mentioned above (see n. 12). While

of persepectives we have outlined. Nevertheless, the varied contributions of this volume, in their spatial range, and their varied analytics, do provide reference points for a global re-orientation to resistance in the Hellenistic East.

2. Contributions

'Cultures of Resistance in the Hellenistic East' is divided into three parts. The first, 'The Big Events: Pattern and Crisis', opens with critical discussions of the two best-known episodes of militarized resistance to the big Hellenistic kingdoms – the Maccabean Revolt in Judea in the late 160s BCE and the Thebaïd revolt in southern Egypt, c.206–186 BCE. The two chapters of this section investigate the nature and ambitions of such indigenous movements, the reasons that in each case tensions coalesced into enduring and powerful military opposition, and the modes of reconciliation or restoration available to the Seleucid and Ptolemaic imperial houses.

Erich Gruen's 'The Maccabean Model: Resistance or Adjustment?' (Chapter 1) explores the extent to which the Maccabean resistance constituted an explicit challenge to the legitimacy and fact of Seleucid governance. Gruen argues that Antiochus IV's actions in Judea must be understood as exceptional within an existing and ongoing relationship, breaking with the normative paradigm of Seleucid-Judean interactions that was established by Antiochus III in his famous 'charter for

---

the contribution of R. Mairs on Bactria in this volume (Chapter 9) deals primarily with historiographic issues of synchronism and causation, there has been much work on the broader historical question of Bactrian resistance and revolts. The (possible) revolt of the Diodotids in Bactria has been discussed in Holt 1999: 18–19, 60, 65, 128–130 and Capdetrey 2007: 124–127. For more recent reassessments of the relationship between the Seleucids and Bactria, see Wenghofer 2018; Strootman 2018: 183–186; Coşkun 2018: 221 and 2019: 472–475. For a broader overview of Bactria in both its Seleucid and broader Asian contexts, see now Mairs 2020. In general, there have also been several works in recent years that have contributed to reassessments of the strength of the Seleucid rule in the eastern provinces, with implications for questions of resistance; for example: Mittag 2006; Feyel and Graslin-Thomé 2014, 2017; Strootman 2018; Coşkun 2019. Although two contributions (Veïsse and Moyer) to this volume treat episodes of revolt and resistance in the Ptolemaic kingdom, several episodes and aspects of resistance are not covered. The best comprehensive overview remains Veïsse 2004; see also above (nn. 9, 14–15, 55, 36).

Jerusalem' after the Fifth Syrian War and continued by Seleucus IV. For Gruen, the ultimate effect of the Maccabean uprising, and so our best guide for its ambitions, was the revival of the mutually beneficial *modus vivendi* between imperial power and subordinate entity that had obtained under Antiochus IV's predecessors.[38] Indeed, Gruen argues, it was Seleucid authorization of Jonathan and Simon that would allow the later Maccabees to act against their domestic rivals in Judea and their local neighbours in the southern Levant. As a mode of resistance, therefore, the Maccabean insurgency commands attention to the problematic, intertwined nature of local assertion within the Seleucid context: this rebellion and its durable outcome were not entirely structured around cultural antitheses, but drew on both local and global discursive strategies.

In 'The "Great Theban Revolt", 206–186 BCE' (Chapter 2), Anne-Emmanuelle Veïsse lays out the evidence for this most long-lasting anti-Ptolemaic movement and the conditions underlying the Thebaïd's hostility to Alexandria. As Veïsse demonstrates, for this revolt, alone of all outbreaks of Egyptian resistance against the Ptolemies, the two successive rebel leaders (if indeed they were not the same individual) proclaimed themselves legitimate pharaohs, took the archaizing throne-names Chaonnophris and Haronnophris, and made repeated reference to the pre-Ptolemaic dispensation, while, at the same time, drawing on Ptolemaic modes of governance for their own state-building activities. Veïsse contextualizes the revolt by reflecting on the role that three developments may have played in its origins and relative success: the growth of Ptolemaic state control over the revenues of the Upper Egyptian temples from the 220s; the reduction of royal subventions to these same temples owing to the costs of the Fourth Syrian War; and the transformation of local elites and promotion of new men by the Ptolemaic state in the course of the third century. The Great Revolt emerges as a politico-religious response to institutional and economic pressures.

---

[38] Our contributors vary in the extent to which they distinguish between the Maccabees and the Hasmoneans, and each contributor follows his or her own terminology accordingly.

The side-by-side discussion of the Maccabean and Theban revolts throws into relief the fundamentally different principles of indigenous resistance and imperial response in each empire. In Egypt, where, as Veïsse puts it, 'there can only be one pharaoh on earth' (p. 68), the Ptolemaic monopolization of monarchic authority produced a contest over the very same sites of power and sources of legitimacy; the Theban revolt was a zero-sum game that, from the Ptolemaic perspective, required total suppression. By contrast, the Seleucid kings, by not permanently occupying the indigenous monarchic positions of their various subject peoples, made possible the accommodation of local resistance to common advantage that we see playing out over many decades in Judea. In Gruen's terms, 'an accord short of unconditional victory or surrender was possible' (p. 49).

In the book's second part, 'The Grounds for Resistance', contributors trace the contours of historical memories and models of kingship and the horizons of expectation that conditioned responses to Hellenistic rule, including the spectrum of strategies of accommodation and resistance. Johannes Haubold begins this endeavour in Chapter 3, 'Memory and Resistance in the Seleucid World', by tracing the shape of historical memory in different parts of the Seleucid world, arguing that responses to Hellenistic rule depended in part on the availability of historical scripts that had been sedimented in layers of previous experience with imperial rule, stretching back into the Achaemenid Persian era, and earlier. Taking the world-historical vision of the *Book of Daniel* as his starting point, he shows how memories of Nebuchadnezzar gave starkly different reference points and relational repertoires to those framing responses to the Seleucids in Mesopotamia and in Judea. While the author(s) of *Daniel* revived the memory of the Neo-Babylonians and Nebuchadnezzar as an anti-Seleucid vision of the present, there were in the case of Seleucid Babylonia itself materials available for constructing between Greeks and Babylonians a common historical ground of imperial succession from bad Assyrians, to good Neo-Babylonians, to bad Achaemenid Persians. Indeed, earlier Babylonian resistance to Persian rule under Darius and Xerxes had already held up Nebuchadnezzar as a model king and aspirational point. The facts on the ground of the Macedonian conquest of the Persian Empire meant that Alexander or a

Seleucid monarch could undo Persian work in Babylon and take on the role of new Nebuchadnezzar. Even in the fragmentation of the Seleucid Empire in the later second century, there is more evidence of a revived discourse against 'the Elamite foe' (a previous formulation of the Achaemenid Persians) than resistance to the Seleucids. Collective memory, in short, played a role in both contesting Seleucid rule and stabilizing it, and in the case of Babylon the particular local contours of that landscape helps to explain the path of non-resistance.[39]

In 'After Him a King Will Arise,' Chapter 4, Kathryn Stevens also observes that, in general, Babylonian cuneiform literature painted a largely 'unnegative' picture of Seleucid rule. There was no resistance literature comparable to the *Book of Daniel* and no major revolt against the Seleucids. The cuneiform sources are, however, partial: tablets of the temple elites survived, while Greek and Aramaic texts on parchment and papyrus did not. Learned and formal cuneiform texts, composed by scribes and scholars allied to the institution of kingship, appear to have maintained an 'eloquent silence' on the Seleucids, accepting them, for the most part, as native rulers. On closer examination, however, Stevens shows that scholars of Babylon, Uruk, and Borsippa did not cede their traditional evaluative role, however circumspect and terse their expression. *Ex eventu* texts such as the *Dynastic Prophecy* are riddled with interpretive difficulties, but combing through the *Astronomical Diaries* and the fragments of Babylonian chronicles reveals 'clusters of negativity', especially around the figures of Seleucus I and Antiochus IV, couched in subtle historical associations and ominous correlations. Antiochus' assertion of royal control over sanctuaries, his transfer of powers from temple assemblies to *politai*, and the cuneiform record of bad omens and reports of trouble that followed, suggest that there was a muted, discursive counterpart in Babylon to the Maccabean Revolt in Judea. Taken together with Greek and Jewish sources, Stevens connects a series of dots that resemble earlier scholarly pictures, perhaps too hastily abandoned with the emergence of cuneiform sources, of Antiochus

---

[39] Eddy's comparative work also highlighted the relative lack of resistance to Seleucid rule in Mesopotamia and Babylon, but offered a rather less convincing explanation in Mesopotamian cultural fatigue and despair. See Eddy 1961: 156–162, 326–328.

Epiphanes as a promoter of Hellenic institutions at the expense of non-Hellenic ones. At the local Babylonian level, however, the reaction was not a matter of Hellenism and anti-Hellenism, but evaluation according to traditional standards of kingship.

The Maccabean Revolt itself, of course, gave rise to several texts, historical and apocalyptic, that were hostile to Seleucid rule, or at the very least, to Antiochus IV. These have long been interpreted as examples of a Judean 'resistance literature',[40] contemporary with the uprising itself. This position has been revived in recent scholarship, but, in Chapter 5, 'Diverging Memories, Not Resistance Literature', Sylvie Honigman questions whether this terminology accurately reflects the historical relationship between the Maccabean crisis and the composition of the texts. Taking 1 and 2 Maccabees and the Animal Apocalypse (1 Enoch 85–90) as examples, she argues that these were not written as exhortations in the moment of struggle, but were retrospective compositions, and, moreover, that they set forth rather different memories of the crisis. For Honigman, 1 and 2 Maccabees were founding myths of the Hasmonean dynasty, who claimed descent from the Maccabees, and represented the revolt in a highly coded narrative, drawing on earlier Jewish/Judean historical works, to indicate the legitimacy of these rulers who 'walked in YHWH's path' and gained victory as a manifestation of divine election. Conversely, the enemies of the Maccabees were illegitimate usurpers. The narrative of the Animal Apocalypse, is also a continuation of an earlier hermeneutic pattern, in this case the more recent genre of apocalyptic eschatology. In contrast to 1 and 2 Maccabees, the Animal Apocalypse downplays kingship, and puts the people's adherence to God and Law, their error and return, at the centre of its explanation of events, and in the midst of a much broader, cosmological view of past, present, and future. Honigman suggests that these texts, bearing the marks of different social and political locations, may even have engaged one another in a contest over the memory of the recent past. In articulating this argument,

---

[40] See Nickelsburg 2001; Horsley 2010; Portier-Young 2011; Collins 2016 for a more recent reassertion of this interpretation of Daniel, 1 Enoch, 1 and 2 Maccabees.

INTRODUCTION 21

Honigman also points out that both texts structured memory and meaning according to local Judean ethical and religious norms, not unlike the local frameworks outlined in other contributions. In 1 and 2 Maccabees, *Hellenismos* and *Ioudaismos* were not so much ethnic labels as *ethical* categories of legitimacy, and in the Animal Apocalypse, the oppression of the nations (among whom the Greeks are scarcely distinguished from the rest), does not follow from a clash of ontological categories, but from human error and divine punishment.

As several contributors show, there is a wealth of evidence that resistance to Hellenistic rule, or at least coded critique, was framed according to local political and religious norms, and that this need not be overwritten with the language of ethnic and cultural antagonism. On the other hand, the hermeneutic strategies of the texts, their social locations, and their often retrospective views make it easy to drive a wedge between 'resistance' on the ground and 'literature' on page or tablet and so to undo a causal nexus between revolt and the culturally located judgements and determinations of its authors. Ian Moyer's contribution to Part II (Chapter 6, 'Revolts, Resistance, and the Materiality of the Moral Order in Ptolemaic Egypt') attempts to bridge that gap by searching out material and documentary evidence for the practice of resistance in Ptolemaic Egypt. He argues that in documentary reports, and damaged documents themselves, it is possible to catch a glimpse of meaningful symbolic actions, undertaken in public ways and places in order to contest the legality or legitimacy of the regime – a counterpart to recondite prophetic texts such as the *Demotic Chronicle* or the *Oracle of the Potter*. The withdrawal of farmers from unfair contracts and the issuance of their refusal from the precinct of a temple suggests not irrational flight, but the quasi-formal registration of protest in a place that was often used for the administration of justice. Evidence of the intentional defacement of inscribed versions of the Canopus decree, erected in the open areas of Egyptian temples, likewise suggests a public rejection of loyal priests' praise for the Ptolemies as good pharaohs. Rebels who forced a guardian of contracts publicly to burn them intended not only to disrupt legal agreements, but also symbolically to reject their authority. Though fleeting, these bits of evidence offer brief insights into the local ethical orientations of specific acts of resistance, acts, Moyer argues, that should be read as far as possible in their own terms.

The book's third and final part, 'The Edges of Resistance', examines the absence of a culturally or ethnically articulated rejection of Seleucid and Ptolemaic suzerainty in the western and eastern limit cases of Asia Minor and Bactria. Laurent Capdetrey, in 'An Impossible Resistance? Anatolian Populations, Ethnicity, and Greek Powers in Asia Minor during the Second Century BCE' (Chapter 7), distinguishes assertions of political solidarity from those of ethnic self-identity. For Capdetrey's carefully striated and comparative study of various population groups of south and southwestern Anatolia – the Carians, Lycians, and Pisidians, in particular – demonstrates the progressive fragmentation and overshadowing of local political forms founded on ethnic identity. We see, instead, a turn to the hegemonic Greek forms of political organization, both civic and federal, which, even if catalyzed or reinforced by the big Hellenistic states, was part of a deeply rooted and regionally specific historical trajectory. The history of these Anatolian populations in this period was, so Capdetrey argues, one of institutional acculturation, not ethnic affirmation.

An even more subtle use of hegemonic Greek culture in the context of limited possibilities for open resistance may be found among the fragments of Greek historiographic responses to Seleucid rule. In Chapter 8, 'Herakles is stronger, Seleucus', Daniel Tober examines the local histories of Pontic Herakleia that were produced by its citizens as they sought to walk the tightrope of independence and self-preservation in the face of Seleucid power and then later Roman pressures and the convulsions that they occasioned in Asia Minor. Such emic local histories had long been composed with protreptic and parenetic aspirations, to sway the policies of (relatively) autonomous city states with a rhetoric grounded in local identity and its past modes of success and survival. In the era of vast Hellenistic kingdoms, the terms were changed. In such a wildly asymmetrical relation, an enigmatic phrase $Ἡρακλῆς$ $κάρρων$ 'Herakles is stronger' – a rebuke delivered to Seleucus I Nicator and recorded by Nymphis in the 240s BCE – becomes a kind of 'hidden transcript'[41]

---

[41] Scott 1985.

rejecting the pretensions of a tyrannical monarch ignorant of Greek culture, and placing Herakliote aspirations in the Dorianism of their Northern League, and a non-confrontational strategy of resistance. Localism, older Greek ethnic identities, and cultural authenticity could thus be the historical ground on which to stand and oppose Hellenistic monarchs, just as well as the broader, panhellenic tropes of Greek freedom found in the Chremonides' decree and Flamininus' speech at Corinth after the second Macedonian War. But in the continuation of Nymphis' history by Memnon, who brought it into the era of Roman conquest, Herakleia's subtle resistance strategy is tragically abandoned, and its status and identity is lost. Between Nymphis and Memnon lie a range of rebellions and secessions that challenged the Seleucid state, including the Maccabean Revolt, and yet, as Tober points out, there appears to be a total absence of emic local historiography by citizens of Greek *poleis* in the second century BCE. Although Herakleides Lembos, at the court of Ptolemy VI, epitomized a group of Aristotelian *politeiai*, this was a synthetic antiquarian exercise in Alexandria, and the historiographic silence of small communities in the old Greek world was perhaps a sign of the local crises and Polybian *symplokê* that they were swept up in, as they found themselves caught between the kingdoms and Rome.

Finally, Rachel Mairs' 'Central Asian Challenges to Seleucid Authority: Synchronism, Correlation, and Causation' (Chapter 9) examines the possibility of discerning patterns in the movements for regional autonomy in Bactria. As Mairs shows, the breakaway of regional or supra-regional imperial blocks – the emerging independence of Diodotus I in 240s, and, finally, that of Eucratides in 170s – passed to a fundamentally different logic than the assertive indigeneities of Judea and the Thebaïd. In distant central Asia, we witness both a replication of the forms of Seleucid statecraft and an inter-ethnic solidarity between regional governors and local populations. Central to this study is an exploration of simultaneity in the historiographic tropes of universalizing histories (ancient and modern), a move that raises the question of whether or not we can consider the synchronisms in Justin's *Epitome of the Philippic History of Pompeius Trogus* of the emancipations of Diodotus and Arsaces I and the movements of Eucratides and

Mithridates as reflections of an actual empire-wide atmosphere of instability conducive to revolt from more local historical perspectives.

3. Cultures of Resistance: Results and Prospects

The contributions to this volume have created a multi-perspectival view of resistance and rebellion across a 'global' Hellenistic world, a world constituted, as in all instances of globalization, out of older landscapes and overlapping cultural conjunctures and disjunctures. Together, they contribute to a broad reconsideration of the explanatory relevance of culture and ethno-cultural assertion to moments of resistance in the history and historiography of the Hellenistic eastern Mediterranean, northeast Africa, and western Asia. What has emerged from this undertaking is a more nuanced and complex picture relative to earlier models of nationalism and ethno-cultural antagonism, and, we submit, this picture shows that 'cultural' dimensions cannot be sidelined as epiphenomenal to the universalized economic, political, and social factors identified from the analytical perspective of the historian. Local identities and the moral, political, and cosmological orders created and sustained by local actors must be more effectively integrated into accounts of resistance. Any analysis of conflict requires the recognition of difference. The inadequacy of simplistic Greek/non-Greek binary identities have long been taken as grounds for subordinating the explanatory value of culture and ethnicity in analyses of resistance to the Hellenistic states. But this is a straw man. For the studies in this volume have shown that indigeneity and cosmopolitanism, local cultural norms, and global Hellenistic norms, were not mutually exclusive, and both were available to subjects in evaluating rulers and considering responses to them, including antagonistic responses. Comparison, moreover, surfaces some commonalities and connections in the responses to particular rulers, in shared pre-Hellenistic pasts that shaped local historicities, and also in the globalizing and cosmologizing worldviews through which historical subjects articulated their prospects and aspirations.

There is, to be clear, little evidence that local responses to Hellenistic rulers involved a straightforward appeal to indigeneity as a justification for resisting foreign rule. Ethnic indigeneity, the idea that a land should be in the hands of native rulers was not, it would appear, taken as a 'natural' or sufficient position on which to base resistance, as other studies have also suggested.[42] However, indigeneity in a cultural mode – indigeneity as a strategic appeal to local cultural norms, historical traditions, and scripts of appropriate kingship – is much more evident. Even if there was not a full-blown, explicit resistance literature in Babylonia, Kathryn Stevens has shown that in the formal and traditional cuneiform texts that have survived scribal elites did comment on Seleucid rulers and at times passed negative judgements through historical and ominological allusion. Such norms of appropriate kingship were also articulated in historical and prophetic texts of Ptolemaic Egypt.[43] Cultural indigeneity, however, was not only a subtle, coded strategy of local elites engaged in the balancing act of maintaining both native traditions and a politics of alliance with the Hellenistic state. In those few cases where resistance and rebellion culminated in the overthrow, brief or lasting, of Hellenistic rule, cultural indigeneity could become a strategy for consolidating power. This is clear in S. Honigman's Hasmonean reading of 1 and 2 Maccabees and the Animal Apocalypse as justifying claims to the fulfilment of divine will and law, and also in the use of mythologically significant royal names and archaizing bureaucratic titles to mark a return to earlier pharaonic norms during the brief rule of an indigenizing pharaoh (or pharaohs) during the Great Theban revolt (A-E Veïsse). Paul Kosmin has argued that the same holds true, also, for the *fratarakā* of Persis and Artaxias I of Armenia.[44] In some cases, as Ian Moyer has argued, it may be possible to read past the retrospective strategies of elite texts to uncover evidence, slight though it may be, of broader segments of the population evaluating the justice of Hellenistic rule according to indigenous moral codes and articulating their opposition in those terms. Cultural indigeneity, as a strategy of resistance, can also be found among Greek communities. D. Tober's contribution has shown that in Heracliote narratives of local resistance,

---

[42] This would be an equivalent to the nationalism rejected by many scholars. See above discussion of the debate over whether 'nationalism' is an anachronistic category.
[43] See, for example, Moyer 2011b: 84–141 and below pp. 150–152.
[44] See, for example, Kosmin 2018: chapter 6.

subtle Dorian shibboleths and mythical allusions were the carriers of a covert rebuke to the tyranny of Seleucus I Nicator. In resisting the great powers, indigenizing Hellenisms were a counterpart, or perhaps a counterpoint, to cosmopolitan, internationalizing Hellenisms, the discursive fields in which both kings and cities manoeuvred and engaged with one another, with each appealing to such cultural norms as the 'freedom of the Greeks'. The decline of indigenizing Hellenisms, as suggested by the second-century disappearance of Greek epichoric historiography, perhaps occasioned the nostalgia for a lost ethic of local autonomy, as expressed in the retrospective celebration of the Achaean Philopoemen as the last of the Greeks.[45]

Appeals to the norms of a cosmopolitan Hellenism as grounds for asserting autonomy against the great powers was not restricted to communities that understood themselves as ethnically Greek, or to those who evinced the traditional values of *polis* autonomy. Erich Gruen's analysis of the broader picture of the Maccabean Revolt shows that Maccabean and Hasmonean indigeneity, especially appeals to religious norms and beliefs, cannot be overwritten with the oppositional language of cultural and ethnic antagonism, since the Hasmoneans who came to rule Judea in the course of the revolt presented themselves, at least in part, according to both biblical models of rule and recognizable patterns of Hellenistic kingship and governance. Gruen argues, moreover, that the revolt itself did not aspire to eradicate Hellenism, whatever that would mean, but to return to the norms of a prior *modus vivendi* of mutual recognition and benefit, and that it was the extraordinary rupture of these norms of government, consonant with normative views of good relations between kings and subordinated communities elsewhere in the Hellenistic world, that lay at the root of the revolt. Far away in Bactria, and under different conditions (as R. Mairs has shown), the ruler of a breakaway satrapy such as Euthydemus could also negotiate continued autonomy from the Seleucids by invoking other shared norms of Hellenistic rule: disavowing unjust revolt, and asserting cultural solidarities against the threat of 'barbarian' nomads (despite signs of cultural accommodation between

---

[45] Pausanias 8.49–52.

rulers and ruled in Bactria). L. Capdetrey's analysis shows that to Anatolian groups in the second century BCE, such as the Lycians and Carians, it appeared that the only viable means to sustain their local identities and maintain some traditions was to adopt federal institutions recognizable to the hegemonic culture. Egyptian priests likewise adopted the Hellenistic political language of honorific decrees to acknowledge and encourage Ptolemaic adherence to pharaonic ideals, and so showed some equivocation about assenting to Hellenistic political universals. Taken together, these examples show broad but varied engagement with Hellenistic culture, even in the process of articulating opposition to Hellenistic rulers. In some cases, if we extend the logic of Gruen's account of the Maccabean Revolt, resistance was a matter of subject peoples attempting to hold rulers accountable for lapses from cosmopolitan norms. The picture of cosmopolitan Hellenism that this entails is not that of a static, bounded and essential culture, but one that was susceptible to varied local reinscriptions.

Each of these differing responses from various local populations shared a basic commonality: all were engaging with similar Hellenistic norms of governance that descended, culturally and historically, from the conquests of Alexander and the establishment of the Successor kingdoms. This substantive dimension of the global frame of our approach (Moyn's and Sartori's first kind of 'global' history, to refer back), is often, as we noted above, treated simply as a series of bilateral relations between local cultures and cosmopolitan Hellenism, and so global considerations of resistance in the Hellenistic world dwell largely in the historian's realm of external, analytic comparison. But one of the questions we have repeatedly raised in the course of this collaborative undertaking was whether there were alternative, non-Hellenistic connections in the substantive and emic dimensions of resistance to Hellenistic rule, that is, in Moyn's and Sartori's second and third kinds of global history. These aspects, especially the latter, emic type of 'global' analysis – as a subjective category of the indigenous communities – have received the least scholarly attention, but there is at least some evidence that it warrants consideration. We can trace the outlines of this with respect to the Hellenistic present, the remembered Achaemenid past, and longed-for futures.

Regarding the Hellenistic present, Kathryn Stevens' careful study has revealed clusters of evidence for negative attitudes to Antiochus IV suggesting that the conduct of this ruler was depicted simultaneously in Babylonian, Jewish, and Greek texts as an exceptional departure from accepted norms of kingship. Although the forms of critique and resistance varied considerably, as we would expect, subjects in distinct regions of the Seleucid kingdom, and sited in different cultural locations, were responding with the same basic judgements on this ruler's transgressions. The text of 2 Maccabees, the epitome of Jason of Cyrene's account of the Maccabean Revolt, even incorporates as parallels for the Judean opposition to Antiochus IV accounts of the revolts of Tarsus and Mallus in Cilicia and the violent resistance of the Persians of Persepolis. These convergences, and the evidence of an indigenous connective perspective, raise the possibility not only that closely parallel historical phenomena can be observed in geographically distant regions, but also that this could be recognized by contemporaries and could contribute to the conceptualization of their own, more localized experiences.[46] Turning to the past, all the regions of the Hellenistic Near East that we are including in our 'global' frame, including Egypt, shared a common history of Persian imperial rule. The survival or re-emergence of diagnostically Achaemenid tokens of kingship among Arsacid, Artaxiad, Persid, and other local elites in moments of self-assertion suggests the trans-regional political valence of remembered Persianisms.[47] Johannes Haubold demonstrates how the highly variable affordances of this terrain could structure local scripts for resistance: the Judean and Babylonian memories of the Persians were vastly different.[48] Finally, and perhaps most spectacularly, we note the common phenomenon of apocalyptic eschatologies issuing from Hellenistic Judea, Babylonia, Iran, and, in a different form, Egypt. These elevated local contests with empire or against rival

---

[46] Kosmin 2016.   [47] See, for example, Canepa 2018.
[48] The memory of the Persians in Ptolemaic Egypt was also generally negative and they served as hostile figures in such texts as the Satrap Stele, several trilingual decrees, the *Demotic Chronicle*, and temple texts from Edfu. See, e.g., Funck 1996: 200–207; Winnicki 1991; Engels 2013: 66–67; Griffiths 1979; Yoyotte 1963: 140–141. Though beyond the scope of this volume, one could even extend Haubold's observation on the variable post-Achaemenid terrain to mainland Greece and the invocation of Persian wars in organizing resistance to Antigonid Macedonia in the Chremonidean War, and other moments.

neighbours to the most profound and totalizing historical and religious significance. Their futurological and prophetic discourses enunciated emic, often globalizing, evaluations of Hellenistic rule from the perspective of indigenous historicities, but at times through shared tropes and historicities, and with similar aspirations.[49]

These tantalizing connections and parallels beg the question of whether there were meaningful contacts and inter-ethnic solidarities between different local populations within and between the Hellenistic kingdoms, especially in prolonged periods of crisis, such as during the internal crises and external pressures of the second century BCE. In part, this is a question of simultaneity: was there in this period a widespread challenge by subject populations across the east Mediterranean and west Asia to the fact and legitimacy of Hellenistic imperial rule? And, if parallel movements and discourses of resistance did exist, to what extent were these atomized phenomena or episodes in an inter-regional movement undergirded by common historical developments and resonances between local indigenous perspectives on the fairness and justice of Hellenistic rule? Answering these questions will require a revived and revised interest in comparative and connective studies of the cultures of resistance in the Hellenistic world, for which we hope this volume will provide an impetus.

[49] See, for example, Kosmin 2018: 137–186.

PART I
THE BIG EVENTS
Pattern and Crisis

1
The Maccabean Model
Resistance or Adjustment?

Erich S. Gruen

The uprising by Judah Maccabee against Antiochus IV Epiphanes, perpetrator of the 'abomination of desolation', the success of which is celebrated annually and joyously as the festival of Hanukkah, serves as a touchstone of our volume. It represents the iconic rejection of the imperial Hellenistic state and thus a model whereby to compare a range of indigenous revolts against Greco-Macedonian suzerainty and to inquire about the parallelism of such examples of native resistance to Hellenic Empire. But does the Maccabean rebellion itself fall into that category? Does our very paradigm, when subjected to close analysis, actually qualify as a quintessential instance of the subversion of imperial rule? Before we employ it as the archetype, we need to question to what degree the Maccabean movement constituted a challenge to the legitimacy of alien governance.

The Jews of Judea came into the orbit of Seleucid power at the beginning of the second century BCE. Antiochus III at that time gained decisive victory over the Ptolemies in the so-called Fifth Syrian War and acquired control over Syria and Phoenicia, including the land of Judea. The Jews who had been under Ptolemaic overlordship for more than a century now shifted allegiance, we are told, to the Seleucid monarch, supplying provisions for his armies and elephants, and troops to help release the Ptolemaic grip from the citadel in Jerusalem.[1] There followed a document of high importance for Seleucid-Jewish relations, the report of which comes to us from Josephus, an item famously referred to by

---

[1] Jos. *Ant.* 12.133, 12.138.

Erich S. Gruen, *The Maccabean Model: Resistance or Adjustment?* In: *Cultures of Resistance in the Hellenistic East.* Edited by: Paul J. Kosmin and Ian S. Moyer, Oxford University Press. © Oxford University Press 2022. DOI: 10.1093/oso/9780192863478.003.0002

Bickerman as 'the Seleucid charter for Jerusalem'.[2] Josephus records a letter from Antiochus III to Ptolemaeus, his governor of Phoenicia and Syria, announcing the benefactions he would bestow upon the Jews for their services to him in the war. They included the reconstruction of the city of Jerusalem after the damages suffered in the war, the restoration of those who had been scattered abroad, the subsidizing of costs for animals, wine, oil, and other necessities for their sacrifices, as well as the provision of flour, wheat, and salt. Equally significant was the king's financing of restorations for the Temple, the relief of various taxes for the Jewish senate (*gerousia*), the priests, scribes, and even temple singers. For the rest, including those returned from exile, taxes would be lifted for three years, and a third of their tribute payments (*phoros*) eliminated thereafter. Further, those Jews who had been captured and enslaved would now be freed and their property restored. The Jews would henceforth be permitted to govern themselves in accordance with their own ancestral laws.[3]

A most generous set of favours, so it would seem. But perhaps not quite so magnanimous. Antiochus III did not act solely out of the milk of human kindness. We leave aside here the question of just how much of Josephus' account can be taken as reliable.[4] The letter, even if accepted as given, serves the king's interests as much as those of the Jews. The tax breaks go essentially to the elite, to the priests, the senate, the scribes, and the temple officials. No mention is made of those below that level of

---

[2] Bickerman 1935: 4–35. Among recent discussions, with bibliographies, see Gera 2014: 23–26; Honigman 2014a: 19–20, 264–269, 306–310; Bernhardt 2017: 100–107. See also Capdetrey 2007: 97–98.

[3] Jos. *Ant.* 12.138–144. On Ptolemaeus, see Gera 1987: 63–73, 1998: 28–34.

[4] Bickerman 1935: 4–35, made a strong case for the letter's authenticity, largely unquestioned since; see e.g. Tcherikover 1959: 82–89; Fischer 1980: 1–10; Seeman 2013: 67–70. But see the doubts of Gauger 1977: 23–151. More than one item causes suspicion. One might wonder, for instance, about the repatriation of Jews who had been enslaved abroad, especially for the alleged purpose of rebuilding the population of the city. It is unlikely that many Jews suffered enslavement in the realm of the Ptolemies. To be sure, the *Letter of Aristeas*, 23–24, claims that Jewish captives were reduced to slavery by Ptolemy I; cf. Jos. *Ant.* 12.29–30. But, even if one were to take that as credible, the author also observes that they were released from captivity by Ptolemy II, long before the Fifth Syrian War. See now the commentary of Wright 2015: 125–128. Portier-Young 2011: 68, takes the idea of widespread enslavement of Jews by the Ptolemies more seriously. The supposed repatriation of Jews to the homeland rings a Jewish, rather than a Seleucid, bell; cf. 3 Macc. 7.6–8. There are echoes here too of the fictitious story of privileges awarded to the Jews by Alexander the Great; Jos. *Ant.* 11.337–339.

society.⁵ It is the political and religious establishment of the city whose loyalty and cooperation Antiochus sought primarily, in order to advance the aims of the crown. But his pronouncements were not simply unilateral decisions. We happen to know, outside the evidence of Josephus, that the benefactions of the king were negotiated through the agency of a Jewish intermediary.⁶ Altruism is not at issue here. The bestowal of advantages to cities and to native cults in the Seleucid realm for the purposes of gaining allegiance and maintaining stability was common practice well before Antiochus III – and well after.⁷ Nevertheless, the favours accorded to the nation went beyond just the elite. Antiochus' letter guaranteed that all members of the *ethnos* shall govern themselves in accordance with their ancestral laws.⁸ There is no need to presume here that Antiochus referred here explicitly to Mosaic law – if he even knew what that was.⁹ Pronouncements guaranteeing freedom, autonomy, and living under ancestral laws were standard expressions of favour by Hellenistic kings toward *poleis* and principalities within their sphere of influence.¹⁰ That Jews would have full freedom of action to determine their own decisions was, of course, never contemplated by either side. The king delivered the pronouncements. The concessions were his to bestow – and his to withdraw.¹¹ There was no hypocrisy here. The reciprocal arrangement, and the slogans that accompanied them, were

---

[5] Indeed no mention is made of those dwelling in Judea outside of Jerusalem. This is sometimes taken to mean that Antiochus imposed taxes without restriction in the countryside and on all levels of society outside the privileged few. So Aperghis 2004: 166–168; Portier-Young 2011: 70–73; Honigman 2014a: 308–309. But the letter directs itself explicitly to bringing relief and restoration to Jerusalem and to the Temple. Inferences about the rest of Judea are speculative.

[6] 2 Macc. 4.11: καὶ τὰ κείμενα τοῖς Ἰουδαίοις φιλάνθρωπα βασιλικὰ διὰ Ἰωάννου.

[7] Some examples, with references, in Gruen 1999: 34–36. See, in general, Sherwin-White and Kuhrt 1993: 132–140. Cf. also Jos. *Ant.* 12.147.

[8] Jos. *Ant.* 12.142: πολιτευέσθωσαν δὲ πάντες οἱ ἐκ τοῦ ἔθνους κατὰ τοὺς πατρίους νόμους.

[9] Bickerman 1935: 27; Tcherikover 1959: 82–84; Portier-Young 2011: 73–75.

[10] See the discussion in Gruen 1984: 133–142; more recently, Dmitriev 2011: 112–141.

[11] It goes too far, however, to maintain that Antiochus was here claiming that Jewish ancestral laws and customs derived their ultimate authority from him and not from Yahweh, as does Portier-Young 2011: 62.

well understood. They do not amount to a false facade for oppression, domination, or exploitation.[12]

As if to underscore the fact, Josephus records a second measure of Antiochus III, this one a general proclamation intended, according to the historian, to be distributed throughout the kingdom. It declared royal sanction for certain Jewish ritual practices, forbidding non-Jews from entering the Temple precincts, and banning the flesh of unclean animals from the city.[13] The provisions are peculiar, and the reliability of the particulars have been properly questioned or reinterpreted.[14] But there is no need to question the general thrust of such a declaration as advertisement of the king's solicitude for peoples who had come under his sway and whose allegiance could be promoted rather than coerced.

The relationship between sovereign and subordinate state proceeded, so far as our information goes, without notable friction or upheaval in the years that followed under Antiochus III and his successor Seleucus IV. The second book of Maccabees, in fact, speaks of complete peace enjoyed by the holy city and the laws observed to the fullest in the era of the Jewish High Priest Onias. III.[15] The text further declares that the kings honoured the site and embellished the Temple with the most elaborate gifts, and it credits Seleucus for paying out of his own revenues the expenses incurred by the shrine for its official sacrifices.[16] Once again the generous benefactions need not represent affection or philanthropy. But the show of respect to the iconic centre of Jewish allegiance was more than window dressing. An inscription from near Beth Shean, from the early 190s, in the reign of Antiochus III, casts important light. It reveals that the king issued orders to various royal officials, including instructions to crack down on those soldiers who were billeting themselves

---

[12] Recent scholarship has placed considerable weight on Antiochus' concerns here with financial considerations; Aperghis 2004: 166–168; Portier-Young 2011: 55–57; Honigman 2014a: 308–310. The interpretation is one sided and does not tell the whole story. On the fiscal structure of the Seleucid Empire, see the important survey by Capdetrey 2007: 395–438.
[13] Jos. Ant. 12.145–146.
[14] Bickerman 1946–48: 67–85; Tcherikover 1959: 84–87; Gauger 1990: 150–164; Schwartz 2001: 53–54; Portier-Young 2011: 57–62. See the very fine treatment now by Gera 2014: 26–39, whose use of both biblical material and evidence from the Temple Scroll adds important dimensions to the analysis. The suggestion of Portier-Young 2011: 61, that the prohibition of animals within the city represented a 'subtle act of resistance in the face of Seleucid occupation' is quite paradoxical.
[15] 2 Macc. 3.1.   [16] 2 Macc. 3.2.

upon the villages and creating havoc among the inhabitants of the area.[17] The orders served to signal in a public document the continued concern of the monarch and the mutual advantage that held between the Hellenistic kingdom and those within its sphere.

Just a single episode in the reign of Seleucus marred this comfortable relationship, according to our chief literary source, 2 Maccabees. The notorious event comes encased in a narrative fable. According to the tale, Simon, the Jewish administrator (*prostates*) of the Temple, picked a fight with Onias the High Priest over market supervision in the city. The matter escalated when Simon appealed to the Seleucid governor of Coele-Syria and Phoenicia, claiming that the treasury at Jerusalem contained untold amounts of cash that did not correspond to the accounting for the sacrifices, and proposed that they could fall under the authority of the king.[18] As consequence of this encounter, Seleucus sent his principal minister Heliodorus with orders to remove those funds, thus triggering a celebrated set of events that issued in divine intervention and a miraculous rescue. Heliodorus' demands for the cash were resisted by the Jewish High Priest, and widespread alarm followed in the city as priests and people, with supplication and sackcloth, appealed to heaven for succour. Heliodorus pressed on, but God came to the rescue, sending a knight in shining armour whose steed sent the minister sprawling with its hooves and, as if that were not enough, two strapping youths beat him to a pulp. Heliodorus was subsequently carried off in a litter, magnanimously spared by the High Priest, and allowed to return to the Seleucid court where he could sing the praises of the Lord.[19]

The miraculous features of the tale can be readily dismissed. But does the fable not indicate tensions and friction stemming from financial exactions by the crown that impinged upon the fiscal autonomy of the

---

[17] *SEG*, 29, 1613. See text and translation in Aperghis 2004: 318–320, with discussion at 269–273.

[18] 2 Macc. 3.4–6. Simon may well have been a Seleucid appointee acting on the orders of the crown; Honigman 2014a: 333–335; Ameling 2012: 355. On his office, see Capdetrey 2007: 327–328. The questions of just which funds were at issue, whether monies supplied for the sacrifices were separate from temple accounts subject to taxation, and what relation held between market regulations and temple supervision are tangled and largely impenetrable. See the interpretation by Bickerman 1980: 159–191, the careful commentary of Doran 2012: 78–90, and the novel reconstruction by Honigman 2014a: 325–344, with further references.

[19] 2 Macc. 3.7–39.

Temple? The question became more acute upon publication a few years ago of a stele dating to 178 BCE, in the reign of Seleucus IV, which contains the king's letter to Heliodorus announcing the appointment of a certain Olympiodorus to oversee the care of the shrines in the satrapy of Coele-Syria and Phoenicia.[20] Seleucus declares that he had seen to it from the start that sanctuaries established in the other satrapies of the realm obtain their traditional honours with the care appropriate to them. But there had been no one authorized to take similar care in the province of Coele-Syria and Phoenicia. The appointment of Olympiodorus would remedy that defect.[21]

Does the text suggest that Seleucus has here undertaken to impose a stricter imperial control over the Temple in Jerusalem, thus compromising Judean autonomy? And did this issue in a major fiscal reform that entailed the levying of heavier taxation upon the land of the Jews? Scholarship since the publication of the stele has speculated that the changes implemented by the king in 178 aimed at shoring up the economic status of the kingdom through more effective fiscal exploitation by the Seleucids which proved eventually to stimulate revolt against the imperial power.[22]

Those broad conclusions rest, however, on a quite slender base. The stele supplies no hint of financial exactions. Seleucus expresses his solicitude for sanctuaries throughout his kingdom, thus to assure the favour of the gods, and declares his support for their traditional practices. And he announces that his new appointee will extend that same solicitude to the shrines of Coele-Syria and Phoenicia. Nothing in the document indicates the need or desire for raising revenues in the

---

[20] See the excellent *editio princeps* of Cotton and Wörrle 2007: 191–216. Important additional fragments were published by Gera 2009: 125–155, who supplied a significant commentary on the whole document. See also the refinements of Jones 2009: 100–104, and, on the formulas and terminology of the document, Bencivenni 2011: 139–153. See further Ameling 2012: 337–359.

[21] See especially lines 20–27: ἵνα μὲν τὰ καθιδρυμένα κατὰ τὰς ἄλλας σατραπείας ἱερὰ τὰς πατρίο[υς] κομίζηται τιμὰς μετὰ τῆς ἁρμοζούσης θεραπ[είας ἐ]ξ ἀρχῆς τυγχάνομεν τεταγμένοι, τῶν δὲ κ[ατὰ Κο]ίλην Συρίαν και Φοινίκην πραγμάτων οὐκ ἐχόντων [τὸν τα]σσόμενον πρὸς τῆι τούτων ἐπιμελείαι, κατε[λαμβάνο]μεν ὅτι σωφρόνως προστήσεται τῆς εὐκοσμίας ταγμ[ά]των Ὀλυμπιόδωρος.

[22] Cotton and Wörrle 2007: 198, 203; Gera 2009: 146–149, 2014: 48–57; Portier-Young 2011: 80–91; Seeman 2013: 70–73; Honigman 2014a: 40, 316–344, 578. A more cautious assessment by Ameling 2012: 350.

interests of the crown. To be sure, a document inscribed on stone and displayed in public would stress royal benefactions, not the raising of taxes, let alone the exploitation of subordinate peoples. But why should one infer unwelcome imperial interference? It is only the fanciful fable in 2 Maccabees with its villainous Heliodorus that suggests a connection. But Heliodorus appears on the stele only as recipient of the king's letter, a man who has oversight for the realm as a whole.[23] The new appointee for the satrapy was Olympiodorus who plays no part in the story told by 2 Maccabees.[24]

Linkage between the inscription and the fanciful tale in 2 Maccabees is an enticing, indeed irresistible, proposition, embraced by each scholar who has written on the subject. Yet it may be wise to curb our enthusiasm. The stele shows only that Seleucus appointed an overseer, Olympiodorus, to bring the administration of shrines in Coele-Syria and Phoenicia generally into proper order, thus to put them on a par with comparable administration of sanctuaries elsewhere in the empire, a policy the king had established from the beginning of his reign. The confrontation in 2 Maccabees, if one trusts the tale, arose from an internal clash between Simon, the Jewish *prostates* of the Temple, and Onias, the Jewish High Priest. A Seleucid official came into the narrative explicitly only when Simon appealed to him and claimed that the monies in the treasury in Jerusalem far exceeded what was required for the sacrifices and should be under the control of the king. The official's report to the king prompted him to send Heliodorus who demanded that the surplus in the treasury should be handed over to the crown, thus triggering the dramatic events that followed. It is something of a leap from the testimony of the stele or from the text of 2 Maccabees, or even

---

[23] Lines 1–2· Ἡλιοδώρου τοῦ ἐπί τῶν πραγμάτων; cf. line 13.

[24] Gera 2009: 148–150, gets around the problem by suggesting that the author of 2 Maccabees simply substituted the name Heliodorus for Olympiodorus, knowing that the former was the more powerful figure in the Seleucid realm generally, thus making for a better story. Cf. also Schwartz 2008: 185–186. But this is speculation, lacking evidentiary basis. Nor does it help to cite the Book of Esther as a possible parallel. Gera also proposed that Olympiodorus obtained the title of high priest, citing comparable cases under Antiochus III; Gera 2009: 133–138, 2014: 41–48; so also Jones 2009: 104; Doran 2012: 90; Ameling 2012: 351–352; Honigman 2014a: 322. Note particularly the appointment of Nicanor as High Priest in the cis-Tauric region of Asia Minor by Antiochus III; SEG, 37, 1010; Ma 2000a: 144–146, 288–292. This is perfectly possible in principle, but the inscription makes no mention of that designation, a surprising omission if Olympiodorus possessed it.

from both together, to infer a systematic Seleucid policy of financial exploitation and a major fiscal reform by the king to raise revenues for the empire – let alone to surmise that such a presumed policy eventually led to revolt in Judea against the Hellenic overlord.[25]

If indeed the Heliodorus fable is to be taken seriously as indicating a rift between the regime and the inhabitants of Judea, it is well to remember that the story has a happy ending. Not only is Heliodorus thwarted, but the High Priest Onias intervenes to save his life, makes a sacrifice on his behalf, sees to his recovery, and sends him back to the king in one piece. The author of 2 Maccabees ascribes to Onias motives that suggest not so much high-mindedness as pragmatism. The High Priest did not want Seleucus to conclude that his minister had suffered grievous harm at Jewish hands.[26] According to the narrative, Heliodorus arrived back at the court safe and sound but praised the miracles wrought by the Jewish god, and advised his sovereign not to send another emissary with demands to Jerusalem – unless it was his worst enemy – for he was sure to be soundly thrashed by the ministers of Yahweh.[27] The narrator may be employing some tongue in cheek here; the tale ends on that amusing note. But the upshot of that encounter was the reestablishment of cordiality between the ruling power and the subordinates. If one is to regard the tale as reflecting, in any significant way, the political relationship, it seems to imply restoration of the *modus vivendi* that had held since the measures of Antiochus III at the beginning of the century.[28]

If the monarchy were tightening the screws on Judea because financial needs dictated exploitation, we have no hint of that in the texts. Moderns point to the heavy indemnity imposed upon the Seleucids as

---

[25] If there had been such a policy, one wonders why it took nearly a decade after attaining the throne for Seleucus to implement it in Coele-Syria and Phoenicia.

[26] 2 Macc. 3.32: ὕποπτος δὲ γενόμενος ὁ ἀρχιερεὺς μήποτε διάληψιν ὁ βασιλεὺς σχῇ κακουργίαν τινὰ περὶ τὸν Ἡλιόδωρον ὑπὸ τῶν Ἰουδαίων συντετελέσθαι προσήγαγεν θυσίαν ὑπὲρ τῆς τοῦ ἀνδρὸς σωτηρίας.

[27] 2 Macc. 3.37–39.

[28] The author of 2 Maccabees does, to be sure, report further friction, but in his construct it is friction within the Jewish establishment, a continued contest between Simon and Onias. And, although he suggests that the Seleucid governor of Coele-Syria and Phoenicia was sympathetic to Simon, it is noteworthy that Onias felt comfortable in going to Seleucus himself in expectation of his support; 2 Macc. 4.1–6.

consequence of Rome's victory and the treaty of Apamea in 188, a whopping sum of 15,000 talents, 3,000 due immediately, and the rest to be paid in annual instalments for the next dozen years.[29] That might seem an imposing burden on the treasury of the Seleucids and an incentive for squeezing the indigenous peoples of their realm. Yet in 173 BCE the government was able to pay off the entire indemnity – well before the uprising of the Maccabees.[30] The king 'once or twice', so we are told, ran a bit short of cash, but that was because of expenditures and gifts that allowed him to be more generous than any of his predecessors.[31] Insolvency did not seem to be a problem.

Hellenistic kings, including the Seleucids, can hardly be reckoned as benevolent despots, their actions governed by philanthropic concern for the welfare of their subject peoples. The robbing of temples and shrines within their spheres of influence, when needed, was a long-standing practice among the Seleucids.[32] On that score the notorious Antiochus IV whose rule began in 175 did not break new ground. He despoiled the Temple in Jerusalem at least once, possibly twice, in 169 and/or 168.[33] The monies were doubtless required to help pay for his expeditions against Egypt. The forceful expropriation of capital from the Temple treasury certainly provoked bitterness and animosity in Judea. The idea that Jews had been seething with resentment at Seleucid overlordship and increasing financial exactions over the past decade or more, however, goes well beyond our testimony. The reign of Antiochus IV proved exceptional. It was not Seleucid business as usual.

---

[29] Polyb. 21.43.19–21; Livy, 38.38.14.
[30] Livy, 42.6.7. It is true that the *stipendium* was somewhat in arrears, but Rome had evidently not put much pressure on the Seleucids for prompt payment. The delivery of the sum in full by envoys of Antiochus IV in 173 is a telling fact. The Seleucids did not seem to be desperate for cash. A peculiar notice in 2 Macc. 8.10 (cf. 8.36) indicates that the government still owed monies to Rome in 165 BCE. Schwartz 2008: 544–545, argues that the *stipendium* paid in 173 was limited to the annual tribute, not to the whole of the indemnity. But that is surely not the obvious meaning of *stipendium... omne*. Even if 2 Maccabees is right that payments were still due in 165, this implies that the Romans were quite flexible in enforcing the terms of the treaty and the Seleucids were not being pressed for expeditious reparations.
[31] 1 Macc. 3.29–30: ἅπαξ καὶ δὶς.
[32] See Le Rider 1999: 1276–1277; Taylor 2014: 222–241, with extensive references.
[33] 1 Macc. 1.20–28; 2 Macc. 5.11–21. Cf. Daniel, 11.28–30; Jos. *Ant.* 12.249; *CAp.* 2.83–84. The despoliation came in 170/169, after Antiochus' first expedition to Egypt, according to 1 Maccabees, but 2 Maccabees sets it after the second Egyptian expedition in 168 (5.1). For Schwartz 2008: 533–536, both refer to the same event.

Money, to be sure, was not irrelevant. The satrapy of Coele-Syria and Phoenicia, which included Judea, regularly supplied tax revenues to the Seleucid regime, as it had to the Ptolemies before. That is a matter quite different from deepening hostility to the regime that ushered in Maccabean violence. Antiochus IV, of course, had additional and unusual needs in undertaking expensive campaigns against Ptolemaic Egypt. The author of 2 Maccabees employs the motif of Jewish leaders bribing Antiochus IV for the sake of their own aggrandizement more than once. As is well known, he has Jason effectively purchase the High Priesthood in 175 BCE, shortly after Antiochus succeeded to the throne, by offering the king 360 talents of silver, plus another eighty from a different source of revenue.[34] Just how to break this down remains controversial and is, for our purposes, unnecessary.[35] The first figure may represent the regular tribute payment and the second a special inducement to the king. Jason also sweetened the pot further by proposing to supply still another 150 talents for the privilege of installing a gymnasium and other Hellenic institutions in Jerusalem, which Antiochus welcomed.[36] We can forgo poking into that hornet's nest. But the money motif is notable, 2 Maccabees reverts to that theme. After three years, we are told, Jason sent Menelaus to the court on matters of some urgency and supplied him with money for Antiochus. But Menelaus trumped the High Priest by adding another 300 talents for the crown, thereby obtaining royal sanction for his own acquisition of the High Priesthood.[37] Whatever the reliability of these suspiciously similar scenarios, the narrative presents them as initiatives by the rival contenders for the High Priesthood, not as exactions imposed by the regime. The issue, for the author of 2 Maccabees, is one of internal friction between competing high priests, each seeking the favour of the

---

[34] 2 Macc. 4.7–8.
[35] See the comments of Schwartz 2008: 218; Doran 2012: 96. On Seleucid *phoros* and *syntaxis*, see Capdetrey 2007: 408–412.
[36] 2 Macc. 4.9–10.
[37] 2 Macc. 4.23–25. On the High Priests Jason and Menelaus, see the careful and thorough discussion by VanderKam 2004: 197–226; cf. also Babota 2014: 48–57, 84–88. The analysis of Gera 2014: 52–55, largely substitutes his own reconstruction for the testimony in 2 Maccabees. The bribery motif occurs again with regard to Menelaus' promise of cash to the royal official Ptolemaeus in persuading the king to dismiss charges against him; 2 Macc. 4.43–47.

king, rather than a financial burden inflicted upon the Jews by the Seleucids.[38] The stunningly ruthless actions taken by Antiochus Epiphanes against the Jews in 168 and 167 occupy central place in the story. The king remains as the iconic figure of unremitting evil in Jewish tradition. As reported in the books of Daniel, 1 and 2 Maccabees, and Josephus, Antiochus ordered devastating assaults upon Jerusalem, installed a garrison, plundered the Temple and defiled it with pagan rituals, banned the exercise of Jewish practices and traditions, slaughtered adult males, sold women and children into slavery, and inflicted unspeakable torments upon those who resisted.[39] Nothing comparable to such actions exists in the record of Jewish experience under the Seleucids. They can hardly be accounted for by fiscal needs or imperial deficiencies.[40] What motivated the monstrous deeds of Antiochus Epiphanes has been endlessly discussed and remains a source of continued controversy. This is certainly not the place to resolve it.[41] Our question is a different one. Did the robust and much celebrated Maccabean movement constitute a revolt against the suzerainty of the Seleucid Empire?[42]

When resistance to the measures of Antiochus Epiphanes began to materialize, its heroic figures, according to our sources, centred upon the

---

[38] Indeed the cost of repressing the Jewish rebellion in 167 caused Antiochus to worry that his treasury would run out of money, thus prompting him to head for Persia to collect tribute; 1 Macc. 3.30–31. That suggests that revenues from Judea had not brought much of a surplus. 2 Macc. 11.2–3 has the Syrian commander express the desire to make sale of the high priesthood an annual source of revenue.

[39] Daniel, 11.29–39; 1 Mac. 1.20–64; 2 Macc. 5.11–27, 6.1–11; Jos. *Ant.* 12.246–256.

[40] To be sure, such actions may not have been unique in the history of Hellenistic warfare or the retaliation of monarchs against recalcitrant foes; cf. Chaniotis 2005: 455–464; Honigman 2014a: 232, 389–390. The examples of Seleucid plunder of temples compiled by Taylor 2014: 222–241, have no parallels to Antiochus' atrocities that followed his despoliation of the Temple.

[41] A summary of various opinions may be found in Gruen 1993: 246–262. And much has been written since. See, e.g., Gera 1998: 153–161, 225–229; Weitzman 2004: 219–234; Nodet 2005: 143–158; Mittag 2006: 230–268; Doran 2011: 423–433, with further bibliography; Aperghis 2011: 68–83; Portier-Young 2011: 130–139, 176–216; Seeman 2013: 74–93; Honigman 2014a: 11–41, 359–361; 2014b: 59–76; Babota 2014: 46–66; Bernhardt 2017: 211–264.

[42] Honigman 2014a: 380–388, has recently revived the theory once propounded by Tcherikover 1959: 186–203, that a popular rebellion broke out in Judea while Antiochus was in Egypt, before the involvement of the Maccabees, a rebellion that triggered the brutal repression, followed by ferocious persecution. So also Schwartz 2008: 250–251, 254–255. But such a putative revolt has left no trace in our sources, and Honigman is obliged to propose that the information was deliberately suppressed.

family of the Maccabees. The immediate objective certainly was to reverse the intolerable policies imposed by the king. But was there something more? Did that resistance direct itself to the eradication of imperial rule or the abolition of Hellenic influence in the land of the Jews? On the latter issue, happily, we need not pause. The idea long prevailed that a deep fissure existed between 'Hellenizing' Jews who opted for assimilation, if not apostasy, and the traditionalists who fought the encroachment of Greek culture upon their treasured heritage, a division highlighted by the Maccabean revolt when understood as a paradigm of cultural conflict in the Hellenistic world. That compelling portrait, drawn by some of the giants in this field, notably Elias Bickerman and Martin Hengel, dominated scholarship for some decades for both those who embraced it and those who challenged it.[43] Fortunately, there is no longer any need to rehearse such a debate further. A strong consensus now holds that Hellenism and Judaism were compatible, that the spread of Hellenism was not Antiochus' objective, and that Judaism, whatever that might be, did not require keeping Hellenism at bay. This was no Kulturkampf.[44]

The more pointed question, and the one more pertinent for our discussion, is whether Judah Maccabee and his followers aimed to topple Seleucid authority in Judea?[45] The idea is expressed once in 1 Maccabees. The text concerns the framing of an alliance between Rome and the nation of the Jews in 164 BCE. It occurs in a digression following Judah Maccabee's dramatic victory over the Seleucid army led by the general Nicanor and before resumption of the narrative in which Judah himself fell in battle. The excursus offers a brief resumé of what Judah may have known about recent Roman history and Roman institutions. And the digression concludes with a prelude to the framing of the alliance in which Judah's motive for the pact is expressed as a desire to have the Romans lift the yoke from them because they saw that the kingdom of

---

[43] See, especially, Bickerman 1937; Hengel 1974. For a recent variation of this view, see Aperghis 2011: 79–81.
[44] See e.g. Will and Orrieux 1986; Gruen 1998; Levine 1998; Grabbe 2002: 52–66; Aitken 2004; Gruen 2010: 53–70; Regev 2013: 18–25.
[45] In the recently expressed view of Regev 2013: 16, Judah did not believe that Jews should live under Seleucid rule.

the Greeks was enslaving Israel.⁴⁶ No comparable statement is to be found elsewhere in the two books of the Maccabees. Should one take it as representative of the movement's meaning? The first objective of the uprising, of course, was to undo what Antiochus had done. The Maccabees, we are told, pulled down pagan altars, reinstituted the practice of circumcision, resisted the blandishments of the conqueror, and began a guerrilla movement to undermine the edicts of the king.⁴⁷ After a stunning victory over the forces of Antiochus, Judah performed his emblematic cleansing of the Temple. He destroyed the pagan altar that had been installed there, discarded the stones that had defiled the premises, rebuilt the shrine, and rededicated the Temple.⁴⁸ That, however, did not terminate the fighting. The contest had just begun. The Maccabees undertook a wholesale series of campaigns in Judea, Samaria, Idumaea, Phoenicia, Galilee, and Transjordan.⁴⁹ This was no mere recovery of lost ground. It was extension of authority.

Who were the enemies against whom they took up arms? The characterization of the Maccabean movement by its leaders and its own historians deserves notice. The appeals for support and the slogans that dominated the movement made repeated reference to the biblical past. They linked its principles to those who stood steadfast as witnesses to the law in the face of oppression.⁵⁰ The depiction of Judah Maccabee by the author of 1 Maccabees plainly sought to evoke the exploits of King David and the glories of ancient Israel.⁵¹ In 2 Maccabees, Judah rallied his forces more than once by alluding to the divine miracle that saved the Israelites from the armies of the Assyrian ruler Sennacherib.⁵² It is noteworthy that the texts repeatedly identify Judah's enemies as *ta ethne*, the 'nations' or the 'nations roundabout', or simply *allogeneis*, 'non-Jews',

---

⁴⁶ 1 Mac. 8.18: τοῦ ἆραι τὸν ζυγὸν ἀπ' αὐτῶν ὅτι εἶδον τὴν Βασιλείαν τῶν Ἑλλήνων καραδουλουμένους τὸν Ἰσραὴλ δουλείᾳ.
⁴⁷ 1 Macc. 2.42–48. ⁴⁸ 1 Macc. 4.34–59; 2 Macc. 10.1–8.
⁴⁹ 2 Macc. 10.15–17. 12.3–16, 12.26–28. 12.32–45. ⁵⁰ 1 Macc. 2. 49–64.
⁵¹ 1 Macc. 3.1–9. On the biblical allusions, see the valuable notes of Goldstein 1976: 293–305; Schwartz 1991: 21–29; and see now Berthelot 2014: 73–85.
⁵² 2 Macc. 8.19, 15.22; cf. 2 Kings, 19.35; 2 Chron. 32.21; Isaiah, 37.36.

a conglomerate foe that would encompass the enemies of the Israelites of yore.[53] They also revert frequently to the term *allophylloi*, used regularly in the Septuagint to mean 'Philistines'. Here the reference is quite clear to the most celebrated foes of David, a deliberate association between Judah Maccabee and the Israelites' greatest warrior.[54] Judah's contests in Idumaea were labelled as wars against the descendants of Esau.[55] He did battle with the Ammonites.[56] He destroyed shrines that long pre-dated the Greeks, like that in Carnaim and that of Atargatis in Philistia.[57] The enemies of the Maccabees include men from Galilee, from the Phoenician cities of Ptolemais, Tyre, and Sidon, and from Joppa and Jamnia.[58] Judah's forces crossed the Jordan to assault and capture numerous cities in that region, rescuing fellow Jews who were held there.[59] The Seleucid army itself, of course, was no monolithic Greek force. It consisted of troops from numerous nations: *pamphylon ethne*.[60] It is striking that *Hellenes* are nowhere identified as the target of Maccabean assault. Judah fostered a different kind of image. He would be the heir of the Israelite champions of old. It is no coincidence that his cleansing and rededication of the Temple in 164 echoed the feat accomplished by Solomon in consecration of the First Temple.[61] The contest, as presented in 1 and 2 Maccabees, is not one that pits the Jewish heroes

---

[53] E.g. 1 Macc. 2.68, 3.10, 3.25–26, 3.36, 3.45, 3.52, 3.58, 4.7, 4.11, 4.14, 4.45, 4.54, 4.58, 4.60, 5.1, 5.9–10, 5.19, 5.21, 5.38, 5.43, 5.57, 5.63, 6.18, 6.53, 7.23, 10,12, 12.53, 14.36; 2 Macc. 8.5, 10.4, 12.13, 13.11, 14.14–15. Cf. also Jos. Ant. 12,327, 12.330. That, of course, is not to deny that *ethne* could occasionally include Greeks, as they do in 2 Macc. 6.1–4, 15.10; cf. 1 Macc. 1.14. But that usage is exceptional. 1 Maccabees, 2.48, observes, quite significantly, that Mattathias, the father of Judah, rescued the law from the hand of τὰ ἔθνη and from that of 'the kings'; καὶ ἀντελάβοντο τοῦ νόμου ἐκ χειρὸς τῶν ἐθνῶν καὶ τῶν βασιλέων. The distinction seems clear. Schwartz 1991: 21–29, stresses the literary character of the portrait in 1 Maccabees and its biblical echoes. But the portrait is not limited exclusively to 1 Maccabees. See the references to 2 Maccabees above.

[54] 1 Macc. 3.24, 3.41, 4.12, 4.22, 4.26, 5.66, 5.68, 11.68, 11.74. An explicit reference to David and the *allophyloi* at 4.30. The term could, to be sure, stretch beyond Philistines to other foes of Israel; 1 Macc. 5.15. It could even, though rarely, include Greeks; 1 Macc. 11.68, 11.74.

[55] 1 Macc. 5.3, 5.65.   [56] 1 Macc. 5.6.   [57] 1 Macc. 5.44, 5.68.

[58] 1 Macc. 5.14–15; 2 Macc. 12.3–9.   [59] 1 Macc. 5.24–54.

[60] 2 Macc. 8.9; cf. 8.16: ἐθνῶν πολυπλήθειαν.

[61] Cf. 2 Chron. 7.1–10. On the biblical echoes in 1 and 2 Maccabees, see now Berthelot 2018: 99–153.

against the denizens of the evil Seleucid Empire – nor is it billed as rebellion against Hellenic rule.[62]

The purification of the Temple and its dedication in December, 164 BCE, did not bring an end to hostilities. The royal armies, unwilling to relinquish their authority in the region, persisted in their contest with the Maccabeans in subsequent years. But it is essential to recognize that this would be no fight to the finish. Nor did either side expect abject surrender to be followed by either wholesale subjection or total toppling of the established order. What needs emphasis is the existence of negotiations and accommodation almost from the start. That is hardly a feature to be given priority by the author of 2 Maccabees, who emphasized uncompromising rigour to the point of martyrdom by his Jewish heroes and heroines. But his text itself offers an alternative interpretation.

The author of 2 Maccabees conveys four revealing letters drawn either from some archive or from a knowledgeable source that shed important light upon relations between the Seleucid court and the Jews. The exact date, the order, and the circumstances of those letters have long been hotly debated, and no fuel will be added to that fire here.[63] Nearly unanimous consensus holds that the letters are genuine, and there is no good reason to imagine fabrication. All are set in the text shortly after the death of Antiochus IV and the accession of the boy successor Antiochus V Eupator. Two of them purport to be composed by the new king himself, though one of them may be by his father. The author introduces them by recording the sentiments of the Seleucid general Lysias who purportedly claimed that the god of the Jews rendered his people invincible, so he was prepared to accept a settlement proffered by representatives of Judah Maccabee.[64] Lysias' letter to the community (*plethos*) of the Jews notified them that he had delivered their requests

---

[62] One might note that 2 Maccabees even conveys the report that 8,000 Jews, presumably mercenaries, joined the 'Macedonians' (i.e. Seleucids) in a battle against the Galatians in Babylonia; 2 Macc. 8.20. This contest is nowhere else recorded, and may or may not be historical. See the discussions of Goldstein 1983: 331–334; Schwartz 2008: 546–548, with further bibliography. But the fact that the author links Seleucid and Jewish forces on the same side is noteworthy.

[63] The bibliography is long and need not be registered here. See the recent review of scholarship and sensible remarks by Doran 2012: 219–230; Seeman 2013: 96–105. A different and novel interpretation is offered by Ma 2019.

[64] 2 Macc. 11.13–15.

to the king and that he himself would see to their implementation, so far as that was within his power.⁶⁵ A letter by young Antiochus to Lysias was particularly compliant. The monarch acknowledged that his father had failed to shake Jewish convictions, and he declared that the Jews can freely enjoy their restored Temple, observe their own laws, and live in accordance with their ancestral practices.⁶⁶ Another earlier letter by king Antiochus, in this case probably by Antiochus IV, to the Jewish council and other Jews, affirmed an amnesty for exiles who would return and a guarantee of secure observance of their dietary laws.⁶⁷ One other letter, directed by Roman envoys to the Jewish people, expressed their assent to the concessions of Lysias and willingness to act on behalf of the Jews at the court in Antioch.⁶⁸

No need to parse these missives in detail. On any reckoning they disclose diplomatic negotiations engaged in by both sides, reciprocal acknowledgements, in short, an effort to restore the status quo ante. As the letters indicate, the monarch could live with the restoration of the Temple and the Jews' adherence to their own laws and customs; and the Jews welcomed the king's endorsement. That endorsement, of course, carried its own significance. These were concessions authorized by the crown – not in any way a sign of Jewish liberation from Seleucid hegemony.

The interchange brought only a temporary truce. Fighting resumed and continued. But that did not preclude bargains, parleys, and attempts to institute agreements. When the forces of Antiochus V and the Seleucid general, Lysias, besieged the Temple in 162, the effort had to be given up because of fear of a palace coup in Antioch. Not only did the Seleucid troops abandon the siege, but, if we believe 2 Maccabees, the king generously agreed to all the terms requested by the Jews, swore an oath to respect all rights, reached an accord, made a sacrifice, honoured the Temple, made benefactions to the site, and welcomed Judah personally.⁶⁹

---

⁶⁵ 2 Macc. 11.16–20.
⁶⁶ 2 Macc. 11.22–26. Note particularly 11.25: κρίνομεν τό τε αὐτοῖς ἀποκατασταθῆναι καὶ πολιτεύεσθαι κατὰ τὰ ἐπὶ τῶν προγόνων αὐτῶν ἔθη.
⁶⁷ 2 Macc. 11.27–33.   ⁶⁸ 2 Macc. 11.34–38.
⁶⁹ 2 Macc.13.23–24; cf. Jos. *Ant.* 12.382.

That was much more than needed to be done just for a temporary ceasefire.[70]

A noteworthy encounter along these lines took place in the following year, when the new Seleucid king Demetrius I sent his forceful general, Nicanor, to install Alcimus as High Priest and to conduct an assault on Jerusalem. In the account of 2 Maccabees an extraordinary event occurred. Nicanor was mightily impressed by the courage of Judah and his followers, and preferred to engage in diplomacy rather than war. And he went further still. In a private meeting between the leaders, Nicanor showed genuine affection for Judah, even offering him advice on marriage, family, and the virtues of domestic life.[71] This delightful scenario is doubtless too good to be true. And indeed the account in 1 Maccabees of this episode provides a nastier picture. In that narrative Nicanor does indeed propose a friendly parley to put an end to hostilities – but it was all a deceitful trick. The general, in fact, planned to kidnap Judah, but the latter got wind of it and foiled the plot, thus rekindling the war.[72] Not surprisingly, most moderns opt for the more cynical version.[73] The two narratives, in fact, however, simply reflect the inclinations of the two works, with 2 Maccabees drawn more to the idea of common ground between Jews and gentiles.[74] We cannot pretend to see into the soul of Nicanor or to affirm the truth of either account. Both, however, attest to the existence of diplomatic exchange, the prospect of reconciliation, and an atmosphere in which an accord short of unconditional victory or surrender was possible – indeed desirable.

Judah Maccabee fell in battle in 160. Diplomacy had broken down once again, and hostilities had resumed. But the contest was no simple one between Jews and Greeks, between troops of the empire and rebels against it. There were internal conflicts on both sides that motivated action and triggered events. The Seleucid throne was contested, and

---

[70] The version of 1 Macc. 6.55–63 gives a somewhat darker hue to the story. Antiochus does consent to the Jews living under their own laws as before, offers peace terms that were accepted, and swears an oath, whereupon the besieged were freed. But the author also has Antiochus subsequently change his mind and demolish the wall that the Jews had constructed before he rushed back to Antioch. Both versions, however, clearly attest to negotiations and concessions.
[71] 2 Macc. 14.11–25.   [72] 1 Macc. 7.26–32.
[73] See, especially, Bar-Kochba 1989: 351, 354–356. But cf. Schwartz 2008: 467.
[74] Cf. Doran 1999: 94–103; Schwartz 2008: 48–49, 466–467.

conflict roiled the empire. The usurpation in Antioch that caused Antiochus V to withdraw forces from Judea had been followed by a still more serious threat when Demetrius, son of Seleucus IV, returned to the east after a decade and a half as hostage in Rome, and claimed the crown for himself. Young Antiochus was swiftly disposed of in 162, and the new king ruled as Demetrius I. The takeover would soon engender further rivals and internal friction. In the meantime, Judah too had faced friction of his own. The new High Priest Alcimus who had succeeded Menelaus angled for the support of Demetrius and also ingratiated himself with various foes of the Maccabees within Jewish ranks. Maccabean leadership had not gone uncontested.[75]

Alcimus' death followed a year after Judah's own. Circumstances took on a somewhat different aspect. Internal battles, both in the Seleucid establishment and in the Judean leadership, had certainly proceeded. But the experience of Judah Maccabee had significant consequences not often emphasized. Periodic disengagement allowed the imperial power and the subordinate entity to revive, at least temporarily, the situation that had held prior to Antiochus IV, a coexistence with mutual benefits. In the Hasmonean period that followed, those benefits became more conspicuous and more substantial.

Two years of peace set in after the death of Alcimus. Jonathan, brother of Judah, became leader of the Hasmoneans. It is noteworthy that he encountered greater difficulties from Jewish opponents of his group than from Hellenistic imperialists. When hostilities broke out again, it was the 'lawless ones', as 1 Maccabees labels them, who took the initiative in soliciting Seleucid troops under Bacchides to help subdue the rival faction of the Maccabees.[76] After an initial defeat, however, Bacchides was prepared to negotiate, and Jonathan eagerly welcomed the opportunity. The pattern repeats itself. Bacchides did more than just arrange terms of a ceasefire. He released Jewish prisoners in his custody and he

---

[75] For struggles among the Jews, see, especially, 1 Macc. 6.18–27, 7.6–7; 2 Mac. 14.3–10. The internal conflicts are rightly emphasized by Wilker 2011: 219–256. The evidence of the Dead Sea Scrolls, especially with regard to 'the teacher of righteousness' and the 'wicked priest', may also reflect conflict between the Maccabees and their enemies within the Jewish community. See Eshel 2008: 13–61. On Alcimus, see VanderKam 2004: 226–239; Seeman 2013: 106–110; Babota 2014: 89–118.

[76] 1 Macc. 9.48–69; Jos. Ant. 13.22–28.

THE MACCABEAN MODEL: RESISTANCE OR ADJUSTMENT? 51

swore an oath that he would do Jonathan no harm for all the days of his life.[77] The rather florid statement may be a bit overblown. But the substance of the narrative has credibility. It was of mutual advantage to seek a *modus vivendi*. The settlement emblematized the character of relations between Jonathan and the Seleucids throughout his years of authority.

Jonathan had a valuable asset. He profited from the fact that claimants to the Seleucid throne continued to battle with one another for that privilege. The support of the Maccabees could be a useful advantage for any contender. Alexander Balas, who claimed to be a son of Antiochus IV, endeavoured to outbid Demetrius I in their power struggle by offering concessions to Jonathan. He named him officially as High Priest of the Jews, gave him the title of friend of the king, and even sent purple robes and a gold crown for Jonathan's investiture.[78] Balas' motives, to be sure, were hardly impeccable. But the public affirmation of Jonathan's status by the pretender to the throne had significant resonance. Demetrius promptly made a counter-offer which included considerable relief from a range of taxes, tithes, and tolls, authority for Jonathan to raise his own troops, and a host of extravagant favours so excessive that Jonathan preferred to go with Balas who seemed more sober and trustworthy, an alliance that endured through Balas' lifetime.[79] The enhancement of Jonathan's position and cordial relations with a Seleucid ruler were naturally hailed by the author of 1 Maccabees. But their significance needs to be underscored. Far from a successful rebellion against the empire, they acknowledged the power relationship that had prevailed since the beginning of the century, interrupted only by the exceptional actions of Antiochus Epiphanes. The regime recognized and supported the High Priest in Jerusalem, brought benefactions to the nation of the Jews, and entrenched the connection between empire and client state. The pattern continued through the years of Jonathan. Rival Seleucid princes fought over the crown, each enlisting the services or at least the neutrality of Jonathan Maccabee by showering distinctions and

---

[77] 1 Macc. 9.71: καὶ ὤμοσεν αὐτῷ μὴ ἐκζητῆσαι αυτῷ κακὸν πάσας τὰς ἡμέρας τῆς ζωῆς αὐτου. Cf. Jos. *Ant.* 13.33.
[78] 1 Macc. 10.1–21; cf. Jos. *Ant.* 13.35–45.   [79] 1 Macc. 10.22–47; Jos. *Ant.* 13.46–57.

titles upon him, including the designation of 'King's friend' or even 'King's kinsman', by awarding territory, by reducing tax payments, and by bestowing other benefits.[80]

These awards counted for more than conventional favours and augmentation of Jonathan's prestige. They were needed to shore up the Hasmonean position in Judea. Just as Seleucid princes and pretenders fought over power in Antioch, the Hasmoneans faced significant opposition in Judea. Rival groups and factions continued to challenge their ascendancy. So, for example, when Alexander Balas in 153 gave Jonathan the right to raise an army, this caused intense alarm among some Judeans.[81] Their concern, quite plainly, was not that Jonathan would employ his forces in the Seleucid cause, but that he would deploy them against home-grown enemies of the Hasmoneans. When Jonathan was treacherously captured and killed by forces loyal to the rebel Tryphon who sought to usurp the Seleucid crown, we are told that 'all the surrounding *ethne*' were planning to destroy the Jews utterly.[82] That was plainly the bitter fruit of Judah's ferocious campaigns against Idumaeans, Galileans, Transjordanians, and others. Jonathan similarly had no qualms about assaulting neighbouring nations. His attack on Azotus (Ashdod) included burning, pillage, and destruction of the venerable temple of Dagon.[83] The Hasmoneans were not contending here with the Seleucid Empire, but taking sides, for their own advantage, with one or another claimant to the throne. Imperial authority and Hasmonean success were in fact fundamentally interdependent.

Full autonomy for Judea in the Hasmonean era was never a realistic possibility – nor indeed aspiration. That may seem contradicted by the author of 1 Maccabees who looked back and identified an ostensible high point for his nation. When Simon succeeded his brother Jonathan as leader of the Hasmoneans in 143, according to the text, he asserted Jewish authority with dramatic gestures, the rebuilding of fortresses, towers, walls, and gates, he obtained a lifting of taxes on the land, and

---

[80] See 1 Macc. 10.59–66, 10.89, 11.27, 11.57; Jos. *Ant.* 13.85, 13.102, 13.124, 13.145–146.
[81] 1 Macc. 10.7–8: καὶ ἐφοβήθησαν φόβον μέγαν, ὅτε ἤκουσαν ὅτι ἔδωκεν αὐτῷ ὁ βασιλεὺς ἐξουσίαν συναγαγεῖν δύναμιν.
[82] 1 Macc. 12.53.
[83] 1 Macc. 10.83–87. Dagon was a pagan deity, with no connection to Hellenic cult.

THE MACCABEAN MODEL: RESISTANCE OR ADJUSTMENT? 53

he secured the right for his people to draw up contracts and agreements with a new dating system, beginning with the 'first year of Simon, great High Priest, general, and leader of the Jews'. 1 Maccabees sums it up with a proud pronouncement: 'the yoke of the nations was lifted from Israel'.[84] For many moderns, that signifies the longed-for and welcome autonomy of the Jews, liberation from imperial rule.[85]

In fact, it was nothing of the sort. The phraseology of 1 Maccabees refers to the release of Israel from the yoke of the nations, *ta ethne*, not of the Hellenistic Empire. That biblical phraseology is no coincidence. Simon had gained ascendancy over his enemies in Judea and over his gentile foes in neighbouring regions. But Hellenic suzerainty was undiminished. Indeed the murderous battles among Seleucid contenders for power in their realm made it all possible. The current conflict raged between Demetrius II and the usurper Tryphon who had eliminated Jonathan and had executed Antiochus VI. The bestowal of honours upon Simon came directly from Demetrius, a valuable step in his own war against Tryphon. This was no Jewish release from Hellenic hegemony, no triumph over the imperial power. One should note, first of all, that the initiative came from Simon who sent his own representatives to Demetrius in order to negotiate for an alleviation of tribute on grounds that Tryphon's exactions had been rapacious.[86] They brought along not only a palm branch to signify peaceful relations, but a golden crown to announce their acknowledgement of Demetrius' royal legitimacy.[87] The author of 1 Maccabees records a formal letter from Demetrius to the elders and to the nation (*ethnos*) of the Jews, addressing Simon as High Priest and 'friend of the king', the latter a conventional title in Hellenistic courts to designate elite local or regional leaders.

In it the Seleucid declared readiness to conclude a prolonged peace, to adhere to all agreements, to sanction the fortifications that Simon had built, and to order remission or cancellation of tribute money that was

---

[84] 1 Macc. 13.33–42. See, especially, 13.41: ἤρθη ὁ ζυγὸς τῶν ἐθνῶν ἀπὸ τοῦ Ἰσραήλ.
[85] E.g. Tcherikover 1959: 236–240; Schürer 1973: 189–194; Goldstein 1989: 318–319. For Regev 2013: 113–117, Simon's High Priesthood represents the institutionalization of Hasmonean rule. Some scepticism is expressed by Rajak 1996: 104–106. Simon's position was a complex and ambiguous one, in the view of Nodet 2005: 85–95.
[86] 1 Macc. 13.34.   [87] 1 Macc. 13.37.

owed, as well all other taxes. The generosity was doubtless welcome. But the power relations went unaltered. In that very letter, Demetrius expressed his graciousness by saying that he pardons all the mistakes and all the violations that Jews have committed down to the present day.[88] This, of course, only confirmed that forgiveness of transgressions was the prerogative of the ruler. And Demetrius concludes the letter quite interestingly by granting Jews the favour of enrolment in the Seleucid army for those who are eligible.[89] The monarch may have been magnanimous in his gestures and policy – but he also made clear who was in charge.

The rosy portrait drawn by 1 Maccabees has Simon preside over a near golden age of peace and prosperity, in which all foes had disappeared and all kings were crushed.[90] Our author even records a lengthy bronze inscription placed on Mt. Zion in 140 BCE that documented the Jewish people's gratitude to Simon for all his accomplishments. It proclaimed, among other things, Simon's bravery in warding off the enemies of the nation, paying for its defenders out of his own pocket, fortifying various cities, raising the heights of Jerusalem's walls, removing hostile forces from the citadel, settling Jews therein, and expelling *ta ethne* from the land. The document also observed that the Jews and their priests showered titles, honours, and powers upon Simon, giving him full control of the government, and denying to anyone else the right to contravene his decrees and decisions.[91] The authenticity of the inscription need not be doubted.[92] But it also contains a most revealing and critical clause. King Demetrius accorded Simon the High Priesthood, made him one of his 'friends', and conferred great glory upon him.[93] The document itself underscored the crucial fact. Simon's achievements were considerable, and support among his countrymen was widespread, but

---

[88] 1 Macc. 13.39: ἀφίεμεν δὲ ἀγνοήματα καὶ τὰ ἁμαρτήματα ἕως τῆς σήμερον ἡμέρας.
[89] 1 Macc. 13.40.   [90] 1 Macc. 14.4–15.   [91] 1 Macc. 14.25–47.
[92] See the treatments of its structure and language by Sievers 1990: 119–127; van Henten 2001: 116–145; more recent discussions by van der Kooij 2012: 29–32; Seeman 2013: 153–161; Babota 2014: 225–231; Bernhardt 2017: 384–394.
[93] 1 Mac. 14.38–39: καὶ ὁ Βασιλεὺς Δημήτριος ἔστησεν αὐτῷ τὴν ἀρχιερωσύνην κατὰ ταῦτα καὶ ἐποίησεν αὐτὸν τῶν φίλων αὐτοῦ καὶ ἐδόξασεν αὐτὸν δόξῃ μεγάλῃ. See the discussion of Babota 2014: 241–245. Bernhardt 2017: 392, rightly sees that Demetrius' endorsement of Simon's High Priesthood underscores the dependence upon and cooperation with the Seleucid.

THE MACCABEAN MODEL: RESISTANCE OR ADJUSTMENT? 55

he ultimately owed his position to the favour of the Seleucid king. Despite the abundance of accolades, the effusive inscription breathes not a hint that Simon had acquired independence for his people from the suzerainty of the Seleucids. Quite the contrary.[94]

We can refrain from going through the subsequent years. It is not our purpose to rehearse the history of the Hasmoneans.[95] I want to return to our initial question. Did the Maccabean uprising represent a model for insurrection against imperial rule, paralleled, duplicated, or even anticipated by comparable rebellions in various parts of the Hellenistic Near East? Or did it constitute instead a form of accommodation, sometimes smooth, sometimes rocky, in which the lesser and greater entities found a route to coexistence and mutual advantage? I have tried to argue that the latter is closer to the truth than the former.

The explosion that occurred in the time of Antiochus Epiphanes proved exceptional rather than paradigmatic.[96] The extraordinary measures implemented by that king did not emerge from a steadily increasing political and financial repression or a growing restiveness that ultimately issued in an effort to terminate Seleucid control. Judah Maccabee and his backers determined to reverse the outrages perpetrated by Antiochus,

---

[94] The letters by Seleucid kings or would-be kings to Jonathan and Simon, with their extensions of privileges, are examined, in interesting fashion, as examples of speech-acts or performative statements by Ma 2000: 95–111. The approach is illuminating, but the notion that they represent the degradation of Seleucid power is difficult to sustain.

[95] Among numerous recent treatments of Hasmonean history, see Sievers 1990; Nodet 2005; Dabrowa 2010: 42–102; Regev 2013: 103–174; Atkinson 2016; Bernhardt 2017: 275–484; Berthelot 2018: 65–340.

[96] Questioning the Maccabean episode as exemplary of indigenous resistance to the imperial power of Hellenistic kingdoms does not, of course, deny the phenomenon itself of native uprisings and attempts to overthrow Hellenic rule elsewhere. The thrust of this contribution is to stress the special circumstances that gave rise to the Maccabean movement, the particular aims of Antiochus IV, and the tenacious attachment of the Jews to their traditional laws and institutions that were violated in so unexpected and flagrant a fashion, altogether unprecedented in Judea under Persians, Ptolemies, and Seleucids alike. Efforts to find parallels and comparisons elsewhere in the Hellenistic Near East need to take account of the unusual character of the Judean situation. The present essay calls in effect for an assessment of the balance between the norm and the exception. Antiochus' singular deeds do not lend themselves readily to extrapolation elsewhere even in Seleucid history. But the events surrounding the Maccabean uprising and its consequences do possess significant features that have resonance for contests on a wider front: local rivalries, appeal to ancient traditions, efforts to negotiate a path between imperial power and regional autonomy, and the aim of restoring a situation that had held prior to the conflagration. On the spectrum between revolt and accommodation, this study leans to the latter.

but they had targets that went well beyond those who ministered to the Hellenistic king. The Maccabean battle directed itself at least as much against internal foes and diverse enemies in Palestine as against the Seleucid regime. Once the Temple was restored and re-consecrated, Judah showed a readiness to conduct negotiations and to conclude agreements with Seleucid officials and commanders. He did not engage in a campaign to eradicate the imperial presence.

The groping for accommodation that Judah pursued in the last years of his life came to fruition under his successors Jonathan and Simon in the next quarter of a century. Contests among rivals for the Hellenistic throne gave an opening to Hasmonean leaders to advance their own interests by propping up pretenders. But the discrepancy in power was never in question. Jewish leaders received their positions, titles, and privileges at the hands of Seleucid princes. The issue was uncontested, and the reciprocal benefits persisted.

Toppling of Seleucid dominion was never on the cards. Nor is there any suggestion that such was the aim of the Maccabees. They nowhere raised the banner of autonomy. Their success rested on the reinstitution of the arrangement that had prevailed before Antiochus Epiphanes. The *modus vivendi* between imperial suzerain and subordinate nation had its own appeal. The Maccabees could live with it. They expected nothing more. And they got nothing more.

2
The 'Great Theban Revolt', 206–186 BCE

Anne-Emmanuelle Veïsse

The domestic uprising known as the 'Great Theban Revolt' that broke out in southern Egypt at the turn of the third and second centuries BCE was both the longest and the most severe that the Ptolemaic state ever had to face.[1] The number of sources that document it is evidence of its magnitude: in his influential article published in 1995, P. W. Pestman gathered more than twenty documents, both papyrological and epigraphical, that explicitly mention the revolt and/or its leaders, and more have appeared since then.[2] Although numerous questions remain, this revolt is much better attested by documentary sources than many other major events of Ptolemaic history. Given the current state of evidence, the Great Theban Revolt is also the only one whose rebel leaders proclaimed themselves as pharaohs.[3] To this day we know fifteen or sixteen documents officially dated according to 'pharaoh Haronnophris' (nine to ten documents) and 'pharaoh Chaonnophris' (five to seven).[4] In order to provide elements of comparison with

---

[1] I would like to thank the organizers of the Maccabean Moment Conference, P. Kosmin and I. Moyer, for having given me the opportunity to come back once again to the 'Egyptian revolts'. The fruitful discussions that have been generated by the conference have contributed to the present study. I am deeply grateful to S. Honigman, W. Clarysse, G. Gorre, P. Kosmin, and I. Moyer for their attentive reading and suggestions, and to R. Birk and L. Uggetti for providing access to their forthcoming studies with me.

[2] See Pestman 1995a. New documents: Farid 2005: n.1; Eldamaty 2005; Chaufray and Wegner 2016. Re-editions leading to new interpretations: Depauw 2006; Chaufray and Wegner 2016. For a possible allusion to Chaonnophris in the fragments of the Judeo-Hellenistic author Artapanus, see also Veïsse 2013.

[3] The so-called 'Pharaoh Harsiesis' who allegedly seized power in Thebes in the 130s is in all likelihood a historiographical myth. See Veïsse 2009, 2011, following a suggestion made by M. Chauveau.

[4] The Demotic contract *P. Brit. Mus.* IV 4 and the letter published by Farid 2005 were written either under Haronnophris or Chaonnophris. Chaonnophris is also mentioned, without the title of pharaoh, in the so-called 'second Philae decree' and in the papyrus *SB* XXIV 15972 ('the

domestic revolts that occurred elsewhere in the Hellenistic world, this article first aims at offering a synopsis of the facts, and then will focus on two aspects that make the Great Theban Revolt particularly worthy of interest: the political-religious concerns displayed by the (from their own standpoint, certainly misnamed) 'rebel' pharaohs and their engagement in a genuine state-building process. Finally, some hypotheses as to why the revolt broke out and why it reached such an extent in the Thebaid will be discussed.

1. The Chronological Outline

Troubles in Upper Egypt started at the very end of the reign of Ptolemy IV (year 16 = 207/6 BCE, or year 17 = 206/5 BCE) – but where precisely remains unknown.[5] In the autumn of 205 BCE a certain Haronnophris seized power in Thebes and assumed the title of 'pharaoh', according to a letter found in Karnak and dated to his first regnal year.[6] Documents in the Theban area were also dated according to Haronnophris' reign in 201 and 199, whereas no documents mentioning the names of Ptolemy IV or Ptolemy V have been found in this area from 207 through the very end of 199. Between 204 and 201/0, the rule of 'pharaoh Haronnophris' is referred to in other places in Upper Egypt as well: in Pathyris (c. 30 km south of Thebes) in 204; in the Coptite nome (c. 40 km to the north) in 202/1; and in Abydos (about 170 km northwest of Thebes) in 201/0.

Then, from 199 BCE, Haronnophris disappeared from the evidence altogether, whereas contracts started to be dated according to the reign of

---

revolt of Chaonnophris'). *P.Brit.Mus.* IV 11, where the protocol is lost, may be attributed either to Chaonnophris or Ptolemy V. All in all, Chaonnophris is mentioned in seven to nine documents, of which five to seven include the title of pharaoh.

[5] For the different sources and the chronological issues concerning the revolt, see Pestman 1995a, 1995b; Veïsse 2004: 11–26, and n. 2 above. For cogent arguments in favour of 206/5 rather than 207/6 for the beginning, see Depauw 2006: 103. The dedicatory inscription of the Horus temple at Edfu records that the doors of the temple were ready to hang in 207/6 BCE and that the work was interrupted by 'ignorant rebels'. But it does not specify where those rebels came from and when exactly they arrived at Edfu: 'Then the troubles broke out after which the ignorant rebels in the South have interrupted the work in the Throne-of-God' (*Edfu* IV, 8, 4–5). The outbreak of the revolt probably also explains the abrupt abandonment of the Bir Samut fortress, in the Eastern Desert: see Redon 2018: 19.

[6] The document has been re-edited by Depauw 2006.

'pharaoh Chaonnophris' who, as P. W. Pestman demonstrated, continued the regnal years of Haronnophris. Thus, the sixth year of Haronnophris gave place to the seventh year of Chaonnophris – and not the first, as we might have expected.[7] It is generally agreed that Chaonnophris was Haronnophris' successor, but it is also conceivable that the two pharaohs were in truth one and the same and that Haronnophris changed his name to Chaonnophris.[8] This hypothesis may be supported by two arguments: first, the continuity in regnal years is very unusual in Egyptian history, and it is all the more surprising given that, as we shall see below, pages 64–65, the rebel king(s) manifestly sought to revive ancient traditions. Second, in the so-called second decree of Philae promulgated on 6 September 186 BCE by a gathering of Egyptian priests in order to celebrate Chaonnophris' defeat,[9] the latter is described as the 'rebel against the gods (...) who began the fight within Egypt', as if one king only had stood at the head of the rebels from 206 to 186 BCE.[10] Besides, the parallel between the names 'Haronnophris' and 'Chaonnophris', even if it suggests at first glance a dynastic succession between two different kings, also allows one to envisage an ideological continuity being expressed by a single individual (see pages 64–65).

All the documents dated according to 'pharaoh Chaonnophris' are Demotic contracts written in the Theban area between 199 and 191 BCE: apparently, only this area remained under the direct control of the rebel king during this period, even though the activity of his supporters is also attested further north, in the Lycopolite nome, where massacres were

---

[7] See Pestman 1995b.
[8] See Veïsse 2013, following a suggestion made by M. Chauveau.
[9] This decree (*Philensis* II) is known from two copies. The one that was inscribed in the 'birth house' of Philae was published independently by Sethe 1904; Müller 1920. The decree was also reproduced on a stele of the Cairo museum, which was published by M. Eldamaty in 2005. Von Recklinghausen 2018 has recently provided a complete re-edition of the two copies of the decree.
[10] Von Recklinghausen, *Philensis* II, § 4.1 (hieroglyphic text): '...gegen den Feind der Götter, Chaonnophris, der den Aufruhr in Ägypten begonnen, Betrüger (um sich) versammelt und alle Gebiete Ägyptens in Unruhe versetzt hatte'. The fact was already noted by Pestman 1995a: 130, n. 90: 'I wonder if Chaonnophris was considered as leader of the whole revolt, once he had taken over the throne in Thebes in 199/198'.

perpetrated at an uncertain date.[11] It is also in Chaonnophris' time that the Ptolemaic counterattack is first documented.[12] In August 199, the royal army besieged Abydos and eventually regained control of the city.[13] In Thebes, the authority of Ptolemy V was temporarily reinstated between the end of 199 and that of 198. But the city was lost again to Chaonnophris and was permanently reconquered only around the autumn of 191.[14] Down to that time, the Ptolemaic response to the revolt had certainly been hindered by the various problems that the Crown had to face both on the domestic and external fronts: the death of Ptolemy IV, the minority of Ptolemy V and the tensions in Alexandria, culminating in the urban riot against the regent Agathocles in 203;[15] the Fifth Syrian War (c.202–198 BCE) resulting in the irreversible loss of Coele-Syria; and the troubles in the Delta. According to the priestly decree of Memphis of 196, this revolt started, like that in Upper Egypt, by the end of Ptolemy IV's reign,[16] but the scarce evidence does not allow us to determine whether there were direct links between the events of Lower and Upper Egypt. Whatever the case, the troubles in Lower Egypt were certainly the most urgent to address. The city of Lycopolis in the Delta had fallen into the rebels' hands and had to be reconquered by the royal army in the summer of 197. Even though its precise location remains debated, we know for certain that it stood at the border of the Bousirite and Sebennytic nomes, that is, in the immediate vicinity of the Greek city

---

[11] As stated by McGing 2016: 151, the papyrus that refers to the massacres (*SB* XXIV 15972) says nothing about Chaonnophris' own movements.

[12] In his new interpretation of the demotic letter from Karnak dated 11 November 205, Depauw 2006: 105 has shown that the camp of the rebellion expected to have to repel a Ptolemaic offensive by that time; given the maintenance of Haronnophris' reign in Thebes after this date, this offensive did not take place, or was unsuccessful. The other letter from Karnak published by Farid 2005 mentions fighting in Thebes but the date is uncertain (either Haronnophris' or Chaonnophris' reign).

[13] The date on which the city was retaken is not known, but one can assume that it preceded the seizure of Thebes by the Ptolemaic troops by late 199.

[14] The last contract bearing the name of Chaonnophris is dated 6 August to 4 September 191 (*P. Eheverträge* 29).

[15] Polybius 15.25–33. See Veïsse 2019.

[16] See the Memphis decree of 196, Greek version, l. 27–28: 'Those who had led the rebels *in the time of his father* and had troubled the land and done wrong to the temples, when he [i.e. the king Ptolemy V] came to Memphis, defending his father and his kingdom, all he punished fittingly at the time he attended the celebration of the proper ceremonies for the assumption of the kingship' (Quirke and Andrews 1988). The rebel chiefs in question were those who had been captured during the seizure of Lycopolis (cf. l. 26–27).

THE 'GREAT THEBAN REVOLT', 206–186 BCE   61

of Naucratis, and not far away from Alexandria.[17] In contrast, from the late 190s Ptolemy V had freer hand to wage war against the rebels of Upper Egypt. As noted above, the city of Thebes was reconquered by the end of 191, and a major offensive led to the final defeat of Chaonnophris on 27 August 186 after a battle fought somewhere in Upper Egypt. Nubian troops took part in this combat on the side of the rebel king.

Whereas in the Delta further military operations had to be conducted against rebel leaders down to 185/4,[18] in Upper Egypt the Great Revolt was now ended, twenty years after it started. Unquestionably, it was a violent episode that led to looting, deaths and destruction, and also drove many people from their homes.[19] However, this revolt cannot be considered only as an explosion of uncontrollable violence, as the Egyptian priests claimed in the second Philae decree. According to the priests, the 'impious rebels' killed, plundered, and desecrated indiscriminately – in other words, turned everything into chaos.[20] But different elements neatly show that the rebel king(s) intended to build a real state and even that he or they were relatively successful in that, especially at the beginning.

2. Building a New State

First, very early in his reign, Haronnophris set up a new chancellery, as revealed by the limestone tablet Cairo 38258 (the earliest document to mention the king), re-edited by M. Depauw in 2006.[21] This tablet, which was found in Karnak, is a Demotic letter mentioning the 29 and 30 Thoth

---

[17] According to the Greek version of the Memphis decree of 196, the city was located in the Bousirite nome, while Strabo and Stephanus of Byzantium set it in the Sebennytic nome.
[18] Saïte nome (Polybius 22.16–17: see Veïsse 2016) and eastern Delta (Memphis decree of 182: see Nespoulous-Phalippou 2015).
[19] See Armoni and Jördens 2018.
[20] Von Recklinghausen, *Philensis* II, § 4.1 (hieroglyphic and demotic text; for the interpretation of the last sentence, see Depauw 2006: 105); Von Recklinghausen 2018: 293; 294–302.
[21] Depauw 2006. The document was first published by Spiegelberg 1912. In view of the large dimensions of the tablet (19 cm wide, 31 cm high and 1.5 cm thick), and atypical epistolary features, Depauw considers that the document was 'not a real letter which was actually sent, but rather a fictive letter by a scribe wanting to exercise his epistolary skills of political correctness now that Thebes was once again ruled by an Egyptian pharaoh'. Depauw 2006: 102.

of his first year, corresponding to 10 and 11 November 205 BCE.[22] Given that the Egyptian year starts on the 1st of Thoth, we may infer that Haronnophris assumed the title of pharaoh on 13 October 205 at the earliest. The letter was addressed by one Peteharmais, son of Petosiris, possibly a *pastophoros* of Amon, to a superior bearing the titles of 'scribe of the king' (sḫ nsw) and 'scribe of the directive' (sḫ pꜣ wḫꜣ). The first one is an archaic title, used here instead of the more modern designation 'scribe of the Pharaoh' (sḫ Pr-ꜥꜣ). The second title appears in Demotic literature, especially in the *Battle for the Armour of Inaros*, 'where its holder seems to be a high official receiving instructions from pharaoh himself only'. A sḫ pꜣ wḫꜣ with similar functions is also found in the so-called *Petition of Petiese*, from the sixth century BCE.[23] M. Depauw identified the sḫ pꜣ wḫꜣ as the head of Haronnophris' chancellery, an office held by the *hypomnematographos* and the *epistolographos* at the Ptolemies' court.

Second, among the crimes that are attributed to the rebels in the second Philae decree, an increase in taxation is denounced.[24] This statement is problematic, however, since no tax receipts have been found for the time of the rebellion.[25] If the priests are to be believed, we must admit that, in one way or another, the rebels either maintained or created administrative structures for the needs of tax collection; in other words that they did not simply engage in plunder but also sought to institute regular sources of income.

Third, the Demotic contracts written in the names of Haronnophris and Chaonnophris show that under his (or their) rule people continued to get married, inherit, buy, etc., carrying on daily life as usual, or almost as usual. We may consider, for instance, the two papyri coming from Pathyris and dated to Haronnophris' reign, which have recently been respectively published and republished by M.-P. Chaufray and

---

[22] For the conversions of Haronnophris and Chaonnophris' regnal years into the Julian calendar, see Pestman 1995b.
[23] Depauw 2006: 99.
[24] Von Recklinghausen, *Philensis* II, § 4.1, hieroglyphic text: 'sie erhöhten die Steuern der Fruchtländer'.
[25] See Clarysse 2004: 6; O'Neil 2012: 146. The permanent state of war can also explain why the new pharaoh(s) did not engage in temple building.

W. Wegner: *P. BM EA* 10486 and *P. Ryl. Dem.* 32.[26] The first one was written at the end of Haronnophris' first regnal year (year 1, 20 Mesore, corresponding to 27 September 204).[27] It is an offer addressed to the priests of Hathor in Pathyris by one Harpaesis son of Thotortaios who applies to become scribe in the temple for one year. The second papyrus is a transfer into private hands of a plot belonging to the temple of Hathor. This deed was written by the same Harpaesis '(in) the name of the priests of Hathor' between 12 November and 11 December 204 (year 2 of Haronnophris, Phaophi). Obviously, the offer made in September had been successful and Harpaesis had started to work as a scribe in the temple. The very ordinary content of these two documents contrasts with the dating according to Haronnophris instead of Ptolemy V. There must have been fighting in the area, and big changes, but in 204, a couple of years after the beginning of the revolt and eleven months after the assumption of the title of pharaoh by Haronnophris, the inhabitants of Pathyris were seemingly carrying on their business as usual.[28] Contracts dated according to Haronnophris or Chaonnophris in the Coptite nome and in the Theban area offer a similar picture as they deal with matters such as marriage, sale of land, agreement concerning a legacy, and debt acknowledgement. Apart from the protocols, only two internal elements may perhaps hint at the new political situation: first, when required, the sums of money are given in silver and not in the new fiduciary copper currency, the value of which was guaranteed by the Ptolemaic state only;[29] second, none of the witnesses has a Greek name, whereas witnesses bearing Greek names occasionally appeared in Theban contracts written before the revolt.[30] These two elements raise further questions: what was the attitude of Haronnophris/Chaonnophris towards the

---

[26] Chaufray and Wegner 2016.
[27] See Chaufray and Wegner 2016: 35. The papyrus had originally been dated to the joint reign of Ptolemy VI and Ptolemy VIII.
[28] Chaufray and Wegner outline that offers similar to that of Harpaesis were addressed both to the priests and to the *epistates* in Soknopaiou Nesos and Pathyris in the second century BCE. As they note, 'as the *epistates* was a royal agent, his absence in the Pathyris' lease offer could have been a consequence of the political change but the *epistates* may also not have been systematically included'. Chaufray and Wegner 2016: 40.
[29] See Gorre 2012: 113, nn. 165 and 167; Gorre 2014: 92.   [30] See Clarysse 1995a.

Greeks and the Ptolemaic power? What was the nature of the authority that he or they attempted to establish?

3. The Nature of Haronnophris/Chaonnophris' Authority

Of all the issues concerning the revolt that remain unsolved, our lack of knowledge about who Haronnophris and Chaonnophris were is certainly the most frustrating one. At the very least, the old view that they were of Nubian extraction is better set aside: not only do we have no positive evidence to support it,[31] but the priests who wrote the second decree of Philae would surely have pointed to the fact insofar as they carefully specify (and implicitly criticize) that 'troops of Nubians' had joined Chaonnophris in the final battle fought against Ptolemy V's army.[32] We have more evidence about how the rebel leaders conceived their action and how, in particular, they sought to revive the 'old order' while remaining at the same time firmly rooted in the present.

The references to the past are reflected first in the features of the new chancellery set up by Haronnophris, which, as noted above, used the Egyptian language and had an archaizing slant. A similar return to the past lies in the new pharaohs' names themselves: Haronnophris and Chaonnophris, that is 'Horus-Onnophris' (*Ḥr-wn-nfr*) and 'Onnophris lives' or 'May Onnophris live' (*Ankh*-Onnophris': *ʿnḫ-wn-nfr*).[33] Per se,

---

[31] In the demotic version of *Philensis* II, the term *sbi*, 'enemy', when applied to Chaonnophris, is complemented by the foreign land determinative in two or three cases: Von Recklinghausen, *Philensis* II, Anhang B, demotischer Text, l. 4, p. 54 (cf. Sethe, *Urk.* II 217, 10, note n); l. 7, p. 57 (Sethe, *Urk.* II 221, 8, note e); and perhaps l. 13, p. 61 (Sethe, *Urk.* II 228, 9, note g). K. Sethe inferred that Chaonnophris 'nichtägyptischer Herkunft war' and that his homeland 'nur in Süden, in Nubien, gewesen sein konnte' (Sethe 1917: 42). He was followed by Préaux 1936: 531, nn. 2 and 532, and by many other authors. But as noted by G. Vittmann, 'Ein Determinativ allein bei einer abfälligen Charakterisierung reicht zu einer derartigen Aussage, die sich anderweitig nicht absichern lässt, nicht aus. Die gleichwohl bemerkenswerte Schreibung dürfte sich einfach daraus erklären, dass man "Rebellion", "Gottlosigkeit" und "Ausland" nach altbewährter Manier in eins setzte, auch wenn im konkreten Falle die Rebellion von innen kam', Vittmann 2005: 208. See also Veïsse 2004: 84–95; Von Recklinghausen 2018: 287.

[32] Von Recklinghausen, *Philensis* II, § 2 and § 4.2.

[33] See Pestman 1995b: 126; Quack 1991: 92–93; Von Recklinghausen 2018: 43. The form 'Chaonnophris' is the Greek transcription of the name, given in the papyrus *SB* XXIV 15972 from Lycopolis ('the revolt of Chaonnophris'), see Clarysse 1978: 245.

these are not uncommon personal names, although Chaonnophris is much rarer than Haronnophris.³⁴ But their parallel structure suggests that they were chosen as programmatic ruler names. Both include the component Onnophris (*Wn-nfr*), an epithet of Osiris, the god that had come to be the model of kingship in the Late Period.³⁵ By adopting these names, the pharaoh(s) Haronnophris/Chaonnophris referred to an ideal past but also challenged the links already established by the Ptolemaic kings with the god Osiris – that is to say, the links established between the god Osiris and the Ptolemaic kings in priestly circles, with the aim of legitimizing both the ruling dynasty and their own support to this dynasty. In Thebes in particular, the parallel between the Ptolemies and Osiris was displayed since the third century on the monumental gates of Mout, Khonsou and Montou;³⁶ the Osirian catacombs of Karnak were also reshaped under Ptolemy IV and the cartouches of Osiris and Isis were associated with the cartouches of the king and of Arsinoe III.³⁷ If the proposal that we are dealing with only one pharaoh is correct, his shift from 'Horus-Onnophris' (Haronnophris) to '*Ankh*-Onnophris' (Chaonnophris) added the meaningful nuance that he was not only the sole legitimate pharaoh associated with the god Osiris, but was still alive in 199, and very much ready to fight, in spite of the first successes of the Ptolemaic counterattack.³⁸ Even under the second scenario (one king succeeding the other) the meaning would have been quite similar: in this

---

³⁴ See Trismegistos NAME 283 and 115.
³⁵ See Clarysse 1978: 252–253; 1995b: 17; Coulon 2010. In the graffito of Abydos referring to the reign of Haronnophris (written in Egyptian with Greek letters), the reference to Osiris contained in the ruler's name is doubled in the epithets: 'Year 5 of pharaoh Hurgonaphor (Haronnophris), beloved by Isis and Osiris, beloved by Amonrasonter the great god' (Graffito P. Recueil 11: 201/0).
³⁶ See Preys 2015.
³⁷ See Coulon 2005, esp. 23–24: 'Sur la paroi fermant à l'ouest cette galerie [i.e. the south gallery], qui peut être considérée comme le point "focal" de l'édifice, une représentation du sanctuaire qu'abrite la butte arborée comprend une corniche ornée de cartouches royaux: de part et d'autre d'un disque solaire aux deux *uraei*, on voit à gauche les cartouches de Ptolémée IV et celui d'Arsinoé III, à droite ceux d'Osiris et d'Isis. Le parallélisme recherché entre les deux couples royaux se veut l'expression de la conception d'une royauté partagée entre le souverain lagide et le dieu qui pour les Egyptiens en est venu à l'époque tardive à être le modèle de la royauté'. See also Coulon 2011.
³⁸ For the contemporaneous appearance of the name Chaonnophris and of Ptolemy V's epithets *Epiphanes* and *Eucharistos* as a reflection of an ideological war between the two camps, see Uggetti, 'Les archives bilingues de Totoès et de Tatéhathyris', PhD, École Pratique des Hautes Études, Paris, 2018.

case, it may be assumed that Haronnophris died in the context of the counterattack, which resulted in the siege of Abydos during the summer 199 and in the first seizure of Thebes by the Ptolemaic forces before the end of the same year.

A similar blend of parallel and opposed elements vis-à-vis the Ptolemaic kings may be identified in the epithets 'beloved by Isis, beloved by Amonrasonter the great god' appearing in the dating formulae of the documents dated according to 'pharaoh Haronnophris' or 'pharaoh Chaonnophris'. The pharaonic titulature of Ptolemy IV, during whose reign the revolt broke out, similarly proclaimed his being 'beloved by Isis'. In contrast, Ptolemy V, under whom the troubles continued, was 'beloved by Ptah', the great god of Memphis, as was his grandfather Ptolemy III before him. As for the epithet 'beloved by Amon', it had disappeared from the Ptolemaic royal titulatures after Ptolemy II's reign.[39] The very presence of such epithets in contracts also deserve attention. In similar documents, indeed, only the 'dynastic' epithets of the Ptolemaic kings were given: Ptolemy IV was 'Philopator', not 'beloved by Isis', whereas Ptolemy V was 'Epiphanes' and (from 199 onwards[40]) 'Eucharistos', and not 'beloved by Ptah'. Similarly, epithets referring to Egyptian gods did not appear in the older Demotic contracts dating from the Saite Period. Hence, we may assume that Haronnophris deliberately took over the Ptolemaic practice of including epithets in dating formulae, while adapting this practice to his own needs (we can safely rule out that the scribes themselves introduced these epithets of their own initiative). Obviously, Haronnophris aimed to advertise loud and clear that he was under the protection of Osiris, Isis, and Amon altogether, and this raises the question of his relations with the priests of Amon in Thebes.

We can state with some degree of confidence that the uprising did not break out in the city itself, since Greek soldiers were still stationed there in 205 BCE.[41] That said, the rebel kings quickly turned Thebes into their power centre. First, Haronnophris must have assumed the title of

---

[39] Clarysse 1978; Veïsse 2004: 96–99.   [40] See Lanciers 2014.
[41] According to *P. Choach.* 12 V°, l. 24–32, Hermias' father 'went away from Thebes to the south, with other soldiers (*stratiotai*), during the *tarache* which took place at the time of the

pharaoh only after he took control of the city, since the first document dated to his reign – and to its first month – is the Theban limestone tablet that we saw above; according to the same document, the new king had his 'palace' (*pr Pr-ꜥꜣ*) in the city. Second, ten of the fifteen or sixteen documents dated according to his or Chaonnophris' names come from the Theban area. Finally, there is positive evidence that the new pharaoh was acknowledged as such by the priests of Amon: some of the contracts dated by his name were explicitly written 'in the name of the priests of Amon',[42] and the person who wrote the aforementioned Karnak letter was connected with the priesthood of Amon.[43] In addition, the epithet 'beloved by Amon' may be taken as evidence that close relations between the pharaoh and the god's priests existed – the epithet can by no means have been an abstract expression of piety. In the case of the Ptolemies, the adoption of the epithet 'beloved by Ptah' under Ptolemy III coincided with his establishing strong relations with Ptah's priests in Memphis.[44] Regarding Haronnophris and Chaonnophris, the extant evidence does not allow us to know whether the rebel leaders were tolerated, welcomed, or actively supported by the priests of Amon, not forgetting that the priestly circles were composed of different families who could have different strategies. All we can say is that so far there is no evidence of a Ptolemaic repression in Thebes after the city was conquered back.[45]

In Pathyris too Haronnophris was acknowledged as pharaoh by the local priests. In this regard, one of the documents already quoted, the transfer of a land plot, could have been a very compromising document, because it was not only written 'in the name of the priests of Hathor' but signed by eight of them, including the fourth prophet of the goddess and the temple *lesonis* (*P. Ryl. Dem.* 32). Yet, like in Thebes, it seems that the

---

father of the kings, the god Epiphanes', Pestman 1995a: 112; the events are set eighty-eight years before the present time (117 BCE). One may assume that the departure of the soldiers was a direct consequence of the installation of Haronnophris in the city.

[42] *P. Cairo* 3 50164 + 50165 (*P. Carnavon* 1+2) (Haronnophris), *P. Eheverträge* 29 (Charonnophris).

[43] See Depauw 2006: 97. The letter was written by ' [...] pastophoros(?) *of Amun-Re-king-of-the-gods*, the great god, the scribe of the trench for the water "of Thebes" Peteharmais son of Petosiris'.

[44] See Gorre 2009b: 605–622; Thompson 2012: 102–143.

[45] Veïsse 2004: 235–240; Birk 2020.

same priestly families remained in place after the revolt.[46] Whatever their attitude towards the uprising, the priests from both areas were apparently successful in preserving their relations with the Ptolemies.

In short, Haronnophris, the first leader of the Great Theban Revolt, if not the sole one, may be credited with a genuine political view, which aimed at building a new state referring to an old, pre-Ptolemaic order while in practice adopting certain Ptolemaic representations of power (cf. the use of epithets in the protocols). Even though the revolt led to a *de facto* secession of the Thebaid, 'secession' cannot have been his stated aim because, according to Egyptian religious thought, there can only be one pharaoh on earth. For precisely the same reason, the Ptolemies could not tolerate the emergence of such usurpers, as the Seleucids did with Euthydemos I in Bactria or the Hasmonaeans in Judea.[47] By putting up with the presence of an alternative pharaoh in Thebes, they would have irremediably undermined their own legitimacy in the eyes of their Egyptian subjects. On the contrary they carried out several campaigns of re-conquest until the complete suppression of the rebellion. A final issue is why the troubles, which, it should be remembered, also affected the Delta,[48] were so acute in Upper Egypt.

4. Why the Thebaid?

There is a long-standing debate whether the revolts that occurred in Egypt under the Ptolemaic rule were 'national' or 'social',[49] but in our view this way of posing the problem is not very satisfactory. On the one

---

[46] Chaufray and Wegner 2016: 38–39 and 42. This seems to be the case for the family of the fourth prophet of Hathor (Peteharoeris son of Peteharsemtheus), and the *lesonis* (Nechtminis son of Sminis), who both signed the *P. Ryl. Dem.* 32.

[47] See Honigman and Veïsse (2021).

[48] Apart from the direct evidence provided by the Memphis decree of 196 BCE (Lycopolis), the Memphis decree of 182 BCE (eastern Delta) and Polybius 22.16–17 (Lycopolis and Saïte nome), there are possible allusions to the troubles in the Delta in the 'Stele of Heracleion' of c.118 BCE (see Thiers 2009: 31) and in Polybius 15.26.10 (see Johstono 2017: 13).

[49] See Veïsse 2004: XI–XIII; McGing 2012, 2016. It is preferable to leave out of this debate the famous explanation given by Polybius 5.107.3, according to whom the Egyptians 'highly proud of their victory at Raphia', were 'no longer disposed to obey orders, but were on the lookout for a leader and figurehead, thinking themselves well able to maintain themselves as an independent power': as C. Fischer-Bovet pointed out, Polybius seems to have conflated the mutiny that took

hand, all the revolts were not necessarily prompted by the same causes; on the other, even in modern times no uprising can be explained by 'nationalistic' motivations only, cut off from social realities. Undoubtedly, the Great Theban Revolt had a politico-religious dimension (rather than 'nationalist', a term quite confusing), since its leader(s) assumed the title of pharaoh and undertook the building of a new state instead of that of the Ptolemies.[50] But why did this politico-religious claim emerge at that time, and not after the conquest, or during the reigns of the first Ptolemies? And why did Haronnophris/Chaonnophris find enough supporters to be able to maintain his/their authority, to a greater or lesser degree, during twenty years in the Thebaid?

In fact, like any uprising, the Great Revolt was certainly due to a combination of factors. Some must have been general ones, since trouble broke out simultaneously in Upper Egypt and in the Delta, and even had echoes in the Fayum.[51] One possible explanation lies in the negative consequences of the Fourth Syrian War, because of the destabilizing social effect of the demobilization of a great number of soldiers, and because of the drying up of the royal treasury due to military expenses. The lack of liquidity could explain why, according to the Memphis decree of 196, the *telestikon*, the tax paid by the priests on assuming office, was increased under Ptolemy IV;[52] the same decree suggests that the payment to the temples of the *apomoira* and of the royal subvention (*syntaxis*) was altered.[53] There are also hints that prices rose in the late

---

place immediately after the battle of Raphia with the inner revolts starting around 206, interpreting the whole thing in light of the 'war of the mercenaries' against Carthage. See Fischer-Bovet 2015a: 212–213; Veïsse 2016.

[50] Due to the scarcity of evidence, we have no means of knowing whether any of the other rebel leaders involved in the trouble in the Delta pursued the same goals as those of Haronnophris/Chaonnophris.

[51] For the Fayum, see Armoni 2013: 23–27 and 68–74.

[52] Decree of Memphis, Greek version, l. 16: '(…) and he [i.e. the king Ptolemy V] has ordered regarding the priests that they should pay no more for the tax for admission to the priesthood (*telestikon*) than what was appointed up to the first year of his father's reign' (cf. Demotic version, l. 9). Quirke and Andrews 1988.

[53] Decree of Memphis, Greek version, l. 14–16: '(…) and he [i.e. the king] has ordered the revenues of the temples and the *syntaxis* given to them each year in grain and coin and likewise the portions allotted to the gods from both vineyards and gardens and from the other properties which belonged to the gods under his father to remain in force' (cf. Demotic version, l. 8–9) (Quirke and Andrews 1988): we may infer that the contributions to the temples had been

third century, either as a consequence of the war or due to more structural, climatic causes.[54]

However, alongside this general context, the Theban Revolt was also prompted by specific factors. The political ambitions and the personality of Haronnophris certainly played a part, but the most important element remains the strengthening of the Ptolemies' authority over the area by the end of the third century, which J. Manning once called the 'Ptolemaicizing' of the Thebaid.[55] This firmer Ptolemaic grip is reflected first in the tighter control of land. The earliest documented 'auctions of Pharaoh' date to the 220s in Upper Egypt. Those were public sales by which the Ptolemaic power assigned ownerless, derelict, or confiscated land. As J. Manning emphasized, the auction, which was introduced in Egypt by the Ptolemies and was administered in Greek, was 'a new institution that the state used to gain control on rights to land'.[56] At about the same time, as K. Vandorpe showed, major changes occurred in the Theban area in the levy of the tax known as 'harvest tax' (*shemou* in Demotic, *epigraphe* in Greek).[57] At the beginning of the Ptolemaic period, this tax in kind was presumably still collected by the 'scribes of Amon', as was the case in earlier times.[58] But from around 220 BCE, the assessment and collection were transferred to governmental officials, and the taxes were brought to the royal granary and not the granary of

reduced (see Agut and Moreno García 2016: 711–712), or at least that it had been envisaged. The situation may have been even more critical for the temples if the *syntaxis* was no longer paid in silver, but in fiduciary copper money as argued by Gorre 2014: 112–113.

[54] On price increase in the late third century, see Hazzard and Huston 2015. Ludlow and Manning 2016 pointed to a possible connection between periods of social unrest in Ptolemaic Egypt and volcanic activity; see also Manning et al. 2017. Did the demonetization of some of the Ptolemaic bronze coinage, which seems to have occurred shortly before the beginning of the revolts (see Gorre and Lorber 2020: 169–170), also play a role in the discontent? Several bronze hoards, containing out-of-use coins, have been found both in Upper Egypt and in the Delta. Lorber 2000; Faucher, Meadows, and Lorber 2017: nn. 183–197. Is this a sign of the unpopularity of the measure? see Picard and Faucher 2012: 50–51 about the burying of demonetized coins in Thasos and Apollonia of Illyria. For J. Olivier and B. Redon, however, the deposit of these hoards can be explained by the closure of royal banks in the regions affected by the revolts, which prevented the owners of coins from exchanging them for the new currencies put into circulation. Olivier and Redon 2020: 136–139.

[55] Manning 2003a: 69, 73. See also Manning 2003b: 164; Moyer 2011c: 119.

[56] Manning 1999, 2003a: 160–161. See also Vandorpe 2000: 194–195; McGing 2016: 149. The *P. Eleph.* 14 (official rules concerning the public sale of temple land and priestly functions) is dated 223 and the *P. Hauswaldt* 16 (actual auction) 221/0.

[57] Vandorpe 2000; see also Manning 2003a: 71 and 2003b: 163–164.

[58] See Vandorpe 2000: 176.

Amon.[59] The royal subvention to the temples, the *syntaxis*, must have been used to compensate for the loss of earnings[60] but, as suggested above, it was probably altered in the aftermath of the Fourth Syrian War due to the drying up of the royal treasury.

There is also evidence of an increased interference of the Ptolemaic administration in the temples' internal management in Upper Egypt – a trend which had occurred earlier in the temples of Lower and Middle Egypt.[61] The fact is well known for Edfu through the activity of two 'commissioners of the temples' (*praktores tôn ierôn*) in the 220s: Euphronios (225–224) and Milon (223).[62] The intervention of these controllers ad hoc was the consequence of the debts owed by the *lesoneis*, the temple administrators, concerning payments on land and on byssos-weaving activity. Despite the royal administration's 'patience' towards the *lesoneis*[63] (three brothers and their father or nephew), the matter ended with the public sale of goods belonging to these members of a prominent local family. In Thebes, R. Birk recently highlighted a major change in the hierarchic structure of the priesthood, with the appearance of new functions, 'great governor of Thebes' and 'second governor of Thebes' whose holders were the new highest authorities of the temple. This creation can be placed around the middle of the third century and the Ptolemies must have had something to do with it since the offices also appeared in other temples in Upper Egypt (Edfu, Denderah) and in the Delta (Tanis, Sebennytos).[64] Further changes affected the organization of the Theban scribal offices in the latter half of the third century. Not only were the 'scribes of Amon' deprived of the levy of the *shemou*-tax but, as C. Arlt showed, this scribal office itself, which was associated with the temple and was hereditary, seems to have disappeared, whereas that of

---

[59] Vandorpe 2000: 174, 176–177 and 194–195. See also Manning 2003a: 71; Monson 2012: 165–167. The oldest receipts date from 219 to 217 (*O. Theb. Taxes* 2 102–105; *O. Wilck.* 1253). The 'harvest tax' was levied on land formally belonging to the temples but practically owned as private property, and on land acquired at the 'auctions of Pharaoh' once they had been instituted.
[60] Vandorpe 2000: 177, n. 20, 2005: 169; Gorre 2014: 112–113; Agut and Moreno García 2016: 710.
[61] See Gorre 2009b; Gorre and Honigman 2014.
[62] See Clarysse 2003; Manning 2003b: 83–85. Manning also suggests that the rebuilding of the Edfu temple may have been a way of asserting financial control on the temple 2003b: 85, 162.
[63] Clarysse 2003: 23.   [64] Birk 2016 and Birk 2020.

'scribe of the Pharaoh', which was attached to the state and non-hereditary, developed.[65]

This is not to assert a straightforward causal link between each of these facts and the outbreak of the revolt, but unquestionably Upper Egypt underwent far-ranging changes in the second half of the third century BCE. Even though, as the Edfu case suggests, the reforms were not necessarily carried out in a brutal way, this set of changes must in some way be connected with a revolt whose leader was precisely intending to restore the ancient order. The proposal that this set of changes was a crucial factor in the outbreak of the revolt is further supported by the fact that the authority of the Ptolemies had long been established in the area, without having caused troubles until then. This leads us to consider that the main causes of the Great Revolt lay in changes in the mode of Ptolemaic domination, and in the moment when they took place, rather than in the domination per se. On the one hand, many changes occurring at the same time were likely to make many people discontent at the same time, albeit for different reasons. On the other, the timing for the implementation of the reforms happened to be particularly ill-chosen, as the Fourth Syrian War interfered in an unexpected way.

5. Conclusions

The Great Theban Revolt was a major event of Ptolemaic history, the only episode during which the power of the Ptolemaic dynasty was challenged from within.[66] Its causes must probably be sought in the articulation between a general context – explaining why troubles broke out at the same time in other parts of the country – and a local context, that is, the tightened grip of the kings on the Thebaid in the last quarter of the third century. In this regard, the Theban Revolt of 206–186 BCE

---

[65] Arlt 2011. See also Gorre 2009a. Arlt suggests that this evolution was accompanied with the loss of importance of the early Ptolemaic scribal families. The situation of the Theban scribes also attached to the temple but acting as notaries was different; they were not in competition with the 'Greek' *agoranomoi* (mostly from Egyptian origin) before the second century BCE.

[66] The causes of the revolt of 88 BCE were probably different. The troubles were more likely connected with the dynastic struggle between Ptolemy IX and Ptolemy X: see Agut and Moreno García 2016: 725; Veïsse forthcoming.

shares numerous aspects with the Judean revolt that broke out in 168 BCE as a result of administrative and financial reforms carried out by the Seleucid kings, as argued by S. Honigman.[67] In either case, the claims of the leaders were expressed in both political and religious terms, however the outcome of each revolt was very different:[68] in Judea, the uprising led to the emergence of a new state and a new dynasty; in the Thebaid, it was crushed and did not stop the process of 'normalization' of the area which, on the contrary, continued unabated throughout the second century.[69]

---

[67] See Honigman 2014a. [68] See Honigman and Veïsse (2021).
[69] See Vandorpe 2000, 2011, 2014.

PART II
THE GROUNDS FOR RESISTANCE

3
Memory and Resistance in the Seleucid World

The Case of Babylon

Johannes Haubold

This chapter considers historical memories that were current in different parts of the Seleucid world in the third and second centuries BCE. I suggest that the shape of those memories correlates with observable patterns of local resistance (relatively weak in some regions, more pronounced in others) and that, in some cases, they may have helped to diffuse popular discontent that elsewhere turned into something more organized and enduring. In pursuing these issues I take inspiration from recent work on political memory in the post-Achaemenid world, which shows that Hellenistic kingship and the loyalty it commanded depended on collective memory as well as on military, administrative and economic muscle. My main focus is Babylon, where the Seleucids seem to have avoided major uprisings, but I shall also reflect on Judea and the Iranian sphere, where things were, on the face of it, rather more fraught.

1. Memory and Resistance

I begin by revisiting the Book of Daniel, a text that features also elsewhere in this volume (especially Chapters 4 and 5). I do not attempt here a close reading of this much-discussed text but simply make two basic points about it.[1] The first is that history in Daniel emanates from a specific point in the past, the sack of Jerusalem under Nebuchadnezzar. The author introduces this event in the dispassionate voice of the chronicler (Daniel 1: 1) and only then goes on to develop his own, much more dramatic, account of history in a series of apocalyptic visions. Just when and why the text was put together in the form we have it remains a difficult question, with recent suggestions ranging from the Maccabean period in the second century BCE to the Hasmonean in the first.[2] But whether Maccabean or Hasmonean, most scholars agree that the Book of Daniel promotes anti-Seleucid sentiment by appealing to canonical Jewish views of history, or we might say: it charts a pathway to resistance against the Seleucids through the familiar landscape of Jewish collective memory.[3]

This brings me to my second point, which is to do with the contours of that landscape. The Book of Daniel envisages history as world history, or rather, as a succession of world empires. Momigliano argued that the basic template was Greek, and that it went back to Herodotus and Ctesias,[4] but more recent work has shown that already Herodotus and Ctesias participated in a conversation about imperial history that was truly global.[5] Certainly, by the Hellenistic period, rulers such as Nebuchadnezzar mattered to many different people.[6] While Jewish observers used him as a peg on which to hang narratives of crisis and restitution, the Seleucids celebrated him very publicly as a positive role model: the court author Megasthenes compared him to Heracles in his *Indica* and when Antiochus III visited Babylon after the disastrous Peace of Apamea he was famously presented with 'a cloak' (perhaps *the* cloak?)

---

[1] For detailed discussion see Kosmin 2018: 139–163, with previous literature.
[2] For discussion see Honigman's contribution (Chapter 5) in this volume, pp. 125–147.
[3] The term 'collective memory', which goes back to Halbwachs 1925 and 1980 [1950], has sometimes been criticized; see Thomas 2019: 22–27, with further literature. Thomas argues that we should distinguish memory as a cognitive process from the production of communally owned transcripts of history; and that actual memories are too diverse to form anything so coherent as a 'collective memory'. These are important considerations, but they do not seem to me to invalidate collective memory as a heuristic tool. Here I use the term, not to suggest that memory was ever uniform in the ancient world, but to draw attention to those aspects of a community's historical repertoire that go beyond 'tradition' (Thomas' own preferred term at 2019: 26) in articulating a shared historical consciousness.
[4] Momigliano 1994.   [5] Haubold 2013: 78–98.
[6] He was not the only Babylonian king who mattered to Hellenistic audiences, though he was the most important: Braun-Holzinger/Frahm 1999; De Breucker 2015; Waerzeggers 2015; Da Riva 2017.

of 'Nebuchadnezzar the king' (*Nabû-kudur-uṣur šarru*).[7] In his darkest hour of need, at what we now think of as the major turning point in Seleucid history, Antiochus III publicly expressed his commitment to Nebuchadnezzar as a model ruler.

Clearly, then, there were conflicting memories of Nebuchadnezzar in the Hellenistic period. While the elites of Babylon regarded him as a model king, Jewish historians associated him with a low point in the history of Israel.[8] The Seleucid rulers, it would seem, were happy to play along with the Babylonian narrative, but in so doing they can have had no interest in offending Jewish sentiment. In fact, the same Antiochus III whom the Babylonians celebrated as a new Nebuchadnezzar after the treaty of Apamea had granted Jerusalem 'its ancient constitution' only some twenty years prior.[9] We must be cautious, then, not to give too much weight to conflicting historical memories when seeking to explain why trouble erupted in some parts of the empire and not others. History is malleable to the needs of different communities. Still, the case of Nebuchadnezzar shows that different ways of reading history in the Seleucid Empire did provide very different templates for the relationship of rulers and ruled – and hence, at least potentially, for organizing resistance to imperial rule. That potential is what I would like to investigate in this chapter, and in order to do so, I suggest we go back all the way to Nebuchadnezzar II himself, the king who ruled Babylon in 605–562 BCE.

2. Nebuchadnezzar and the Shape of History

Whatever else he may have been – patron of the temples, gifted general, charismatic king – Nebuchadnezzar was certainly adept at promoting himself. In his inscriptions he mentions not just his accomplishments in

---

[7] AD -187 rev. 11'; for discussion of the episode see Madreiter 2016; Haubold 2017.
[8] This is not to say that they always denigrated him personally: see Stökl 2013.
[9] Josephus, *Jewish Antiquities*, 12.3.3, discussed in Bickerman 2007; Honigman 2014a: 302–310. Both scholars comment that the settlement was not especially favourable toward the city, though Honigman notes that hindsight would make it appear more generous.

war and construction but also the sense of wonder he confidently assumed they would instil.[10] He calculated correctly: his conquests were widely admired, and his palace and the garden attached to it became one of the seven wonders of the Hellenistic world.[11] Nebuchadnezzar himself quickly attained the status of a model ruler. Already Nabonidus presented him as one in his most important royal inscription, the so-called *Babylon Stele*, and, when Cyrus marched into Babylon, the priests of Marduk declared him a new Nebuchadnezzar in the so-called *Persian Verse Account*, a pamphlet against Nabonidus.[12] It was not necessary to be of Babylonian descent/come from Babylon in order to impersonate Nebuchadnezzar. It was rather the other way round: Cyrus became legitimately Babylonian by acting like a new Nebuchadnezzar. I return to this point below.

The initial alliance between Persian kings and priestly Babylonian elites did not last: Darius mentions two rebellions in Babylon, in his Behistun inscription, both of them led by men who called themselves 'Nebuchadnezzar, son of Nabonidus'.[13] The names betray a programme: if Nebuchadnezzar had been invoked to rally Babylon around Cyrus after the battle of Opis, his name now served to mobilize Babylonian patriotic sentiment against Persian rule. This was not simply a matter of pitting native Babylonians against a foreign regime: one of the two usurpers was in fact Armenian.[14] In other words, the problem with Darius was not that he was not ethnically Babylonian but that he seemed unwilling to play the role of a good Babylonian king in the mould of Nebuchadnezzar.

Darius crushed the rebel kings but Babylon continued to be restive. Further revolts erupted under Xerxes, and met with a draconian response. Existing elite networks were dismantled across Northern

---

[10] E.g. Nebuchadnezzar 15 col. VII.36 (Langdon), where the king describes his own palace as *bīt tabrât nišī*, a 'house admired by the people'.

[11] Rollinger and Bichler 2005; Rollinger 2013.

[12] For Nabonidus and Nebuchadnezzar see the *Babylon Stele*, No. 3.3 col. VI (Schaudig). For Cyrus as a new Nebuchadnezzar see the *Persian Verse Account* VI.6' (Schaudig).

[13] DB i.16 and iii.49.

[14] Cf. Waerzeggers 2015: 182–183 on the non-Babylonian backgrounds of Neriglissar and Nabonidus.

Babylonia,[15] and the damage to the social fabric suggests a more thoroughgoing *damnatio memoriae*. Certainly, Herodotus and Ctesias do not seem familiar with Nebuchadnezzar, or indeed any other aspect of Neo-Babylonian history as we know it, leaving us instead with ethnographic titbits and court intrigues involving Chaldeans, eunuchs, and domineering women.[16] This is of course a typically Greek way of approaching Eastern history, but it does add to the suspicion that Nebuchadnezzar and the Neo-Babylonian Empire became anathema under Darius and Xerxes.

The pendulum swung back in the Hellenistic period. Already Alexander seems to have portrayed himself as reversing the work of destruction that the Persians had allegedly perpetrated in Babylon.[17] Seleucus I made the city his first powerbase,[18] and although he later founded a new residence on the Tigris, this did not spell the end of Babylon, despite what some ancient sources suggest.[19] Babylon seems to have flourished under the Seleucids. The cuneiform chronicles and *Astronomical Diaries* attest to some further building work in the city, involving Seleucid royalty.[20] They also show that the Seleucids sponsored Babylonian cult and occasionally visited the city.[21] Local intellectuals responded by reintroducing Nebuchadnezzar as a model king.[22]

The arrangement proved remarkably stable. I am not suggesting that there was no friction between the Seleucids and their Babylonian subjects. Under Antiochus V we hear of clashes between the Greek community and the local population.[23] These may have arisen in response to administrative changes that were made in the second century BCE, when

---

[15] Waerzeggers 2003, 2015; Beaulieu 2017: 410–412.
[16] For Herodotus on Babylon see Rollinger 1993, 2014; for Ctesias see Haubold 2013: 91–94.
[17] The stories that circulated about Persian prevarication appear to have been largely fictitious (Kuhrt and Sherwin White 1982, 2014, *pace* George 2010); but they do seem to capture real frustrations at the lack of Achaemenid patronage; see Waerzeggers 2015: 195–202.
[18] Sherwin-White 1987. Kosmin 2018: 26–44 draws attention to the fact that the Seleucids dated the beginning of imperial time to the moment that Seleucus returned to Babylon from exile.
[19] Boiy 2004: 135–136.   [20] Kuhrt and Sherwin-White 1991: 81–82
[21] Visscher 2019.
[22] Most visible to us is Berossos F 8a, with discussion in Kuhrt 1987; Dillery 2013, 2015: 271–293; Haubold 2013: 173–176, 2017; but Megasthenes too must have been drawing on Babylonian sources when declaring that Nebuchadnezzar outdid Heracles (F 1); see Haubold 2013: 131–132.
[23] *BCHP* 14 obv. 1–7.

a Greek *polis* was founded in Babylon and local elites lost some of their prerogatives.[24] There were also local rivalries, notably between Babylon and Uruk.[25] Mesopotamia was not a Seleucid paradise. But tensions did not boil over into major uprisings – or at least not in comparison to earlier and more radical rebellions against Persia, let alone the great Egyptian revolt of 205–186 BCE.[26] Our sources are fragmentary and partial, but we would surely know it if uprisings on that kind of scale had occurred. Mesopotamia stayed quiet, though not because of apathy or exhaustion, as Eddy suggests.[27] Nor was it simply the case that the Seleucids were more adept at pandering to their Babylonian subjects than the Persians had been. Broader patterns of historical allegiance were arguably at stake.

3. A Shared View of the Past

Seleucid Greek and Babylonian policymakers, I suggest, became locked into a stable alliance not just because that was expedient to both sides but because historical memory favoured such an arrangement. From a Seleucid perspective, the overriding problem was how to deal with the legacy of the Achaemenid Empire. Like Alexander, the Seleucids certainly sought accommodation with the old Iranian elites.[28] But as Tuplin stresses, they had learned to treat Iranian imperial tradition with caution.[29] After Alexander's experiments with Achaemenid court protocol, those traditions could no longer serve as a unifying bond for the Empire: cautionary tales to that effect circulated widely among Hellenistic Greeks and provided ammunition to those who wished to denounce the Seleucids as an essentially barbaric dynasty. The Ptolemies and their court authors were good at this game, and they passed on the habit to others.[30]

---

[24] Clancier 2007, 2017.   [25] Stevens 2016 discusses articulations of Urukean pride.
[26] Noted by Mehl 1999: 31 ('Tiefgreifende und anhaltende Spannungen zwischen den Seleukidenkönigen und ihren syrischen und babylonisch-mesopotamischen Untertanen hat es jedenfalls nicht gegeben'.). For the great Egyptian revolt see this volume, Chapters 2 and 6, pp. 57–73 and 148–174.
[27] Eddy 1961: 157–162; for a more nuanced review of possible factors see Kosmin 2018: 189.
[28] Plischke 2014.   [29] Tuplin 2008; Eckhardt 2015.   [30] Barbantani 2014.

Against the backdrop of *Vergangenheitsbewältigung* in the Iranian east, the picture in Babylon stands out as distinctly less problematic. Babylonian historical memory too was of course complicated, but it was not fraught in the same way. In fact, it must have struck ancient Greek observers as really rather compatible with their own canonical histories of empire. The Assyrian period was fairly well established in Babylonian thought as a time of oppression under a foreign regime.[31] Not everyone in Hellenistic Babylon loathed the Assyrians, but a critical stance was mandatory if one accepted, as most people did, that Nabopolassar and Nebuchadnezzar were Babylonian national heroes.[32] The Seleucids' Greek elites would certainly have been happy to distance themselves from Assyria (which Ctesias, for one, had associated with debauchery and gender inversion in his influential *Persica*).[33] Nebuchadnezzar was a blank slate to them, but in a context where any known traditions of kingship in Asia were regarded with suspicion that was if anything an advantage.

When it came to memories of the Achaemenid Empire, the roles were reversed: here, Babylonian thinking was less clear-cut, but as Caroline Waerzeggers has shown it could certainly accommodate the Greeks' more pronounced distaste for all things Persian.[34] With a little bit of accommodation, then, it was possible to arrive at a shared view of imperial history that alternated between peaks and troughs (broadly speaking: Assyrians bad, Neo-Babylonians good, Persians bad again) and which culminated with the Seleucids themselves. This is indeed how Berossos described the succession of empires in his *Babyloniaca*.[35] His narrative need not have been acceptable to all, but it articulated a convergence of historical memory that was sufficiently robust to weather even major historical storms.

From a Babylonian perspective, Berossos' Assyrian and Persian kings could easily be construed to have behaved badly: the Assyrians by

---

[31] The classic statement of anti-Assyrian sentiment is Nabopolassar's é.PA.GÌN.ti.la cylinder, C 12.17–21 (Da Riva); see also Nabonidus 3.3 cols I–II (Schaudig) and Berossos *BNJ* 680 F 7.
[32] In fact, their Babylonian credentials are really rather suspect. On Nabopolassar's background in the pro-Assyrian circles of Uruk see Jursa 2007; Da Riva 2008: 4–5; Da Riva 2017 collects and discusses literary traditions about Nabopolassar.
[33] Rollinger 2017.   [34] Waerzeggers 2015.   [35] Haubold 2013: 163–176.

sacking Babylon, abducting its king and setting up an imitation of the city in the far west; the Persians by destroying the walls of Babylon with the express purpose of making it less 'difficult to conquer'.[36] By contrast, the Chaldean kings of the Neo-Babylonian Empire, and especially Nebuchadnezzar, did what good Babylonian kings had been expected to do since time immemorial: enrich the city and strengthen its defences.[37] Granted, Berossos also stressed that the quality of Neo-Babylonian rule declined after the death of Nebuchadnezzar – with short-lived rulers like Labashi-Marduk behaving badly and being killed as a result.[38] Here Berossos offered a (typically Babylonian) cautionary tale about the importance of good counsel and the education of the king.[39] Rather than disqualifying Chaldean rule, this further served to make it an object lesson for the Seleucids, for better *and* for worse.

We should not assume that any of this was self-evident to Babylonians, as though Berossos' view of history could simply be plucked from their collective memory. Histories are grounded in lived reality, and there are signs that the Achaemenids had taken measures to neutralize those memories that had framed successive revolts under Darius and Xerxes. Beyond the immediate backlash, Artaxerxes I took at least three Babylonian wives, whose children became serious contenders to the throne after Artaxerxes' death.[40] Eventually, one of them became king: after the assassination of Crown Prince Xerxes II, the half-Babylonian Darius II Ochus emerged victorious from a power struggle with two of his brothers, both of them also born of Babylonian mothers. Ochus' wife had a Babylonian mother too, so that from then on the Achaemenid Dynasty was effectively half Babylonian – though the predominantly

---

[36] Berossos *BNJ* 680 F 7 and F 9a; discussion in Haubold 2013: 170–172 (Sennacherib as arch-enemy of Babylon) and 163–164 (Cyrus is unfit for kingship, despite his *philanthropia*).
[37] Da Riva 2008: 114–115, on the self-portrayal of Babylonian rulers in their inscriptions.
[38] Berossos *BNJ* 680 F 9a with Haubold 2013: 82 and 137. Waerzeggers 2015: 216–218 discusses the long-running debates in late cuneiform literature about the merits of Nabonidus and other Neo-Babylonian kings; see also De Breucker 2015.
[39] The *locus classicus* on 'counsel' in Babylonian political thought is SB *Gilg.* X.272–277, which contrasts the fool with the king. At 277, the fool is characterized as lacking in counsel (*amāt milki lā iš*[*u*]).
[40] Zawadzki 1995–6 discusses the circumstances of Ochus' accession; see also Briant 2002: 588–591; Brosius 2002: 64–65.

female and less than fully legitimate Babylonian element merged into the Achaemenid line like a recessive gene.[41]

Away from dynastic politics, the cuneiform evidence suggests that the Achaemenids enjoyed some success in dampening Babylonian resentment.[42] However, the Neo-Babylonian past was not forgotten. In fact, Berossos revived precisely some of the memories that had sustained successive Babylonian rebellions against Darius and Xerxes: Nebuchadnezzar as a national hero, Assyrians and Persians as occupying regimes. The aim, however, was not to rekindle Babylonian nationalism but to ensure that Greek readers had a stake in this very Babylonian template of history. Assyria provided an early point of convergence: Berossos dismissed the works of the glamorous Semiramis as the product of historical fantasy (*BNJ* 680 F 8a) and turned Sennacherib into an enemy of Greece as well as Babylon (*BNJ* 680 F 7c). As for Nebuchadnezzar, Berossos described his reign in strikingly Seleucid terms as one of military prowess and benefaction (*BNJ* 680 F 8a). He also subsumed the Median Empire of Herodotus and Ctesias into that of Nebuchadnezzar by means of a dynastic marriage (*BNJ* 680 F 8a). If Ctesias had presented Babylon as the female element in the Achaemenid line, Berossos saw to it that Media now got to play that role – except that the operative trope, for him, was not palace intrigue but royal romance. By telling his readers how the homesick queen Amyitis got the Hanging Garden as a present from her loving consort, Berossos removed the Median Empire from recent history in a way that Hellenistic readers would have found hard to resist.

With that, most of Berossos' work was done. He may not have said much about the Persians,[43] but they hardly required comment: for Greek readers they could not provide much more than a negative foil to the Seleucid present. The resulting account of imperial history could speak to them as well as to Babylonians: they shared a vision of history where the high points and the low points coincided – or at any rate could be made to coincide. Berossos tweaked the details to ensure a close fit, but he could only do so successfully because the raw material was favourable to

---

[41] More on how this informs the works of Herodotus and Ctesias in Haubold 2013: ch. 2.
[42] Beaulieu 2017: 411–412.   [43] Waerzeggers 2015: 207.

his plans. What ultimately mattered was not the cross-cultural appeal of individual anecdotes like the Hanging Garden but the overall shape of historical memory: from Assyrian oppression to Babylonian liberation and Persian occupation. The template locked the details into place – and put the Seleucids on the right side of history.

4. Seleucid Dissolution and 'The Elamite Foe'

I have argued elsewhere that the *Babyloniaca* offered a powerful *political* blueprint for Greco-Babylonian collaboration, with the (Macedonian) 'friends' of the Seleucid king sharing responsibility for the stability of the empire with his Chaldean experts.[44] I now argue that he also proposed a *historical* concordat to serve as a frame for political action. This was not wishful thinking on Berossos' part, nor was it confined to the honeymoon period of early Seleucid rule. Berossos' scheme worked because it chimed with existing patterns of historical memory on both sides; and it was still in place a century later, when Antiochus III visited Babylon and was hailed as a new Nebuchadnezzar (188/7 BCE). Indeed, there is reason to believe that it endured even further. The Astronomical Diaries – the closest approximation we have to an official version of history from a Babylonian perspective – describe the Egyptian campaigns of Antiochus IV (169/8 BCE) and Demetrius II (145/4 BCE) in language that recalls Nebuchadnezzar's victorious wars in the west.[45]

But if a convergence of Seleucid Greek and Babylonian historical memory persisted until the middle of the second century BCE, did it also endure into the turbulent period of Seleucid decline that started immediately after? The question is worth asking, not just because sustained periods of political instability tend to change how people perceive themselves and hence redirect political loyalties, but also because Babylonian historians posed the question themselves – albeit indirectly. I refer here to two passages on the obverse and reverse of one single cuneiform tablet, the Astronomical Diary for the year 145/4 BCE.

---

[44] Haubold 2016.
[45] AD -168A rev. 14–15 (Antiochus IV) and AD -144 obv. 35'-36' (Demetrius II).

The first of these passages reads like a clear reaffirmation of Greco-Babylonian historical memory as Berossos had articulated it over a century earlier (AD -145 obv. 35'-36'):

35' ITU B[I.... ¹De]-⌐met¬-ri LUGAL ina URU^(meš)šá KUR Me-luḫ-ḫa
36' [šal-ṭa]-niš GIN.GIN-ak
35' That month [....] king Demetrius marched around the cities of Egypt
36' victoriously.

As I have shown elsewhere, the language of this brief note harks back, via the Diaries' own description of Antiochus IV's Egyptian campaigns, to the form of words that Babylonian chroniclers had used to describe the Western wars of Nebuchadnezzar in the sixth century BCE.[46] Whether rightly or wrongly, its authors clearly assume – or perhaps we should better say: affirm – that Seleucid and Babylonian memory still share the same understanding of high and low points in imperial history; and that Seleucid kings are still acting on that shared knowledge. However, that certainty is put to the test on the reverse of the same tablet, where we learn that the following events take place in Babylonia while the king is on campaign in Egypt (AD -144 rev. 201):

20 [ITU BI?]
21 ¹Ka-am-ma-áš-ki-i-ri LUGAL KUR NIM-MA^(k[i]) ina URU^(meš) u ÍD^(meš) šá KUR URI^(ki) šal-ṭa-niš GIN.GIN-ak
20 [That month?]
21 King Kammaškiri of Elam marched victoriously around the cities and rivers of Babylonia.

---

[46] Haubold 2019: 274–275. In the Babylonian Chronicles the expression *ina* GN *šalṭāniš ittallak* first appears in connection with Nabopolassar's conquest of Assyria in *Chronicle* 22.54 and 59 Glassner, perhaps as a deliberate allusion to Assyrian imperial discourse (cf. the passages from Neo-Assyrian royal inscriptions cited in *CAD s.vv. šalṭāniš* and *šalṭiš*). It then encapsulates Nebuchadnezzar's achievements during his Syrian campaigns (*Chronicle* 24 obv. 12–13, 16, 23(?), rev.' 5 Glassner). Assyrian and later Neo-Babylonian, Persian, and Hellenistic Chronicles prefer formulations that are less obviously encomiastic, such as 'PN marched to GN' (PN *ana* GN *illik, Chronicles* 15.13' and 25.4 Glassner), or 'the king of Assyria went down to the land of X and pillaged city Y' (*urdamma ... iḫtabat, Chronicle* 17.4'-5' Glassner).

It is not difficult to see that this note echoes the description of Demetrius' military prowess on the obverse of the tablet. The echo is deeply unsettling: an enemy king should not be 'marching victoriously' through Babylonia at a time when the Seleucid king marches victoriously through Egypt. The problem, here, is not simply that Demetrius fails in his duty to protect Babylon from invasion but that his actions call into question the very terms of the Greco-Babylonian concordat. Berossos had insisted that it was beneficial for everyone to have a Seleucid king who acted as a latter-day Nebuchadnezzar. Yet, all of a sudden the king's campaigns in the west allowed an enemy ruler to claim the legacy of Nebuchadnezzar in the most shocking way. We might expect this to be the starting point for expressions of anti-Seleucid sentiment. If the Seleucid king could no longer guarantee the safety of the city, why not replace him with a local ruler? Yet, there is no sign of a backlash in the cuneiform sources, no rewriting of history in a hostile key. It is possible that the evidence for Babylonian resentment has simply been lost, but if resentment there was, then the priests of Marduk played no role in expressing it.

One question here concerns the degree of influence the Babylonian priestly elites still wielded at this moment in time and, consequently, how we should judge the literature they produced. Even if we accept that men like Berossos set the initial terms of what I have called the concordat between Seleucid Greek and Babylonian historical memory, was the thinking of his peers still relevant in the increasingly chaotic environment of the 140s–120s BCE? There is some ground for scepticism, partly because the Babylonian priests wrote in the rarefied medium of cuneiform Akkadian (as far as we can tell, no other Mesopotamian intellectuals tried to repeat Berossos' feat of writing Babylonian history in Greek); and partly because of the long-term decline of the Babylonian temples in political, economic and religious terms.[47] If Babylonian intellectuals working in cuneiform were no more than political dinosaurs, this would surely affect the argument advanced in this chapter: perhaps there *was* popular resistance which our sources fail to capture; or, if there wasn't, the reasons for the relative lack of upheaval may have had

---

[47] See for example Clancier and Monerie 2014; Robson 2019.

nothing to do with the view of history promoted by the priests of Marduk.

Two points seem worth making in relation to these uncertainties. The first concerns the danger of underestimating the evidence we *do* have in pursuit of what we assume has been lost. It is true, of course, that very little survives from Babylonia *c.*170–120 BCE apart from the cuneiform sources. Literature in other languages must once have been abundant. Aramaic and Greek were the main languages of politics and commerce in the region, and anybody wanting to mobilize popular resistance to Seleucid rule would surely have used one or both of these. No doubt, the cuneiform sources were intended for circulation only within a very small group of people. However, they were not therefore cut off from the lives of 'real' people in the region. In fact, they show a keen interest in those lives: they record weather conditions, commodity prices, and historical events in and around Babylon that affect the welfare of 'the people' (Akk. *nišū*) 'in the land' (*ina māti*). The Astronomical Diaries return to these issues with an obsessive insistence.[48] As part of their tracking programme, they record the Parthian conquest, Seleucid counterattacks and the temporary occupation of Babylonia on the part of Hyspaosines of Characene, a breakaway Seleucid governor.[49] They also note instances of civil unrest, such as the citizens of Seleucia turning against a disloyal Parthian general, or a charismatic prophet appearing in Borsippa and Babylon.[50] While we can concede that they may miss or deliberately pass over *some* events, they would certainly have noted any significant rebellions, coups or takeovers in the region – whether the diarists themselves supported them or not.

My second point is that the priests of Marduk, as well as offering a fine-grained analysis of historical events in and around Babylon, were perfectly capable of gauging the popular mood in the region – though rather than attesting to widespread anti-Seleucid, or anti-Greek, or even anti-Parthian feeling, they report a deep-seated loathing of the 'Elamite

---

[48] See Haubold, Steele, and Stevens 2019.

[49] AD -140A (Parthian takeover); AD -137 'rev.' 8'-11' (Seleucid counterattack); AD - 124A (Hyspaosines in Babylon); for the career of Hyspaosines see Schuol 2000: 291–300.

[50] AD -140C rev. 29'-35' (the citizens of Seleucia turn on Antiochus); AD -132 (the false prophet).

foe'. In AD -144 rev.' 22 we hear, apropos of the first Elamite invasion, that 'there was panic and fear in the land (ḫattu u gilittu ina māti ibši)'. In AD -140D 'obv. 11' 'panic of the (Elamite) foe prevailed in the land' (ḫattu nakri ina māti šaknat). Three years later 'panic of the Elamite foe was strong in the land, and panic of the enemy fell on the people' (ḫattu nakri Elamî ina māti dannatma nišū ḫattu nakri imqussunūtu AD -137D 'obv. 12') – and so on.[51] At one point the diarist gleefully reports that there was general joy and well-being in Babylon while there was panic in Elam.[52] Everything suggests that loathing of 'the Elamite foe' went well beyond the priestly circles of Babylon.

But those circles still mattered, as Boiy and Mittag show,[53] not least because they had access to the city's deep past. The authors of the Diaries must have known, for example, that animosity towards Elam was deeply engrained in Babylonian historical consciousness. The theme can be traced back to Nebuchadnezzar I (ruled 1125–1104 BCE), who defeated Elam and recovered the statue of Marduk.[54] Nebuchadnezzar's achievement spawned an entire literature which lodged enmity toward Elam in the imagination of educated Babylonians, to be sure, but quite possibly in the popular imagination too.[55] There is evidence to suggest that memories of Nebuchadnezzar I and his victory against Elam stoked resentment against Persian rule, which some Babylonian observers construed as 'Elamite'.[56] Memories of the Elamite *Erbfeind* were also alive in the Hellenistic period. A Hellenistic calendar treatise associates Elam with Tiamat, the chaos monster of the Babylonian national epic *Enūma eliš*;[57] and when the former Seleucid province of Elymais emerged as an independent and politically aggressive kingdom, the authors of the Astronomical Diaries wrote about it in a way that suggested history was repeating itself – that is to say, the 'Elamite foe' had once again

---

[51] The Elamite threat finally subsided in 125 BCE; see AD -124 'rev.' 12'-20'.
[52] AD -137D rev.' 3.   [53] Boiy and Mittag 2011.
[54] Nielsen 2018; Reynolds 2019: 80–92.
[55] Nielsen 2018: 105–112; Reynolds 2019: 80–101.
[56] Nielsen 2015 and 2018: 132–134; Waerzeggers 2015: 221–222.
[57] Reynolds 2019 *passim*, e.g. p. 245, with reference to Calendar Treatise § 3 i 10'.

exploited a moment of Babylonian weakness to wreak chaos and destruction.[58]

It seems, then, that at a time when other regions of the Seleucid Empire turned against the central government, Babylonian sentiment focused obsessively on one of Mesopotamia's most long-standing *external* enemies. The Elamite king had usurped the role of Nebuchadnezzar for himself (*ina* GN *šalṭāniš ittallak*), and this most alarming of historical reversals called for urgent remedy. From a Babylonian perspective, the Seleucids were in a good position to appreciate this, for they too had had their problems with Elam. Shortly after Antiochus III visited Babylon in 188/7 BCE he was killed on a visit to Elymais, allegedly while attempting to collect money from a temple.[59] Later, under Antiochus IV, we hear again of a Seleucid king running into difficulties while trying to raise revenue from Elymaean sanctuaries.[60] The Seleucids may have lacked any deep cultural memories of 'the Elamite foe', but when Elymaean armies started harassing Babylonia, their interests yet again fell into natural alignment with the interests of the Babylonians themselves.

The point, however, was not Babylonian allegiance to the Seleucids so much as allegiance to whoever was prepared to take on Elam. The Parthians took control of Mesopotamia in 141 BCE, yet the only 'foe' who appears in the Astronomical Diaries for the year is the 'Elamite foe'.[61] Loyalties shifted at this point, just as they shifted in other parts of the Seleucid Empire, but in Babylon the focus was not on the imperial centre and its cultural trappings but on external attack. Indeed, Babylonian observers detected the same set of priorities in their neighbours in Seleucia. The Astronomical Diaries report that the citizens of Seleucia arrested the general Antiochus after learning that he had defected to the Elamite side (AD -140C rev. 29'-35'). That Antiochus was a *Parthian* general allegedly did not matter to them – what mattered was his betrayal of the anti-Elamite cause. Now, Antiochus may not have

---

[58] For the question of how Elymaean thinkers viewed this process see below, p. 93 with n. 69.
[59] Diodorus Siculus 19.15. The particulars of Diodorus' story are problematic, but the outcome is not in doubt; for discussion see Potts 2016: 610–613, Reynolds 2019: 99.
[60] Potts 2016: 613–614 discusses the evidence.
[61] The formulation occurs for the first time in AD -140D 'obv. 11', just after the Parthian takeover.

been the bare-faced traitor which the Diaries portray,[62] but the account still suggests an important fact: the turmoil that engulfed Mesopotamia after 145 BCE did not foster Babylonian resentment toward the Seleucids, or indeed their Parthian successors. We hear of tensions between 'Syrian' (i.e. Babylonian) and Greek communities in Seleucia during the Parthian period,[63] and we know of at least one indigenous revival in Southern Mesopotamia.[64] But the evidence for trouble in Seleucia is late, and that for indigenous revival is limited in scope. The priests of Marduk, we can assume, had nothing to do with it. Their writings articulate a longing for central authority.[65] That the king was absent was seen as a problem. That he should be replaced with someone more local, and more properly 'Babylonian', was not a thought that gained consensus in Hellenistic Babylon.

5. Conclusions

Historical memory, I have argued in this chapter, can help to explain what did, and perhaps more importantly, what did not happen in Hellenistic Babylonia during the so-called 'Maccabean period' on which this collection focuses. I have made three main points. First, there is no evidence of major anti-Seleucid uprisings in Babylonia. Second, there *is* evidence that Greeks and Babylonians converged on a shared vision of imperial history that oscillated between the lows of Assyrian and Persian occupation and the highs of Neo-Babylonian and Seleucid rule. My third point is that the re-appearance on the world stage of an aggressive Elam rekindled memories of a long-standing Babylonian trauma, and strengthened loyalty to the incumbent king at a crucial moment of transition.

It is possible to see Babylonian inactivity in part as the result of economic and demographic factors: Seleucid Babylonia was prosperous

---

[62] Shayegan 2011: 78–79.   [63] Goodblatt 1987.   [64] Kosmin 2018: 197–203.
[65] Haubold 2019.

and well settled.[66] If it is true, as some scholars have argued, that the Seleucids did not levy troops in the region, this too may have contributed to keeping it quiet.[67] Yet another consideration may be that ethnic and cultural fragmentation made serious resistance more difficult to organize in Mesopotamia than elsewhere.[68] Still, the relative lack of political resistance in Babylonia contrasts sharply with the situation in neighbouring regions to the east and west. Elam/Elymais was restive since the 180s BCE and after further problems under Antiochus IV staged a hostile breakaway in the 140s. There are signs that this process was fuelled by appeals to an imperial longue durée, though the details remain elusive.[69] We do know that historical memory played a part in Persis, another eastern neighbour of Babylonia that may have gained independence at around this time. The chronology is uncertain, but however precisely we date the various stages of Persis' 'movement away from the Seleucid Empire',[70] there can be no doubt that it was motivated not only by Seleucid decline but also by memories of the Achaemenid past.[71]

Pivoting from Western Iran to the Levant, we note a similar lack of alignment between Jewish and Seleucid historical memory. Not only was the Achaemenid period, which was problematic from a Seleucid perspective, a time of restoration in much of canonical Jewish literature, but the reign of Nebuchadnezzar which formed a low point for Israel also marked a high point in Seleucid readings of imperial history, as I have shown. These dissonances were not in themselves a reason for war, and were, in any case, open to negotiation: as Jonathan Stökl has argued, *some* Jewish authors could portray even Nebuchadnezzar in a positive light.[72]

---

[66] Pirngruber 2017 discusses the overall fairly benign economic development of Seleucid Babylonia. For demography see Aperghis 2004: 36–40, who emphasizes the prosperity of the region as a whole but notes that the old Babylonian heartlands appear to have done somewhat less well than the area around Seleucia and the Diyala (p. 40).

[67] Bar-Kochva 1976: 52 notes that our sources do not mention Babylonian contingents in the Seleucid army. Engels 2019: 426–429 suggests that Babylonian soldiers may have fought in the Macedonian phalanx and that this may be why they remain invisible to us.

[68] Kosmin 2018: 189.

[69] Significantly, one of Elymais' most important military leaders, the much-hated Pittit, bore an Elamite name; see Potts 2016: 632.

[70] Wiesehöfer's formulation (1994: 138). Wiesehöfer sees the process of emancipation as roughly parallel with what happened in Elymais; for discussion and alternative views see Eckhardt 2015: 274–278.

[71] Kosmin 2018: 203–219.   [72] Stökl 2013.

Historical memory was multiform and malleable, in Judea as well as everywhere else – but there were limits to historical claims and counter-claims. What versions of history were available for reuse had a bearing on whether popular resentment turned into collective revolt.[73]

One point seems to me worth stressing here: not all historical memory is manufactured opportunistically, and with hindsight. As Silverman and Waerzeggers put it: 'The past is indeed shaped by the needs of the present, but within the constraints of historical givens'.[74] Collective memory can itself be such a given. To be sure, the past can be rewritten, but it cannot be re-invented wholesale and overnight. The present is, as the author of Daniel insists, a future past – it is determined by the past and it is to be understood through the past. When the Ptolemies, for example, claimed to have recovered sacred objects that the Persians had stolen from Egypt,[75] they did not just engage in facile propaganda but rather explained to themselves and others what their actions *could* mean, and what they hoped they *might* mean, in view of historical memories that most of their subjects could share. Just so, we should allow that memories of the past motivated political action and – indeed – inaction in Seleucid Babylon. Exactly what pushed people to act as they did in different parts of the Seleucid Empire is not something we can always fully understand. What seems certain is that historical memory played a part, both in the Seleucids' own efforts to stabilize their rule and in the efforts of others to support or dislodge them.

---

[73] Jewish authors reinvented Achaemenid tradition to exaggerate the conflict with the Seleucids (see Eckhardt 2015: 286–292); but like Berossos, who harmonized Babylonian and Seleucid Greek history, they could not have succeeded without drawing on established patterns of collective memory.
[74] Silverman and Waerzeggers 2015: 3.
[75] See *OGIS* 54.20–24, discussed in Eckhardt 2015: 272.

4
'After Him a King Will Arise'
Framing Resistance in Seleucid Babylonia

Kathryn Stevens

The last few decades have seen the disruption and rewriting of 'resistance' narratives across the Hellenistic east.[1] As the editors note in their introduction to this volume, while Samuel Eddy's landmark study framed insurrections by non-Greek populations within the Hellenistic empires in cultural and religious terms, subsequent scholars have increasingly moved away from cultural factors as prime motivators for revolt, emphasizing that their role in the rhetoric of revolts may not always reflect their causal importance.[2] In Egypt, the Great Theban Revolt (205–186 BCE) and smaller episodes of unrest under Ptolemaic rule have been analyzed in socio-economic terms, as the product of tension arising from tighter fiscal control by the Ptolemies and/or even climatic changes which led to failure of the annual Nile flood.[3] In Judea, the Maccabean Revolt and the events which triggered it – crucial to Jewish self-definition in antiquity and beyond as an example of resistance to cultural destruction and analysed in this vein well into the twentieth

---

[1] The final version of this chapter was submitted in January 2019; it has therefore not been possible to take account of more recent bibliography.
[2] Eddy 1961; Kosmin and Moyer (this volume). On rhetorical versus causal importance, see especially Collins and Manning 2016: 3, who stress the multiple causes usually in play in episodes of rebellion, and the possible disjunct between the rhetoric used by actors (often religious) and the factors driving their actions (often economic or more broadly social).
[3] Socio-economic factors: more recently Manning 2003: 164–171; Veisse 2004, but this line of scholarship has a long history before becoming the dominant paradigm (e.g. already Préaux 1936). Climate change: Ludlow and Manning 2016; Manning et al. 2017 (but based on ice core data which does not allow the necessary chronological precision to make exact correlations). For treatments which emphasize cultural, religious, and/or 'nationalistic' elements to a greater extent, see Peremans 1978; McGing 1997.

century – have been variously repositioned as a local conflict which the Seleucid authorities mismanaged, a show of strength by Antiochus IV to bolster his international position, or the product of fiscal measures by the Seleucid kings which triggered unrest in the region.[4]

Yet, just as the explicit rhetoric of resistance is not necessarily to be taken at face value, neither is its absence. In parallel to the studies which have reinterrogated supposedly 'anti-Hellenic' expressions or events in the Hellenistic world, there has also been a move to re-evaluate evidence previously analysed in terms of co-operation or collaboration between local groups and Hellenistic rulers. Ian Moyer shows in his contribution to this volume that the Ptolemaic priestly decrees, which on the surface seem to encapsulate a harmonious collaboration between elite and ruler, are 'slyly' rewriting Ptolemaic rule in Egyptian terms.[5] In Babylonia, where the lack of evidence for significant economic or social disruption in the cuneiform sources had been taken as indicative of a consistently positive relationship between the Seleucids and the Babylonian elite, Philippe Clancier and Julien Monerie have traced a narrative of increasing interference in the early second century BCE, whereby the Seleucids denuded Babylonia's temples and their personnel of political, judicial, and economic power.[6] At the same time (and following to some extent in Eddy's footsteps) a number of Hellenistic Babylonian texts in Akkadian and Greek have been viewed as muted or coded critiques of contemporary imperialism.[7] It is to this latter body of work that the current paper aims to contribute, by revisiting 'resistance' in Seleucid Babylonia through the lens of the cuneiform scholarly texts.

In Hellenistic Babylonia, the difficulty is not one of unpicking the logic of texts which on the surface seem to call out for the downfall of the foreign rulers, or assessing the weight of isolated expressions of dissent and dissatisfaction against an otherwise apparently positive source tradition. Rather, one faces what seems initially to be an eloquent silence.

---

[4] See e.g. Gruen 1993 (show of strength). Ma 2000 (intra-elite conflict); Honigman 2014 (fiscal measures). See also Gruen (this volume, Chapter 1).
[5] Moyer, this volume, Chapter 6.
[6] Clancier 2012, 2014, 2017; Clancier and Monerie 2014.
[7] E.g. Beaulieu 1993 (Uruk Prophecy); Cavigneaux 2005 (Uruk Chronicle); Dillery 2015 (Berossus as proto-apocalyptic).

As has frequently been noted, the surviving sources from the region provide less evidence of discontent than those from other regions of the Hellenistic world. We know of no large-scale Babylonian uprisings comparable to the Maccabean Revolt in Judea or the Theban revolt in Egypt, and there is no evidence that locals supported the Parthians when they conquered Babylonia. Nor are there any clear-cut examples of 'resistance literature': Akkadian cuneiform texts offer no analogue to Gabriel's promise of the terrible punishment awaiting Antiochus once the measure of the successors' sins is full, or the proclamation in the *Oracle of the Potter* from Egypt that 'the city of the Girdlewearers (Alexandria) will be abandoned like my kiln because of the crimes which they committed against Egypt'.[8] Eddy's conclusion was that the Babylonians *didn't* really resist; rather, they 'remained generally passive under the Hellenic regime, although they did continue to tell stories about an heroic age, and protested feebly against what they considered wrong'.[9] He attributed this to various factors, including the Babylonian ideology of kingship and a cultural crisis whereby allegiance to older religious and cultural traditions was fading.[10] Approaching the issue from a rather different perspective in *From Samarkhand to Sardis*, Amélie Kuhrt and Susan Sherwin-White reached comparable conclusions about 'resistance' in Babylonia, stressing the lack of interpretative clarity in much of the surviving material.[11] In particular, they criticized historical reconstructions that followed Greek and Latin authors' claims about Seleucid neglect or Babylonian discontent; Sherwin-White elsewhere emphasized the 'unnegative' attitude to Seleucus detectable in the Babylonian Chronicles.[12]

On the level of open revolt and rebellion there does seem to be a lack of 'resistance' in Seleucid Babylonia, and to some extent we must take this seriously and interrogate the possible reasons behind it.[13] But our source record from Babylonia is also more partial than elsewhere. By this

---

[8] *Daniel* 8.25; *Oracle of the Potter* 32–33 (trans. Burstein 1985: 137); see further below on the lack of Babylonian analogues.
[9] Eddy 1961: 104.   [10] Eddy 1961: 157–162.
[11] Sherwin-White and Kuhrt 1993: 137–139 (but noting possible evidence from the Diaries for revolt/unrest in the 230s).
[12] Sherwin-White 1987: 15.   [13] See Haubold, this volume, Chapter 3.

period, the primary spoken and written language was Aramaic (and increasingly Greek), written mainly on parchment or papyrus which has not survived due to the climatic conditions. Apart from a handful of Greek and Aramaic inscriptions, our only textual sources are thousands of cuneiform tablets, containing texts in Akkadian and Sumerian. These represent the writings of a very socially restricted group: the elites associated with Babylonia's temples, where Akkadian and Sumerian survived as languages of ritual and scholarship.[14] This restriction is particularly relevant since the Aramaic or Greek texts may have been more likely to voice negative views: the cuneiform sources are for the most part traditional liturgical and scholarly compositions and were written by temple elites generally cultivated by the new rulers. If our source material from Ptolemaic Egypt was restricted to the hieroglyphic and hieratic texts – a traditional and culturally conservative corpus produced by the temple elites, which presents a close parallel to the cuneiform sources – our picture of relations between the Ptolemies and their Egyptian subjects would also be far more positive. The hieroglyphic and hieratic material focuses on liturgical and learned compositions and when the Ptolemies appear at all it is usually in positive, Pharaonic mode;[15] in Egypt the evidence for anti-Ptolemaic critique and resistance comes primarily from texts in Demotic and Greek, languages of everyday discourse and documentation for which the partial source record leaves us no analogue in Hellenistic Babylonia.

In what follows, I revisit some of the cuneiform sources that have been brought into discussions on this topic, looking partly at the question of 'resistance' but also thinking more generally about evaluations of the Seleucid rulers. Do these sources suggest, however subtly, moments of tension, flashes of anti-Seleucid or anti-Hellenistic feeling? I will argue that, far from reflecting positive or passive acceptance of the present or a gentle nostalgia for a lost past, cuneiform literary sources of the Hellenistic period show us Babylonian elite scholars consistently

---

[14] For overviews of the cuneiform sources from Hellenistic Babylonia, see Oelsner 1986; Oelsner 2003; Boiy 2004: 13–39; Clancier 2009: 28–44 (Uruk), 123–169 (Babylon); Pirngruber 2017: 3–22 (economic texts).

[15] Although expressions of resistance have also been detected in the hieroglyphic sources: see e.g. Griffiths 1979.

engaging with Seleucid kingship in an evaluative way. Using past, present, and future, they constructed a paradigm of correct royal action against which each ruler could be judged, and not all rulers were judged favourably. The exact force of each text can be hard to understand, because their laconic and allusive nature often leaves interpretive multiplicity. Yet if we look for clusters of negativity, a striking pattern emerges around particular rulers – although we may still wish to hesitate before classing any of this as 'resistance', anti-Hellenic or anti-Hellenistic.

1. The 'Unnegative' Picture: Seleucid Kings in Cuneiform

The first challenge to understanding how Babylonian scholars evaluated the Seleucids and whether they framed any critiques in anti-Seleucid or anti-Hellen(ist)ic terms is that there is no explicit dynastic evaluation in the cuneiform material. In Mesopotamia there certainly existed the concept of a dynasty as a line of kings ruling from a given centre, and scholars were interested in transitions of power between different dynasties: texts like the *Sumerian King List*, which was originally composed in the third millennium BC but was still copied in the Hellenistic period, are devoted to charting their rise and fall.[16] What are absent, in Hellenistic cuneiform texts as in those from other periods, are *evaluations* of dynastic behaviour. There is no Babylonian equivalent to the sorts of characterizations Greek and Jewish authors made of the various dynasties: the decadent Ptolemies or virtuous Attalids we find in Polybius, for example, or even the coded and compressed vision of the Macedonian kingdoms in the Book of Daniel. This reflects the nature of the relationship or 'contract' between king and gods in Babylonia, which, as Maria deJong Ellis has observed, was viewed as short-term and dependent on the behaviour of the human partner.[17] Mesopotamian observers were interested in how each individual ruler measured up to

---

[16] On the *Sumerian King List* and its textual history, see Wilcke 2001; Steinkeller 2003; Glassner 2005: 95–96; Marchesi 2010.

[17] Ellis 1989: 173–177. It may also reflect the absence of a conception of a dynasty in *familial* (as opposed to geographical) terms, also noted by Ellis (p. 175).

the ideal of the good king who would preserve justice, strengthen the land, and honour the gods.

Even if they did not write about them *as* a dynasty, however, the scholars associated with the temples of Babylonia consistently observed and recorded the actions of their latest foreign rulers. We see this most clearly in the sources from Babylon, where reports about the actions of individual kings appear in two types of Akkadian text: Astronomical Diaries and Chronicles. The Astronomical Diaries contain nightly observations of the heavens that were compiled by scholars in Babylon over an astonishingly long timespan: five hundred years, from the mid-sixth to the mid-first century BCE. While they focus mainly on nightly observations of particular astronomical phenomena, at the end of each month scholars also recorded selected events on earth: prices of certain commodities at Babylon; changes in the level of the river Euphrates; and, sometimes, events of political or cultural significance, which usually involved the king or the royal family.[18] The Late Babylonian Chronicles, also probably compiled in Babylon, record the same sort of information as the historical sections of the Diaries; they survive in much smaller numbers and with very uneven preservation.[19]

It is from these texts that one gains a generally 'unnegative' impression of the Seleucids. One basic indicator is the terminology used to introduce them. Based on the Diary and Chronicle references, Seleucus and his successors seem to have been accepted as legitimate rulers of Babylonia: they are all simply described as 'king of Babylon' (Akk. *šar Bābili*), or simply 'king' (*šarru*), like native kings of previous centuries, and are never given foreign ethnics or described pejoratively. For example, a Chronicle probably written in the 280s BCE describes how 'the son of the king, his troops, his wagons, and elephants removed the debris of Esagila'; a later third century Chronicle records Seleucus III's donations for sacrifices at

---

[18] The Astronomical Diaries from the Hellenistic period are published in Sachs and Hunger 1988, 1989; 1996. Their historical sections are re-edited with commentary in Van der Spek, Finkel and Pirngruber forthcoming. On the purposes, context and development of the Diaries see also Rochberg 2011; Pirngruber 2013, and the papers in Haubold, Steele, and Stevens 2019.

[19] On the Babylonian Chronicles see Grayson 1975a; Glassner 2005; Waerzeggers 2012. New or revised editions of all the Hellenistic Chronicles are being published by Irving Finkel and Bert van der Spek in Van der Spek, Finkel, and Pirngruber forthcoming.

Esagila, which were communicated on 'a parchment letter of the king that he had received before'; in 177 BCE a Diary records sacrifices in Babylon 'for the life of king Seleucus (IV), his wife and his sons'.[20] Importantly, no Seleucid ruler ever receives the ethnic 'Hanean' – an archaic term for an enemy people on the Upper Euphrates which, as Amélie Kuhrt has shown, is applied to Greeks and Macedonians in the Diaries and Chronicles when they behave in a harmful way towards Babylon or its inhabitants.[21]

The Diaries' and Chronicles' consistently positive, or at least neutral, way of referring to their Macedonian rulers over 150 years of Seleucid rule is the closest we get to a dynastic evaluation. Beyond that, Babylonian scholars' views on the Seleucids need to be pieced together from specific comments about individual rulers. Those direct comments, however, are few and laconic. The Astronomical Diaries and Chronicles are usually brief in the extreme and do not offer any explicit judgement on the events described. That does not mean that there is no judgement: these texts are very interested in royal behaviour, especially towards the temples of Babylon, and they are almost certainly assessing it. The Diaries and Chronicles have connections with Akkadian divination texts, and may be intended as a kind of database for future predictions, establishing correlations between different events.[22] Alternatively, they may be more historiographical, a record of Babylon's changing fortunes and the merits and demerits of its kings. Either way there is an implicit evaluation of those royal deeds.

The difficulty is identifying the evaluation in each case. We can extrapolate to a certain degree by reading these texts against traditional Babylonian royal ideology. When Antiochus I as crown prince repaired the crumbling brickwork of Esagila or Antiochus III took part in the New Year festival, they were enacting the cultic duties of good Babylonian rulers like Nebuchadnezzar, and we can infer that the evaluation was positive.[23] But often the tablets are broken or their interpretation

---

[20] *BCHP* 6 obv. 7'-8'; *BCHP* 12 obv. 4'; *ADART* II -178C rev. 21'.
[21] Kuhrt 2002: 25–28.   [22] Drews 1975; Rochberg 2011.
[23] Antiochus I: *BCHP* 6 obv. 7'-8'; Antiochus III: *ADART* II -187A rev. 5'-18'.

equivocal. For example, an Astronomical Diary for 278 BCE tells us that there was 'panic and fear in the land'.[24] But is this local trouble connected with royal policy? The entry says nothing further. Even when it is clear that high Hellenistic politics *is* causing tensions or suffering on the ground, it is hard to tell from the reports whether this reflected poorly on the Seleucids. A Diary for 274/3 BCE reports the movement of troops and resources to Eber-nāri, 'Beyond the River' (the satrapy west of the Euphrates), where the Seleucids were fighting the First Syrian War against the Ptolemies, then follows it with a description of famine, disease and silver shortages in Babylonia:[25]

> That year, the king left his [...], his wife and a notable official in the land of Sardis to strengthen the guard. He went to Beyond the River against the troops of Egypt [30] which were encamped in Beyond the River, and the troops of Egypt withdrew before him. Month XII, day 24, the satrap of Babylonia brought out much silver, cloth, goods, and utensils?[31] from Babylon and Seleucia, the royal city, and 20 elephants, which the satrap of Bactria had sent to the king, to Beyond the River [32] to the king. That month, the general gathered the troops of the king which were in Babylonia and went to the aid of the king in month I to Beyond the River.[33] That year, purchases in Babylon and the (other) cities were made with copper coins of Ionia. That year, there was much *ekketu*-disease in the land.

Clearly the author saw a connection, but no explicit comment is made on the situation. Did the scholars who recorded these events view them as the consequences of foreign occupation, or unavoidable results of war in which the legitimate kings of Babylon were doing their best? Most of the comments in the Chronicles and Diaries are of this type, making it hard to identify the evaluative nuances or construct a coherent narrative. So far, so 'unnegative'.

---

[24] *ADART* I -277A obv. 6.
[25] *ADART* I -273B rev. 29'–33' (translation slightly adapted).

2. Babylonian 'Resistance Literature'? The Case of the Dynastic Prophecy

Babylonian scholars of the Hellenistic period did construct more explicit narratives about correct and incorrect models of royal behaviour, however: they just did not set them in the present time. One literary tool used by the subjects of Hellenistic empires to articulate views of present rulers was prophecy, often *ex eventu*. In Seleucid Judea, the detailed 'predictions' of Persian and Macedonian rule in the *Book of Daniel* culminate in a real prophecy which expresses Jewish hopes for deliverance from Seleucid rule, while making plain the failings of Antiochus IV: sacrilege in the temple, altering the 'set times and the laws'.[26] From Egypt, the *Oracle of the Potter* (originally written in Demotic during the Hellenistic period but surviving in later Greek translation) also couches criticism of the present in 'predictions' which highlight the cultural failings of the Ptolemies: the relocation of statues to Alexandria, and the 'crimes' of the 'crowd' of girdle-wearing Greeks who have come to Egypt. Like *Daniel*, it then offers a genuine prophecy of the foreign dynasty's downfall and the desertion of Alexandria, the foreign 'city by the sea'.[27] From Hellenistic Babylonia two Akkadian *ex eventu* texts of this type have survived. One offers 'predictions' relating to the Macedonian conquest, and, on one interpretation, is the most explicit evidence for Babylonian negativity towards Hellenistic rule.

The text in question is the so-called *Dynastic Prophecy*. Preserved on a tablet from Babylon dating from the late fourth century or later, it 'predicts' the reigns of kings from the Neo-Babylonian period onwards, most of whom can be identified securely.[28] Thus, in col. ii 11–16 the king who will 'establish the dynasty' of Harran (l.12) must be the last Neo-Babylonian king Nabonidus (r. 556–539); he is then overthrown by 'the king of Elam', Cyrus I (col. ii 17–24), after which there is a break in the tablet, and the text resumes at the end of the Achaemenid Dynasty with

---

[26] *Daniel* 7–9. [27] Burstein 1985: 136–137.
[28] On the *Dynastic Prophecy*, see in general Grayson 1975b: 24–37; Van der Spek 2003: 311–333; Neujahr 2005; Neujahr 2012: 58–71. The edition here largely follows that of Van der Spek.

Artaxerxes IV and Darius III (col. v 1–8).[29] Then comes the crucial, but fragmentary passage:

Col. V

4. 2 mu.an.na^(meš) [šarrūtu ippuš]
5. lugal šá-a-šú ^(lú)ša-re-[ši .. .. ..]
6. [a]-a-um-ma ^(lú)nun^(ú) [...]
7. zi^(am)-ma a[š.te iṣabbat]
8. 5 mu.an.na^(meš) lugal-[ú-tu ippuš]
9. ^(lú)erín^(meš) kur ḫa-ni-i x [...]
10. zi^(meš) u? [..]-ú?-tú? ú?[-...]
11. ^(lú)erín[^(meš)-šú (?) ...]
12. [ḫ]u-bu-ut-su i-ḫab-ba-t[ú šillatsu]
13. i-šal-la-lu ár-ka-nu ^(lú)e[rín^(meš)-šú ...]
14. ú-kaṣ-ṣar-ma ^(giš)tukul^(meš)-šú í[l]
15. ^(d)en-líl ^(d)utu u ^(d)[Marduk(?)]
16. da ^(lú)erín^(meš)-šú gin[^(meš)-ma]
17. su-kup-tu ^(lú)erín^(meš) ḫa-ni-i i-[...]
18. šil-lat-su ka-bit-tu₄ i-šal-l[a-al-ma]
19. a-na é.gal-šú ú-[še-reb(?)]
20. ^(lú)un^(meš) šá lum-nu i-[mu-ru(?)]
21. dum-qa (blank) [immarū(?)]
22. líb-bi kur [iṭâb]
23. za-ku-tú [...]

4. For two years [he will exercise kingship].
5. That king a eunuch [will murder].
6. A certain prince [...]
7. will arise and [seize] the thr[one]
8. Five years [he will exercise] king[ship]
9. Troops of the land of Hana [...]
10. will arise a[nd?..]-ship? th[ey will? ...]
11. [his] troop[s they will defeat;]
12. booty from him they will take [and his spoils]
13. they will plunder. Later [his?] tr[oops x]
14. will assemble and his weapons he will ra[ise]
15. Enlil, Šamaš and [Marduk(?)]
16. will go at the side of his army [and]
17. defeat of? the Hanean troops [...].
18. Extensive booty from him he? will car[ry off and]
19. into his palace he? [will bring it?]
20. The people who had [experienced] misfortune
21. [will enjoy] well-being.
22. The heart of the land [will be happy].
23. Tax exemption [...]

What 'should' happen next is that Alexander the Great overthrows Darius, and indeed the passage seems to begin this way: the 'troops of the land of Hana' (Macedon) arise and defeat Darius. However, then someone masculine singular assembles 'troops', and the Babylonian gods 'go at his army's side', and presumably lead him to victory (v 13–17).[30] Since the last 'he' mentioned was Darius, it is commonly suggested that the person supported by Babylonia's deities in this section is him too, so that here the text stops being *ex eventu* to offer a genuine – and

---

[29] Following Van der Spek, I assume an original six-column text with all the Persian kings treated in the break; an alternative reconstruction posits a four-column text with a shorter break and more selective treatment (Neujahr 2005; 2012; Grayson 1975b is equivocal).

[30] The main verb is missing, but when gods 'go at the side of' rulers this denotes assistance and, usually, success (see *CAD* A1: 319–320).

ultimately ahistorical – prediction about Darius defeating Alexander and his Hanean troops and regaining control.[31] Such a prediction would be excellent evidence for negative Babylonian impressions of Macedonian rule (although not necessarily of Seleucid rule). But there are real problems here.

First, according to the logic of the text, if anyone defeats Alexander it is very unlikely to be Darius. As Van der Spek has pointed out, it is stated clearly (col. v 8) that Darius reigned for five years in total, which in this text is usually the formula that precedes the appearance of a new ruler and a transfer of power.[32] Nor is it clear that Alexander or the Macedonians *are* defeated. Alexander could be mentioned in the break in line 10, becoming the victorious person with the Babylonian gods at his side in line 16. Alternatively, the Hanean troops might be the victorious ones: the broken verbs in lines 18–19 are usually restored as singular, but they could be plural, with the Hanean army returning to plunder Darius again (certainly, 'his booty' (l.18) refers not to plunder taken *by* the unnamed male protagonist but rather booty taken *from* him).[33] This section might not even describe a change of rule at all: notably, no new *king* is announced (the army of the Haneans occupies that place in the structure). The end of the Persian Empire was protracted and messy, with Darius killed not by Alexander but by the usurper Bessus; it is possible that the text reflects this, and indeed Susan Sherwin-White suggested that the end of Darius is lost in the break.[34] It is possible that the text recognized no king until Seleucus.

Most importantly of all, the internal logic and structure of the *Prophecy* make the idea of a genuine prediction problematic. Typically in *ex eventu* prophecy texts, there is a switch to 'genuine' prophecy in the final section, which predicts a single episode of salvation or restoration and is signalled by more universal and generic language, as with the downfall of the 'little horn' and restoration of Jerusalem in Daniel or the downfall of the 'Girdlewearers' in the Oracle of the Potter. But in the

---

[31] Thus Grayson 1975b; Neujahr 2005; Neujahr 2012: 58–71.
[32] Van der Spek 2003: 327.
[33] Following this interpretation, one might even read 'defeat – the army of the Haneans will bring about', rather than 'the defeat of the army of the Haneans he will bring about' in l.17.
[34] Sherwin-White 1987: 11.

Dynastic Prophecy the text originally continued for around forty lines beyond this column; although this section is fragmentary, enough is preserved to show that several further reigns are described, which has deterred most adherents of the victorious Darius hypothesis from viewing the final section as a genuine prediction.[35] In his influential reassessment of the *Prophecy* Matthew Neujahr has argued that an 'original' version of the text ended with a prophecy predicting Darius' victory and return, but was later 'updated' with additional sections when this proved incorrect.[36] Yet this is contrary to the logic of *ex eventu* prophecies, in which the accuracy of the historical 'predictions' in the *ex eventu* section establishes authority for the genuine prophecy to come; retaining a blatant ahistoricism in the middle of the text would destroy that authority. The parallels adduced for this kind of updating seem quite different in kind: the changing of the numbers of days until the 'end times' in different sections of the Book of Daniel, or the addition of Rome to an originally ten-kingdom scheme which looks forward to the restoration of Jerusalem in the *Sibylline Oracles*.[37] These are not really parallel cases: numbers could be easily altered or reinterpreted (particularly in an ancient Jewish or Babylonian scholarly context, where this was a common exegetical strategy) and it is much easier to explain a delay to a predicted event than a completely incorrect prediction about an event that has already happened. All this would tell against a redacted *Prophecy* embedding an ahistorical defeat of Alexander and then continuing with further predictions.

Whether this text offers a negative view of Alexander and/or his successors ultimately seems questionable at best. What it definitely *does* do is articulate traditional paradigms for royal behaviour found in many earlier Akkadian literary texts and royal inscriptions: good kings look after the temples and the land is content; bad kings neglect their cultic duties and both they and the land suffer.[38] In other words, it provides evidence that the Babylonian scholar(s) of the early

---

[35] E.g. Sherwin-White 1987: 11, 14.   [36] Neujahr 2005, 2012: 66–71.
[37] Neujahr 2012: 68–70.
[38] A parallel from Ptolemaic Egypt is the so-called Demotic Chronicle (P.Chronik), a partly *ex eventu* text probably produced during the third century BCE. This composition, set in the reign of Nectanebo I and Tachos (365–362 BCE), contains 'predictions' of the reigns of Egyptian

Hellenistic period who produced and used this text, and who probably came from the same group who produced the Diaries and Chronicles, found such paradigms a meaningful way of thinking about contemporary kings, and quite probably had them in mind when they recorded the actions of their Macedonian rulers in and beyond Babylon. But whether the Prophecy was written as a negative commentary on Macedonian rule, an expression of hope at the beginning of a new dynasty, or even a celebration of a particular Seleucid king, is very hard to establish.

Far from offering random observations of current events or vague hopes for a better future, the Diaries, Chronicles, and *Dynastic Prophecy* show us concern among Babylonian scholars of the Hellenistic period with the behaviour of contemporary kings. The *Dynastic Prophecy* offers explicitly positive or negative comments, and to a Babylonian reader the reports of the Diaries and Chronicles may have been similarly transparent. The problem is that the gaps in the evidence make it very difficult to extract the evaluative nuances in each individual case. One way forward, however, is to focus not on individual texts but on significant clusters of texts or comments, where the cumulative impression of a group of sources can compensate for the equivocal interpretation of some of the individual pieces of evidence. When the cuneiform sources are approached from this perspective, it is possible to detect 'clusters of negativity' around particular Seleucid kings.

3. Antiochus IV and the Problematic Politai

One such cluster is around Antiochus IV, particularly in the sources from Babylon. Philippe Clancier and Julien Monerie have argued convincingly that Antiochus IV's reign saw a significant increase in royal control over the sanctuaries in Babylon, and a shift where powers

---

rulers between the end of the first Persian period and the dramatic date of the Chronicle, followed by general pseudo-prophetic statements about the Persian and early Ptolemaic period which cannot be assigned with certainty to particular rulers and culminate in a genuine prediction of an ideal pharaoh. As such, the Chronicle's primary concern seems to be to articulate an ideology of kingship against which any ruler could be judged, rather than offering an assessment of individual kings. See further Johnson 1983; Moyer 2011b: 129-133.

formerly given to the temple assembly were increasingly taken over by the *politai*, the inhabitants of a newly formalized Greek civic community in Babylon.[39] One might expect this to have caused concern among the Babylonian priestly elite, and several episodes recorded in cuneiform texts from the 170s and 160s BCE combine to suggest a halo of negativity around Antiochus IV and the *politai* he introduced to Babylon.

Beginning in the late 170s BCE, there are signs that the *politai* in Babylon, or rather the changes that accompanied their arrival, were a concern for the Babylonian elite. One is the so-called Lehmann text, a tablet written in 173/2 BCE which preserves a copy of a monument recording tax exemptions and land grants given to the 'Borsippans, Babylonians and Cutheans' by king Antiochus II and his family in the mid-third century BC.[40] Importantly, the royal decision recorded in this text also grants the tithe of the harvest to the main temples of these cities. Bert van der Spek has convincingly suggested that the reason the Babylonians were recalling the grants a century later was that the land had been reassigned to the *politai* by Antiochus IV and the Babylonians were attempting to dispute it by providing evidence of their royally sanctioned claim.[41]

A tantalizing reference to the *politai* and 'weeping/mourning' (*bikītu*) a few lines later in a small chronicle fragment concerning 172 BCE may also be part of this picture.[42] The fragmentary remains mention the *politai*, the Great Gate (of Esagila, typically mentioned in Diaries or Chronicles in the context of offerings), bricks, another gate (probably again the Great Gate of Esagila) and then weeping (*bikītu*). Although the state of the text is rather desperate, *bikītu* is a strong word that is rare in the Diaries and Chronicles; it also appears twice in *BCHP* 3, a Chronicle which describes the unsettled conditions in Babylonia during the conflict with Antigonus, in the phrase *sipdu u bikītu ina māti*, 'there was weeping and mourning in the land'.[43]

---

[39] Clancier 2012; Clancier and Monerie 2014. Debate continues over whether the *polis* in Babylon was founded by Antiochus IV or Antiochus III, but it seems to be under Antiochus IV that the shift in local administration takes place. Clancier 2017 is the most recent and comprehensive treatment of the topic, with a useful summary of previous positions.

[40] Full edition and commentary: Van der Spek and Wallenfels 2014 (a duplicate tablet survives, but cannot be dated exactly).

[41] Van der Spek 1993: 71–77.   [42] *BCHP* 13.   [43] *BCHP* 3 r24' and r37'.

The occurrence of the word (and possibly the whole formula) here suggests that we are dealing with conflict or unrest of some kind. It is even possible that the construction work mentioned is related to the new Greek community (as opposed to restoration work at Esagila, the typical focus of Diary reports about the moulding of bricks)[44] and that this caused difficulties locally. Overall, the tablet is too fragmentary to extrapolate any narrative with confidence, but even if only the interpretation of *bikītu* is correct, it offers evidence for tensions in Babylon during these years.

At the beginning of the 160s, evidence from the Diaries also suggests increasing royal control of Esagila. A Diary for 169 BCE records that Antiochus IV had appointed a *zazakku* (official in charge of temple revenues, an office which seems to have been obsolete in the earlier Seleucid period):[45]

> That month, day 6, a Babylonian, a jeweller, a brother of the *šatammu* of [Esag]ila, who p[erformed] the office of *šatammu* in his place, was entrusted with the office of *zazakku* by a message from the king. That day, gold from the dedications [from] the property of Esagila was given to this *zazakku* and the assembly of the goldsmiths for the making of a wig, a great [...] of Bel.

As the brother of the *šatammu*, the new *zazakku* is drawn from within the current temple elite; the appointment therefore does not seem to be a move to disrupt the existing local hierarchy by inserting royal sympathizers (although one should not necessarily assume this was *not* the case – witness near-contemporary affairs in Jerusalem with Onias and Jason).[46] Nonetheless, as a number of scholars have observed, the addition of a royal appointee with direct access to the temple funds represents increased royal involvement in temple administration; previously temple personnel had been appointed internally by the temple

---

[44] The sign after é in obv. 4 is *ni*; one possibility is *bīt niṣirti* 'treasure-house', although the Chronicles and Diaries typically use *bīt bušê* for this.
[45] *ADART* II -168A rev. 12'-14' (translation slightly modified).
[46] Pirngruber (2012: 260) notes that in the first decade of the first century BCE a *šatammu* was also occasionally replaced by his brother.

assembly.[47] Of course it is possible, especially given the fragmentary state of the Diaries, that there was a *zazakku* throughout the period and the earlier attestations happen not to have been preserved. Yet it is striking that a *zazakku* is so far only attested in the 160s, the same decade as the other evidence suggesting an increase in royal interference and shift of power away from the temple hierarchy towards the *politai* and royal officials.[48] As is usual for the genre, there is no explicit evaluation of this episode in the Diary, positive or negative. But we may note the encroachment on temple autonomy as significant, a potential negative in the ongoing balance sheet of royal behaviour recorded in the Diaries.

Combined with the arrival of the *politai*, the reintroduction of the *zazakku* might well be expected to cause consternation among the priestly elite who for the first century of Seleucid rule had enjoyed considerable autonomy and consistent royal patronage. Indeed, to judge from what survives of the Astronomical Diaries from the following years, the scholarly community of Esagila may well have felt that all was not as it should be in Babylon. Passages in Diaries from 166 to 163 BCE record an unusual cluster of ominous happenings: destructive storms; locusts; the appearance of a comet (Halley's comet, in fact) in 164 just before Antiochus IV's death, and two eclipses – usually very negative, according to Mesopotamian divinatory principles – shortly afterwards in early 163.[49] As Reinhard Pirngruber has observed, in the Diaries such events tend to cluster in periods of political or economic difficulty;[50] the most notable such cluster in the Late Babylonian Diaries is shortly after the time of the Parthian conquest, but these few years in the mid-160s also seem to offer an unusually concentrated set of extreme or ominous phenomena. Of course, the source record is partial, and natural phenomena either occur or do not; one cannot invent a comet or a solar eclipse. Nonetheless, the Diaries' records of weather and terrestrial

---

[47] E.g. Eddy 1961: 135–137; Geller 1991: 2–3; Boiy 2004: 224; Pirngruber 2012: 260; Clancier 2014: 435–436.

[48] Pirngruber 2012: 260. The *zazakku* is also mentioned in *ADART* III -163C$_2$ rev. 17.

[49] Storm: *ADART* II -165A rev. 8' ('Adad devastated'; unusually strong wording to describe a storm/flood, and recalls the language of omens); locusts: *ADART* II -164A rev. 4'–5'; comet: *ADART* III -163B obv. 16–17; -163C$_1$ obv. 9'. eclipses: *ADART* III -163B rev. 8' (solar), 20'–21' (lunar).

[50] Pirngruber 2013: 202–204.

events always represent a selection of phenomena, observed and recorded through a particular interpretive filter. We might compare for instance the cluster of bad omens reported by Tacitus at the end of the year of the Fire of Rome: lightning flashes, monstrous births, and a comet heralded coming disaster.[51] The sum of phenomena the Babylonian priestly elite selected for record in these years is similarly negative and creates the impression of an unsettled city.

And finally, just after Antiochus' death, local tensions erupted. In 163 BCE, the first year of Antiochus V, a Chronicle from Babylon reports that the *politai* in Babylon 'did battle with the prefect (*šaknu*) and the people of the land who were in Babylon'.[52] The precise scale and context of the conflict described are unclear, but the Chronicle reports that women and possibly also the *boulē* of the *politai* were evacuated from the city, which suggests that it was not simply a minor skirmish.[53] We should be cautious about reading this episode in terms of cultural conflict or 'resistance' by the Babylonians. For one thing, the fighting may not have involved the priestly elite at all: the 'people of the land who are in Babylon' probably refers to Babylonians from the countryside as distinct from the citizens of Babylon itself,[54] and we hear nothing in the surviving text about the Esagila community. Nonetheless, the precise description of the 'Greeks, as they are called, the *politai* who anoint with oil just like those in Seleucia' fighting the 'people of the land who are in Babylon' does seem to position the conflict to some extent along ethno-cultural lines. Moreover, and particularly relevant for our purposes, the writer's decision to describe the problematic *politai* as those who entered Babylon 'at the command of king Antiochus (IV)' is significant.[55] In these laconic texts, nothing superfluous is included, and this reference looks pointed: the Greeks are causing problems, and Antiochus was the one who brought them into Babylon... Granted, this is a subtle way of

---

[51] Tacitus, *Annals* 15.47.   [52] *BCHP* 14 obv. 2–7.   [53] *BCHP* 14 obv. 9–12.
[54] Van der Spek, comm. ad loc.
[55] *BCHP* 14 obv. 3. Since the Diaries and Chronicles do not distinguish between homonymous Seleucid kings, the Akkadian here (*An šarri* 'Antiochus the king') could refer to Antiochus III, but the important point is the connection between royal action and local unrest that seems to be being made.

criticizing Antiochus, but subtlety and implicit evaluation are the Diaries' standard register.

Each of the individual points in this cluster of evidence is somewhat equivocal in interpretation, some very much so. Yet taken together, these cuneiform texts offer a decade's worth of hints that Antiochus IV, and his 'Hellenizing' policies, which disrupted traditional land ownership and social and legal structures, were not well received in Babylon. Thus, in a more muted way than contemporary Judea, Babylonia experienced tensions parallel to those that spurred the Maccabean Revolt.

Strikingly, the two issues raised in these Babylonian sources – the interference with temple revenue, and the promotion of Greek political and cultural institutions – chime exactly with the sources on Antiochus IV from outside the region, where he appears in Greek and Jewish texts as a temple-robbing Hellenizer. Polybius' account of Antiochus' magnificent games at Daphne in 166 BCE concludes with the sting in the tail that the king had paid for it all by 'despoiling most of the temples' in Egypt, while in 1 and 2 Maccabees and Josephus, Antiochus steals the temple treasures from Jerusalem and supports Hellenization in the city.[56] As noted above, recent scholarship on the Maccabean Revolt has tended to minimize its culturally Greek aspects, as part of the general turn away from cultural towards economic explanations for Hellenistic revolt and resistance.[57] Taking the Greek, Jewish, and cuneiform evidence together, however, raises the question of whether one should revisit the older view of Antiochus as a deliberate 'Hellenizer'.[58]

Although the most memorable Classical sources on Antiochus IV are the striking anecdotes about the bad behaviour of 'Epimanes', Greek and Roman authors also emphasize Antiochus' commitment to Greek culture: Polybius claims that he surpassed all his predecessors in sacrifices to cities and honours to Greek gods, while Livy catalogues his magnificent gifts to an array of Greek cities.[59] On that note, it is worth observing that all the temples Antiochus is recorded as plundering or attempting to plunder may belong to non-Greek deities: the temples of Egypt, the

---

[56] Polybius, 30.26.9; 1 Macc. 1.21–23; 2 Macc. 5.16, 21; Jos. *Ant.* 12.250–253.
[57] See above, p. 97 with n.3.
[58] As found in e.g. Bevan 1902 2: 162–174; Bengtson 1960: 482; Eddy 1961.
[59] Polybius, 26.1.10–12; Livy, 41.20.6–9.

temple of Nanaya in Elam, the temple in Jerusalem, and perhaps also Esagila if the *zazakku* episode is to be interpreted along similar lines.[60] Together the Greek, Jewish, and Babylonian sources provide a coherent picture of a ruler – for whatever reason – systematically promoting Greek political and cultural institutions across his domain, and reducing the political and fiscal independence of non-Hellenized groups. Greek observers like Polybius commended Antiochus' Hellenism even as they deplored his unkingly conduct. The 'people of the land' in Babylon met the *politai* with violence. And the priestly elite of Esagila registered it all in the scholarly texts which had acted as a barometer of the health of their land and the worthiness of its rulers for over five hundred years before the *politai* came to Babylon.

4. Trouble from the Start? Seleucus I Revisited

In this light – concern over 'Hellenization', or the changes that accompanied the influx of Greek settlers or creation of Greek political institutions – it is worth revisiting finally another Seleucid ruler whose reputation has evolved markedly since the cuneiform evidence became available. Antiochus IV's philhellenism in the west is matched in the Greek sources by that of one earlier Seleucid king: the dynastic founder, Seleucus I. Yet, unlike Antiochus IV, some Classical sources explicitly portray Seleucus as unpopular in Babylonia, suggesting an early phase of positive relations and a later phase that was not quite so positive. Diodorus describes how Seleucus' generosity towards the inhabitants of Babylonia as satrap created goodwill, *eunoia*, which helped him to retake the region from his rival Antigonus in 311–310; Appian, too, claims that the Babylonians 'received Seleucus with enthusiasm' on his return to the region.[61] But according to the Greco-Roman authors, the foundation of Seleucus' new capital at Seleucia on the Tigris spoiled this beautiful relationship. Strabo and Pliny speak of the ruinous effects the foundation

---

[60] Egypt: Polybius, 30.26.9 (although this could refer to Greek temples as well). Elam: Polybius, 31.9; App. *Syr.* 66; Jos. *Ant.* 12.354–359; 1 Macc. 6.1–16, 2 Macc. 1.13–17.
[61] Diod. Sic. 19.91.1–3; App. *Syr.* 54.

of the new Seleucid capital had on Babylon;[62] Pliny even emphasizes that this was Seleucus' intention from the beginning: Babylon was 'drained' or 'exhausted' (*exhausta*) by its proximity to Seleucia, which was 'founded for that purpose by Seleucus'.[63] Appian preserves a story in which the Babylonian priests foresee these terrible consequences of the new foundation and attempt to thwart Seleucus' plans by tricking him into starting the building on an inauspicious day.[64]

Before the cuneiform evidence from Babylon was available, modern historians had tended to follow the narrative of the Classical sources, assuming that Seleucus' reputation in Babylon suffered during his final years.[65] But as the publication of more Hellenistic cuneiform texts revealed that Babylon was far from moribund during the Seleucid period, this negative view of Seleucia and Seleucus faded, and the material about his positive earlier reception in Babylonia has tended to be emphasized instead.[66] Yet the fact that Babylon was not depopulated or ruined after the foundation of Seleucia is not incompatible with the foundation of a new Greek city in northern Babylonia causing concern or resentment locally, particularly among the local elites who had most to lose if the regional centre of power shifted. Indeed, if one examines the cuneiform scholarly texts closely, it is possible to detect something of a halo of negativity around Seleucus, albeit – as ever – faint and allusive.

While the evidence suggesting Babylonian scholars' concern about Antiochus IV is concentrated in texts from Babylon, hints of unease about Seleucus I can be detected in cuneiform texts from several cities. In Uruk, two texts which were copied and/or composed in the early Seleucid period have been interpreted as coded attacks on the first Seleucid ruler. The first is another *ex eventu* cuneiform text, the so-called *Uruk Prophecy*. It survives in a copy that is probably Seleucid, from the house of a priestly family who lived in Uruk during the late fourth and third centuries BCE.[67] The text has a simple format and structure: various rulers 'arise'; good ones make the right decisions for

---

[62] Strab. 16.1.5; Pliny, *HN* 6.121–12.   [63] Pliny, *HN* 6.122.   [64] App. *Syr.* 58.
[65] E.g. Bevan 1902; Eddy 1961.
[66] See e.g. Sherwin-White 1987: 14–21; Sherwin-White and Kuhrt 1993: 10–12.
[67] *SpTU* 1, 3. The tablet was found on the fourth century level, but Seleucid-period tablets which had fallen down from upper levels were also found here.

the land and support the temples; bad ones oppress it, and so on. The brief and formulaic descriptions of each king make it difficult to identify the kings with certainty, and several different sequences have been proposed, but the text does seem to be describing the reigns of historical rulers of Babylonia during the first millennium BCE.[68] For our purposes the key section concerns the final three rulers, whose reigns are 'predicted' as follows:[69]

> After him a king will arise, but he will not perform justice for the land; he will not make the (right) decisions for the land. He will rule the four quarters (of the world), and the (four) quarters will tremble at his name.
>
> After him a king will arise in Uruk and he will perform justice for the land; he will make the (right) decisions for the land. He will establish the rites of the Anu cult in Uruk. He will bring the eternal protective goddess of Uruk from Šuanna; in Tirana, in her sanctuary he will let her dwell. He will give her her own people as a gift. He will rebuild the temples of Uruk and restore the sanctuaries of the gods. He will renew Uruk. He will build the gates of Uruk out of lapis lazuli. He will fill the rivers (and) cultivated meadows with abundance and plenty.
>
> After him a king, his son, will arise in Uruk, and rule the four quarters. He will exercise [ruler]ship and kingship in Uruk; his dynasty will be established forever. [The king]s of Uruk will exercise rulership like the gods.

A compelling case has been made that these three rulers represented in the first instance three Neo-Babylonian kings: Nabopolassar, Nebuchadnezzar and Nebuchadnezzar's son Amel-Marduk.[70] Nabopolassar ended Assyrian rule over Babylonia and founded the Neo-Babylonian Dynasty, but seems to have been viewed negatively in later Uruk; Nebuchadnezzar

---

[68] On the interpretation of the *Uruk Prophecy* see in general Hunger and Kaufman 1975; Goldstein 1988; Ellis 1989; Beaulieu 1993; Scurlock 2006; Neujahr 2012: 50–58.

[69] rev. 9–18 (trans. after Neujahr 2012).

[70] Hunger and Kaufman 1975, followed by Beaulieu 1993; Neujahr 2012: ch. 2 (for alternative reconstructions see Lambert 1978; Goldstein 1988).

was celebrated there for his patronage of local cults and enjoyed a positive reputation in Babylonia which lasted down to the Hellenistic period.[71] But when the text was copied in the Hellenistic period, were these identifications the only ones its writer made? Surely it would have been hard to interpret two foreign conquests as part of the eternal rule of the Neo-Babylonian Dynasty. A solution proposed by Paul-Alain Beaulieu is that these final kings took on alternative or additional identifications for their Seleucid copyist. The king who 'rules the four quarters' but does not make the right decisions for the land could also be equated with Seleucus I: an imperial ruler with a vast domain who neglected local needs. The Prophecy would then express a perceived neglect of Uruk by Seleucus I, who did focus on northern Babylonia, and end with a new hope for the city's ascendancy under Antiochus I and his successors (or alternatively a hope for a new native dynasty from Uruk that would break free from Seleucid rule).[72]

Another Akkadian text from Uruk, again from the circle of scholars associated with the city's main temple, the Rēš, may reflect similar disquiet about Seleucus. This is a chronicle which survives in a copy made in 251 BCE by a junior scribe for his father, a priest at the Rēš; the colophon states that the tablet was copied from a previous exemplar, which puts the likely date of composition in the early third century.[73] The Uruk tablet deals with the reign of Šulgi, a king of the Ur III Dynasty which ruled Uruk and the rest of Babylonia during the third millennium BC.[74] Šulgi's reign begins well enough: he defeats Babylonia's enemies, the kings of Subartu. But he then commits sacrilege in both Babylon and Uruk, stealing temple treasures and improperly altering the cultic regulations. For this, he is punished with a horrible disease by the god Anu, patron deity of Uruk:[75]

---

[71] On Nebuchadnezzar as a model in Seleucid Babylonia, see Dillery 2013; Haubold 2016; Haubold this volume, Chapter 3.
[72] Beaulieu 1993.
[73] *SpTU* 1, 2. The text may also have been composed earlier, but even if so, the choice to recopy it would indicate its continued significance.
[74] Part of the reign of Šulgi's son is also described, and the tablet has a catchline, so it may belong to a series which originally dealt with the whole Ur III Dynasty.
[75] *SpTU* 1, 2 obv. 3–20. When gods 'clothe the body' of humans with something it is usually a skin disease (typically leprosy, which can probably be restored here).

[The divine Š]ulgi, king of Ur, son of Ur-Nammu, exercised [ki]ngship over all the lands... He conquered -bangar and Rabsisi, the kings of Subartu, and plundered the [citie]s of the enemy land. He took out as booty the [property] of Esagila and Babylon; he built and perfected the [E]gišnugal, the temple of Sin in Ur; he constructed the wall of Ur and made fi[rm] Ur's foundations. The divine Šulgi, son of a daughter of king Utu-ḫegal of Uruk, with the blind Lu-Nanna, the scholar [...] – there was [ev]il in their hearts! – improperly alte[red] the rites of the cult of Anu, Uruk's cultic regulations, the [sec]ret knowledge of the scholars, and put down in writing the [for]ced labour exacted by Sin, lord of Ur. [During] his [re]ign, he composed untruthful stelae, insolent writings, [concerning the rit]es of purification for the gods, and left them to posterity. [But Anu], the king, whose decisions are great, regarded him with anger and [...] his great punishment [...] he clothed his body with [...].

Stories about former kings appear in cuneiform literature of all periods, so finding a narrative about an ancient king in a scholarly tablet collection is not surprising. But in Mesopotamia, such stories often had a paradigmatic force and contemporary resonance with the time at which they were written or copied.[76] Narratives about past rulers could be used as a means of commenting on the present, since one king could become an avatar for another: for instance, Marc Van de Mieroop has shown that compositions criticizing the third-millennium king Sargon of Akkad which circulated in the reign of his first-millennium namesake seem to be a means of criticizing the latter.[77]

Several aspects of the Šulgi Chronicle certainly resonate strongly with its early Seleucid context. In the Chronicle Uruk is under the rule of another state, just as at the time the tablet was copied, and the text anachronistically stresses the importance of the cult of Anu, which had been reorganized during the Achaemenid period; indeed, Paul-Alain Beaulieu has interpreted both the Chronicle and the *Uruk Prophecy* as

---

[76] On this aspect of Mesopotamian historiography, see Van De Mieroop 1999; Glassner 2005: 10; De Breucker 2015.
[77] Van De Mieroop 1999.

part of a cluster of texts designed to bolster the prestige of the Late Babylonian cult and its personnel.[78] In the Chronicle, Šulgi supports another city, Ur, at the expense of Uruk and Babylon, even stealing the resources of Babylon's temple to fortify his rival city. Might the Urukean elite have seen an analogue with Seleucus' promotion of his new city, Seleucia? Antoine Cavigneaux has in fact suggested that here Šulgi is an avatar for Seleucus I (enhanced by the phonetic similarity of the consonants in their names, via a type of wordplay common in Mesopotamian scholarship), and that the ancient king's neglect of Uruk and its cult was correlated by the priests of Anu with contemporary actions of Seleucus.[79] As such, the Chronicle seems to serve a similar function to contemporary local histories from the Greek world, which provided *poleis* with a means of self-assertion and a way of expressing expectations for treatment by external powers.[80] It asserts Urukean identity under Seleucid imperial rule, and sets up a paradigm of royal behaviour against which claims for privileges might be made, and by which contemporary kings were to be judged. It also makes clear the awful punishment for rulers who fail to treat the god (and by extension, his priests and the city) with the proper reverence, as, perhaps, the Urukeans feared their new foreign rulers might.

Through their *ex eventu* predictions and reshaping of the remote past, texts like the Prophecy and Chronicle offered a medium for Babylonia's priestly elite to articulate concern or veiled critique about contemporary rulers. In my view, there are sufficient resonances to suggest that the Prophecy and Chronicle are both alluding to the reign of Seleucus in particular. Yet these allusions must remain uncertain, particularly since both texts are somewhat free-floating chronologically. If we move north, however, more pieces of evidence join the cluster, this time with a firmer temporal anchor. At Borsippa, the so-called Antiochus Cylinder, a

---

[78] Beaulieu 1993. For the Seleucid resonances of the Chronicle's narrative, see further Stevens 2019: ch. 7.
[79] Cavigneaux 2005.
[80] On this aspect of Greek local historiography, see e.g. Boffo 1988; Chaniotis 1988; Clarke 2008, ch. 6; Dillery 2005, 2015: 136–148, 183–192 (arguing that the works of Berossus and Manetho can be read in a similar way); Tober, this volume, Chapter 8. For a fuller argument that the Šulgi Chronicle should be viewed as comparable to Hellenistic Greek local historiography, see Stevens 2019: ch. 7.

'AFTER HIM A KING WILL ARISE' 119

cuneiform royal inscription composed in 268 BCE to celebrate Antiochus I's restoration of the local temple to Nabû, gives Antiochus himself the titulary of a legitimate Babylonian king with no comment on his ethnicity, but describes Seleucus I explicitly as 'the Macedonian'.[81] While this may be part of a claim to royal status (the ethnic *Makkadunāya* 'Macedonian' follows 'king', *šarru*, in a slightly awkward arrangement which suggests that it may be meant to qualify it), the fact that only Seleucus is described in this way while Antiochus is 'king of the world, king of Babylon, and king of the lands', is striking.[82] A more pointed reference comes in the Chronicle from Babylon which records Seleucus' departure in 281 BCE for 'Macedon, his land'.[83] Were these texts hinting that even after several decades as 'king of the land' Seleucus' cultural allegiance still lay elsewhere? It is worth recalling here that, as we have seen, the Chronicles and Diaries never otherwise specify the Seleucids' foreign origins.

On the topic of cultural allegiance, it is striking that the surviving Babylonian Chronicles from Seleucus' reign all mention the settlement or other activities of Greeks/Macedonians in or near Babylon, most of them in proximity to statements about problems or otherwise negative occurrences in Babylon. The 'Antiochus and Sin temple Chronicle' records the resettlement of Macedonians from Babylon in Seleucia, followed immediately by a reference to heavy taxation in Babylon;[84] the 'Antiochus, Bactria and India Chronicle' reports offerings made 'in the Greek fashion' in Babylon, possibly by Seleucus, who is mentioned in the following line;[85] the 'Juniper Garden Chronicle', in a very broken context, records a Greek apparently mustering people involved with the service estate of the god, which seems to have led to problems ('weeping and mourning' in the estate is reported immediately afterwards).[86] The 'Ruin of Esagila Chronicle' mentions a Greek acting at the command of Seleucus I in a fragmentary context, as well as someone (possibly

---

[81] BM 36277 i.5 (most recent edition and translation: Stevens 2014: 68–69).
[82] On the varying interpretations of *Makkadunāya* and its connection with *šarru*, see Stevens 2014: 76–77 with references. Antiochus' royal titles: BM 36277 i.1–3.
[83] *BCHP* 9 rev. 1'–3'.   [84] *BCHP* 5 rev. 6'–10'.   [85] *BCHP* 7 rev. 3'-4'.
[86] *BCHP* 8 rev. 13' (note here the occurrence again of *bikītu*, 'weeping'). Van der Spek (comm. ad loc.) suggests that this tablet records a complaint about the removal of temple personnel for royal purposes.

Seleucus) making offerings on the ruin of the Esagila temple and falling over.[87] The latter is probably an inauspicious sign, and indeed the Chronicle records other negative omens: a lightning strike in the most sacred quarter of Babylon, Eridu, and 'five bitches in the palace' on the fragmentary reverse.[88] It is also significant that the Chronicle records the person who fell making an 'offering in the Greek fashion' in the temple[89] – a practice, which, although never explicitly evaluated in the cuneiform texts, may well have been considered by the Babylonian priesthood as sacrilegious.[90] Did Seleucus's reign ultimately cause disquiet among the Babylonian temple elites for a troubling commitment to Greek culture, or a perceived disregard for local rights and traditions? Was his promising record of the early years, just as the Classical authors imply, overwritten by his foundation of a new, Greek capital, his neglect of the urban metropolis of the south, and the fact that he brought Greeks and Greek customs into the heart of Babylon?

Once again, each of the textual witnesses we have examined is equivocal, but together they suggest that activity one might loosely describe as 'Hellenizing' was a focus of interest and concern among the scholarly elite of Babylon in the later stages of Seleucus' reign, just as under Antiochus IV.

5. Conclusions

The images constructed here are admittedly a patchwork of scraps. The sources are difficult, and the interpretation of many individual cases equivocal. But when these cases cluster together, the cumulative impression of negativity or tension becomes more compelling. Despite the differing mode and intensity of the responses in each region, it seems as if similar shifts in Seleucid policy under Antiochus IV provoked a

---

[87] *BCHP* 6 obv. 13' (Greeks); obv. 4'–5' (falling). The person who falls over is usually taken to be the crown prince Antiochus, who appears in obv. 7'–9', but the subject is lost in the break and as the Chronicle cannot be dated exactly it is possible that Seleucus was present too.

[88] *BCHP* 6 obv. 10', rev. 2'.   [89] *BCHP* 6 obv. 6'–7'.

[90] See e.g. Van der Spek's commentary on *BCHP* 6 obv. 9', which collects all reports of this practice.

negative judgement on his kingship among the priestly elite in both Judea and Babylonia. And a similar judgement may well have been passed by the Babylonians on the 'Hellenizing' figure of Seleucus I. It is not clear that it is helpful to class any of these cases as 'resistance literature', unless the definition of the latter is weakened to the point where it embraces such heterogeneity as to lose its value as a category. What I think *is* helpful is to locate them along a spectrum from positive to negative in terms of local reactions to Seleucid imperialism. At a local level, the clusters of concern or critique around Antiochus IV and Seleucus I in the Babylonian scholarly texts add nuance to the blanket picture of 'unnegative' acceptance of the Seleucids we might otherwise posit for the elites of Babylon and Uruk, and fit well with the more differentiated economic and political history of Seleucid Babylonia emerging from recent scholarship.[91] Beyond the region, they connect the temple elites of Babylonia with counterparts in Judea and Greece in terms of the features of individual rulers' reigns (or of Hellenistic imperialism more broadly) that they identified as significant or problematic: the introduction or support of Greek cultural forms; the appropriation of religious resources and interference in cultic practice. While the precise form taken by the local reaction might be different (outright violence; coded critique; prophetic hopes for a brighter future), the recurring pattern provides further evidence that the history of Hellenistic (and broader ancient) imperialism and local elite reactions to it needs to be written from a cross-regional and cross-linguistic perspective.[92]

It is noteworthy that from different sources and by different routes these clusters have brought us close to the same rulers whom Eddy identified as problematic fifty years ago. It is striking, too, that working from the cuneiform texts alone one arrives at the same rulers who have a negative reputation in the Greek and Latin sources. There is something of a methodological point here. Although we should resist overprivileging what Classical authors say about Babylonia or simply slotting the

---

[91] See especially Clancier and Monerie 2014; Clancier 2017; Monerie 2017.

[92] An approach increasingly prevalent in recent studies: see apart from the current volume Strootman 2014 (courts and elites); Lavan, Payne, and Weisweiler 2016 (imperial strategies for co-opting local elites); Ludlow and Manning 2016 (revolt and resistance); Stevens 2019 (Hellenistic imperialism and intellectual culture).

cuneiform evidence into their narratives, there is increasing evidence that abandoning the Greek and Latin sources at the first hint of contradiction with the cuneiform evidence is also premature. After cuneiform sources revealed that Babylon was not decimated by the Persians, Greek and Latin material which reported Xerxes' violent actions against the city's temples was rejected or reinterpreted, yet Caroline Waerzeggers' study of the 'end of archives' in northern Babylonia showed conclusively that a significant number of priestly elite families suffered severe reprisals after the revolts under Xerxes, while the archaeological evidence suggests that the stairways of the ziggurat Etemenanki were demolished during his reign, precisely as suggested by Strabo.[93] The stories recorded by Strabo, Herodotus, and the Alexander historians may well be exaggerated and, in the case of later authors, recast to portray Alexander in a positive light, but they can still preserve a genuine reflex of the trauma suffered by the Babylonian priestly class under Xerxes.[94] The cuneiform evidence from Antiochus IV's reign aligns well with his portrayal in the Greek sources, and so there may be some grounds for revisiting Pliny, Strabo, and Appian on Seleucus. The Classical texts are, like all sources, likely to be misinformed and biased, but there has perhaps been something of an overreaction against them. We should be less apologetic or afraid about restoring them to some place in the overall narrative.

What of that narrative? Given the state of our evidence, it may never be possible to write a differentiated history of relations between the Seleucids and the Babylonian elite; it is certainly impossible to write a coherent history of Babylonian 'resistance', however coded or implicit. We may never know exactly what the priests of Esagila were thinking as they offered a crown to Macedonian kings or watched sacrifices 'in the Greek fashion' being carried out in their temple. What I think we *can* do

---

[93] Positive re-evaluations of Xerxes in Babylonia: Kuhrt and Sherwin-White 1987; Kuhrt 1988a (followed by most later works). Xerxes, the 'end of archives' and the impact on the Babylonian scholarly elite: Waerzeggers 2003; Robson 2017, 2018 (anticipated by Dandamaev 1993's prescient challenge to Kuhrt and Sherwin-White's revisionist reconstruction, even though the evidence was not yet available to confirm it). Etemenanki: George 2005; George 2010; cf. Strab. 16.1.5 ('tomb of Belus' but the description clearly refers to the ziggurat).

[94] Strab. 16.1.5; Hdt 1.183 (Xerxes removes a statue from the temple of Bel); Diodorus, 17.112.1–3 (temple of Bel destroyed by 'the Persians'); Arrian, *Anab.* 3.16.4 (Alexander restores temple of Bel); cf. also Aelian, *Varia Historia* 13.3 (Xerxes opens the tomb of Bel).

'AFTER HIM A KING WILL ARISE' 123

is nuance the idea that Babylonian elite views of the Seleucids were 'unnegative'. There were certainly moments of positive interaction, like Antiochus III at Esagila. But it is also possible to detect darker phases, where the cultural or economic policies of certain rulers disrupted life in Babylonia and caused concern among its elites.

The final question is whether such phases and the moments of tension or critique we have detected in the sources should be viewed as 'anti-Seleucid', 'anti-Hellenic', or 'anti-Hellenistic'. It is difficult, on balance, to argue that they should. First, both the kings who attract clusters of negative comments were not very 'Seleucid' or 'Hellenistic' in their policies of poliadization and their promotion of Greek settlement and cultural institutions. As has often been remarked, Antiochus IV is more of an anomaly than the rule as far as Seleucid rulers were concerned.[95] In some ways, so too was Seleucus – as a dynastic founder, his need for legitimacy and consolidation spurred city foundations and Greek settlement that did not need to be repeated under his successors. More importantly, from a Babylonian perspective, perhaps these two rulers were simply anti-Babylonian. They fell down not because they were 'Hellenizers' who sponsored Greek culture but because their policies disrupted traditional religious and socio-economic norms. In short, they failed to live up to the standards against which rulers of Mesopotamia, native or otherwise, had always been judged – standards constantly reaffirmed in the accounts of previous kings which the scholars of Hellenistic Babylonia copied and studied. The past of Nebuchadnezzar, and of Šulgi, was still live.

As Johannes Haubold has shown, the Seleucids themselves were alert to this, and played to it with some success.[96] But the real point was not the past itself, but the paradigm it established. Nebuchadnezzar was the ideal king because he rebuilt temples, provided lavishly for the gods, and made Babylon great. One had to do more than venerate his robe to fill the part. Some of the Seleucids, like the good kings of the prophecies, understood this and invested the right amount of care (and money) in their performance as kings of Babylonia. As scholars in Uruk and

[95] E.g. Bickerman 1979: 61–62; Gruen 1993: 238.
[96] Haubold 2016; Haubold, Chapter 3, this volume.

Babylon knew, however, good reigns come interspersed with bad, and so there were also the avatars of Šulgi who might start off well but would later neglect the gods. But the important thing was that in the end, they would be brought down – by a nasty skin disease or a human agent – and that ultimately, a king would arise who would set everything right.

5
Diverging Memories, Not Resistance Literature

The Maccabean Crisis in the Animal Apocalypse and 1 and 2 Maccabees

Sylvie Honigman

1. Introduction

Until the mid-1970s, the Book of Daniel was thought to be the earliest Jewish (Judean) apocalypse.[1] Given that it refers to Antiochus IV's alleged religious persecution that prompted the Maccabean revolt in the 160s BCE, and that its composition is thought to be contemporary with those events, scholars inferred that the apocalyptic genre emerged in this context as a type of resistance literature. J. T. Milik's publication, in 1976, of Aramaic fragments of the Astronomical Book that had been found among the Dead Sea Scrolls (the Qumran library) and were paleographically datable to the early second century – that is, prior to the revolt – disproved this causal link between the persecution and the genre.[2] However, while it is now indisputable that the genre's emergence predated the Maccabean crisis, the definition of apocalypses as resistance literature was upheld by some commentators. It was forcefully reasserted by George Nickelsburg in his commentary of 1 Enoch, published in 2001, and promoted further in the early 2010s by Richard Horsley and

---

[1] I am grateful to Christophe Nihan for reading an earlier draft of this paper and offering helpful comments. I also thank the book's editors and the anonymous readers for their useful comments. Any errors remaining are my responsibility.
[2] Milik 1976: 7. See Nihan 2009: 669–670.

Sylvie Honigman, *Diverging Memories, Not Resistance Literature: The Maccabean Crisis in the Animal Apocalypse and 1 and 2 Maccabees* In: *Cultures of Resistance in the Hellenistic East*. Edited by: Paul J. Kosmin and Ian S. Moyer, Oxford University Press. © Oxford University Press 2022.
DOI: 10.1093/oso/9780192863478.003.0006

Anathea Portier-Young, respectively, who explicitly referred to James Scott's concept of hidden transcripts.[3] It is that view that I wish to question in the present article. According to this model, the apocalypses were composed at the height of crises caused by economic oppression and religious persecution to comfort the victims. They were authored by priests who were critical not only of the foreign, Hellenistic (and Roman) domination, but also of the temple's corrupt and Hellenized priestly establishment who collaborated with empire, to the point that these censors rejected the temple institution and cult. They formed either marginal groups, or a separate form of religion dubbed 'Enochic Judaism', which supposedly emerged in the late fourth century BCE.[4]

Although debate persists over what are the defining features of apocalypses, for the present purpose I will adhere to the prevailing definition, which characterizes that genre as a combination of revelation and eschatology, conveyed within a narrative framework. Revelation is mediated by an other-worldly being (a divine messenger) to a human recipient (an illustrious figure of the past, such as Enoch[5] or Daniel), and the revealed knowledge may bear upon scientific matters (such as the calendar, cosmology, or angelology), and eschatological themes (such as the hidden meaning of history and the heavenly world; the end of history; God's final judgement and recreation of the world; the fate of the righteous and wicked; and life after death).[6]

The resistance theory is problematic on several grounds.[7] In particular, it ignores the generic affinities between the early Judean apocalypses and contemporary genres that emerged in Egypt and Mesopotamia respectively.[8] More crucially, it ignores affinities between the interpretative techniques used in the early Judean apocalypses and other genres

---

[3] Nickelsburg 2001; Horsley 2010; Portier-Young 2011. See also Horsley 2008; Collins 2016. The reference is to Scott 1990.

[4] This extreme version is endorsed by Portier-Young 2011.

[5] According to Genesis 5:19–21, Enoch was the seventh antediluvian patriarch.

[6] See the influential definition of the genre of apocalypses by J. J. Collins (1979: 9) and A. Y. Collins (1986: 7). For a survey of the debated aspects of the genre's definition, see DiTommaso 2007: 238–247; and Nihan 2009: 662–669.

[7] For a critical discussion of its premises as applied to pre-Maccabean times, see Honigman 2020.

[8] For overviews, see Nihan 2009: 671–672; DiTommaso 2007: 265–269. See further Hellholm 1983; Neujahr 2012.

that flourished in Judea at about the same time, in particular wisdom and mantic (divinatory) wisdom.[9] Based on these affinities, an alternative school of commentators understands apocalyptic literature as being primarily a method of interpretation.[10] The decisive factor in the emergence of various competing hermeneutics in Judea in early Hellenistic times were the compositions of the Pentateuch and of corpora of prophetic oracles attributed to various prophets of old in Persian times.[11] While these texts had acquired an authoritative status among Judean scribes, they were difficult to read, and required explanation and commentary. The shift from prophecy to apocalypses has been described as a shift from oral, performative interpretation, to a hermeneutic based on the written medium.[12]

That said, Annette Yoshiko Reed has pointed to a shift in the content of the esoteric knowledge disclosed through divine revelation between the earliest apocalypses – that is, antedating the Maccabean crisis, such as the Book of Watchers (1 Enoch 1–36) and the Astronomical Book (1 Enoch 72–82) – and those that were written after, and to a large extent commented upon, the Maccabean crisis – the Animal Apocalypse (1 Enoch 85–90), the Apocalypse of the Weeks (1 Enoch 93:1–10 and 91:11–17), and Daniel.[13] While revelation in the works of the third century referred to scientific knowledge of that era – astronomy, the calendar, and cosmology – the post-Maccabean works 'equate heavenly secrets with ethical pronouncements, historical predictions, and eschatological prophecies'.[14] On the face of it, it might be argued that although apocalyptic literature emerged as an interpretative method, the shift to

[9] See Silverman 2012: 11, 20–22.
[10] For a recent, forceful statement of this view, see Silverman 2012.
[11] On the promulgation of the Pentateuch as a Torah, see Nihan 2010; Carr 2005: 111–173, 201–214.
[12] Silverman 2012.
[13] 1 Enoch is a composite text canonical to the Ethiopian Orthodox Church, which preserves the only extant complete version of these four early apocalypses, in Geʿez translation. As just noted, Aramaic fragments were discovered in Qumran. They also included fragments of a hitherto unknown Book of Giants, and attest that the custom of grouping together various works relating to the patriarch Enoch began in Hellenistic times. See Milik 1976. The Book of Daniel is the only text classed as an apocalypse by modern scholars that is included in the Hebrew Bible – as a prophetic book. Two historical apocalypses identified among the Dead Sea Scrolls have been tentatively dated to the mid- and late second century BCE, respectively. See Henze 2009.
[14] Yoshiko Reed 2004: 47.

historical apocalypses starting from the Maccabean crisis is evidence that by this time, this genre became resistance literature. To show that the classification of the historical apocalypses as resistance literature also is problematic, in this paper I discuss the Animal Apocalypse (1 Enoch 85–90, hereafter An-Apoc), which is deemed to refer to the Maccabean crisis in 1 Enoch 90.6–18. According to proponents of the resistance paradigm, the work was composed at the height of the crisis to comfort the victims of Antiochus IV's alleged religious persecution.[15]

Like all commentators, I compare An-Apoc with 1 and 2 Macc. – except that my comparison is based on a revised interpretation of the latter. Moreover, in contrast to commentators who treat these texts as complementary, I argue that An-Apoc, on the one hand, and 1 and 2 Macc. on the other, reflect two contrasting memories of the crisis. Before we compare the texts, it will be useful to summarize their respective versions of the Maccabean crisis.

2. Rereading 1 and 2 Maccabees

According to 2 Macc, the pious high priest Onias III was overthrown in 175 BCE by Jason, who obtained the high priesthood from Antiochus IV. Jason established a *polis* and a *gymnasion* in Jerusalem, and instituted a regime of *Hellenismos* that disrupted the temple cult. Three years later, Menelaus ousted Jason, and was appointed high priest in his stead by the king. To pay the increased tribute that he had pledged to Antiochus, Menelaus stole the temple's holy vessels, and further used this booty to have the pious high priest Onias assassinated. In 168 BCE, Antiochus, who was on his way back from Egypt, attacked Jerusalem, in the mistaken belief that it was in revolt, and 'some time later' he allegedly tried to

---

[15] Most scholars date An-Apoc to the years 168/7 to 161/0 BCE (that is, between the year of the so-called religious persecution and the eve of Judas Maccabee's death), except the section held to refer to the Maccabean crisis in 90.6–18, which is usually seen as an interpolation added shortly after the composition of the work. On this passage, see section 3, pp. 133–135, and n. 30 below. On the dating of An-Apoc, see Nickelsburg 2001: 360–361; Tiller 1993: 61–79; Bryan 1995: 37–38; Mermelstein 2014: 134, n. 1; see further references in Portier-Young 2011: 347, n. 347. A notable exception is Assefa 2007: 214–215, who argues that the composition of the work (except 90.6–18) antedates the said religious persecution.

force the Judeans to abandon God's laws. Judas Maccabee led the struggle for *Ioudaismos*, and within two years had recaptured Jerusalem and purified the temple altar, allowing the continual sacrifices to be resumed. He then went on to win further victories against the Seleucids, with God's support for him and his warriors manifested in epiphanies before decisive battles.[16]

As I have argued elsewhere, both the narratives of 1 and 2 Macc. are shaped by a highly codified narrative pattern which, in the Judean literate (and literary) tradition, was used to indicate the legitimacy or illegitimacy of a ruler. According to the political ideology encapsulated in this narrative pattern, a ruler was legitimate if he was chosen by YHWH to build or rebuild his temple. The deity made his choice based on the ruler's righteousness – namely, if he 'walked in YHWH's path' (to use the biblical wording) – and victory was the manifestation of this divine election. Moreover, usurpers asserted their own legitimacy not only by advertising their rebuilding of the temple, but claimed that their deposed predecessors had lost their position because they had gone bad – that is, had neglected their duties toward the patron-deity, the temple, and the people of the land.[17]

---

[16] For this summary, see Honigman 2014a.

[17] On this narrative pattern in general, see Honigman 2014: 95–118. In 1 and 2 Macc, see Honigman 2014: 119–181. Jan Willem van Henten and Katell Berthelot respectively objected that while they could easily identify the narrative template of the ruler rebuilding the temple in 1 Macc., it was far more elusive in 2 Macc. (personal communications, August 2018; September 2019). In support of my reading of 2 Macc, I should clarify that the said narrative pattern is evident in the description of the rededication of the temple in 10:1–8, which to my mind is the starting point of the discussion (see Honigman 2014: 123–127). Likewise, the second story of Judas refounding the temple composing 2 Macc. (14:1–15:37) is a textbook example of the narrative template in question (Honigman 2014: 149–159), and it may well be that its juxtaposition with the founding myth of the Hanukkah festival in 2 Macc. (4:6–13:26) aimed specifically to make the work's message more explicit to the readers, namely the regal status of Judas Maccabee. The fact that the narrative pattern is contrived in the main section of 2 Macc. (the Hannukkah story) may be explained by the author's dependence on a source (Jason of Cyrene). This analysis of the literary structure of the book assumes that the key passage of 2 Macc. 10:1–8 is actually part of the original composition and not an addition, and moreover that its place in the text is correct. For an overview of the claims that this section is an interpolation – or was for some reason moved – see Trotter 2017, who provides a thorough refutation. The identification in 2 Macc. of the narrative pattern commonly used in the Judean literary tradition to legitimize forms of rules and specific rulers is reliable evidence not only that, like 1 Macc, it was composed in Judea, but also that its author was at the service of the Hasmonean court. For further arguments supporting this view, see Honigman 2014: 115–117. For assorted diverging views about the social identity of the author of 2 Macc, see, inter alia, Schwartz 2008; Doran 2012; Collins 2016; Bernhardt 2017. For a recent historiographical survey, see Eckhardt 2018.

The fact that 1 and 2 Maccabees are shaped by this narrative pattern indicates that the story of Judas Maccabee reconsecrating the temple altar had become the founding myth of the Hasmonean Dynasty, which claimed descent from the Maccabees. By this token, Jason, Menelaus, and Alkimos, the three men who ruled as high priests between Onias III and Jonathan and Simon Maccabee (Judas's younger brothers) are depicted as illegitimate usurpers. In 2 Macc., the author claims that the temple altar refounded by Judas had been desecrated not only by Antiochus IV, but by these wicked high priests as well. In particular, Jason's establishment of the *gymnasion* in 2 Macc. is depicted as the foundation of an anti-temple through a literary construction alluding to biblical texts that described the ceremonies of dedication for the Jerusalem temple.[18]

By this logic, in 2 Macc. *Ioudaismos* and *Hellenismos* do not mean 'Judaism' and 'Hellenism', respectively, but rather are two abstract words that capture the notions of political legitimacy and illegitimacy that had been traditionally expressed through the narrative pattern of temple founding as described above. Precisely, *Ioudaismos* denotes the righteous social order established by Judas Maccabee when he refounded the Jerusalem temple that had been defiled by both Antiochus IV and the high priests Jason and Menelaus, and in which the Hasmoneans ruled. Conversely, *Hellenismos* signifies the wicked social order established by Jason when he founded a *gymnasion* (and the *polis*) in Jerusalem. Moreover, in 2 Macc. this wicked social order is associated not only with Jason, but with Menelaus and Alkimos, as well. Jason's *gymnasion* caused the priests to neglect the temple service as they ran to the *palaistra* at the sound of the gong every day; Menelaus stole the temple's holy vessels and served as Antiochus's guide when the king looted the temple; and Alkimos was intent on demolishing the temple's wall when God had him die to foil his wicked plot.[19] The relationship between the contenders to power and the late Onias III in 2 Macc. follows the same line: the wicked Jason ousts him from the high priesthood unjustly, and Menelaus assassinated him, whereas Onias III acknowledged Judas

---

[18] For a detailed discussion, see Honigman 2014a: 199–214.

[19] On the portrayals of Jason, Menelaus, and Alkimos in 1 and 2 Macc, see Honigman 2014a: 197–228. For a positive historical reappraisal of Menelaus as a political and religious leader, see Honigman 2014a: 92–93, 287–288, 349–350, 376–379, 387–390; Ma 2019.

Maccabee as his worthy heir by appearing to him in a dream vision on the eve of his last decisive battle.

As this list shows, *Hellenismos* in 2 Macc. is equated with the semantic realm of 'wickedness'. Admittedly, when compared with the traditional notions of 'righteous' and 'wicked' rulers associated with the old narrative pattern of temple founding, the terms *Ioudaismos* and *Hellenismos* unquestionably add an ethnic connotation. However, ethnicity is here manipulated in a polemical manner: with the term *Ioudaismos*, Judas – and his heirs, the Hasmoneans – are presented as the true guardians of the ancestral traditions, while the term *Hellenismos* is used to otherize their internal political rivals and equate them with their external enemies. Strikingly, neither the king nor the Seleucid generals or soldiers in 2 Macc. are characterized as 'Greeks' – that label is reserved for the wicked Judeans.[20]

3. The Animal Apocalypse (1 Enoch 85–90): Content and Date

An-Apoc purports to be a dream vision by Enoch, offering an account of history based on a tripartite periodization: from the Creation of humanity until its destruction in the Flood; from its recreation after the Flood until the end of history; and its final recreation after God's Last Judgement. History ends with the Maccabean crisis. Until the first destruction of the temple in the Neo-Babylonian period, the author follows the biblical account – from the book of Genesis to 2 Kings and prophetic books. For recent history – for which he lacked an authoritative source – he used a historiographic genre typical of his time, by dividing time into four sub-periods, which he further subdivided into seventy 'hours' or 'weeks' (12 + 23 + 23 + 12).[21] The four periods are that of exile under the Babylonians; the return and rebuilding of the temple

---

[20] The king's men are defined as *allophyloi*. For the detailed discussion, see Honigman 2014: 141–146. On the modern reinterpretation of the ancient nomenclature of 'wickedness' as 'Hellenization', see Honigman 2014a: 62–63.

[21] This historiographical genre is found in MT Daniel's reference to four kingdoms, and the late Akkadian prophecies (or predictive texts). For further parallels, see Dimant 2001: 109–112.

under the Persians; a first Greek period under the Ptolemies; and a second one under the Seleucids, including the Maccabean revolt. Peoples and historical characters are allegorized as animals – hence the work's name. Each one of the three ages begins with a founding figure in the form of a white bull: Adam in the primeval age (1 Enoch 85.3), Noah after the Flood (1 Enoch 89.9), and an eschatological figure (either a New Adam or the Messiah) after the Last Judgement (90.37–38). Abraham and Isaac are also white bulls (89.10–11). Beginning with Jacob, Israel is allegorized as a flock of sheep, and God as the Lord of the sheep. The seventy hours are associated with seventy shepherds (wicked angels). The nations are depicted as wild animals – the Babylonians as lions, and the Greeks as birds of prey.[22]

The leading thread in the author's survey of recent history is disclosed in 89.51–58: when the sheep stray off the path of the Lord, He[23] initially sends sheep (prophets) to bring them back, but they refuse. So the Lord of the sheep abandons the flock[24] – handing the care of the sheep over to 70 shepherds (wicked angels), each being appointed for one 'hour', in turn. In addition, He appoints another 'man' (angel) to keep record of the shepherds' misdeeds in a book (89.59–64). During the first period (the Babylonian era – 12 hours, 1 Enoch 89.65–72a), the nations devour most of the sheep, and demolish the house and the tower (i.e., Jerusalem and the temple). In the second period (the Persian era – 23 hours; 89.72b–90.1), two sheep (Joshua and Zerubbabel) return.[25] They rebuild the house and the tower, and resume offerings and sacrifices (bread), 'but all of the bread upon [the table of bread-offering] was polluted and impure' (89.73).[26] Moreover, 'the eyes of the flock had become blind, so that they could not see' [i.e., that the temple was impure] – nor could their shepherds – and the flock continues to be devoured (89.74). No specific event is singled out in the third period (Ptolemaic times – 23 hours; 90.2–5), other than the birds of prey preying on the sheep.

---

[22] On the allegorical imagery, see Olson 2013: 1–3; and Bryan 1995: 41–167.
[23] Pronouns for God are capitalized when the standpoint of the ancient authors is quoted or summarized. They are not capitalized when the sentence represents my own stance.
[24] This understanding of history is typical of that found in the prophetic books, Kings and Chronicles.
[25] I follow Olson's reading (2004: 202, at 89.72).
[26] Translations here and henceforward are per Olson 2013, unless otherwise stated.

DIVERGING MEMORIES, NOT RESISTANCE LITERATURE 133

The fourth period (the Seleucid era – 12 hours; 90.6–19) begins with the white sheep giving birth to lambs, who open their eyes and see, and cry out to the sheep, but the sheep do not listen to their words, and remain blind (90.6–7). The following verses refer to events that occur on the eve of the Maccabean revolt and during it, and must be quoted in full (90.8–19):

> 8. Then in the vision I saw how the ravens swooped down on those young lambs, and they seized one of those young lambs. And they dashed the flock to pieces and devoured them. 9. And I watched until horns emerged on those young lambs; but the ravens were crushing their horns. I watched until a large horn sprouted on one of the *sheep*,[27] and their eyes were opened. 10. And it had regard for them, and their eyes were unbound. It cried out to the flock, and the male sheep saw it, and they all ran to it. 11. In spite of all this, those eagles, falcons, ravens, and kites continued to snatch at the flock, swooping upon them and devouring them. But the flock kept silent, while the male sheep were protesting and crying aloud. 12. And those ravens battled and contended with it, and they wanted to eliminate its horn, but they did not prevail against it. 13. And I watched until the shepherds [*wicked angels*], the eagles [*Macedonians*], the falcons [?*Thracians/ Anatolians*], and the kites [*Ptolemies*] came, and they called upon the ravens [*Seleucids*] to smash to bits the horn of that male sheep. And they did battle with it and waged war, and as it fought against them it cried out for its help to come. 14. And I watched until that man came who was writing the names of the shepherds and bringing them up before the Lord of the flock. And he helped it and revealed everything to it: the help of that male sheep came down. 15. And I watched until the Lord of the flock came upon them in wrath. And all who saw him fled, and they all fell away, into the shadow before his face. [vv. 16–18

---

[27] Olson 2013 – whose translation I otherwise follow here – has 'lambs'. However, Tiller (1993: 349) noted that 'it is clear from the text that [the pious warrior] springs from among *the still-blinded* sheep' (his emphasis – I substituted 'the pious warrior' for the original's 'Judas'). See, likewise, Nickelsburg 2001: 388; Olson's earlier translation of v. 90.9a (2004: 207); and his commentary on the verse (2013: 212). Tiller sought to refute commentators who postulated a continuity between the lambs and the new warrior – a view that would preclude the warrior's identification as Judas Maccabee. See below pp. 143–144.

are a recapitulation.²⁸] 19. And I watched until a great sword was presented to the flock. And the flock went out against all the wild beasts to kill them. And all the beasts [*the earlier nations*] and the birds of the sky [*the Greco-Macedonians*] fled from before their faces.

There follows God's Last Judgement (90:20–27); His 'folding up' the old house (Jerusalem) and building of the new house, where all the sheep who had dispersed throughout the world gather, along with the beasts and the birds. The sheep have now turned white – i.e., pure – and their wool is thick (presumably as a token of prosperity) and pure (90:28–36). The horned ram is carried up to heaven by three angels (90.31), and the sheep lay down the sword and return it to the house (90.34). The narrative ends with the coming of a white bull (i.e., marking the advent of a new age, like at Creation and after the Flood), and as all animal species are transformed into white bulls, the first bull becomes a wild ox (90:37–39).

The date of this section is disputed. In the late nineteenth and early twentieth centuries it was suggested that the 'horned ram' of v. 90.9 is the prophet Elijah or the Hasmonean ruler John Hyrcanus. However, since Milik's publication of Qumran's Aramaic fragments of the book of Enoch in 1976, there is general agreement that the reference is to Judas Maccabee, because Milik dated the earliest Qumran fragment of An-Apoc (4QEn^f) to the third quarter of the second century on palaeographical grounds.²⁹ As a consequence, to reconcile this identification with the premise that apocalyptic works are resistance literature composed in the midst of crises to comfort the victims, numerous scholars see the section of 90.6–18 as an interpolation: while most of An-Apoc was composed between 168/7 and 161/0 BCE, the passage taken to refer to Judas Maccabee was composed slightly thereafter.³⁰

---

²⁸ I endorse Bryan's understanding of these verses (1995: 39, 181). Tiller's alternative proposal that these verses are doublets is discussed below pp. 135–136.
²⁹ See Milik 1976; and Vanderkam 2010. For a survey of the early historiography, see Tiller 1993: 4–13.
³⁰ See, for instance, Mermelstein 2014: 134, n. 1. For a survey of the historiography on this section, see Tiller 1993: 63–79. See further Tiller 1993: 4–13.

However, in contrast with Milik's dating, Patrick Tiller cites two alternative opinions of scholars, who respectively date 4QEn^f to the end of the second or early first century.[31] The other scrolls preserving fragments of An-Apoc (4QEn^{c-e}) were dated by Milik to the first century BCE.[32] For my purpose, even Milik's early dating of 4QEn^f allows for a partial overlap with John Hyrcanus's years of rule (134–104 BCE). Whereas the revised, lower dating of 4QEn^f would even more neatly allow us to envisage that the text was composed in Hyrcanus's days.[33]

4. Animal Apocalypse vs. 1 and 2 Maccabees: The Integrative Reading

The identification of the horned ram as Judas Maccabee has been further defended on grounds of content. Once it was agreed that An-Apoc refers to the revolt, 1 and 2 Macc. were searched to decode the historical allusions found in vv. 90.6–19 – both for their own sake, and to refine the dating of the work. Because the text does not refer to Judas Maccabee's death, most scholars have inferred that An-Apoc was composed before 161 (or 160) BCE – the year of his death, according to 1 Macc. To refine the dating further, Tiller, followed by Daniel Olson, has revived an old suggestion that vv. 90:13–15 and 16–18 are literary doublets. According to this view, the first edition was composed between the outbreak of the Maccabean revolt in 167 (allegorized as the rising of the horned ram, 90.9–12) and late 165 BCE. To illustrate their method, here is Olson's summary of Tiller's discussion:

> The last historical events of the original apocalypse are the battles of 90:11–12 (166–165 BCE). The author believed the end was drawing near, and he wrote verses 16–18 not as history but as genuine

---

[31] Milik 1976: 5; Tiller 1993: 61. On the imprecise nature of palaeographical dating, see further the critical remarks in Wise 2003: 55–58; and 2010: 98–99.
[32] Milik 1976: 5. See also VanderKam 2010: 256.
[33] See below, pp. 146–147. Of course, the down-dating of the manuscript does not rule out the possibility that the text was composed much earlier, but it does open the possibility that its composition was later than was previously assumed.

prophecy. But Judas went on to score victories at Beth-zur in early 164 (1 Macc. 4:29–34; 2 Macc. 11:6–12) and later on at Carnaim in mid-163 (1 Macc. 5:43–44; 2 Macc. 12:22). Someone, perhaps the original author, then updated the allegory in order to reflect these battles (our vv. 13–15). Subsequent copyists had both editions and simply kept the readings of both versions... [Verse 19] reflects the battle of Adasa in March, 161 (1 Macc. 7:39–50; 2 Macc. 15:15–17) and serves to update the latter part of verse 18 further.[34]

According to this view, the first edition was composed between the outbreak of the Maccabean revolt in 167 and late 165, while the revised one was promulgated between either the battle of Carnaim in summer 163 or the battle of Adasa in March 161, and before Judas's death in late 161. This tight chronology is, of course, premised on the tenet that An-Apoc is a sample of resistance literature composed to comfort the victims of Antiochus IV's persecution, and on the assumption that An-Apoc and 1 and 2 Macc. are transparent windows on historical events. Hence, the battles described in 1 and 2 Macc. are read into the allegorical imagery employed in 1 Enoch 90:13–18 on the basis of various narrative details. However, this method is convincing only if one believes that an allegory is nothing more than a term-for-term encoding of the historical reality, that is, that its allegorical aspect is irrelevant to its meaning. Moreover, it is assumed that as transparent windows on 'what happened', they can either corroborate or complement each other, but not diverge from each other.

This chronological reconstruction may be faulted on several grounds. First, An-Apoc is a highly elaborate response to events, both in terms of its literary quality, and more importantly, in terms of its intellectual reflection on history. This makes it very unlikely that it was composed at the height of the crisis. In stark contrast with the sense of chaos and disruption that pervades the persecution accounts included in other sources (1 Macc. 1:41–64; 2 Macc. 6:1–11; and Dan 11:29–39), the tone

---

[34] Olson 2013: 216–217. See also Olson 2004: 206 at vv. 90:13–15 and 16–18; and Tiller 1993: 61–79.

of An-Apoc conveys scarcely any sense of urgency.[35] Moreover, as modern commentators have regularly stressed, the allegorical figures used as ciphers to designate Israel's succession of oppressors reference precise images borrowed from a variety of biblical books. One can only wonder how a scribe living through such painful upheaval would consider an arcane allegory of ravens and eagles composed in prose as the most appropriate literature to bring comfort to survivors of massacre. One might argue that sung poetry – psalms or lamentations – would have resonated more effectively with his audience. Second, Judas's death as a *terminus ante quem* is not compelling: 2 Macc. also ends before Judas's death, but can hardly have been composed before that event[36] An-Apoc is a quintessential *ex eventu* prophecy – namely, one written in hindsight.[37] To sum up, this modern method of reading clues of the date of the work's composition in the recounted events attributes an objective perception of time to ancient scribes that was alien to them.[38] The fact that the author placed the end of history at the end of the Maccabean crisis is no hindrance to dating An-Apoc's composition to several decades after this event.[39]

More crucially, even if we may readily accept that the passage 90.6–19 of An-Apoc refers to the Maccabean crisis, its account is not easily reconcilable with those of 1 and 2 Macc. Rather than being complementary, these accounts are genuinely different. In particular, the respective portrayals, in An-Apoc and 2 Macc., of the victorious warrior who

---

[35] The persecution accounts carried in 1 and 2 Macc. speak explicitly of massacres and of survivors seeking refuge in hidden places (1 Macc. 1:53). We are also told that persons found with a Torah scroll in their possession were slain on the spot (1 Macc. 1:57). I doubt that any scholar living through such troubled times would have found the peace of mind to compose such a complex work with battles raging around him and distressful news pouring in.

[36] According to the accepted chronology, Judas died in 161 or 160 BCE, whereas the account of 2 Macc. mentions the emergence of Demetrios I as contender to the Seleucid kingship and the appointment of Alkimos as high priest in 162 BCE, and the death of Seleucid general Nicanor, which is traditionally also dated to 161 BCE. Such a short span hardly allows enough time to accommodate not only the composition of 2 Macc. itself, but also that of the longer work produced by Jason of Cyrene, which 2 Macc. purports to epitomize.

[37] On the use of time in *ex eventu* prophecies, see for instance, Neujahr 2012: 1–10.

[38] Cf. the author's computation of the four periods (12 + 23 + 23 + 12 weeks of seven years each), which is certainly wrong according to an objective time reckoning. On the modern misunderstanding of the ancient scribes' method of computing time, see the critical remarks in Wise 2003: 62–64 and 2010: 99–100.

[39] In 1 Macc, messianic times are achieved under Simon Maccabee (143–c.134 BCE). See 1 Macc. 14:4–15, with Honigman 2014a: 169–174.

vanquishes the nations with God's help, are incompatible – to the point where it is uncertain whether this figure (the horned ram) in An-Apoc is intended to represent Judas Maccabee, or some other prominent figure from the time of the revolt, whose memory was expunged in 1 and 2 Macc.[40] That said, in my view these basic differences between the two accounts (treating 1 and 2 Macc. as a single one) may be understood in two ways – each having a different bearing on An-Apoc's date of composition and on how it should be understood. However, prior to exploring these two alternative interpretations of An-Apoc, we need to dwell on a complementary issue, namely how modern scholars reconstruct its view of history.

5. The Place of the Maccabean Crisis in the Animal Apocalypse's View of History

In his commentary of An-Apoc, Olson noted that the 'rehearsal of the past' in the Judean literate tradition was 'a characteristic way of articulating theology'. In the opinion of numerous scholars, the subject matter of An-Apoc is, as he puts it, 'the outworking of God's plans for his creation. It is a story of sin and salvation'. Disagreement remains about a few issues, whose phrasing discloses the theological, not to say Christianizing, slant of the scholars taking part in this debate: for instance, whether the work is about the salvation of Israel or of humanity in general; or what role, if any, do *the Mosaic covenant* or *the temple* play in God's plan of salvation.[41] This emphasis on theological issues serves

---

[40] Thanks to Josephus, we know with certainty that 1 and 2 Macc. obliterated the existence of Onias IV, the high priest Onias III's son, from their record. In addition, there are grounds to believe that 2 Macc. attributed to Judas acts of leadership that in all likelihood were those of the high priest Menelaus. We cannot rule out additional omissions in 1 and 2 Macc. On Onias IV, see Honigman 2014a: 154. On Menelaus, see above, n. 19.

[41] Olson 2013: 3–15 (p. 3, n. 5, and p. 5, for the quotations). Emphases are mine. This dispute was revived by Nickelsburg's commentary (2001). To take one example, Nickelsburg (2001: 405) infers from the fact that only the house is rebuilt, while the tower (temple) is not, that the building of the eschatological house marks the end of the sacrificial custom (i.e., of the Mosaic covenant). In contrast, based on parallels in Qumran's sectarian works (the *Temple Scroll*, but see also 4QMMT), Dimant (1981–1982) interprets the eschatological image in An-Apoc as meaning that the entire city of Jerusalem becomes a temple. Nickelsburg's theological reading was further refuted by Himmelfarb (2007: 228–232).

the premise that An-Apoc was written to comfort the victims of religious persecution in real time. But at the same time, the terms of the theological debate aim to buttress the tenet that the authors of apocalypses were dissident priests who had broken with the Jerusalem temple and the Mosaic covenant.[42]

In 1995, David Bryan put forward a totally different line of analysis, by paying due attention to how the animals shaping the allegorical imagery in An-Apoc were chosen – arguably a key issue to understanding this text, but one which is ignored in the theological debate.[43] Bryan demonstrated that the underlying principle was the classification of these animals as either clean or unclean according to the priestly laws of purity set out in Leviticus 11 and Deuteronomy 14.[44] Clean animals were used to represent the righteous, and unclean animals and monsters to represent the wicked.[45] Drawing on Mary Douglas's understanding of the Leviticus laws of purity as a system defining God's orderly cosmos, Bryan argues that the dominant theme of An-Apoc is the motif of order – that is, God's orderly creation – and the threat of chaos posed by mixing together and confusing distinct kinds.[46] The narrative structure of An-Apoc is composed of cycles enacting the sequence of initial order, intrusion of chaos, and reestablishment of order.[47] In contrast with Olson's (and Nickelsburg's) claim that the An-Apoc rejects the

---

[42] Arguably, the terms of this theological interpretation are wholly incompatible with the assumed historical context. Foreign aggression is hardly the appropriate occasion for an author to engage in a lofty reflection about the salvation of humanity in general, let alone in a dramatic moment in which the social group to which he belongs perceives the aggression as an attack on the core elements of its identity, a factor that the 'persecution accounts' make clear. Granted, this latter objection is irrelevant if one believes that the author of An-Apoc broke away with the Mosaic covenant and the temple. But why then, to paraphrase 2 Macc, would he care for those who fought for *Ioudaismos*? In other words, to whom did he intend to offer comfort? Is it plausible that he cared for the salvation of humanity while caring to console members of a demographically narrow, dissident group?
[43] Bryan 1995: 34–185.
[44] These priestly regulations are surveyed, Bryan 1995: 130–143.
[45] See his detailed commentary, Bryan 1995: 41–97.
[46] Bryan 1995: 144–166. Olson (2013: 8, n. 18) rejected Bryan's reading on the grounds that the choice of clean animals for Jews and unclean for Gentiles was 'a simple artistic choice' drawing 'on deep-seated cultural associations', 'picking symbols with positive connotations on the one hand and symbols that inspire repugnance and ridicule on the other'. This objection fails to address Douglas's claim that purity and impurity is a system, not a matter of 'cultural associations'.
[47] Bryan 1995: 171–183.

Mosaic covenant, in Bryan's interpretation the cause of chaos is Israel (the Judeans) straying from YHWH's path. Foreign oppression is the punishment, rather than the cause of suffering – and thus An-Apoc is no more resistance literature than that of the great prophets of old.

According to the paradigm of order and chaos, recent and traumatic events (the Maccabean crisis) are made comprehensible through their insertion in a reassuringly familiar pattern of action. This historiographical device was common in the ancient Near East, and may be described as a 'helical' view of history.[48] Consequently, while it is undeniable that the Maccabean crisis is presented as a harbinger of eschatological times, the author's propensity to see recent events as a reenactment of old patterns makes it unclear whether he perceived the Maccabean crisis as exceptional in essence, or simply uses it to display his hermeneutic. For a more precise understanding of how the Maccabean crisis was perceived in An-Apoc, we must analyse 1 Enoch 90.6–19 in detail. As previously noted, I offer two alternative readings here. Both are in line with Bryan's understanding of the text's hermeneutic. Moreover, in both readings, the comparison with 1 and 2 Macc. is crucial.

---

[48] 'Helical' rather than 'cyclical', because it combines cyclical repetition of the interpretative pattern with the notion of chronological succession. I hereby correct earlier comments I made on this matter (Honigman 2014a and elsewhere). Mermelstein (2014: 133–153) characterizes this representation of history as 'timeless', noting that its particular organization into 'a set of recurrent events or paradigms' (p. 135) enabled the author to 'link the present with the past' (p. 136). Mermelstein further endorses the view that the author was writing in the very midst of the troubles, 'to diminish the frightening novelty of his present condition' (p. 135), and to reassure himself and his readers that, despite all appearances, 'God had *not* abandoned his flock' (p. 136). However, Mermelstein's interpretation of the text also works if we assume that the author was writing a meditation on history *after* the event. Notably, on the heels of Knibb (2009), Mermelstein argues that the author of An-Apoc considered the rebuilt temple as 'inconsequential' because it was much smaller than the original, and that he perceived the entire period of its existence as a continuation of exile. See Mermelstein 2014: 136; Knibb 2009: 194–197. This periodization de-emphasizes the moment of crisis under Antiochus IV and it is easier to understand how the author adopted it when we assume a hindsight perspective. That said, Knibb's idea of 'exile' after the return is odd, and therefore the underlying issue is likely to be a political one. However, as I argue below, the author of An-Apoc seems to downplay kingship, and consequently the issues that the author sought to address in the last three periods of history in the text remain as yet unclear. Whatever the case, in itself this aspect does not explain why the ancient author describes the sacrifices in the rebuilt temple as impure (89:73; Mermelstein 2014).

6. The Memory of the Maccabean Crisis in 1 Enoch 90.6–19

The sequence of events as told in 1 and 2 Macc. is substantially different from that of An-Apoc. According to 2 Macc., Antiochus IV attacked Jerusalem on his return from a campaign in Egypt (in 168 BCE). He massacred people, plundered the temple, and returned home. This is when Judas Maccabee withdrew to the wilderness with his supporters (2 Macc. 5:27). 'Some time later', Antiochus dispatched one Geron to Jerusalem to compel the Judeans to relinquish their ancestral laws. More people were killed, and the temple was desecrated (2 Macc. 6–7). 2 Macc. 8 shows Judas recruiting pious warriors and winning his first victory, which leads to the rebuilding of the temple (10:1–8). In 1 Macc., the spotlight turns to the Maccabean family (starting with Mattathias, Judas's father, in ch. 2) immediately after the persecution account in 1:41–64.

In contrast, An-Apoc dwells with some insistence on a preliminary phase, in which a group of reformers allegorized as white lambs 'began to open their eyes, and to see, and to cry out to the flock' (90.6) – like the prophets of old, but to no avail.[49] Verse 90.8 can only be understood as alluding to the leader of these reformers being put to death by the Seleucids ('ravens'). Based on 1 and 2 Macc., some scholars identify these reformers as the 'Hasidim' – a group of pious men who joined Judas Maccabee in the early stages of the rebellion (1 Macc. 2:42–44; 7:13–17; 2 Macc. 14:6) – and the lambs' fallen leader as Onias III, whose assassination is recounted in detail in 2 Macc. (4:33–36). However, these identifications contradict each other, because nowhere is it stated in 1 or 2 Macc. that the Hasidim were linked to Onias III. Moreover, the former interpretation is inconsistent with 1 and 2 Macc., and the latter clashes with other aspects of An-Apoc.[50] The identification of the lambs' leader

---

[49] See the translation of the passage above, pp. 133–134.
[50] See Olson 2004: 204, at 90:6, and 205, at 90.8.

as Onias III is a good illustration of how efforts to combine the narratives of An-Apoc and 2 Macc. lead to an impasse.[51]

As I have argued elsewhere, in 2 Macc. the portrayal of Onias III as an ideal pious high priest is part of that work's discursive strategy of legitimizing the Hasmoneans, in two ways. First, it serves to besmirch the memory of Jason and Menelaus, the Hasmoneans' rivals: the former is accused of deposing Onias, and the latter of assassinating him. Second, Onias is depicted as acknowledging Judas as his legitimate heir in a vision delivered in a dream (2 Macc. 15:12–16).[52] In contrast, in An-Apoc the temple rebuilt in Persian times is said to be impure, and the sheep who accepted this temple are blind (89.73–74). Although, as Himmelfarb has noted, the author does not blame the desecration of the temple on the priests' improper observance of purity laws – all the sheep are collectively stigmatized for their blindness – he had no particular interest in priests.[53] In this context, it is improbable that he singled out Onias III as the Suffering Servant put to death by the Seleucids (the ravens) in v. 90.8.[54] The allegory of the lamb being 'seized' by the ravens pertains to the leader of a group that saw itself as the truly righteous. As modern commentators have speculated, the author of An-Apoc may have identified with this group, but he may also be simply alluding in this verse to an episode that had become a site of memory for some – but which had been omitted in 1 and 2 Macc. 1 and 2 Macc. focus on the Maccabees as the only champions of the rebellion – again as part of their strategy of legitimizing the Hasmoneans. The fact that some literate circles in Judean society chose to commemorate other groups and other leaders was certainly not to their authors' taste. Conversely, in the account of the days preceding the emergence of the ram in An-Apoc,

---

[51] Moreover, an association between the temple's high priest and what appears to be a group with a self-contained identity is implausible. Olson 2013: 210–212 refrains from identifying the lambs, but endorses the identification of the leader with Onias III, albeit cautiously.

[52] Honigman 2014a: 153–156.

[53] See Himmelfarb 2007: 231–233. Her comment responds to the claim that apocalypses were composed by dissident priests rejecting the temple and the priestly establishment altogether. According to Himmelfarb, An-Apoc's 'critique of the Second Temple is more like the prophetic critique of the cult: even sacrifices offered properly are repulsive to God when the people offering them continue to sin' (233).

[54] The Suffering Servant is a traditional prophetic image which appears in the accounts of Antiochus IV's persecution in 1 and 2 Macc. See Honigman 2014a: 239.

there is no record of the wicked, Hellenizing high priests (Jason and Menelaus) – who, in the pro-Hasmonean version of 1 and 2 Macc., were key to establishing the dynasty's legitimacy.[55]

The second crucial difference between An-Apoc and 1 and 2 Macc. is their respective portrayals of the horned ram and Judas Maccabee. Although in 1 and 2 Macc. Judas is depicted as a pious warrior who won victories thanks to God's epiphanic support on the battlefield, the emphasis is on his royal (or quasi-royal) status – namely, he rebuilds the temple.[56] Similarly, in the dream vision that he receives on the eve of his final battle in 2 Macc. (15:12–16), Judas is acknowledged as a worthy heir to both Onias III, the late pious high priest, and to the kings of old. While, in the dream, Onias III extends his hand to bless him and his army, Jeremiah hands him a sword, thereby granting him the status of king by divine election.[57] In contrast, nowhere in An-Apoc is the horned ram depicted as rebuilding the temple. Not only that, but, as we have just seen, it is stated that the temple was polluted ever since its reconstruction in the second period (Persian times, v. 89.73): accordingly, the desecration of the temple by Antiochus IV, which is a key episode in 1 and 2 Macc., receives no mention whatsoever. Given that the blind sheep are held as collectively responsible for the pollution, no single human being could be qualified to purify it. The fate of the temple is sealed by God himself in eschatological times (90.28–36). Moreover, the wild ox in eschatological times is a patriarch (like Adam and Noah) – not a king. In other words, An-Apoc decidedly downplays not only the priesthood and the high priesthood, but kingship, as well. Instead, the depiction of the horned ram in An-Apoc stresses that its eyes were open, arguing that it was deemed worthy of the Revelation through the 'man' (righteous angel) that the Lord of the sheep had appointed to record the shepherds' misdeeds (90.14). As far as I can discern, nothing in 1 and 2 Macc. hints at Judas receiving, or potentially receiving, a revelation. Finally, the ram does not die (nor, interestingly, does Judas in 2 Macc., although the

---

[55] That is, by delegitimizing their rivals. See my summary of 1 and 2 Macc. in Section 2 above, Rereading 1 and 2 Maccabees, pp. 128–131, and Honigman 2014a: 197–228.
[56] The ideological meaning of this act is explained in Section 2 above, pp. 129–130. See also Honigman 2014a: 95–141.
[57] For an analysis of this key passage, see Honigman 2014a: 153–156.

intention there may be different), but rather ascends to heaven, accompanied by the three angels who guided the seer (i.e., the narrator of the dream vision of An-Apoc).[58]

As we see, the man who delivers victory with God's help is portrayed very differently in An-Apoc compared with 2 Macc., and I see no way of reconciling the two renditions. There are two possible explanations of this difference. One is that – like Enoch, Jeremiah, and other prophets of old – the figure of Judas in Judean society of Hellenistic times had begun to function as a site of memory, which the author of An-Apoc and the court historian who wrote 2 Macc. each appropriated differently, to suit their respective ideological needs. The other is that the ram in An-Apoc does not refer to Judas.

To sum up our discussion thus far, the comparison between An-Apoc and 2 Macc. leads to two basic conclusions: first, the Judean revolt against Antiochus IV was, unsurprisingly, remembered as a major event among different, and presumably all, parts of Judean society. Second, because it was a major event, it was interpreted in different ways by different circles of scribes. As a shared site of memory in Judean society, different circles of scribes projected their respective social and political ideologies onto it.

Through their respective portrayals of the righteous warrior, the two authors gave their own interpretation of the victorious war against the Seleucids. As one might expect from a work of court historiography, 2 Macc. interprets the causes of revolt against Antiochus IV as the consequence of impious usurpers (the high priests Jason and Menelaus) seizing power by ousting the legitimate and pious ruler with the support of a wicked king. Moreover, these wicked usurpers and king are shown to be greedy and cruel: they raise taxes, plunder the temple, and massacre the people. Every aspect of the denunciation of Jason and Menelaus on the one hand, and of the Seleucids on the other, are hallmarks of Judean royal ideology.[59] For his part, the author of

---

[58] In this way, his fate is equated to that of the prophet Elijah, which is recorded in 89.51–58.
[59] For a detailed exposition of this interpretation, see Honigman 2014a. The issue of taxes as a major cause in the Judean rebellion against Antiochus IV is pervading in 1 and 2 Macc. For a discussion of the loci, see Honigman 2014a: 259–281. On the place and role of taxes in the rebellion, see also Girardin (forthcoming).

An-Apoc interprets the events through the lens of Israel's (the Judeans') faithfulness or unfaithfulness to God's path. The cause of all disorders was that Israel went astray, causing the temple rebuilt in the Persian period to be impure. This is why God abandoned Israel to the oppression of a long series of foreign peoples – the Babylonians, the Persians, the Ptolemies, and the Seleucids. The fate of Israel finally changed for the better when a group of faithful ones emerged, and when one of their own gathered the people around him and won victories with God's help.

If we assume, as my first interpretation of An-Apoc does, that this text provides an independent version of events, it can – indeed, must – be dated to before the time when the pro-Hasmonean version of the events that is found in 1 and 2 Macc. was formulated. As I have argued elsewhere, the authors of 1 and 2 Macc., as court historians, were instrumental in the creation of that version, and therefore the date of the pro-Hasmonean version coincides with the composition of 1 and 2 Macc., meaning the early years of John Hyrcanus's rule (134–104 BCE).[60] Consequently, An-Apoc must have been composed between the 150s to 130s BCE.[61] It is an interpretation of history – an intellectual speculation in line with the apocalyptic hermeneutic. Although the importance of the Maccabean crisis is acknowledged by the fact that it marks the end of history, the specificity of the crisis is ironed out by its inclusion in a succession of historical cycles, rather than singled out as it is in 1 and 2 Macc.[62] In particular, the claim that the temple was impure from the outset de-emphasizes the incident of its desecration by Antiochus IV – which, conversely, is pivotal in MT Daniel, and in a slightly distorted manner, in 1 and 2 Macc.[63] Likewise, the image of foreign kings oppressing (devouring) the Judeans (the sheep) is interpreted as a consequence of the Judeans abandoning God's Torah – and God abandoning them in return – and this foundational disorder is said to occur before the exile to Babylonia. No intrinsic distinction is drawn between oppression suffered

---

[60] Honigman 2014a. John Hyrcanus is alluded to in the concluding verses of 1 Macc. (16: 23–24).
[61] Yoshiko Reed 2004: 47 and Himmelfarb 2007:79, respectively, date An-Apoc to this period.
[62] Cf. the respective interpretations of Assefa 2007 and Mermelstein 2014: 135–153.
[63] In these works, the desecration is attributed first and foremost to the wicked high priests, and only secondarily to Antiochus IV.

by the Judeans at the hands of the Babylonians, the Persians, the Ptolemies, or the Seleucids. The change in allegorical images – from wild beasts to birds of heaven – to depict the Ptolemaic and Seleucid periods is the only intimation that Greek rule was seen as different, in some way, from earlier kingdoms. Finally, the narrative downplays the role of priests, high priests, or native kingship.

7. The Animal Apocalypse as a Response to 1 and 2 Maccabees?

An-Apoc may be just that: a historical apocalypse with a peculiar social ideology. However, the revised dating of the earliest Aramaic scroll of An-Apoc found in Qumran to the late second century BCE invites us to consider the possibility that the work was composed under John Hyrcanus's rule. Such a late dating would cast a totally different light on the work's peculiarities – while, at the same time, provide an easy explanation for them – by allowing us to read An-Apoc as a response to the pro-Hasmonean version promoted in 1 and 2 Macc. In this way, An-Apoc would acquire an overtly political, and polemical slant. The oddities of its historical survey would appear to be a deliberate excision of all the elements that were key to Hyrcanus's legitimizing discourse – namely, Judas's refounding of the temple, and possibly Judas himself; the priesthood (and high priesthood) and kingship; and even *Hellenismos* (as defined in Section 2 above, Rereading 1 and 2 Maccabees, p. 131).

According to Josephus (*War* 1.68–69; *Ant* 13.300), John Hyrcanus claimed for himself the threefold status of high priest, king, and prophet – and it is the latter claim that stirred opposition. His name was included in a list of false prophets cited in the Dead Sea Scrolls (4Q339), and it seems that another text of historical tenor (4QTestimonia) was a polemic against his prophetic claims.[64] Thus, we should not rule out the

---

[64] On 4Q339 (or 4QList of False Prophets), see Wise 2003: 69. On 4QTestimonia, see Berthelot 2009.

possibility that An-Apoc was composed in this context, as a hostile response to Hyrcanus's claim.

9. Conclusions

1 and 2 Macc. on the one hand, and An-Apoc on the other, document not the Maccabean revolt per se, but different – and possibly competing – memories of this event. Under the Hasmoneans, this episode acquired the status of a founding myth – for the ruling dynasty, as well as for society at large. Given that the dynasty derived its legitimacy from the story of Judas refounding the temple that had been desecrated by Antiochus IV and (allegedly) by the wicked priests Jason and Menelaus, we can readily imagine that various groups appropriated the seminal episode of resistance in deliberately divergent fashion. Depending on how we date An-Apoc, its version may or may not have been contentious. But whatever the case, the fact that this work, like 1 and 2 Macc., referred to the rebellion against Antiochus IV does not necessarily mean that it was a piece of resistance literature – at least, not according to the definition of this concept promoted afresh by Nickelsburg, Horsley, and Portier-Young.

6
Revolts, Resistance, and the Materiality of the Moral Order in Ptolemaic Egypt

Ian S. Moyer

The revolts and disturbances (ταραχαί) of Ptolemaic Egypt have, over the last decades of scholarly debate, become more convulsive and spasmodic. They are more likely than ever to be explained as natural responses to material and social privations of various kinds: losses of economic resources, of power, or simply of sustenance. They have become voluntary only in a limited and mechanical sense. They are 'triggered' by various material causes: resistance results from the oppressive exactions of the Ptolemaic state to fund foreign wars; from encroachments on the finances of the temples and the prerogatives of their traditional stewards; from agricultural crises and food shortages caused by climatic disturbances. In some cases, the timing of an outbreak of resistance is also conditioned by opportunity: a state weakened by the loss of overseas territories, invasion, or dynastic strife. This swing toward materialist explanations of revolt is, in part, a reaction against the previously prominent, and now widely rejected, cultural-ethnic explanation: Egyptian nationalism. Though wisely regarded with caution as a modernizing translation of ancient relations between inter-ethnic tension and collective action, reflecting on this broad historiographic shift still begs a basic question: did Egyptians – and other ancient people – only revolt when they were hungry, when they felt the pinch of taxes, or when they lost fiscal control in major institutions?[1] E. P. Thompson long

---

[1] See McGing 2016: 153 citing Bayly 1988: 188. McGing has long urged Hellenistic historians to consider or reconsider nationalism or proto-nationalism among the causes of Egyptian revolt (see McGing 1997, 2006, and 2012), and it is true that the politics of cultural and ethnical

ago warned that 'spasmodic' interpretations of popular 'riots' in eighteenth-century England had the shared weakness of 'an abbreviated view of economic man', and argued that acts of resistance were the result not only of deprivation, but also outrages to shared assumptions about social norms and obligations, and the proper roles of various members of a community – what he described as a 'moral economy'.[2] Historians of Ptolemaic Egypt, and the wider Hellenistic world, can leave aside the well-canvassed arguments for and against (proto-)nationalism as a cause, and still ask whether local cultural norms, and perceived affronts to them, played a part in the chains of causation that led to Ptolemaic revolts. And if so, can they be found in our sources? I would like to suggest that an answer to this question lies in an expanded view of the materiality of resistance to Ptolemaic rule and a closer examination of the practices of resistance.

Several studies of the revolts against Ptolemaic rule have pointed to the admittedly limited evidence that Egyptians did express grievances and their redress in the language of Egyptian religious traditions and political theology, and this language does include implicit or explicit moral evaluations. For example, the names of the rival pharaoh or pharaohs of the Great Theban revolt of 206–186 BCE, Haronnophris (*Ḥr-wn-nfr*) and Chaonnophris (*'nḫ-wn-nfr*), both incorporated the Osirian epithet

identity cannot be ignored simply because such identities have been fully historicized and interpreted as social constructs (see the Introduction, p. 6, n. 17). In this article, however, I would like to argue that these are not the only options among 'cultural' (vs. materialist) explanations of revolt. Proponents of social and economic causes have generally held the field (e.g. Manning 2003b; and Veïsse 2004, though note, of course, her nuanced appreciation of kingship discourses in this volume). The very successful comparative work on Hellenistic revolts in different states, regions, and cultural contexts has also tended to use economic, institutional, and social categories to organize and frame the comparanda (see e.g. Gorre and Honigman 2013; Fischer-Bovet 2015b). McGing, on the other hand, takes another comparative approach and applies the basic question of C. A. Bayly 'did Indians only revolt when they were hit in their pockets or stomachs?' to Ptolemaic Egypt. One answer would be to point to the correlation between revolt and volcanic eruptions and their attendant climatic disturbances, discussed in Ludlow and Manning 2016. The correlation is statistically significant, but it is also worth pointing out that according to their reckoning (Ludlow and Manning 2016: 16, fig. 1) there are twelve episodes of resistance that are 'volcanic', and fourteen that are 'non-volcanic'. The latter are *explananda* at the very least, and I shall argue that they all are, since social and economic pressures are not necessarily direct causes, but conditions of a decision-making process that judged the morality of the ruler by traditional pharaonic norms in periods of crisis.
[2] Thompson 1971: 78–79.

Onnophris (*Wn-nfr*), thus affiliating the new regime with a return to mythical paradigms and norms of legitimate kingship.[3] The basis of this legitimate kingship should not be confused with the legitimation of modern states as defined by Weber, but a belief in norms and conformity to these norms did matter.[4] This conformity did not entail reference to the explicit or implicit assent of the people. Rather this was a social and political system grounded in the divinity of the ruler, and in the ruler's cosmic role as guarantor of lawful order, or Ma'at, which included correct patterns of the transmission of power from one ruler to another.[5] The name Haronnophris (*Ḥr-wn-nfr*) attaches the Osirian epithet to the name of Osiris' son, Horus, and so invokes the principle of legitimate descent and inheritance epitomized in the myth of Horus' struggles with Seth, which culminates in Horus' justification, before a divine tribunal, as the true heir to Osiris. Conversely, the mythical reference implies that the Ptolemies are to be identified with Seth, the murderer of Osiris and the unjust usurper of his throne. The *Oracle of the Potter* uses even clearer moral language. The potter's *ex eventu* prophecy is hostile to Ptolemaic rule and predicts its overthrow, even if specific connections to a revolt of Harsiesis in 131/130

---

[3] See Veïsse, this volume, pp. 64–66; Clarysse 1978 and 1995b: 17–18.

[4] For the basic distinctions between legal, charismatic, and traditional legitimations of domination, see Weber 1958: 78–79. As Weber repeatedly pointed out, these 'ideal types' almost never exist in their pure form, and Pharaonic kingship is easily recognizable as grounded in a combination of traditional and charismatic legitimation, but it also had a dimension of legal legitimation in reference to the cosmic-religious notion of Ma'at. For a searching critique of the application of Weberian and Marxist notions of legitimation and ideology to pre-modern states, see Pollock 2006a: 282–286 and 2006b: 511–524. One of Pollock's central arguments is that legitimation and ideology, as concepts derived from reflection on modern states, function to bridge a gap between political (or economic) norms and facts by sustaining (false) beliefs about the way things are. This gap is, in his view, not to be assumed in pre-modern states that have not undergone the ruptures of general consensus seen as defining the historical development of (Western) modernity. This is not to say, however, as he points out, that belief and culture were uniform in any given pre-modern context – that was certainly not the case in the Hellenistic oecumene any more than in pre-modern South Asia. On the other hand, kingship as a form of domination or government was far more legible and less in need of legitimation than in modern contexts. The justification of a particular king's rule, or of various modalities of kingship vis-à-vis others, could clearly be points of a much less revolutionary form of contention.

[5] Texts such as the *Demotic Chronicle* make it clear that in the Ptolemaic period, there was a continuation of a Late Period conception of 'law' (*hp*) which pharaohs could transgress with negative consequences for their reigns. The standards of this law were applied to Egyptian as well as Greek rulers. See Johnson 1983. Therefore, Egyptian claims regarding 'legitimacy' are not cover for some other 'real' explanation, i.e. that the Ptolemies are illegitimate because they are foreign.

BCE can no longer be regarded as part of its historical context.⁶ The coming troubles for Egypt include agrarian crisis and economic ills, but the prophecy also laments the many crimes that will occur under the Greek 'Girdle-wearers', who are described as 'Typhonians', followers of Seth-Typhon. Egypt is wronged with such terrible maltreatment that even the sun is darkened, as he averts his gaze from the evils done in the land. And when the great god of Memphis comes to drive the Greeks to the sea, he does so because they are 'impious' (ἀσεβεῖς).⁷ In broad terms, then, this evidence, along with other texts such as the Demotic Chronicle and the Prophecy of the Lamb, show that in the later period, the rule of any given pharaoh or dynasty, regardless of culture and ethnicity, was not quite absolute, but depended on the fulfilment of various obligations, in default of which, it could, by the will of the gods, be superseded.⁸ Texts that specifically evaluated Ptolemaic rule, for better or for worse, did so within this framework, and these should not be taken as cover for rejection of rule on solely ethnic or cultural grounds in the absence of direct positive evidence that this was the case. Such local frameworks of judgement vary from context to context, and each has its own sedimented history of rulership, but they are nevertheless a common feature of the terrain in which revolt and resistance erupted in the Hellenistic world.⁹

These bits of evidence are well known, and almost always mentioned in analyses of resistance to Ptolemaic rule, but (with the exception of earlier 'nationalist' arguments) they have rarely led to conclusions about the causes of revolt. Moralizing religious objections to Ptolemaic rule do

---

⁶ For the text and connection to the revolt of Harsiesis, see Koenen 1968 and 1970; Koenen and Blasius 2002: 169–170. English translations of the text are available in Burstein 1985: 136–139 and Kerkeslager 1998. The analysis of Veïsse 2004: 48–52 and 2011 has shown that the evidence adduced for the existence of a rebel pharaoh Harsiesis in 131/130 BCE is not at all secure and so Harsiesis should be removed from the list of rebels against the Ptolemies. Nevertheless, the *Oracle of the Potter* does envision the overthrow of Greek rulers, and does ground its prophecy in actual events through other references to Ptolemaic history, such as the invasion of Antiochus IV.

⁷ P₂ (P. Rainer (G.19 813)) col. I, ll. 12–16: [...ταῦτα ἔσται γ]άρ, ἐπεὶ ὁ μέγας θεὸς Ἡφα[ισ]τος ἐ[β]ο[υ]λήθη [εἰς τὴν] [πόλιν ἀνελθ]εῖν καὶ ἑαυτοὺς οἱ ζωνοφόροι ἀνελοῦσι⟨ν⟩ ὄν[τες Τυφώνιοι......]λατος κακωθήσεται· μετελεύσεται δὲ ποσὶ [πρὸς θά][λασσα]αν [ἐν τ]ῷ μηνί⟨ει⟩ν καὶ πολλοὺς καταστρέψει αὐτῶν [ἀσεβεῖς] [ὄντας].

⁸ The *Dream of Nectanebo* could also be seen as an example of this principle, since Nectanebo II appears to be punished by the gods for failure in his pharaonic duties of maintaining and improving temples. For discussion see Moyer 2011a: 137–138, 170–171; Matthey 2011: 310–315 and more broadly the sophisticated analysis in Matthey 2012.

⁹ See, especially Stevens (Chapter 4) and Honigman (Chapter 5) in this volume.

not easily fit the social scientific containers into which many historians sort the causes of conflict and revolt, so they are often treated as epiphenomenal, or as epichoric translations of underlying, universal categories of historical analysis.[10] Thus the *Oracle of the Potter* can be read as 'a response, in religious terms, to political, socioeconomic, climatic, and environmental conditions that obtained during the second century BCE'.[11] Since this evidence of moral contextualizations of revolt originated with would-be rulers or literate priesthoods, the responses are at times assigned to these elite milieux, and not taken to represent the social and economic concerns of the broader population.[12] The latter position presumes either that revolts against Ptolemaic rule had roots in a populace with little interest in high-flown ideologies, and/or that such moral justifications for revolt as are evident in the sources were secondary elaborations created by elite leaders who organized and gave coherence to inevitably complex motives for resistance. B. McGing, who is sympathetic to the idea that a kind of proto-nationalism was part of a complex mix of causation in revolts, once put it as follows:

> Taxation, debt, law and order all have their part to play in the discontent of the Egyptian people... Not only are the people oppressed, but they are oppressed by a foreign regime. Giving expression to their anger is the voice of Egyptian religious nationalism. This is the stick with which they beat their foreign oppressors, but it is not necessarily what put the stick in their hands in the first place.[13]

---

[10] On historical knowledge lost in translation, see Chakrabarty 2008.

[11] Ludlow and Manning 2016: 164. See also Manning 2003b: 165–166. It is interesting to note that McGing 2016: 146 who is open to complex causation in ancient revolts, including ancient equivalents to 'nationalism', puts religion in a secondary or supplementary role: '... the temple estates of Egypt had age-old economic and social networks, and the priests might easily find the new Ptolemaic modes of economic control and exploitation highly objectionable. And then religion could be brought into play as part of the ideology of revolt'. See also McGing 1997: 288 quoted below.

[12] Manning 2003b: 166. Likewise, authors who recognize that there was a significant alliance of interests between the priesthoods and Ptolemies regard anti-Ptolemaic statements as exceptions to a general rule, and thus the origin of the revolts are attributed to discontent among the masses. For a summary of this view, see, e.g. Hölbl 2001: 153–154.

[13] McGing 1997: 288. Somewhat earlier, McGing describes nationalist opposition to the Ptolemies as 'led by religious leaders presenting themselves as messiahs ushering in a new golden age'. See also McGing 2016: 146, quoted above, n. 11.

In either case, these interpretations run the risk of underestimating non-elite culture, a culture that was, in some measure, attuned to elite representations owing to popular participation in the public dimensions of temples, such as dramas and festivals that enacted mythical episodes, as well as visual and dramatic celebrations of the pharaoh's role in protecting and caring for Egypt, and maintaining cosmic order through ritual. The instructions for cult honours for members of the Ptolemaic Dynasty, for example, refer not only to the cult offered by the priests, but also to the broader participation of the populace.[14] Within the moral frameworks of such a popular culture, is it not possible that a range of dire circumstances were understood as failures of kingship, or that the ruler failed in his obligations in a time of crisis, and that these considerations were part of the desperate calculus, along with the economic and social privations themselves, that led Egyptians both ordinary and elite, to run the risk of raising violent opposition to the Ptolemaic state?

The process of getting any closer than these speculative questions to the voices, let alone the 'moral economy', of the Egyptian crowd is plagued by well-known methodological problems. The few existing ancient narrative histories that describe and explain Egyptian revolts were written by Greek authors, and their accounts of cause and motivation focus, not surprisingly, on the military and courtly matters that interested them most. Polybius famously attributed the rebellion after the battle of Raphia to Ptolemy IV's decision to arm Egyptians for

[14] For example, in the first known decree, enacted at Alexandria in 243 BCE, provisions are made for statues of the 'Beneficent Gods' (Ptolemy III and Berenike II) to be carried in procession in a special shrine during the major festivals, and on the birthday and accession date of Ptolemy III there is also a provision that the people of Egypt should honour the models of this shrine of the royal couple in their homes 'so that it may be clear that all the people of Egypt honour the Beneficent gods as it is custom to do' (hieroglyphic version, lines 19-20; demotic, lines 110-113; see el-Masri, Altenmüller, and Thissen 2013: 21, 25, 48-49, 63-64, 143-146). Similar measures for domestic cult are also taken in the Raphia decree (demotic: see Simpson 1996: 256-257), the Memphis decree of 196 (Greek: *OGIS* 90A 52-53; demotic: *Urk.* II.197.1-6; Simpson 1996: 270-271; hieroglyphic: *Urk.* II.197.1-6), and in the first Philae decree (see von Recklinghausen 2018: 164-165). The Canopus decree mentions the festivals decreed in 243 BCE, and the Greek version (very fragmentary in the 243 decree) refers to them as ἑορταὶ καὶ πανηγύρεις δημοτελεῖς 'festivals and public assemblies' (see Pfeiffer 2004: 121-127 for Greek, demotic and hieroglyphic texts, German translations, and commentary on the public nature of these festivals). Likewise, the image of the princess Berenike is to be carried in procession at festivals, so that everyone may see it and worship it (Greek: ὅπως ὑπὸ πάντων ὁρώμενον τιμᾶται καὶ προσκυνῆται; demotic *mtw rmt nb nwy r-r=f mtw=w wšt iw=w ti pḥw n-im=f*; hieroglyphic: *r-nty mꜣ-s bw-nb sn-tꜣ m ḏsr=f*; see Pfeiffer 2004: 163-167). Examples could be multiplied.

his war with Antiochus III, and to Egyptian soldiers' pride in their accomplishments. Diodorus Siculus described the revolt of Dionysius Petosarapis solely in terms of an Egyptian courtier's ambitions for the throne at a time of weakness after the invasion of Antiochus IV, and a fragile joint rule under Ptolemy VI and his brother, Ptolemy VIII.[15] The strategy of reading against the grain of official texts issued by and for the Ptolemaic state poses other predictable challenges. Royal and priestly decrees use terms such as 'rebels', 'impious' and 'enemies of the gods' to vilify opponents of the regime, and these effectively obscure the reasons for resistance as the rebels themselves saw them.[16] Nevertheless, among the many royal 'benefactions' detailed in priestly decrees and in royal amnesty decrees (φιλάνθρωπα), a preponderance of which were aimed specifically at priests and temples, there were also general remissions of taxes and debts to the crown, and measures against abuses by agents of the state. In their historical context, they are quite reasonably interpreted as efforts to address the grievances of the wider populace in troubled times.[17] In the texts themselves, however, they are described as benefactions motivated by the pharaoh's traditional care for the land and its people, not as concessions to popular discontent or rebel demands, so an interpretive step is required to pass from the correlation of revolt and benefaction to an account of grievances from the perspective of the rebels. Economic rationalism can fill that gap, but it does not produce an entirely sufficient account, since it skips over the primary discursive strategy of the text: painting a picture of conformity to the traditional morality of Egyptian kingship. This higher-order message of the decrees was also tacitly addressing a grievance. The Egyptian populace may have risked revolt as an act of calculated self-interest in the context of extreme

---

[15] Though influential for earlier Ptolemaic historians, Polybius 5.107 has more recently been found problematic, based as it is in the limited and distant perspective of a Greek historian. See Veïsse 2004: 5–7; Fischer-Bovet 2014. Veïsse 2004: 126–127 points out that this passage is one of only two ancient narrative sources to offer explanations of the causes of Egyptian revolts. The other is in Strabo's *Geography* 17.1.53, in which he attributes a revolt in 29 BCE to the imposition of tribute, though this was a revolt against the Roman governor Cornelius Gallus rather than the Ptolemies. For discussion of the revolt of Dionysius Petosarapis, see Veïsse 2004: 28–32, 99–112.

[16] On the range of terms applied to the rebels, see Veïsse 2004: 112–126. See the Philensis II decree and the Rosetta Stone, discussed by Pestman 1995b: 120. On the term 'enemy of the gods' (θεοῖσιν ἐχθρός) see Koenen 1959: 106–112, but with the important corrective of Veïsse 2011.

[17] See e.g. McGing 1997: 287, 296; Hölbl 2001: 157; Ludlow and Manning 2016: 163.

privation, but the rhetoric of the text implies that they also believed that taxes and other impositions had crossed a line between the just and unjust exercise of pharaonic rule. Documentary texts provide another archive of evidence, but they are terse and usually indifferent to the motives for revolt. Greek documents that mention such an event most often call it simply a ταραχή, a 'disturbance' or 'disorder', a term also used in the Memphis decree of 196 BCE.[18] At first sight an anodyne abstraction, this term could also be read as part of what Ranajit Guha has called the 'prose of counter-insurgency'[19] – an ostensibly unadorned official reportage that is in fact full of commentary hostile to those whose acts of rebellion seem to irrupt spontaneously into historical documents. Coupled with the terms of vilification noted above, ταραχή becomes a dehumanized, turbulent force opposed to the divine order of the regime. At the very least, it is an abstract disorder that renders the agency, consciousness, and interests of the rebels illegible.

To bridge these silences in the Ptolemaic documents, it can be productive, as Roger Bagnall pointed out some time ago,[20] to make comparisons with better-documented times and places and their literatures in order to inform and broaden the historical imagination and develop a more nuanced picture of the lived experiences and conscious decisions that lie behind acts of resistance. Bagnall himself used as his example an episode documented in a papyrus from the Zenon archive (*PSI* V 502), a small dossier of correspondence sent by Panakestor, steward of the Fayyum estate of the Ptolemaic finance minister Apollonios, to Zenon, who would soon become the estate's manager. The dossier details an apparent case of *anachoresis*, or the withdrawal of cultivators from the

---

[18] For the range of terms used to describe revolt in Greek as well as demotic and hieroglyphic texts, see Veïsse 2004: 114–120. ταραχή is attested twelve times. Towards the end of the second century BCE, this tends to be replaced by the equally vague and rather curious abstraction ἀμιξία / ἀμειξία (attested nine times), apparently signifying a lack or cessation of normal communication and interaction. By contrast, terms with more overt Greek political connotations, such as στάσις or ἀπόστασις occur rarely (ἀπόστασις once and στάσις perhaps twice), although there are about eleven references to rebels in the terminology of ἀπόστασις (ἀποστάται, ἀποστάντες, ἀποστάς). In the Memphite decree, ταραχή is translated *thth* (confusion), and in Philae II, the term *bks* is used. McGing 2016: 150 briefly suggests that ταραχή as official language could be used 'to play down the importance of resistance'.
[19] Guha 1983.   [20] Bagnall 1997.

land in the middle of the third century BCE, before the first known outbreak of a major revolt in Ptolemaic Egypt. The farmers withdrew in response to the imposition of advance estimations of the rents to be paid from the crops produced rather than a straightforward partition of the produce after the harvest. The new practice shifted the risk inherent in agriculture from the state-backed landlord to the farmers. While a much earlier study had used a now-outdated anthropology to analyse the act of *anachoresis* as 'instinctive' and characteristic of the 'archaic' mentality of the Egyptian peasants,[21] Bagnall suggested that Pramoedya Ananta Toer's novel, *Child of All Nations*, can give clearer insights into the experiences of disrespect and coercion that lead to peasant acts of refusal and resistance.[22] Neither study, however, makes much of the fact that the flight of the peasants was not simply a withdrawal *from* the land and the newly imposed payment regime; it was also withdrawal *to* a temple. If we illuminate this withdrawal with Thompson's study of the moral logic of direct actions taken by eighteenth-century English 'crowds', this moment of *anachoresis* can be read not simply as a refusal, but as a symbolic action with its own logic. Thompson pointed out that organized popular uprisings in times of food shortage were often characterized not by sheer plunder, but by 'setting the price'. Grain and other goods were indeed taken, but they were taken to be sold at a price fixed by the protestors, sometimes with the forced (or even willing) oversight of authoritative figures such as constables, mayors, or soldiers. These were prices that the protestors clearly considered 'just', and the general procedure echoed earlier paternalistic practices of provision that had been taken by the crown or other authorities, and that were being superseded by 'free market' practices and ideologies as the eighteenth century progressed. These direct actions were, in short, not incomprehensible, spasmodic 'riots', but moments of resistance and self-help that enacted, in semi-formal ways, social and economic justice according to

---

[21] Bingen 2007 [1970].
[22] Bagnall's study is also, in part, informed by the work of Scott 1985, whose careful ethnographic work on peasant resistance in Malaysia can also provide insights into subaltern strategies of resistance and the consciousness and agency of otherwise illegible historical actors. Scott's work on subtle, even hidden, strategies of resistance is especially helpful to understanding the dynamics behind the episode described in Panakestor's report, but less suitable for the instances of open, violent revolt discussed below.

traditional moral economies. A similar effort to enact justice, rather than an irrational flight or blunt refusal, may lie behind Panakestor's brief report of the Egyptian farmers' reaction to Apollonios' new rent-taking practice. Temples like the one to which they withdrew, could in some cases be sites of asylum,[23] but the public areas of the temple (the areas to which the farmers could plausibly gain access without violating temple protocols) were also traditional Egyptian sites for jurisdiction and other means of arbitrating disputes. In the words of Panakestor's report, the farmers, after considering the new estimation procedure for a few days, 'took up seats in the temple, and said they would not undertake any estimation, just or unjust, but would abandon the crop, since there was an (existing) agreement with [Apollonios] that they would pay a third of the produce'.[24] This description suggests a considered decision rather than an irrational flight, and the farmers may well have sat and made this statement in the shade of the temple's 'gate of giving justice', the site where the pharaoh was often depicted making the offering of Ma'at to the gods, and where courts of priestly judges had long met to adjudicate legal disputes, and the elders of temple associations met to arbitrate between their members.[25]

Read in this way, with an eye to the practice of resistance, its material contexts, and their local cultural logics, some sources may be able to give fleeting insights into the moral world of the Egyptian 'crowd' – or at least confirm that such a world did exist and could provide a framework for collective action. The episode in Panakestor's report was a peaceful expression of resistance to injustice, but in the context of the wider 'disturbances' that would later erupt in Ptolemaic Egypt, temples were at times sites, or even targets, of violence.[26] During the great revolt of 206–186 BCE, according to the Memphis and Philae II decrees, temples

---

[23] See Rigsby 1996: 541–544, who points out in his study of the Ptolemaic Egyptian *asylia* grants that there does not appear to be an earlier pharaonic tradition that presumed a 'right of asylum' in temples for those fleeing arrest or enforcement actions. In the Ptolemaic period, some cases do appear in the documents that suggest such asylum, but it is not clear that every temple enjoyed this privilege, and Rigsby notes that the case under discussion (attested in *PSI* 5 502), is not a certain case of asylum.

[24] *PSI* 5 502, lines 21–23: καθίσαντες εἰς τὸ ἱερὸν οὐκ ἔφασαν οὔτε δικαίως οὔτ' ἀδίκως συντιμήσεσθαι, ἀλλ' ἔφασαν ἐκχωρήσειν τοῦ σπόρου· ὁμολογίαν γὰρ εἶναι πρός σε αὐτοῖς ἐκ τοῦ γενήματος ἀποδώσειν τὸ τρίτον.

[25] See, e.g. Sauneron 1954; Allam 1991; Quaegebeur 1993; Derchain 1995. On the tribunals of associations, see de Cenival 1972: 194–197.

[26] For discussions, see McGing 1997: 283, 289, 292–293; Veïsse 2004: 135–142.

were attacked.[27] The revolt of the 160s that followed the invasion of Antiochus IV saw the temple of Amun at Moeris in the Fayyum attacked and seriously damaged by rebels.[28] Although attribution to rebel actions cannot be certain, the temple of Medamud was destroyed around the time of the Theban revolt, and there was also damage to the enclosure wall at Medinet Habu.[29] While Panakestor's farmers may have issued their collective refusal from a temple in order to stake a claim to justice, violent actions taken against temples during periods of revolt – at least at first glance – seem to demand a different interpretation. Indeed, whether such attacks had any significance at all as acts of resistance can be difficult to disentangle from the complex of other possible motivations. The fact that the temples targeted by rebels were ostensibly 'Egyptian' has been a problem for straightforward nationalist interpretations of the revolts, although perhaps less so if priestly elites and temples as institutions were viewed as collaborating with the Ptolemaic regime.[30] As part of the broader argument against cultural and ethnic antagonism as root causes of revolt, scholars have pointed to these attacks and suggested that they are evidence of the material grievances behind the revolts. Temples were, after all, concentrated sites of wealth, and individuals or groups may have intentionally or opportunistically sought gain by targeting them. The description of the attack on the temple of Amun at Moeris, for example, mentions the removal of doors, door fixtures, and boarding. Such actions can be difficult to distinguish from plunder, though, as noted earlier, it is methodologically prudent to be suspicious of explanations that simplify rebel actions down to the mechanical dynamics of an appetitive and lawless mob, even if (or especially when) such characterizations are inscribed in the sources.[31] From the rebels' perspective, property taken from the temples could have been seen as an equitable

---

[27] Memphis decree, line 23 in the Greek; line 13 in the demotic Egyptian; Philae II, hieroglyphic 9c-10b; demotic 7e-8b. For the latter, see now the text, translation and commentary of von Recklinghausen 2018: 61–69.
[28] P. Tebt. III 781.   [29] See Vandorpe 1995: 222, 232; Veïsse 2004: 141 n. 83.
[30] McGing 1997: 283.
[31] See the discussion in Veïsse 2004: 141–146, in which she notes the blurred lines between rebel actions and brigandage, including comparisons made between rebels and brigands in documentary sources. These provide important insights, although it is important to consider the motivations behind these characterizations.

re-distribution of wealth, and fixtures carried away from the Amun temple at Moeris may have been viewed as necessary materiel to supply rebel war needs. Much would also depend on the identities of the rebels and how they understood the ownership of temple wealth.[32] On a more general level, Egyptian temples were often furnished with substantial enclosure walls in the Late Period,[33] which would have made them logical sites of defence and targets of attack for tactical reasons. Indeed, soldiers were at times garrisoned in temple precincts, especially during times of mobilization against external or internal threats.[34] But, as I have been arguing, the actions and decisions of the Egyptian crowd must be grounded in more than material considerations. Just as in the episode of resistance recorded by Panakestor, actions taken in the context of the temple must be considered in relation to these places as sites for the creation of authoritative meaning. Temples served religious functions (most notably royal cult) that were inseparable from the state's authority, but they also served as sites for the constitution and enunciation of authority in other ways, such as legal proceedings. The sacerdotal decrees characterize attacks on temples as acts of impiety and sacrilege against the gods, but temples were also logical sites for a material struggle over the legitimacy, authority, and power of the pharaonic state, a struggle that was parallel to the discursive counterclaims made against Ptolemaic legitimacy through the titles of Haronnophris (*Ḥr-wn-nfr*) and Chaonnophris (*'nḫ-wn-nfr*). In attacking and defending temple precincts, Ptolemaic forces and rebel groups alike were laying claim to a 'high ground' that was as much symbolic as physical, since the public

---

[32] On the latter interpretation, see McGing 1997: 292–293. Note that the Amun temple at Moeris is described as belonging to the forty-five aroura-holders, and thus it is possible that it was targeted because of its association with this privileged class of cleruchs. In general, G. Gorre (2009b, esp. pp. 543–547) has argued that local vs. state control of temple wealth and the funding of temple building programs changed during the Ptolemaic period, and also varied geographically (Upper Egypt vs. Lower Egypt and the Fayyum, in particular). Much of this analysis depends on prosopographical study and the assignment of officials to different categories of 'state'or 'temple/priest' that could be debated, but if these distinctions were perceived by the historical actors involved in revolts, it may well have made some difference to their understanding of the morality of seizing temple property.
[33] Arnold 1999: 93 with examples throughout; Zivie-Coche 2008: 1–2. This tradition of building large fortified enclosures began in the Twenty-ninth and Thirtieth Dynasties in order to protect Egyptian sanctuaries from foreign invasion, but they could also serve the same purpose for internal conflicts.
[34] Fischer-Bovet 2014: 263–269.

areas of temples – the processional ways, gates, and forecourts – often served as the central places of Egyptian towns for social, legal, and economic business of all kinds. They were, in short, the functional equivalents of public space.[35]

In this sense, the temples that are mentioned briefly in various sources as targets of attack or scenes of conflict were perhaps no less sites of a specifically *political* violence, structured by a sense of moral outrage, than the palace, squares, theatres, and stadium in Alexandria. There, in 203 BCE, contemporary with the early years of the Theban revolt, a discontented populace, enraged by the crimes of Agathocles, the guardian of the young king Ptolemy V, began to gather in open areas around the palace, in the stadium, in the main road, and in the open area before the theatre of Dionysus. Macedonian soldiers at first seized the gate of the palace that was intended for the conduct of official businesses and audiences (the *chrematistikos pylon*), in order to demand the appearance of the young king Ptolemy V.[36] The exact form of the Ptolemaic palace, almost entirely concealed by modern Alexandria, is unknown, but to judge from literary sources and contemporary comparanda, the *chrematistikos pylon* was probably a monumental portal with a large peristyle courtyard before it.[37] When they discovered that the young king, together with Agathocles and his retinue, was holed up in a passageway between the palace and the theatre, the soldiers then moved there to seek the young Ptolemy. The boy king was eventually produced, and the Macedonians led him on horseback to the stadium, where he was greeted with shouts and applause by the assembled people. Eventually this crowd made Ptolemy consent to give up to the people anyone guilty of offences against him or his mother. Agathocles, Agathoclea and others were

[35] On the centrality of the temple in Egyptian urban space, especially in the Late Period and Ptolemaic and Roman Egypt, see Mueller 2006: 108; Alston 2002: 196–218.
[36] Polybius 15.31.2–4: τὸ μὲν οὖν πρῶτον οἱ Μακεδόνες ἐξαναστάντες κατελάβοντο τὸν χρηματιστικὸν πυλῶνα τῶν βασιλείων· μετὰ δέ τινα χρόνον ἐπιγνόντες ποῦ τῆς αὐλῆς (ἦν) ὁ βασιλεύς, περιελθόντες τὰς μὲν πρώτας τῆς [πρώτης] σύριγγος ἐξέβαλον θύρας, ἐγγίσαντες δὲ τῆς δευτέρας ἠτοῦντο τὸν παῖδα μετὰ κραυγῆς. The previous night, Agathocles, on hearing the tumult of the crowd, had taken the king, a few bodyguards, and members of the family to a passage way behind three sets of locked gates.
[37] For an overview of the scattered archaeological finds in the palace quarter of Alexandria, see McKenzie 2003: 47–50 and 2007: 68–71. The remains do not permit any clear reconstruction of the layout of the palace and its gates, or the spatial relations of the palace, theater, and stadium.

brutally killed there in the stadium. This was undoubtedly a violent episode and could be described as a riot, but the proceedings were not without a certain moral logic as the army and the people of Alexandria seized traditional spaces of political practice and public spectacle, and extorted an authorization of their para-judicial actions from the young boy king, in order to punish those whom they saw as wrongdoers. Without a detailed narrative source such as Polybius, we are left to wonder whether there was a similar logic to any of the 'disturbances' that resulted in acts of violence visited on temple precincts during times of revolt.

We can supplement this speculative comparison to Polybius' narrative, with two examples from material and documentary evidence in which, I argue, it is possible to glimpse dimensions of the practice of resistance and revolt that are otherwise obscured by our sources. Both involve the destruction of documents in a public context, in a way that suggests neither mob violence nor rationalizing economic behaviour are sufficient explanations. Given the official nature of the texts, and the public contexts in which they were destroyed, these were symbolic attacks on the authority and legitimacy of the state.

The first example involves the intentional defacement of inscribed versions of the sacerdotal decrees.[38] Of the six known versions of the Canopus decree of 238 BCE, two were found in the Theban region: one at Karnak and one about 60 miles (100 km) to the south at Elkab. The Karnak example, a large stele of pink granite (2.23 m high, 1.59 m wide and 55 cm thick), was discovered in 1929 under pavement in the southwestern part of the great hypostyle hall at Karnak, evidently buried during a renovation at some point broadly in the Ptolemaic or Roman period. The stone now stands on display in the hypostyle hall near the third pylon, although the text has never been fully published. The excavators were able to make out that it bore the cartouche of a Ptolemy, but it took at least another thirty years before the text was identified as a copy of the Canopus decree. The reason for this is that the inscription is almost illegible, owing to severe damage to the stone,

---

[38] In an earlier article (Moyer 2011b: 117–118, 124), I have discussed these examples of the intentional destruction of the decrees, and critiqued the assumptions of prior 'nationalist' interpretations without taking the risk of offering my own interptetation. Whether the following is an improvement on that safer approach remains to be seen.

which appears to have been beaten repeatedly with a hard object.[39] The identification was finally confirmed by S. Sauneron only through the careful study of plaster and latex impressions – a testament to the thoroughness of the destruction. The Elkab version, discovered near the gate of Nectanebo I at the temple of Nekhbet in 1946, is a fragment broken away from a larger stele. While the hieroglyphic side appears to have been obscured by natural wear, the Greek part shows signs of being intentionally chipped and scraped away with a chisel. One of the edges of the fragment also bears the marks of a chisel used to break it away from the rest of the monument.[40] The scholars who originally published the find suggested that at first the Greek letters were mutilated, and then at some later point the entire fragment was broken away and removed from the larger monument to which it had been attached.

The intentional destruction of these inscribed versions of the trilingual decrees struck the earliest scholars who studied them as acts of 'nationalist' resistance to the Ptolemaic regime, and on occasion they imagined the fury of a crowd attacking a monument and text that honoured their foreign oppressors.[41] That such images of nationalist fervour presented themselves to these scholars was perhaps the product of their contemporary moment of decolonization and general patterns of historiography that now seem anachronistic and dated. Scenes of riot or revolt are,

---

[39] Chevrier 1929: 145; Lauffray et al. 1970: 73–75. See also the brief discussions in Simpson 1996: 3, 17–18 and Pfeiffer 2004: 39. Curiously, only the hieroglyphic portion of the text, and the first lines of the demotic version were completed; the Greek text was never engraved. Does this in itself suggest some foot-dragging on the part of those charged with creating and erecting the stele at the great temple of Amun at Karnak?

[40] Capart 1947: 354; Bayoumi and Guéraud 1947. The plate accompanying the latter article shows the damage to the Greek text. See also the brief discussions in Simpson 1996: 3, 18. Pfeiffer 2004: 39 n. 76 doubts the intentional nature of the damage since only part of the Greek text is damaged. Nevertheless, the damage, however interpreted, is clear in the published photo of the inscription.

[41] Bayoumi and Guéraud 1947: 382: 'Sans qu'on puisse rien affirmer, bien entendu, devant la mutilation, d'abord du texte grec, puis de toute cette stèle élevée en hommage à des souverains helléniques, nos yeux évoquent instinctivement l'image d'une foule exaltée, protestant, à la manière simpliste qui est celle des foules de tous les temps, contre l'oppression étrangère, au cours d'une de ces révoltes nationales qui· soulevèrent l'Égypte dès le IIe siècle avant J.-C'. See also Sauneron 1957: 70: 'Sans doute, les foules hostiles aux souverains étrangers se sont-elles acharnées avec un fanatisme particulèrement efficace sur ces documents qui proclaimaient la divinité de leurs officiels oppresseurs'. Cf. Lauffray et al. 1970: 74–75: 'La stèle, en granit rose de bonne qualité, a été sauvagement martelée... Cela témoigne, une fois de plus, de la violence avec laquelle la Thébaïde a réagi à la promulgation des décrets lagides'.

moreover, precarious images to conjure from marks left on a stone, when it is impossible even to be certain of the agent(s) of destruction, let alone their motivations. The exact moment of the destruction has not been narrowed down in the El Kab fragment, and for the Karnak stele the best estimate is rather broad: it must have happened at some point between the promulgation of the decree in 238 BCE and the stone's burial beneath the Roman-period renovations of the great hypostyle hall.[42] But the historian is not left with nothing: there are circumstantial clues. These two copies of the Canopus decree were, after all, found in a region that was central to the most extensive revolt in Ptolemaic history (206–186 BCE), and that was affected by the revolts of c.165 BCE, and 88 BCE.[43] The damaged inscriptions were located at temples whose divinities had broad significance for the ideology of pharaonic kingship. Thebes was, of course, one of the great dynastic seats of pharaonic Egypt, and the stele from Karnak was found at the temple of its great god Amun, the god who appeared in the epithet of the rebel pharaoh(s) Haronnophris/ Chaonnophris in the dating formulae of documentary texts ('beloved by Isis, beloved by Amonrasonter the great god') as a counter-discourse to Ptolemaic epithets and their assocation with Ptah, the god of Memphis. The appeal to Amun could also be seen as reviving an older pharaonic order of Theban/Ammonian rule. The priests of Thebes, moreover, appear to have had close relations with the rebel regime during its brief existence.[44] Ptolemaic Elkab is much less well documented both in texts and material remains than Thebes, but was nevertheless closely connected with other major centres in the Theban region.[45] The ancient city, known as Nekheb in

[42] On the caution with which these damaged exemplars of the Canopus decree must be treated, see Veïsse 2004: 141 n. 83.
[43] As noted above (n. 6), the revolt of Harsiesis dated to 131/130 BCE is now in doubt, but if still accepted, that revolt also involved Thebes. Even without the case of Harsiesis, the Theban region can still be considered as an area that was prone to revolt in the Ptolemaic era. For discussion, see Veïsse 2004: 240–243, who suggests quite persuasively that the revolts did not necessarily break out in Thebes, but it became involved in the revolts because of the strategic advantages of the city and the Thebaïd more widely as a repository of wealth, strategic strong points, and ideological value.
[44] See Veïsse 2004: 86–87 and Veïsse, this volume, Chapter 2, pp. 57–73.
[45] For an overview of the texts from Elkab, see Depauw 2003: 29–32; for an overview of the archaeological remains and the history of excavations, see Limme 2008. The fabric and formulae of tax receipts on ostraka from Elkab suggest connections with Edfu and southern Upper Egypt. Though there are only a few ostraka from the Ptolemaic period, onomastic evidence from the more plentiful Roman period ostraka suggest connections with Thebes (Depauw 2003: 31).

Egyptian and Eileithyaspolis in Greek, was located just across from ancient Nekhen (Hierakonpolis), about 55 miles (90 km) south of Thebes, following the course of the river. Though in earlier pharaonic times Nekhen and Nekheb were important upper Egyptian capitals in their own right, they were governed in the Ptolemaic period from Edfu/Apollonopolis Magna, which was another 12 miles or so (20 km) further south along the Nile. Although no texts explicitly connect Elkab with revolts in the Theban area, it was almost certainly affected by the Great Theban revolt, given its proximity to Edfu.[46] As a site of symbolic significance for Egyptian kingship, Elkab has ancient roots, since the vulture goddess of the main temple, Nekhbet, developed from an Upper-Egyptian regional goddess of predynastic times to become one of the Two Ladies, the dual protectors of the king of Upper and Lower Egypt, who were the protective uraei who sat on the king's crown, and presided over one of the names of the five-fold pharaonic titulary.

These were, therefore, attacks on monuments at important religious sites implicated in pharaonic kingship ideology, but the specific nature and location of the targets can give us further insights into the symbolic dimensions of violence in temple precincts. Unlike the reports of attacks on temples discussed earlier, it is hard to imagine that the damage inflicted was incidental to some other purpose. The damaged stones were left more or less where they were originally placed (see further, below, pp. 165–166), so they do not appear to have been carried off to be used for their material. Both inscriptions also show an attempt to deface and render illegible the text on the stone. This kind of damage is not easily explained as the results of incidental contact in the course of attack or defence of a fortified position. Defacement can therefore plausibly be interpreted as the primary goal of the acts that left the marks on the stone. Most important of all, the text of the decree and the places where these stelae were found confirm that these were *public* acts of

---

[46] For what is known of the extent of the revolt at various times, see Pestman 1995b. Just how far to the south the territory of Haronnophris extended is not entirely clear. He controlled at least as far as Pathyris, and there is evidence of disturbances at Edfu: notably interruptions in work on the temple of Horus there (Pestman 1995b: 103, 110–111, text e), and evidence that a soldier had to abandon his house at Edfu (Pestman 1995b: 103, 124, text bbb).

defacement. In the surviving Greek versions of the instructions for inscription and display, the Canopus decree is to be set on stelae in Greek, demotic and hieroglyphic and placed in the temples of the first, second, and third ranks 'in the most conspicuous place' (ἐν τῷ ἐπιφανεστάτῳ τόπῳ).[47] This phrase is a standard expression in Hellenistic honorific decrees that refers in general terms to a highly visible place, often further specified as 'of the city', 'of the agora', 'of the temple' and so forth, where statues and decrees of various kinds were placed.[48] In the Ptolemaic sacerdotal decrees, the demotic Egyptian translation of the phrase follows the Greek fairly closely: *n pꜣ mꜣꜥ nty wnḥ n pꜣ irpy*: 'in the place that is open (or visible) in the temple'. Rather than this glossing periphrasis, the hieroglyphic translation uses a more specific architectural term: the decrees are to be placed in the *wsḫt-mšꜥ*, the court (or hall) of the people.[49] The term appears to refer to the public area of the temple, where the people could meet the gods when they made their appearances in various festival processions, and its more usual name was, accordingly, the *wsḫt-ḥbyt* or festival court or hall.[50] The find spots of both the Karnak and Elkab versions of the decree suggest that their original placement was in one of these public areas of the

---

[47] The instructions for the placement of the stelae are common to the decrees in general. Either it is to be placed 'in the most conspicious place' as just noted, or it is to be placed next to a statue that has been previously stipulated as an honour for the king. In the latter case, the instructions for the *statue* say that it is to be set up 'in the most conspicuous place' (ἐν τῷ ἐπιφανεστάτῳ τόπῳ) in all the temples of Egypt (the Memphis decree, 196 BCE). In Philae I (184 BCE) there is even a chain of references that builds on a previous decree (Memphis).

[48] On typical *epiphanestatoi topoi* of the Hellenistic city, see Ma 2013a: 75–98.

[49] This term does not appear to have been widely used outside of the decrees. Dictionaries and lexicographical studies on Egyptian architectural terms only cite the decrees as evidence. See Spencer 1984: 77, 95 n. 150. The last reference is a citation of Erman and Grapow 1926–1963: vol. 1, p. 461, 10. For that reference, the *Belegstellen* only cite the Canopus and Philae decrees. At the temple of Edfu, the forecourt area is called the *wsḫ.t ḥby.t* or 'festival hall', referring to its ritual function, and this term is widely used in other temple inscriptions. This raises the intriguing possibility that *wsḫt-mšꜥ* was used intentionally in the decrees to draw even more attention to the idea of the space as 'public'.

[50] This would make some sense of the Demotic periphrasis, which in its roundabout way captures the meaning of ἐπιφανής, but also alludes to this ritual aspect of the public space of the temple. The term *wnḥ* (related to *wn-ḥr* – open the face) may refer to both openness and to the epiphany that occurred in the forecourt of a temple when a procession of the god's image moved out the gates and along the dromos.

temple,[51] as was the case with other decrees that have been found roughly *in situ*.[52]

At whatever moment these decrees were damaged, whether it was during one of the revolts that affected the Thebaid or not, the act of mutilation took place in a public area of the temple, and therefore either the action or its results would have been visible not only to priests but to members of the general populace of Thebes and Elkab. This was, therefore, very likely a dramatic public performance of violence, but what did it mean? We have no direct evidence of motive, but we can say more about the nature of the document attacked. As mentioned previously, the texts on the stone were copies of the Canopus decree, which was not a traditional Egyptian decree. It was a version of the widespread Hellenistic genre of the honorific decree that a synod of priests gathered from all over Egypt near Alexandria, at Canopus, had adapted to the political, linguistic and cultural circumstances of the Ptolemaic kingdom.[53] In this

---

[51] The location of the *wsḫt-ḥbyt* within the structure of a temple seems to have varied somewhat, but it could include the first hypostyle hall of a temple, or the more open forecourts and processional ways that preceded them along the central axis of the temple. For the architectural referent of *wsḫt* in Demotic and hieroglyphic Egyptian, see Gallo 1987: 37, who notes that it often refers to the initial columned hall(s) of a temple. According to the evidence assembled by Spencer 1984: 71-80, the term *wsḫt* on its own can refer to any hall or court along the axis of the temple, while the area accessible to non-priests during festivals is called the *wsḫt-ḥbyt* or festival hall/court. Karnak location: Although *wsḫt-ḥbyt* was used of the Twenty-second-Dynasty forecourt of Karnak (Spencer 1984: 84) which precedes the great hypostyle hall, it appears that the hall where the damaged stele of the Canopus decree was discovered was also publicly accessible on certain occasions. In the later history of the temple, probably in the Ptolemaic period, a kiosk, such as those used as stopping points in processions, was added to the central aisle of the hypostyle hall extending from the antechamber of the third pylon and connecting the first three columns on either side of the aisle. See Barguet 1962: 77. Brand 2001: 1-3 also notes that the massive gates to the second pylon, the outermost entryway to the hypostyle hall, had been destroyed during some violent episode (perhaps the sack of Thebes by Ashurbanipal in 663 BCE), and were only repaired under Ptolemy VI. Without doors to close it off, the hypostyle hall probably become part of the more public festival court. Elkab location: its discovery near the gate of Nectanebo I at the temple of Nekhbet places it at the first pylon that gave passage through the enclosure wall to the sanctuary, and so the decree was positioned along the dromos or processional way of the temple, also in public space.

[52] Though few of the inscribed copies of the decrees have been discovered in controlled archaeological excavations, contexts are known for a few other decrees. Several years ago a new copy of the Canopus decree was discovered roughly *in situ* at the temple of Bubastis (Tell Basta) – and it was located at the entrance to the forecourt (Tietze, Lange, and Hallof 2005). The Philae decrees did not follow the instructions to the letter: rather than on a stele, they were inscribed on the southern part of the east wall of the birth house at Philae. Nevertheless, they face the forecourt of the Isis temple, and so conform to the spirit of public display (von Recklinghausen 2018: 11-13, 359).

[53] See Clarysse 2000; and Moyer 2011b: 117-125.

decree, they took on, in formal terms at least, the usual role of the assembly or council of a Greek *polis* or *koinon* in order to issue a decree praising Ptolemy III for his benefactions to Egypt, and enacting a number of measures, primarily cultic, in his honour and in honour of his recently deceased daughter, the princess Berenike. This was, as I have argued elsewhere, a complex document in which Egyptian priests adopted the role of a Greek state to honour a Macedonian king as an Egyptian pharaoh.[54] In their translation of a Greek genre into an Egyptian context, however, they made various commensurations between key terms of the genre and Egyptian concepts, which suggest a polite equivocation, or 'sly civility' on the part of the priests in not quite assenting to the universality of Greek political discourse.[55]

These priestly honorific decrees, passed in temples and displayed in the 'most conspicuous place', in the 'court of the people' of Egyptian temples, seem to have borrowed some of the language of Egyptian jurisdiction to translate the Hellenistic genre. Immediately after the dating formula of the decree comes a word that announces the genre. In the Greek text, the word is *psêphisma* (decree), while the Egyptian equivalents given are *sḫꜣw* in the hieroglyphic version and *wt* in the demotic, each of which sheds light on how the texts were understood from a specifically Egyptian perspective. The hieroglyphic term *sḫꜣw* is a substantive related to the verb 'remember' and so it is usually translated as 'remembrance' or 'memorial'. This is significant in itself, since it represents the stele as a material embodiment of memory, the destruction of which, in the Egyptian practice often loosely termed *damnatio memoriae*, was not just an act of forgetting, but a magical negation of existence, a relegation to the realm of non-being that was often directed at enemies, criminals, or rulers deemed illegitimate.[56] This is a possible explanation of the logic of mutilating decrees, but since there is no clear evidence that the name or image of Ptolemy III was specifically and ritually targeted in this case, the fit is not exact.[57] On a more mundane

---

[54] Moyer 2011b: 123–124.   [55] On sly civility, see Bhabha 1985.
[56] For an overview of the practice, see Bochi 1999. Note also the various examples in Ritner 1993: 141, 148, 200, 213.
[57] There is at least one known case of this: the defacement of Ptolemaic cartouches in tomb chambers at Tuna el Gebel/Hermopolis West. See Huss 1994: 143.

level, the term *sḫ3w* can also in Late Egyptian refer to an official report, apparently one that was used in an administrative or juridical context,[58] and this overlaps to a certain extent with the demotic Egyptian term used. Although the demotic word *wt* derives from the classical Egyptian *wḏ* 'command', it has a wider semantic range in demotic, and was used for the written decisions that panels of Egyptian priestly judges, known in Greek sources as the *laokritai*, produced and gave to the successful party in a lawsuit.[59] Given the temple context in which the decrees were issued and displayed, and the formal Egyptian terminology used to translate the structure of a Hellenistic honorific decree as though they were issued by a panel of *laokritai*, the texts present themselves as records of a quasi-legal decision that awarded honours to the Macedonian king on the basis of his correct fulfilment of his role as a good pharaoh. If that is the case, the destruction of the decrees would have amounted to a rejection of the judgement that they recorded and an attempt to nullify the decision. In other words, this would have been a public, material communicative act expressing the belief that Ptolemy III was not a good pharaoh and had not carried out his responsibilities to the people and gods of Egypt.

This does not bring us closer to narrowing down the temporal moment in which the Canopus decrees at Karnak and Elkab were attacked. It could have happened under Ptolemy III at any point after the publication of the Canopus decree, as there is evidence of tensions

---

[58] The term is used of various kinds of official reports in the hieratic ostraca from Deir el Medina, and many of these recorded unlawful acts, suggesting that they were documents intended to be used in the course of legal proceedings. While several of these memoranda appear to outline crimes or 'charges' against an individual, none contains a judgment or decision. See McDowell 1990: 16–18; Hudson 2014: 80–84; Haring 2003: 108–110. The Coptic word ⲥϩⲓ (written copy, diploma) may be derived from *sḫ3w* (see Crum 1939: 383b; Černý 1976: 173)

[59] This usage is attested, for example, in the *Hermopolis Legal Code*, a demotic Egyptian legal manual of the third century BCE, and in later trial transcripts. P. Mattha V, 2; VIII, 12; the template for such documents, which is provided in the manual, even uses the label '*wt*' at the beginning of the document as in the practice of the Ptolemaic decrees. For transcription and translation of this passage, see Donker van Heel 1990: 87. In the transcript of a trial from Siut, the term is used in this sense as well (P. dem. BM 10591 vo IV 1; Thompson 1934: 54). On the meaning of *wt* in the legal context see also Lippert 2004: 80–81. For discussion of the terms *sḫ3w*, *wt* and ψήφισμα in the decrees see Pfeiffer 2004: 56, 74–75; el-Masri, Altenmüller, and Thissen 2013: 79; von Recklinghausen 2018: 34.

and even of a possible revolt early in his reign.[60] On the other hand, the attacks could just as well have happened posthumously – a retrospective indictment of his rule or of the general character of the dynasty. Nor do we come closer to identifying the agents of the attack. Interpreting the defacement as a response to the genre, terms, and content of the decree would seem to require that the agent(s) be able to read one or more of the scripts and languages used, and be familiar with the conventions of legal documents. A member of the literate priesthood, who thought that the Ptolemies had not conducted their rule in accordance with Maʻat would be an obvious possibility. On the other hand, in a society where writing was an ubiquitous part of everyday life,[61] fully functional literacy would not necessarily be required to understand the content of a publicly displayed decree, as well its genre and some of its formal features. Anyone who had occasion to conduct legal or other business in and around the public areas of the temple could, in theory, become aware of what the decree represented through a combination of observation and oral communication, and be able to situate the textual and material form of the inscription in a framework of everyday practices related to this public context. Though agents and timelines remain open questions, this perspective does make the moment of resistance more comprehensible. Given the public context, whoever damaged the decrees must have done so with the assistance, or at least tacit approval of others present, or even against the protestations of others present. The scene may or may not have been tumultuous, but if we make even a modest effort to accord the agent or agents reason and morality on their own terms, a plausible case emerges that the attack had meaning and was a considered public gesture, rather than a spasmodic, angry reaction to whatever general or

---

[60] Two years prior to the first surviving sacerdotal decree (the decree of 243 BCE), there occurred the first known episode of resistance to Ptolemaic rule, the *domestica seditio* of 245 BCE (Justin *Epit.* 27.1.9). As pointed out by McGing 1997: 274–277, little is known about what happened, and it seems unlikely that this was a major event. He points to the episode in PSI V 502 discussed earlier and similar evidence as indications of 'normal' tensions and disputes, rather than major outbreaks of violence. See also Huss 1994: 142–143 who sees the destruction of the decrees as acts of resistance regardless of when they occured. Indeed, he argues that the Karnak example of the Canopus decree was damaged shortly after the promulgation of the decree in 238 BCE, thus at a high point of Ptolemaic rule.

[61] Bagnall 2011.

particular indignities and deprivations may have been antecedent to the decision to mutilate the inscriptions.[62]

The final episode of resistance that I would like briefly to discuss provides a parallel to the destruction of the decrees as a deliberate, public symbolic action. The episode is documented in *P. Amherst* 2.30, which is dated to the time of the revolt of Dionysius Petoserapis and the contemporary troubles in Thebes that followed the invasion of Antiochus IV in the 160s BCE.[63] The events described were therefore right in the heart of a broader period of disturbances in the Hellenistic world, as well as a more local crisis of pharaonic kingship precipitated in part by a foreign invasion of Egyptian territory. The papyrus is a fragment of a report on the resolution of a dispute between two individuals with Egyptian names: Thembos and Tesenouphis. At issue was the ownership of a house in Soknopaiou Nesos (Dime). In the course of this proceeding, testimony was given by the village elders that the house belonged to Marres, the father of Tesenouphis, 'before the war', probably before the war with Antiochus.[64] The documents (*syngraphai*) for the house, however, had been held by a certain Kondylos, a fisherman. This Kondylos gave additional testimony that in the city, presumably the nome capital Krokodilopolis/Arsinoe (Medinet al Fayum), he had been forced by the 'Egyptian rebels' to bring the documents forward and to burn them.[65] This Kondylos was probably a *syngraphophylax*, a guardian of contracts, who, in Greek practice, was one of the witnesses who held the

---

[62] There is a possible comparandum in the destruction of the Babylonian copy of Darius' Behistun inscription, which was shattered into small pieces. It was also erected in a public space – on the Great Processional Way inside the Ishtar Gate. Seidl 1999: 114 dated its destruction to one of the Babylonian revolts against Xerxes. For further details on this inscription, which showed efforts to adapt the Behistun inscription to the Babylonian context, see Seidl 1999 and Granerød 2013: 467–470. I thank Paul Kosmin for drawing my attention to this fascinating parallel.

[63] The dating of this document to the time around the revolt of Dionysius Petoserapis goes back to the original editors (Grenfell and Hunt 1900–1901). One of the individuals, named Tesenouphis, also appears in P. Amh. 2.33.5, a document dated to *c*.157 BCE. Marres, the father of Tesenouphis, is also attested in P. Amh. 2.42 and 2.43, dating to 179 and 173 BCE respectively, so the chronology fits.

[64] McGing 1997: 290.

[65] P. Amh. 2.30, col. 2, ll. 23–36: ... τοὺς ἐκ τῆς κώμης πρεσβυτέρους, προσεμαρτύρουν τὸν τοῦ Τενεσούφιος Μαρρῆν πατέρα κατεσχηκέναι τον οἰκίαν πρὸ τοῦ πολέμου. ὁμοίως καὶ Κονδύλου ἑνὸς τῶν ἁλιείων, προσεμαρτύρει ἔχειν τὰς τοῦ πατρὸς τοῦ Τεσενούφιος συνγραφὰς τῆς δηλουμένης οἰκίας καὶ ἐν τῆι πόλει ἠναγκάσθην ὑπὸ τῶν Αἰγυπτίων ἀποστατῶν ἐνέγκαι τὰς συνγραφὰς καὶ ταύτας κατακαῦσαι.

REVOLTS, RESISTANCE, AND THE MATERIALITY   171

authoritative copies of agreements, in case of dispute between the parties.⁶⁶ Since the report in the papyrus was in Greek and may have been prepared for a legal proceeding before Greek officials, it seems probable that the burned contracts were being kept by a guardian according to Greek practice, but there is a possible parallel to the *syngraphophylax* in Egyptian law, the ꜥrbṯ ('trustee' or 'document holder'), so it is possible that Kondylos may have held demotic contracts, especially since the parties involved had Egyptian names.⁶⁷ In either case, these were legal documents which could have been produced either in a Greek or in an Egyptian lawcourt, had they not been burned.

Several scholars have compared the destruction of these documents to other social revolutions in which there was an effort to cancel debts or redistribute property,⁶⁸ and this may well be the case, but the specific details of this act of resistance merit closer examination. This was a violent, dramatic, public performance that destroyed the legal documents that Kondylos held, documents whose authority was ultimately backed by the Ptolemaic regime. The rebels could presumably have seized and destroyed the documents themselves, but they compelled Kondylos, the guardian or trustee of the contracts of Thembos and Tesenouphis, and perhaps others, to bring them forward 'in the city', and burn them himself. If Kondylos was acting in the capacity of a *syngraphophylax*, his duty would be not only to keep the contract, but

---

⁶⁶ Rostovtzeff 1941: 2.722 suggested that Kondylos was a *syngraphophylax*. On this official and Ptolemaic notarial practice, see now Claytor 2014: 31–34.
⁶⁷ See the *Chicago Demotic Dictionary* s.v. ꜥrbṯ for references. One of the earliest discussions of this title is by Nims 1938: 72–82, who pointed out two demotic letters of agreement in the University of Michigan papyrus collection that originate from Philadelphia in the Fayum, and are dated c.190 BCE: both deal with the sale of houses, and refer to the ꜥrbṯ as the keeper of the letters of agreement and other documents. The role of the ꜥrbṯ appears to be to hold a set of documents until the terms of an agreement are met, and then to relinquish them as stipulated in the agreement. Thus the ꜥrbṯ may not simply be a neutral third party who holds the documents for reference, but may be involved in the process of managing the fulfilment of the agreement through his handling of the documents. Whether Kondylos was a *syngraphophylax*, or an ꜥrbṯ, the destruction of documents in his possession could have resulted in him having to give testimony about the documents in a legal arbitration.
⁶⁸ See Veïsse 2004: 136, 139ff. McGing 1997: 293 suggests a mixture of social revolution and nationalism owing to the presumed Greek identity of Kondylos and/or the documents he keeps, although neither identification can be entirely certain (see previous note). The interpretation of the burning of the documents as part of a social revolution goes at least as far back as Rostovtzeff 1941: 2.722.

to produce it in a court of law if required.⁶⁹ The role of *syngraphophylax* had already become subject to state regulation over a century earlier (*c*.275 BCE), so this was a formalized position, and his duties would be familiar to anyone who had made a Greek contract.⁷⁰ The act of forcing a *syngraphophylax* to produce and then destroy contracts in the nome capital seems to instrumentalize his usual role in order to create a parody of an official act. Rather than a trial at which the documents produced help the presiding officials to render a verdict, the performance over which the rebels presided dramatized a harsh verdict against the documents and whatever practices had authorized them as legal instruments. Social revolution and an intervention in property rights may well have been intended, but the ritualized action of the rebels also aimed to make a vivid statement that the legal documents of the Ptolemaic regime were no longer valid, and perhaps even that they had been authorized by an unjust and illegitimate government. Some forty years earlier, the rebel pharaoh in Thebes, Haronnophris, shortly after he claimed his throne, instituted a new, archaizing chancellery and documents in his territory began to be dated by his regnal years and with his epithets.⁷¹ Had the revolt of the mid 160s BCE been more successful, perhaps the public destruction of documents in the nome capital would have been the beginning of a similar effort to create a rupture in practices of authorization, a break with the practices of rulers judged to be unlawful and illegitimate.

These examples all reveal that the Ptolemaic state was weighed and found wanting not only through the medium of a few recondite prophetic texts that circulated among literate elites. There were public practices of resistance that made use of the authoritative places, documents, and officials that constituted the state's power in order to protest the unfairness of its dealings, to contest claims of the ruler's good

---

⁶⁹ This can be inferred from two examples of testimony from *syngraphophylaktes*: *M.Chr.* 28.23–27 and *P.Heid.* VIII 414.

⁷⁰ It is unclear whether an ꜥrbṱ would be expected to produce documents in a law court in the same way as a *syngraphophylax*, but since the duties of such a trustee appear to include rendering documents to the appropriate parties on the fulfilment of the terms of an agreement, the act of compelling Kondylos to produce and destroy documents would also have played on his formal role in some way.

⁷¹ See Depauw 2006 and Veïsse, this volume, Chapter 2.

conduct, or to reject its legality. By situating acts of resistance in their local material and moral contexts, the motivations and considerations that led the Egyptian crowd to refuse demands or take the desperate gamble of violent action become somewhat more legible. In none of the cases that I have explored is it self-evident that moral evaluations of the Ptolemies were simply cover for ethnic hatred or cultural antagonisms.[72] The few insights into the practices of the Egyptian crowd that we can wring from the evidence suggest a far more considered reaction to the Ptolemaic state. Food shortages, fiscal oppression, losses of social power and standing all created stresses that undoubtedly contributed to outbreaks of resistance, but they also would have occasioned critical evaluations of the pharaoh and his performance of his role by traditional standards. These latter considerations should not be left out of the complex of factors that influenced the Egyptian crowd to revolt. To do so would be to overwrite their voices with presumed universals, or simply to regard their voices as incomprehensible. The larger historiographic conversation to which this volume of essays contributes at one point took S. K. Eddy's book *The King is Dead* (1961), as a reference point: the last monograph to undertake a systematic comparative investigation of resistance and rebellion in the Hellenistic world. Eddy found many causes for resistance to Ptolemaic rule in economic exploitation, class tensions, oppressive governance, and ethnic and cultural antagonism between Greeks and Egyptians, but the core of his broader comparative enterprise, as well as his analysis of Ptolemaic Egypt, was the study of religious resistance to Hellenistic rule and the pursuit of restored native kingship as a means to protect indigenous laws and traditions, and to remedy social and economic ills. Although the work is out of date in its method, theory, and evidentiary base, and has its flaws, including an uncritical use of sentiments and terminology derived from the then-contemporary conflicts of a decolonizing world, and constant slippages between his central theme and national or cultural-ethnic antagonisms, the virtue of Eddy's work was to take seriously the indigenous paradigms

---

[72] In this respect, my conclusions are similar to those of Stevens in this volume, Chapter 4.

of kingship, religion, and law through which Persians, Jews, and Egyptians formulated their horizons of expectation and aspiration in response to the new conditions of Hellenistic rule. If we are to do more than render revolt mechanical or incomprehensible, we would do well to follow this impulse and try to understand local moral frameworks and logics of resistance.

PART III
THE EDGES OF RESISTANCE

PART III

THE EDGES OF RUSSIANNESS

7
An Impossible Resistance? Anatolian Populations, Ethnicity, and Greek Powers in Asia Minor during the Second Century BCE

Laurent Capdetrey

The second century BCE is a tipping point and a time of reconfiguration in the heart of the Hellenistic period and it is interesting to observe the effects in Asia Minor. This region, from the Aegean to Anatolia, made up a particular territorial sub-group because of its political fragmentation and even more so by the presence of several ethno-cultural layers.[1] Nevertheless, it remains difficult to perceive the degrees of identity construction of the different populations of Asia Minor in the second century, even though the partially accessible material culture can supply a few limited clues that are always delicate to interpret. In fact, while ceramics, funerary practices, epichoric languages, and architectural forms can in fact be read as ethnic signs and identity markers they are never explicit markers of a transparent ethnicity.

These issues cannot be tackled if the more or less recent[2] developments in the theoretical field concerning collective identities, and in particular ethnic and cultural identities, are not taken into account.[3] To put it briefly, while the constructivist consensus may not be in question today, it nevertheless masks clear differences in approach or in the

---

[1] Debord 1999; Briant 2006. [2] Already Besançon-Pisa-Rome 1983; Barth 1969.
[3] Cf. Müller 2014. Also Malkin and Müller 2012; McInerney 2014.

Laurent Capdetrey, *An Impossible Resistance? Anatolian Populations, Ethnicity, and Greek Powers in Asia Minor during the Second Century BCE* In: *Cultures of Resistance in the Hellenistic East*. Edited by: Paul J. Kosmin and Ian S. Moyer, Oxford University Press. © Oxford University Press 2022.
DOI: 10.1093/oso/9780192863478.003.0008

detailed understanding of concepts of ethnicity and ethnic identity, which are often confused.[4] Here we will use these two notions of ethnicity and ethnic identity by following S. Jones[5] and taking ethnicity to be the complex *process* of construction and production of *ethnic identities*, which are never fixed or transcendent. This is a process which leads to the emergence of realities that are both objective and subjective, assigned or claimed, for an ethnic group that is both aware of itself and perceived and designated as such.[6] With a view to comparison with the other regions of the Hellenistic Middle East, and in particular with the situation in Judea, at question is also the desire and the ability of Anatolian populations to maintain or to (re)build an eventual ethnic identity, at least partially. C. Morgan's work on the archaic period has questioned the link between the process of ethnic constructions and political frameworks. Memorial networks, religious structures, and confrontations with otherness would have played a much more important role than *political* structures in the building of the ethnicity-process of the *ethnê* in mainland Greece and in southern Italy.[7] In other words, anthropological dynamics and social and cultural interactions, rather than institutional and political impulses, would be more salient in the emergence of collective and ethnic identities.[8] With the distance lent by time the case of Asia Minor, in the heart of the Hellenistic period, provides an exemplary case for testing hypotheses like those which, on the contrary, associate perceived reality and affirmation of ethnic identities primarily with their articulation in a political framework.[9]

In order to think through the forms of ethnicity in second-century Asia Minor we must examine the possible link between the process of regional affirmation/fragmentation and potential identity dynamics. And of course, we must ask the basic question of what role conflict and identity consciousness played in these processes. We must be careful however not to confuse identity *revival* and conflict, if only because

---

[4] Cf. Müller 2014; Hall 1997: 20–26; Hall 2002: 1–29. Also Luce 2007: 11–23.
[5] Jones 1997: 84–87.
[6] In this paper, the use of ethnic appellations such as 'Greek', 'Lycian', etc. should be taken as assuming this understanding of ethnicity.
[7] Morgan 2003.   [8] Azoulay 2014.   [9] Prost 2007: 112–113.

forms of resistance can be multiple (political, military, cultural, etc.). If a common criterion must be defined, rather than war, it is better to identify the ambiguous affirmation of a polymorphic otherness in relation to politico-cultural norms purveyed by the Greco-Macedonian powers.[10] The central question therefore consists in asking whether, in the second century, the populations of Asia Minor and Anatolia manifested the desire to define themselves – even partially – as being different from the Greeks, to perceive this, and to transform this perception into a position of opposition with political stakes: in other words into an 'identity moment'. And we must ask whether the indisputable regional affirmations (in the Anatolian kingdoms, Lycia, and to a lesser extent in Caria and Pisidia) can be explained by the expression of an ethnic-cultural identity rather than by questions of territory or by economic, fiscal, or administrative factors, independent of identity issues. Contemporary fascination with the issue of identity in fact too often leads to the neglect of powerful forces which cannot simply be reduced to this one topic any more than they can be reduced to a political expression of identity. In addition to re-examining their basis, the questioning of regional solidarity or identities also raises questions about the forms they could take. We know, for example, that Hasmonaean power was able to regain many of the categories and characteristics of Greek royal power as a means of political affirmation. This reflects more contemporary practices that saw liberation or decolonization movements based on the discourses and organizational methods of the colonial powers, for example. In other words, it was a question of borrowing the tools of the dominant to challenge domination. Asia Minor of the second century offers examples of this type of transfer and hybridization that deserve to be explored precisely. Finally, still from the point of view of modalities, it is necessary to question the role of violence, which was always possible without being a necessary means or an inevitability. And one may wonder in particular whether, unlike the situation in Judea, the revolts in Asia Minor were impossible, useful or inappropriate given the specific characteristics of identity and/or regional constructions.

[10] Jones 1997: 84.

1. All Greek? The Dynamics of Ethnicity during the High Hellenistic Era in Western Asia Minor

With a certain sense of provocation, the question could be put differently: how could one not be Greek in Asia Minor of the second century? In fact, the situation was somewhat more complex and we would obviously be wrong to want to reduce the cultural processes at work to a uniform unhindered conquest by Greek political and cultural norms.[11] Ancient Asia Minor was, above all, a moving mosaic composed of neighbouring populations, sometimes overlapping,[12] with fairly clearly defined identities[13] that were nevertheless deeply mixed together. From the Classical period onward the practices of the western Anatolian populations were sometimes profoundly influenced by dynamics that were differential from the point of view of ethnic or cultural crystallizations or redefinitions, beginning with their elites. This can be observed especially in dynastic Lycia of the fourth century, in the case of Pericles of Limyra in particular.[14] And the violent context of territorial construction of the Hellenistic kingdoms helped to accelerate a certain number of earlier developments. The local populations (Greeks from the coastal cities, Carians, Lycians, Pisidians, Phrygians, Bithynians, etc.) were periodically subjected to phenomena they could not control: submission to different royal powers, forced mobility, the settlement of Macedonian, Greek, and also Celtic populations.[15] Only the regions held by the Anatolian or Pontic kings enjoyed relative political and territorial stability, partly because they were away from Macedonian powers, but certainly because they sheltered from certain kinds of violence linked to the confrontation with Greek cities on the coast and with Hellenistic kings.[16]

---

[11] Mitchell 1993; Elton and Reger 2007; Sartre 2003.
[12] On Carians and their neighbours: Rumscheid 2009; Ratté 2009.
[13] For Herodotus, the Carians had a perfectly clear identity. They claimed their indigenousness, possessed a sanctuary to Zeus *Karios* at Mylasa (Herodotus, 1, 171) and at the time of the Persian conquest they met at *Leukai Stelai* then at Labraunda at the sanctuary of Zeus *Stratios* (Herod., 5, 118–119). Lycian urbanism: Kolb 2013: 113–124; Borchhardt 2003: 63–64. On Pericles: Briant 1996: 626–627 and 689–692.
[14] Kolb 2003: 212–213; Kolb 2000.
[15] Billows 1995: 146–182; Briant 1999. Cilicia: Sayar 2007; De Giorgi 2011.
[16] Hannestad 1996; Scholten 2007: 18–20; Marek 2009: 35–36.

Yet this powerful maelstrom, with long-lasting effects, hides deeper currents.

The first element of continuity lies in the opposition between a western maritime Asia Minor, deeply marked by the Greek presence and by the density of cities, and an interior, Anatolian Asia Minor, which for some time had remained apart from political and cultural hybridization.[17] One of the paradoxical effects of the Macedonian conquest was that it reinforced the opposition, at least at first, all the while modifying the geographical contours. The settling of colonies or the founding of cities mainly concerned the coastal regions, the western plains and the main valleys, notably in Lydia and in southern Phrygia,[18] as well as in the plains of Cilicia.[19] This effort left aside the more difficult zones which were less useful and more hostile, such as the mountainous region of Pisidia, a large part of inner Lycia, central Phrygia, and even most of Mysia, not to mention the northern Anatolian kingdoms.

This implantation was the source of an undeniable spread of new populations – populations with Macedonian, Greek, and Thracian identities – the scope of whose influence, it must be admitted, is difficult to discern.[20] However, the display of Macedonian identity in many of the colonies during the imperial era suggests the maintenance of a strong feeling of ethnic belonging, of a settler identity.[21] But, between the end of the fourth century and the end of the third century, there were at the most only a few tens of thousands of veterans and colonists who were settled in the valleys of Asia Minor and western Anatolia.[22] Numbers were not high enough to deeply impact the demography of different regions in Asia Minor.[23] Therefore it is not the distribution of new populations that could strongly modify regional forms of ethnicity. Other, more profound forces were also at work.

---

[17] Marek 2009: 35–36.
[18] Cf. Cohen 1995: 145–409; Billows 1995: 179–180. Also Thonemann 2013b: 17–18.
[19] Sayar 2007; De Giorgi 2011.
[20] Macedonian and Thessalian colonists in South Phrygia, in Dokimeion's territory: Thonemann 2013: 17–18. In Pisidia: Talloen 2015: 85–86.
[21] Cf. Macedonian shields at Sagalassos: Waelkens and Kosmetatou 1997; Kosmetatou 2005. North and central Phrygia: Thonemann 2013: 24. About Macedonians in Asia Minor: Mitchell 2018; Mitchell 2019.
[22] Billows 1995: 153–154; Bosworth 2002: 64–97.   [23] Bosworth, 2002: 64–97.

In fact, it is during the course of the fourth century in Asia Minor that we note a phenomenon of hybridization of political and cultural forms, in particular in the south-west. We must remember that Greek had already been the language of power of the dynasts in Hecatomnid Caria. In architectural and artistic matters, a kind of Ionian *koinê* was also developed in this same Hecatomnid space in the first half of the fourth century.[24] Still in Caria, we note a clear reduction and then the abandoning of the use of Carian in inscriptions from the third century onwards.[25] So, in local communities Greek names tended to be substituted for the Carian onomastics from the third century and even more so during the second century[26] even if at Milas they kept up the habit of giving Carian names until the end of the Hellenistic period.[27] The case of Lycia is both similar and yet quite different. While before Alexander's conquest Lycian inscriptions were numerous and were an important marker used by Lycian elites alongside Greek,[28] we know of no Lycian inscriptions after the end of the fourth century.[29] This obviously does not mean the end of the spoken language and even less that of Lycian onomastics, which partially continued,[30] especially in central Lycia.[31] But, like Caria or Phrygia,[32] between the end of the fourth century and the third century Lycia saw an increasing linguistic shift towards Greek in public documents. It is clear that the administrative use of Greek by the Hecatomnid dynasts in Caria and then in Lycia had the effect of accelerating a process which was itself continued by the Macedonian kings and the regional elites at the beginning of the Hellenistic period. In Pisidia, however, the outline was different since Pisidian dialects were

---

[24] Pedersen 2013; Hellström 2009; Henry 2013a.
[25] Piras 2009: 241–248; Benda-Weber 2005: 63–66. Of course, we are aware that language use and onomastics are often, but not always, means of signalling or detecting ethnicity. They remain *indicia* rather than absolute *criteria*, to use the terminology adopted by Jonathan Hall in his work on Greek ethnicity (1997 and 2002).
[26] Debord et al. 2001; Robert 1963: 82; Blümel 1994: 85–86.
[27] In contrast, they disappear much earlier in Kaunos: Bresson 2007a: 219–220; Robert 1963.
[28] Le Roy 1987: 263–266 and Le Roy 2004b: 8–9. [29] Bryce 1986: 42–98.
[30] At Xanthos, two lists of 141 subscribers' names found at Letoon and dating from 150–120 BCE, included twenty names which were not Greek (Lycian, Carian, Persian): Bousquet and Gauthier 1994: 355–356. Cf. Briant 2006: 323 and Colvin 2004.
[31] Kolb 2007: 288.
[32] Brixhe 2013: 59. Peter Thonemann showed that Phrygian was no longer used as a written language from the end of the fifth century or the beginning of the fourth century. In its written form, this language only re-emerged in the second century. Thonemann 2013: 12–13.

definitely kept alive until the imperial age,[33] at least outside urban centres,[34] even though a process of Hellenization of the language and the onomastics was clearly happening during the third century and into the second century.[35] Bithynia and Pontus seem to have followed the same trajectory with a time lag, towards the lower Hellenistic era.[36] The first half of the Hellenistic age therefore saw multilingualism maintained in western Asia Minor but it was unequal depending on the regions and Greek always prevailed in public usage. In this sense, in the second century the use of Greek was no longer a clear ethnic identity marker whereas the use of indigenous languages – little attested but nevertheless quite real – clearly fulfilled this role.[37]

Unsurprisingly, this phenomenon of cultural hybridization in favour of certain Greek norms can also be found in the religious field. Apparently the substratum of very ancient divinities was maintained but often through a process of adopting and transforming Greek gods who partially took their place[38] without totally smothering them,[39] particularly in the great Anatolian sanctuaries.[40] This pattern is widely attested and perfectly described in Caria and Lycia,[41] and also in Pisidia.[42] In Lycia at the end of the Classical period and more so during the Hellenistic age, Apollo became an essential figure in regional religious identity and doubtless also in a kind of ethnicity, following a fairly complicated process of indigenous identity reappropriation that was

---

[33] Pisidia: Mitchell 1991: 121; Talloen 2015: 82-83. Caria and Lycia: Marek 2013.
[34] Bracke 1993: 23-24.   [35] Mitchell 1991: 121.   [36] Marek 2009: 36-37.
[37] Cf. Celtic languages and Galatian ethnicity: Strobel 1996: 139 and Strobel 2009: 138-139.
[38] Cf. Prost 2007: 103-106. Le Roy 2004a: 263-274. The links between Zeus in Caria and Luwian and Carian gods: Debord 2009: 252-257.
[39] On the continuance of indigenous religions in the rural Pisidian world in the Hellenistic era: Talloen 2015: 357-358. On Maeonia where the indigenous religious tradition remained very much alive: Robert 1963: 321-322.
[40] Debord 1982: 54-55 and 163-165; Magie 1950: 139-142. Pessinus: Virgilio 1981; Welles 1934: nn. 55-61. On the link voluntarily maintained by Philetairos with the cult of Cybele in Pessinus, in particular by the foundation of a sanctuary near Pergamos and by the construction of a first temple on a new site in Pessinus itself, in association with the citadel of the priestly family: Verlinde 2010 and Verlinde 2015: 65-72, where the author underlines the solution of continuity with the Phrygian antecedents, both by the location in the valley and by the monumentalization that is beginning to take place. Also on the cult of Cybele: Roller 1999; Tsetskhladze 2018. The existence and importance of this cult in the Inner Troad, at the foot of Mount Ida, is known as early as the fourth century: Ellis-Evans 2019: 65-66.
[41] Lycia and Xanthos: Le Roy 2004b: 12-13; Bryce 1983b.
[42] Talloen 2015: 93-101 and 113-115.

associated with belonging to a system of legendary and mythological links with the Aegean Greek world.[43] In Caria it has been shown that religious acculturation in the Classical era was based on constant contacts leading to the progressive fixing of a mythological fabric around different Carian Zeus figures, for example, but this was a fabric that was still not fixed in the Hellenistic age.[44]

In this field, the main break took place elsewhere. In fact, the high Hellenistic period saw certain major western Anatolian sanctuaries taken over by the cities. At Labraunda, from the middle of the third century, control of the sanctuary was seized by the city of Milas with the support of successive royal powers, to the detriment of the priestly family.[45] And the same thing could be seen at Xanthos with the Letoon. In other words, although the sanctuaries obviously played a role in the maintenance and the structuring of local indigenous identities in Asia Minor, this was absolutely not in opposition to the Greek norms, dominant since at least the end of the Classical age. This was the continuation of a wider phenomenon: that of the spread of the civic and para-civic model of organization. It is evident that from the end of the fourth century in Caria and in some regions of Lycia,[46] in the third and second centuries in Pisidia,[47] in Pamphylia,[48] in Cilicia,[49] and in the more inland regions, the norm of community organization was that of the city.[50] The haste of the Phrygians from the Tyriaion plain to have their city status recognized by Eumenes II at the beginning of the second century, around 188 BCE,[51] is a reminder of how the civic model was considered as the institutional norm to be attained for reasons that were both statutory and cultural. Recognizable everywhere throughout western Asia Minor (in Phrygia, Lycia, Caria, and Pisidia, as well as in Nicomedian Bithynia[52]) in the second century this phenomenon was independent of any external political constraint,[53] even if its royal basis and the powers' preference for the civic model reinforced this norm and even though the

---

[43] Prost 2007: 105–106; Debord 2003: 130–131. Pontus and Bithynia: Marek 2003: 101.
[44] Cf. Laumonier 1958: 205; Debord 2003: 131; Rivault 2016: 365–370.
[45] Cf. Boffo 2007.   [46] On Kyaneai: Kolb 2003: 231–236.   [47] Talloen 2015: 78–79.
[48] Grainger 2009: 85–108.   [49] Salmeri 2003: 265–293.
[50] Laodicea on the Lykos: Corsten 2007.   [51] *I.Sultan Dağı* I, 393 (*SEG* 53, 1504).
[52] Scholten 2007: 20–21; Marek 2009: 36–44.
[53] Termessos in North Lycia: Corsten 2013: 83.

AN IMPOSSIBLE RESISTANCE? 185

Pergamenian power perhaps played a role in the implementation of forms of civic urbanism.[54] This process clearly sped up over the second century. The markers of an acceleration in the adoption of Greek institutional norms[55] include: the changes in civic spaces in inland and western Lycia,[56] the appearance at the end of the second century of *bouleuteria* in many Pisidian towns,[57] and the appearance of religious architecture directly inspired by Greek models.[58]

It would, however, be wrong to understand the success of the civic model as the acceptance of a uniform norm from all points of view. In the Lycian case, the presence of *perioikoi* on the fringes of certain civic spaces[59] shows that the shape of the city was redesigned according to local socio-political situations.[60] There was a Lycian, a Pisidian, and even a Carian model of the *polis* and even variations within these regions.[61] In Lycia, until the second century, the city was above all the affair of local elites as the civic model conveniently chimed with the socio-political development of Lycian communities, which, during the third century, had seen the disappearance of dynasts and 'tyrants' in favour of oligarchic forms. Moreover, it is recognized today that the essence of the phenomenon of *poliadization* of the urbanism in Lycia,[62] like in inland

[54] S. Mitchell sees the influence of Pergamon in the trapezoidal agoras of Selge, Termessos and Sagalassos and the commercial buildings in Selge, Pednelissos and Adana: Mitchell 1991: 140–145. M. Waelkens on the contrary highlights the existence of Anatolian antecedents and also the role of integration into the Asia province in the latter third of the second century: Waelkens 1993: 24–28; Waelkens and Vandeput 2007: 99–100; Waelkens 2004: 450–455, 467–468.
[55] The institutional developments of Pisidian cities in the second century: Bracke 1993: 15–29. For S. Mitchell, between the second and first centuries all the Pisidian cities had an enclosure, a *bouleuterion*, one or several temples for Greek gods, *stoai* and Greek style institutions: Mitchell 1991: 140–145; Mitchell 1992: 22–26.
[56] Corsten 2013: 78–80 (Kibyra, Boubon, and Oinoanda). Olympos and Kyaneai: Kolb 2013: 122–124.
[57] Bracke 1993: 22–23. Waelkens 2004: 453–458.
[58] On religious architecture in second-century Pisidia and particularly on Ionian and Pergamenian influences: Mitchell 1991: 126 and, with many reservations: Waelkens 2004: 461–463.
[59] Xanthos, Telmessos, Limyra: Kolb 2013: 124; Wörrle 1978: 237–243.
[60] On the institutional particularities of Pisidian cities (Selge, Termessos, Sagalassos) in the third and second centuries: Waelkens 2004: 454–455.
[61] Keen 2002: 29–34.
[62] By 'poliadization' we mean the phenomenon of community transformation according to civic models not only in the field of institutions, but also in those urban forms and community representation practices.

Phrygia or in Pisidia,[63] must be set in the second century, while in western Caria or in Lydia this occurred much earlier.[64] The cultural hybridization process therefore acted to reveal regional particularities[65] and it ended in a differential erosion of the local and regional sub-layers. The examples of Pisidia[66] and Phrygia[67] from the third and second centuries clearly show this, where *poliadization* was very uneven and rather late as regards its architectural and spatial interpretations.

The Carian and Lycian examples of the fourth century are a reminder that the spread of the civic model was no kind of a brake on the emergence of ethnic or identity consciousness but nor was it an indispensable condition for these identities to emerge.[68] This awareness was not expressed, or just not stated, in institutional or even linguistic terms, but it was the extension of an old and deeply rooted identity. That there was, at least partially, a Lycian ethnic consciousness in the Classical age is a fact that is supported by the appearance, in a few Xanthos documents in Lycian, of the ethnonym Termilai (*TPMMAI*) used by the Lycians about themselves,[69] without however the term ever having been used in a political sense.[70] This identity of a cultural nature lay first of all in the sharing of practices (languages, religions, funerary architecture, etc.) and was not the clear basis of an ethnicity claimed in opposition to outsiders, even less as a political unit on a regional scale. Maybe it only firstly concerned the westernmost part of Lycia, around the Xanthos valley before it spread to inland Lycia over the Classical period, meaning that Pericles of Limyra could present himself, at least formally, as the 'king of the Lycians' in the first third of the fourth century.[71] Of course, we know that the title of 'king of the Carians' existed in pre-Hellenistic Caria.[72] When Alexander conquered western Asia Minor at least part of the

---

[63] Talloen 2015: 80–82.
[64] On Sardis at the beginning of the third century: Berlin and Kosmin 2019: 236–238.
[65] Potter 2007: 82–83.   [66] Cf. Mitchell 1991; Waelkens 2004: 448–449.
[67] Rheidt 2008: 118–121; Thonemann 2013b: 24–26.
[68] *Contra* Prost 2007: 106 about Lycia.
[69] Laroche 1976: 15–19 and Frei 1993: 88–90. On the ethnonym 'Lycians': Bousquet 1992: 155–187. Cf. Bryce 1986: 22–23.
[70] Kolb 2003: 210–212.
[71] Wörrle 1991: 206. Cf. Keen 1998: 148–170. Bryce 1983a highlights the role of the Persian domination in the emergence of a common identity throughout Lycia.
[72] Cf. *infra*. Marek 2015: 9–10 and Nafissi 2015: 30–40.

Carian *ethnos/koinon* was sufficiently united to be embodied by Ada, whose traditional regional legitimacy was recognized by Alexander at least in the inland mountainous part of Caria.[73] Finally, the study of Carian tombs shows clearly that it was in the fourth century that they gained a singular identity founded on a common model, partly influenced by the Greek world.[74] In south-western Asia Minor,[75] the fourth century thus saw the emergence of an articulation between ancient identities and a kind of partial political incarnation. The episode of the agreement between Ada and Alexander however had no sequel. The Greco-Macedonian conquest, and even more so the administrative and territorial recompositions of the third century afterwards, had differential effects throughout Asia Minor. In the centre and the north-west, resistance by the indigenous dynasts or settlement by Galatians[76] allowed the structuring of territory and perhaps the affirmation of kinds of regional identities.[77] In Caria or Lycia, however, despite the fact that the Seleucid or Ptolemaic units were able to extend these geographical entities, the effect of the high Hellenistic period was to fragment or to conceal the political forms founded more or less partially on an ethnic identity, without destroying some of the cultural bases of these identities.

From the point of view of ethno-cultural questions, Asia Minor in the early second century is a picture of contrasts. The impression of fractured identity and geography often dominates even in those regions, like Caria, which had known partial sorts of political unity. Basically, the process of ethno-cultural unification begun in the Persian era in Caria and Lycia[78] was slowed down in some places, hindered, or even abolished by the effects of the Greco-Macedonian conquest. Moreover, in most regions of Asia Minor it is difficult not to conclude that there was a weakening of some kinds of the more visible forms of ethnic identity, especially in the uses of indigenous writing but also in specific funerary

---

[73] Diod. 17.24.2-3; Arr. 1.23.8. Cf. Capdetrey 2012: 230-231.
[74] Henry 2009: 177-178.   [75] Cf. Briant 1996: 689-694.
[76] Strobel 1996; Darbyshire et al. 2000.   [77] Strobel 2002.
[78] Lycia: Zimmermann 1992: 27-51; Potter 2007: 82-83. From the point of view of the material culture, in Lydia, the example of Sardis shows that at the time of the Macedonian conquest the population had worked out a hybrid ceramics (Lydian-Greek-Persian): Berlin 2016. It is in fact necessary to wait for the Seleucid period to read a clearer break in favour of Greek-style tableware: Berlin and Kosmin 2019: 236-238 and Berlin 2019: 55-57.

architecture.[79] On a very local scale however this process was more complex than we might think. Regarding Dokimeion in Phrygia at the beginning of the Hellenistic age, P. Thonemann has shown that a certain number of inscriptions reveal the presence of Macedonian and Thessalian colonizers as well as the adoption of an archaeo-Phrygian style for some of the funerary steles.[80] However, in the second century, many of the regions that had lagged behind in adopting Greek norms became engaged in these changes. S. Mitchell has shown this for Pisidia[81] and the process had also largely begun in Gordium.[82] Nevertheless, despite the strong effects of Hellenization the cultural sub-layers continued to be operative elements even in the regions longest exposed to Greek influence, but this was often at the price of a redefinition of their expression according to new norms and models. We can probably consider that from an architectural and artistic viewpoint the claimed cultural hybridization had become one of the Carians' ethno-cultural identity characteristics, just like the Lycians (or at least their elites), from the fourth century onwards.[83] But these elements of identity or cultural distinction, which continued partially until the second century, objectivized by us observers, in themselves are only a very partial aspect of the process of identity construction. Strictly speaking, they do not authorize us to talk of ethnicity. This supposes an awareness or a desire for affirmation or confrontation, violent or not, against the otherness of Greco-Macedonian royal powers, who, from the high Hellenistic period

---

[79] Benda-Weber 2005: 72–85. Nereid Monument and Mausoleum: Prost 2013. Also Kolb 2003: 212 and 237.

[80] *MAMA* IV, 49. Cf. Thonemann 2013b: 18. In Pisidia, on the territory of Sagalassos, the site of Düzen Tepe reveals a stable spatial organization from the fifth to the second centuries and the maintenance of a Pisidian material culture that does not seem deeply affected by the inflections of the political chronology: Vanhaverbeke et al. 2010: 119–125. At the same time, Sagalassos – the large neighbouring community – is undergoing much more important transformations: Waelkens 2004: 448–466.

[81] Cf. production of olive oil, probably associated with needs in the gymnasium, from the end of the fourth century at Sagalassos: Mitchell 2005: 92–93. But one has to wait until the late second century to see a monumentalization of civic space.

[82] Thonemann 2013b: 20–21.

[83] We can speak of the Carianization and the Lycianization of Greek influences but also of Iranian ones. Cf. Potter 2007: 83–85. Research into funerary architecture in Caria, Lycia, and Pisidia highlight the integration from the fourth century onwards of external factors (Ionic columns and decor in particular) in cave tombs or the end of Lycian-type burials. Cf. Tietz 2009: 170–172; Carstens 2009: 393–394; Kolb 2007: 275; Henry 2009: 178–179; Henry 2013b. Pisidia: Talloen 2015: 107–108.

onwards, were themselves eager to modify or redefine certain forms of ethnicity.

2. Identity and Otherness in the Second Century: The Meaning of Violence

One observation must be made: in the second century there was no structured revolt based on ethnic or religious claims against the Greco-Macedonian powers or against the Greeks in Asia Minor or in Hellenistic Anatolia. The first example of violent coordinated action against a section of the population, the Italians, would not take place until the Mithridatic crisis at the beginning of the first century, and this was for reasons which escape a purely ethnic logic. We must recall that Alexander's conquest and the setting up of kingdoms had, at first, caused as much resistance among Greek populations – remember the siege of Halicarnassus and the resistance of Pontic cities to Antiochus I, etc. – as in more inland areas such as Pisidia, Phrygia and Cappadocia.[84] Regarding the founding of Anatolian kingdoms, in Bithynia and in the Pontus, these were more of a response to a need for protection and territorial affirmation of local powers than an ethnic or identity reaction.[85]

And yet, since the Classical period, Greek sources based an important part of the ethnicity of Anatolian peoples (Carians, and especially Lycians, Phrygians, and Pisidians) on their strong defence of their territory or even on their cultural inclination towards independence and rebellion.[86] Obviously, one must be cautious. Of course, demographic power,[87] or the Pisidians' particular ability for and specialization in war, all explain why they would have been widely deployed in the

---

[84] In 333 BCE, Termessos and Sagalassos united against Alexander because Selge supported the conqueror. Cf. Arr. *Anab.* 1, 27, 5–28, 1–2.
[85] Marek 2003: 30–43.
[86] Herodotus, 1, 171: The Xanthians against Harpagos. On Pisidians: Diod. 11, 61, 4 (in 465 BCE); Xen. *Hell.* 3, 1, 13; Xen., *Anab.* 1, 2, 4–5; 2, 5, 13; 11, 61, 4; Arr. *Anab.*, 1, 27, 5–28; Strab. 12, 7, 3.
[87] Towns of Pisidia: Waelkens 2004: 450–451.

armies of the Diadochi,[88] the Seleucids, and the Ptolemies.[89] This is made manifest[90] by the development of massive and complex defence systems in Pisidian towns in the fourth century and in the high Hellenistic[91] period. In fact, specializing in war made some populations regular actors in Asia Minor conflicts in the third and the second centuries. But we also know that after the Peace of Apamea the Greek cities of the lower Meander valley (Miletus, Heraclea, Priene) clashed over territorial issues.[92] It was the same issues which, during the second century, led Pisidian and Lycian communities to clash, and sometimes to make alliances with the Attalid king for support.[93] Moreover, the towns in northern Lycia seem to have feared more than anything invasions by the Pisidians and, from this point of view, the royal Greco-Macedonian powers represented a potential protection, as they had been for those Greek cities facing raids by the Galatians or the Bithynians from the third century onwards. In second-century Lycia, the affirmation of a regional identity was reinforced by this northerly threat which partly allowed Lycian fringes to be integrated into horizontal systems of alliance and solidarity. It might have been thought that the relative weakening of constraining powers – since Pergamon did not have the military weight of the Ptolemies or the Seleucids in the third century – would have played in favour of re-establishing some regions' ability to withdraw from an order that had been imposed on them. Certainly, everything indicates that Eumenes II, like Attalus II, had difficulty in controlling Pisidia[94] and in ending piracy in Pamphylia.[95] Nevertheless, it seems that Attalid influence in Pisidia and on the edges of this region was no weaker than that of the Seleucids.[96] And yet, conflict internal to this region did not fall

---

[88] In 321, Alketas gathers an army consisting of Pisidians at Termessos: Arr. *Succ.* 1, 41–42; Diod. 18, 29, 2; 41, 7, 44, 1; 46; Plut. *Eumen.* 4, 1–3; 5, 1.
[89] Cf. Bracke 1993: 19–20. For example, soldiers from Etenna with Achaios in 218 BCE: Pol. 5, 77, 1.
[90] Cf. Waelkens 2004.   [91] Diod. 18, 46, 1, about Alkatas in 319.   [92] Baker 2001.
[93] The support of Attalus II at Termessos is particularly well known especially because of the erection of a *stoa*: Kosmetatou 1997: 28–29. Cf. Bringmann and Steuben 1995, n. 303. On Olbasa and the Attalids versus the Pisidians: Kearsley 1994: 48–49. Amblada and Eumenes II: Welles, 1934, *RC*, n. 54.
[94] Waelkens 2004: 446–448.
[95] Bracke 1993: 17 and Kosmetatou 1997: 25. On Amblada: Welles 1934, n. 54.
[96] Waelkens 2004: 442–443, 466–468. On the defensive armour attributed to the Attalids: Mitchell 1992: 24–26. Also Talloen 2015: 86–87.

AN IMPOSSIBLE RESISTANCE? 191

away and is widely attested, but in no way did it concern ethnic or identity claims. The partial mobilization of Pisidian cities, for example, was never based on an affirmation or a contestation of a particular, integrating ethnicity.[97] When there were conflicts they were firstly internal to these regions according to the logics that mobilized territorial and political resources.[98]

However, forms of violence played a role in the emergence of identity representations. For example, in the years around 270 threats from Galatian tribes had led coastal Greek cities to identify this enemy and to mobilize the solidarity of the Greeks against the barbarians.[99] The Galatian raids on the Attalid kingdom in 168–167 and then in the following decades were exploited in a similar way.[100] These examples demonstrate that the representation of otherness was also, if not above all, the action of Greeks in the cities and the royal powers, as is clearly shown in Alexander's letter to the Prienians in 334.[101] Of course, practically speaking, things were more complex as the barbarians (Galatians or Pisidians) depicted as threats – which they obviously were – were largely integrated into the armies of the Greco-Macedonian kings from the third century onwards.[102] But the gigantomachy frieze of the Great Altar in Pergamon has been interpreted as a depiction of the victory of the Attalids over the Galatians.[103] A certificate of Hellenism for the dynasty, this representation belongs to an artistic genre where the figure of the defeated or wounded Galatian provided the means, in Athens, Delphi, Ephesus, or Pergamon, of affirming Greek identity by representing the savage and threatening identity of the Galatians.[104] It is tempting to make a link between the Greeks' obsession with the Galatians and the

---

[97] On the monetary particularity of Selge within Pisidia (retaining the Persian standard) from the end of the fourth century: Kosmetatou 1997: 17–18, 31.
[98] Olbasa grants privileges to an Attalid *strategos*, Aristarchos, and to Sotas, maybe a local dynast: Kearsley 1994: 49, l. 6. Cf. Also: Savalli-Lestrade 2001: 79–80.
[99] Strobel 1994: 67–87. On Galatians: Coşkun 2014; Kistler 2009; Mitchell 2003.
[100] Strobel 1994.
[101] Thonemann 2013a: 23–36, where P. Thonemann shows that Alexander founded privileges on ethnic belonging.
[102] Kosmetatou 1997: 20–24; Avram and Tsetskhladze 2014.
[103] Queyrel 2005: 130–136.
[104] The reference to the Galatians is explicit in the Attalid *ex-voto* on the Athenian Acropolis: Cf. Queyrel 2005: 133; Bringmann and Steuben 1995: 66–68, n. 30; Oberleitner 1981: 57–104.

fact that, of all the populations settled in Asia Minor, the Galatians were the ones who preserved their language, material culture, and an organization distinct from Greek norms.[105] In one sense, like a terrifying Gorgon, the territorial pressure of the Galatians, associated with the conservative practices that were both Celtic and indigenous,[106] stimulated the ethnicity of the Greeks or of those who claimed to be such. The counterpoint to the *galatization* of Anatolia[107] was a spike in *Hellenicity* further west.

Essentially, the second and first centuries witnessed the reactivation and the distancing of the threatening figure of the barbarian in particular from Asia Minor. And so, in 188 BCE the distinction made between Greeks from the cities and the other populations of western Asia Minor remained a structuring factor in the Treaty of Apamea. In fact, the topic of eventual liberty granted at the time of the Peace was only ever raised for the city Greeks and never for other populations, whatever the degree of their adoption of Greek political and cultural norms.[108] At best, they were only semi-Greek and unworthy of political freedom. In the second century this conception and this opposition still had the operative strength of being implicitly obvious.

But the threat personified by the barbarians was based also, and more deeply, on the fact that, in the eyes of some Greeks, they imperilled a certain idea of Hellenism. In the first century, Dionysius of Halicarnassus was thus led to denounce the corruption of rhetoric by clumsy Asian rhetoricians.[109] We also know how reticent the Rhodians were in integrating the lands of South Caria into their own territory at the end of the third century because of the linguistic and cultural differences between

---

[105] Mitchell 1991: 13–21, 42–59; Darbyshire et al. 2000: 81–93.

[106] The question of the galatization of Inner Asia Minor is much discussed today. According to some studies, the idea of Celtic cultural imports into Asia Minor in material culture should be reconsidered. In this field, Phrygian and Pontic elements would have remained dominant: Coşkun, Altay 2014. On the contrary, for the sense of a Galatean cultural affirmation: Strobel 2009.

[107] Strobel 2009: 119.

[108] Pol. 21, 19, 5 (Eumenes' discourse); 22, 7 (The Rhodians' discourse); Liv. 37, 53, 3 (Eumenes' discourse); 54, 17–24 (The Rhodians' discourse). Cf. Bresson 1998: 66–67.

[109] Dionysius of Halicarnassus, *De antiquis oratoribus*, I, p. 4 l. 17 Teubner. Cf. Bresson 2007a: 223–224.

AN IMPOSSIBLE RESISTANCE? 193

the Carians and themselves.[110] Thus, at the same time as Hellenism was enjoying multiform success, some Greeks turned around and claimed a purer and more demanding form of Hellenism, simultaneously showing their contempt for the populations engaged, in their eyes, in an unfinished process of Hellenization. These reactions were in fact part of a wider movement, which in the second century rather more so than in the third century, led the Greeks of Asia Minor to claim they belonged to a triumphant Hellenism, doing so notably by signalling and claiming *syngeneiai* or by euergetic practices in favour of grand sanctuaries or cities.[111] It appears that in this race towards conspicuous Hellenicity, which seems to have concerned all of Asia Minor, those who felt they lived as real Greeks sometimes wished to underline this ontological difference.[112]

Mention has been made of the Aristonikos war (132–129 BCE) as an example of a confrontation based on opposition which was social in nature but also partly ethnic since Aristonikos brought together freed slaves and indigenous dwellers in a very violent clash with Rome and cities across Asia Minor.[113] The conflict cannot be summarized as the simple contesting of the will of Attalos by a disinherited heir.[114] Its repercussions were so profound that conflict enflamed all of western Asia Minor, from the Propontis to inland Caria, long after the capture of Aristonikos-Eumenes III.[115] While the hypothesis of the widespread mobilization of slaves on the side of Aristonikos remains open[116] – though rather unlikely – we can nevertheless emphasize the effect of the uprising on the inland regions where the message of resistance to Roman power or to that of the cities met with a certain success. But the motive for the mobilization cannot have been the affirmation of a

---

[110] Bresson 2007a.
[111] Cf. Bringmann and Steuben 1995: 552. On *syngeneia*: Curty 1995; Curty 2005.
[112] Strabo clearly opposes the Greek peoples (Aeolian, Ionian) and the 'others' (Carians, Lycians, Lydians): Strab. 12, 1, 3.
[113] Strab. 14, 1, 38. Cf. Will, 1979–1982: 419–425. Robert and Robert 1989: 29–35. Cf. Briant et al. 2001: 252–255 and Mileta 1998.
[114] Mileta 1998.   [115] Briant et al. 2001.
[116] On the 'city of slaves': Robert and Robert 1989: 37–38. On political divisions in Asia Minor under Aristonikos, Dreyer, and Engelmann 2003, 66–89. On Aristonikos' success among Macedonian colonies: Coşkun, 2011, 110–111.

regional or local identity. What can be suggested at best is that Aristonikos and his supporters, in their desire to succeed, knew how to exploit the denunciation of forms of domination – economic, fiscal, statuary – from which doubtless all the *chôra* and the innermost regions suffered, in favour of the cities and of Pergamon.[117] How can we otherwise understand the clauses of the Pergamon decree which, in the context of the beginning of the war, granted the right of city residence to the Macedonians, the Mysians and the Masdynians?[118] Moreover, we notice that most of the coastal cities sided with Rome (Bargylia, Ephesus, Smyrna, Sestos, Cyzicus) and above all that Aristonikos found his main allies in Mysia and Lydia (Apollonis, Thyateira, Stratonikeia on the Kaikos), regions marked by Macedonian military colonization.[119] Essentially, if the role of an ethnic criterion must be recognized in the mobilization of communities, this was more the case for the Macedonian colonies than for other actors. Some of them seem to have supported Aristonikos' claims against what perhaps had been Greek cities' hopes of seeing the Attalid power disappear in favour of a more far-off power.

One point must be made: the link between ethno-cultural identity and conflict is rather flimsy and in Asia Minor in the second century the dynamics of violence do not correspond at all to ethnic and identity divisions. While violence remains an important fact in relations between communities in these regions, the internal splits in regional sub-groups and the weakness of identity focus, undermined by the conquest and its aftermath, explain the absence of any rebellious movement based on a feeling of cultural or ethnic otherness. The roots of conflict are mostly linked to issues of territorial control, defence, or regaining autonomy, in a grand continuity of the Classical era. This is explained notably by the fact that the process of Hellenization did not arise from a political will, against which identity had to be built or reinforced. And building of ethnic or cultural otherness into the justification for conflicts, when there were any, was basically a fact that was external to local dynamics, a fact based on the representation of the barbarian and on an artificial image of otherness.

---

[117] Ferrary 2001: 98–99.   [118] *OGIS* 338, l. 11–16. Cf. Robert 1962: 265.
[119] Cohen 1995: 45–46 and 232–242.

3. The Strategies of Identity: Regional Unity and Paradoxical Ethnicity

In Asia Minor the ethnicity question and its political translations are posed in very different terms from Babylonia, Judea, and Egypt. Anatolian regional sub-groups were marked by many internal splits. Only Hecatomnid Caria in the fourth century could have constituted a unit before the conquest. The existence of the Carian *koinon*, bringing together many western Carian communities from the end of the fourth century, is a situation which had no contemporary parallels.[120] Up until the middle of the Hellenistic era, Lycia had no political unity and remained divided into several regional sub-groups. This was also true for Pisidia, where political or cultural unity was not achieved before the imperial age.[121] As for Phrygia, the effect of setting up Greco-Macedonian foundations in the plains and along major routes leading to inner Anatolia was to accentuate yet again the internal fractures in the region. And yet, just like the decisions taken in Apamea, the Hellenistic administrative network helped in constructing western Asia Minor into sub-units and giving these sub-areas a unity which they had perhaps never had in Caria or in Lycia.[122] The Ptolemies undoubtedly had an administrator in Caria to control their possessions in the region.[123] Ptolemaic Lycia was run by two *oikonomoi* in the third century, doubtless one for eastern Lycia and one for the west.[124] Above all, granting Caria and Lycia to Rhodes through the Treaty of Apamea constituted territorial groups, and conferred a hitherto unknown unity.[125]

To these categories, defined by the big powers, must be added a certain number of significant changes in the reformulation of collective identities. The spread of the civic model and its local adaptation had the effect of calling into question some of the elements of the traditional functioning of local communities. But there is nothing to support the idea of

---
[120] The Carians' *koinon*: Debord 2003: 118–125; Debord 2005: 262–264; Capdetrey 2012: 233–237.
[121] Cf. Waelkens and Vandeput 2007: 102–105.
[122] Debord 2005: 270–277; Debord 2009: 260–263.
[123] Robert and Robert 1983, n. 3: 118–124.   [124] Wörrle 1977: 43–44.
[125] Under Rhodian domination there was a *hagèmôn epi Karias* and a *hagèmôn epi Lykias* (about 185 BCE): *IG*, XII, 1, 49, l. 59–64.

deliberate hostility on the part of royal Greco-Macedonian powers even if, when they had to arbitrate between the cities and priestly powers, the kings tended to support the cities, as in Mylasa in the third century,[126] for reasons of efficiency in controlling the territory. But these powers also played on local identities and, to a certain extent, reinforced or transformed them. In Caria, religious links between the communities in the west had existed at least since the early fourth century,[127] in the context of the Carians' *koinon*.[128] One of the effects of the Macedonian conquest was the dislocation of the proto-federal Carian system, at least initially. From the third century, and doubtless with the support of the Ptolemaic and Seleucid powers, other systems of solidarity (re)emerged in western Caria. These had religious and not political bases,[129] notably the *koinon* of the Chrysaorians around the Zeus *Chrysaoreus* sanctuary in the territory of Stratonicea.[130] In the third century and still in the second century, this *koinon* operated as a powerful confederating structure able to integrate several communities into a system of solidarity and also was able to make itself the relay of royal powers in central Caria.[131] But this was more of a religious regional identity than one of actual ethnicity.[132] In the same spirit, the attention that Hellenistic kings paid to establishing close links with the Zeus sanctuary at Labraunda, continuing Hecatomnid practices,[133] shows how these powers were also keen to maintain the expression of a powerful Carian religious identity. After 166 BCE epigraphic documents reveal the success and the influence of the Zeus *Karios* sanctuary at Panamara over a large part of Caria.[134] This success was in response to a Carian ethno-religious dynamic that was still powerful, in the continuation of the Carians' *koinon*,[135] but which did not contradict religious or political affiliations, since the *koinon*

---

[126] Capdetrey 2007: 172.
[127] Two inscriptions at Sekkoÿ, dated 354/3 BCE, bear lists of Carian cities and communities associated in a *koinon*: *IK*, 34-Mylasa, 11 (Debord and Varınlıoğlu 2001, n. 90); *IK*, 34-Mylasa, 12 (Debord and Varınlıoğlu 2001, n. 91).
[128] On Asandros and this *koinon*: Capdetrey 2012: 233–235.   [129] Debord 2003.
[130] Strab. 14, 2, 25. Cf. Debord 2003: 125–141; Robert and Robert 1983: 223–224; Gabrielsen 2011b.
[131] Capdetrey 2007: 105–106.
[132] The influence of the religious identity is explicit in the *Amyzon* 28 text at the beginning of the second century: Robert and Robert 1983: 217–227.
[133] Hellström 2009: 278–280.   [134] Cf. Van Bremen 2004.   [135] Debord 2003: 125.

integrated Kallipolis which was then under the control of Rhodes.[136] In Caria, the maintenance of federal and regional *koina* and the multiplication of more local *koina*[137] bear witness to the fact that the undeniable adoption of the model of the *polis* was accompanied by a kind of partial resistance by the Carian sub-layer and by forms of organization that were different, parallel, or complementary.[138]

Therefore, in the third century, the south-west of Asia Minor saw a fairly clear double movement: on one hand, the construction of administrative units bearing on regional unification and imposing a sort of top-down identity, and on the other hand, the (re)emergence of local and regional identities that the royal powers knew how to recover or control, if only by supporting a Hellenized form of these expressions. Things were clearer in Lycia where from the end of the third century the Lycian *koinon* gradually emerged around the federal sanctuary of the Letoon, with the backing of the Ptolemaic power.[139] This process must be placed in chronological relation to the architectural recomposition of the sanctuary of the Apollonian triad.[140] Thus we observe the reconstruction of the three temples according to a model which kept pre-existing Lycian elements embedded, as so many symbols of Lycian religious memory. The interior of the temple of Leto in fact conserved the first foundation of a chapel.[141] In Apollo's temple the *cella* contained the foundation of a Lycian temple in wood or in plain brick. As for the temple of Artemis, its

---

[136] Debord and Varınlıoğlu 2001, n. 84, 208–210, n. 89, 212–216. Importance of the Zeus Carios sanctuary: decree of Panamara: *IK*, 21,-Stratonikeia, 7; decree of Kallipolis: Debord and Varınlıoğlu 2001, n. 84 and decree of the *koinon* of the Laodiceans: Debord and Varınlıoğlu 2001, n. 89.

[137] On an intra-regional scale the history of identities in Caria in the third and second centuries is also that of the structuring of local *koina*, which were more or less widespread. Cf. the *koinon* of the *Panamareis* near Stratonicea, the Chersonasian *koinon* in Rhodian Peraia around the sanctuary at Kastabos (Held 2013: 93–97 which highlights the role of Rhodes in the emergence of this local identity), that of Pisyetai-Pladasseis, that of Tarmianoi, etc…: Debord et al. 2001, nn. 3 and 4, 106–113, nn. 37, 38. Cf. Debord 2003: 142–170. This only concerned very local identities where the structuring into *koina* allowed both organization and representation.

[138] Dignas 2003: 86–90.

[139] Classic Lycia: Behrwald 2000: 9–46. On cooperation between Lycian cities in the third century and the part played by Ptolemaic power: Behrwald 2000: 69–80. The Lycian *koinon*: Bresson 1999: 111, who defends the hypothesis of an early constitution, at the end of the third century at the latest. Cf. Debord 1999: 182.

[140] Cavalier and Courtils 2013: 143–152.   [141] Cavalier and Courtils 2013: 144.

cella was entirely occupied by an outcrop of rock crowned by a statue.[142] So, at the very time when the Letoon was being transformed into a Greek looking sanctuary, the Lycians were adopting for their temples an architectural form that was a perfect metaphor of the adaptations of Lycian identity to dominant forms of expression and organization marked by Hellenism. These observations in Caria and Lycia were not without intellectual consequences. They show clearly how these solidarities and religious identities constituted the pre-existing base and the indispensable driver for all forms of political translation of an ethnic identity, as C. Morgan showed for archaic western Greece.[143] They also show how, afterwards, the Greco-Macedonian powers – probably more the Lagid power than the Seleucid – and Rome knew how to exploit this sub-layer by transforming it into a way of structuring territories, in other words, into a political instrument.

The Lycian example is more explicit here without being an isolated case, however.[144] In Lycia, doubtless since the end of the third century and definitely during the Rhodian domination, a federal structure appeared, at first on a religious foundation, around the Letoon sanctuary.[145] It was after the liberation of the Lycians in 167 BCE that this *koinon* assumed its full dimensions by adopting a political organization that was better known in the second half of the second century.[146] It was therefore a decision of the Senate which validated and reinforced the Lycian political identity by giving it a means of expression and granting its claims. The Lycian *koinon* conferred a partial political unity on the different regions in Lycia without however suppressing local identities or, in particular, the autonomy of the cities which maintained their own citizenship.[147] The appearance of an army and also federal coinage,[148] which had no equivalent in Hellenistic Asia Minor, demonstrates relatively well-developed integration and the clear affirmation of an ethnic and regional identity. In Pisidia it was not until the imperial age that a Pisidian *koinon* appeared, set up by Rome. The forces that led to the

---

[142] Le Roy 1991: 341–351; Chr. Le Roy 2004a.   [143] Morgan 2003.
[144] Pisidia: Waelkens and Vandeput 2007: 98.
[145] Rousset 2010: 76–77. Institutions of the *koinon*: Strab. 14, 3, 3 (C 665).
[146] Behrwald 2000: 89–105; Behrwald 2015; Rousset 2010: 76–77; Baker and Thériault 2005.
[147] Bresson 2007b: 76–78.   [148] Troxell 1982.

AN IMPOSSIBLE RESISTANCE? 199

emergence of a Lycian *koinon* are obviously many, both internal and external. A regional logic of response to threats certainly played a role. It was a question of facing incursions by Pisidians in particular (especially the conflicts with Termessos[149]) in the north of Lycia, and definitely also one of affirming unity when facing Rhodes at the beginning of the century. But the affirmation of a *koinon* also constituted a powerful relay point and then, once the province of Asia had been created, it was an instrument for organization and control of the region for Roman administration.

One point also has to be made: the *koinon* method of organization, and the role played by the Lycian cities in this federal system, largely reproduced the structure of contemporary Greek *koina*.[150] In Asia Minor there was a system of solidarity like the Ionian *koinon*, very active at the end of the third century and early second century,[151] which constituted a model for association and regional cooperation for the Lycians even if, from the angle of political, military, and institutional organization, the most explicit parallel seems to have been the Achaean *koinon*.[152] So, everything seems to point to the affirmation of Lycian identity through the *koinon* as being a result of adopting Greek norms but also of the submission of all of Lycia to the Ptolemaic power during the third century. This is a phenomenon which must be linked to the spread of the civic model of which it is clearly a corollary. Lycia – and the regions of Caria to a lesser degree – was thus inscribed in a wider movement of regional or sub-regional structuring around federal systems founded on religious solidarities and geographical identities. And, far from being related to an apparent desire for ethnic affirmation, the development of a Lycian *koinon* must first of all be interpreted as the product of a long process of institutional acculturation.[153] As it had for the Chrysaorians, this process had given the Lycians the means of claiming their identity and their autonomy and of structuring their region, with the words, the

---

[149] Cf. Decree of Araxa for Orthagoras: *SEG* 18, 570. Cf. Rousset 2010: 96–98.
[150] Beck and Funke 2015; Behrwald 2015.
[151] Metcalfe 2005; Müller and Prost 2013; Hallmannsecker 2020.
[152] Knoepfler 2010: 705; Behrwald 2015: 406.
[153] On the distinction between ethnicity and federalism: Hall 2015: 48.

institutional instruments, and the conceptual means of the Greeks, in particular thanks to vocabulary for institutions and family links.[154] Doubtless, this is also an observation which can be made, to a certain degree, for the emergence of the Hasmonean kingdom in Judea, and perhaps also for the kingdom cities of Phoenicia.[155] From this angle, and despite the absence of any associated conflict in the case of Asia Minor, it is not excessive to underline a partial parallel between the situations in southern Syria and in Asia Minor, as if in the second century identity crystallization had partly followed the paths traced by the effects of a long-term institutional acculturation, and as if the adoption of Greek practices and norms had been conceived as a means of regional and identity resistance. But in Asia Minor this resistance had a price: the disjunction between cultural and regional identity. The partial reformulation of cultural identity to preserve a regional political unity led to ethnicity dwindling to a simple local consciousness, integrated into the rest of the Greek world, globalized through *syngeneiai*, *koina* and pan-hellenic religions. To take up the categories of F. Barth, there was no longer an adequate *frontier* or *otherness* around which to construct a clear, recognizable, and meaningful ethnic identity.

4. Conclusions: From Ethnicity to Local Identity, Hellenistic Fractures

In the Asia Minor of the second century, it is not possible to identify an opposition movement to the Greco-Macedonian powers based on a cultural otherness or on the construction of a distinctive ethnicity. In truth, even when ethnic discourses may be mobilized in the context of violent conflict, there are almost always several other factors at play. The effects of an already longstanding Hellenization were such in the western part of Asia Minor and in the more inland urban centres that it was hard to build politically or culturally against practices imbued with norms.

---

[154] Jones 1999: 66–72. The Lycians: Behrwald 2015: 407.
[155] Jones 1999: 72–80; Sartre 2010: 110–116. See also Gruen's essay in this volume and earlier work, e.g. 'Hellenism and Hasmoneans', in Gruen 1998.

So we will not find here any source for conflict. Moreover, the internal splits in the regional sub-units did not really favour the emergence of an identity which from the outset would have had to be defended, consolidated, and unified before even being affirmed in the face of the powers in place. The case of Lycia is therefore even more interesting even if only because from the second century it heralded the destiny of other regions of Asia Minor in the imperial age. Unlike Caria, Lydia, or Pisidia, where during the Hellenistic period there was no political translation of cultural sub-layers, though there were indeed ancient traditions of this kind, Lycia witnessed the affirmation of a federal unity based on an identity under construction. But this affirmation should not be interpreted as a reaction to an external, foreign power. On the contrary, this Lycian identity should be understood, not without paradox, as the product of cultural transfers at work in the fourth century, that Roman politics had skilfully backed throughout the second century and even more so in the first century, by systematically deploying a strategy drawn up in the third century by the Ptolemies and the Seleucids.

And yet, the later Hellenistic period and even more so the imperial age saw ethnic cultural traits maintained and even reaffirmed in Asia Minor. We first observe that the imperial administrative division of Asia Minor and Anatolia conserved regional units that were partly based on a perceived or assumed ethnic coherence.[156] We also know that regional funerary practices, religious solidarities,[157] specific dress habits,[158] and the partial maintaining of onomastics and epichoric languages[159] were still attested in late Hellenistic and imperial Anatolia.[160] In Phrygia as in Pisidia, funerary monuments and religious cults then remained as identity markers.[161] In central Lycia local architectural traditions were kept up under the Empire, founded on the widespread use of wooden architecture.[162] In Caria traces of an indigenous cult were preserved in particular on coinage where references to certain gods belonging to

---

[156] Cf. Vitale 2012.
[157] In Phrygia, around the sanctuary of Pessinous: Brixhe 2002; Brixhe 2010.
[158] Phrygian funerary steles: Masséglia 2013.
[159] Salmeri 2000. About the Lydian language: Thonemann 2013b: 13.
[160] Ruggieri 2009. Lycian aesthetic patterns in the imperial era: Schürr 2013: 39.
[161] Kelp 2015: 209–219; Talloen 2015: 363–364.   [162] Kolb 2007: 290–291.

local tradition reappeared.[163] Yet, in all these regions these identity characteristics were maintained by using forms of expression adapted to the Greco-Roman world. For, in fact, a break occurred during the third and second centuries and these partly reinvented identity markers were really only the products of a kind of cultural inertia,[164] except no doubt for Galatia.[165] They therefore only fed a kind of theatrical ethnicity for the Anatolian populations who, since the Hellenistic age, had been as concerned to integrate themselves into a Hellenocentric cultural universe as they had been to affirm specific identity traits. Following a process which has since been widely recognized, these markers only served to help find a place in a distended world to which one had to belong, with no conflict.[166] If the example of Lycia in the second century BCE shows sufficiently that the adoption of a dominant cultural and institutional language was a sure and efficient means to maintain, affirm, and defend a regional and political identity, it appears just as clearly that this process of political affirmation bore within it the collapse of Anatolian populations' forms of ethnicity, and it must be concluded that this depletion accelerated during the Hellenistic period and more particularly during the second century.[167] In this western Asia Minor of the second century, the institutional expression of an ethnic identity, when it took shape, basically had the contradictory and paradoxical effects of an ambiguous *pharmakon*.

---

[163] Rivault 2016: 370.
[164] D. Piras has shown that in the second century at Mylasa in Caria there was an acceleration in the changes in funerary architecture around the principle of a Greek architectural *koinê*: Piras 2010: 20–21.
[165] Strobel 2009. [166] Whitmarsh 2010: 1–16. [167] Kolb 2010: 89–90.

8
'Herakles is stronger, Seleucus'
Local History and Local Resistance in Pontic Herakleia

Daniel Tober

In the thirteenth book of his history of Pontic Herakleia, Memnon recounted an altercation between the Herakleotai and Seleucus I Nikator, whose recent defeat of Lysimachos at Koroupedion (281 BCE) had given him nominal control of the *polis*. Suspicious of Herakleia's loyalty, Seleucus reprimanded a contingent of local ambassadors who happened to be at court. The leader of the group, the well-known Peripatetic Chamaileon, was unfazed. Ἡρακλῆς κάρρων, Σέλευκε, he replied: 'Herakles is stronger'. According to Memnon, Seleucus was confounded; understanding neither the Doricism nor the reference – Chamaileon was alluding archly to a line from one of Sophron's mimes – the king turned away in anger. Herakleia, in response, turned toward the Greek communities of the region, laying the groundwork, as Memnon frames it, for what would become the 'Northern League' and initiating a series of diplomatic negotiations through which it managed to maintain its autonomy until the Mithridatic Wars.[1]

---

[1] *FGrHist* 434 F1.7.1–2 = Phot. *Bibl.* cod. 224.7.1–2: Ἐν τούτῳ δὲ Σέλευκος Ἀφροδίσιον πέμπει διοικητὴν εἴς τε τὰς ἐν Φρυγίᾳ πόλεις καὶ τὰς ὑπερκειμένας τοῦ Πόντου. ὁ δὲ διαπραξάμενος ἃ ἐβούλετο καὶ ἐπανιών, τῶν μὲν ἄλλων πόλεων ἐν ἐπαίνοις ἦν, Ἡρακλεωτῶν δὲ κατηγόρει μὴ εὐνοικῶς ἔχειν τοῖς τοῦ Σελεύκου πράγμασιν, ὑφ' οὗ Σέλευκος παροξυνθεὶς τούς τε πρὸς αὐτὸν ἀφικομένους πρέσβεις ἀπειλητικοῖς ἐξεφαύλιζε λόγοις καὶ κατέπληττεν, ἑνὸς τοῦ Χαμαιλέοντος οὐδὲν ὀρρωδήσαντος τὰς ἀπειλάς, ἀλλὰ φαμένου, Ἡρακλῆς κάρρων, Σέλευκε (κάρρων δὲ ὁ ἰσχυρότερος παρὰ Δωριεῦσι). ὁ δ' οὖν Σέλευκος τὸ μὲν ῥηθὲν οὐ συνῆκεν, ὀργῆς δ' ὡς εἶχε, καὶ ἀπετρέπετο· τοῖς δὲ οὔτε τὸ ἀναχωρεῖν οἴκαδε οὔτε τὸ προσμένειν λυσιτελὲς ἐδόκει. ταῦτα δὲ Ἡρακλεῶται πυθόμενοι τά τε ἄλλα παρεσκευάζοντο καὶ συμμάχους ἤθροιζον, πρός τε Μιθριδάτην τὸν Πόντου βασιλέα διαπρεσβευόμενοι καὶ πρὸς Βυζαντίους καὶ Χαλκηδονίους. For Chamaileon's identity, see below n. 59; for the likelihood that he was intending here to

Memnon published his history of Herakleia late in the Hellenistic period,[2] and the exchange between Chamaileon and Seleucus that he here envisages, an episode cribbed, along with much of the first thirteen books of his history, from the *On Herakleia* of Chamaileon's compatriot and younger contemporary, Nymphis (*FGrHist* 432),[3] would have occurred well before the crises of the second century BCE on which this volume concentrates. Yet Memnon's narrative has survived with remarkable clarity: in the ninth century CE, it elicited from the Patriarch Photios, who had only partial access to it, one of the longest epitomes of his *Bibliotheke* (cod. 224).[4] And since it is among the few remains of Greek local historiography that directly engage with the Seleucids (or indeed with any of the Macedonian kings), it offers us a fresh perspective on local resistance. On the one hand, it allows us insight into Greek, as opposed to Near Eastern, responses to Seleucid rule, particularly into the ways a *polis* on the edges of the empire (Herakleia, founded by Megara and Boiotia in the mid sixth century BCE, lay on the Bithynian coast of the Black Sea[5]) might reframe its cultural memory to accommodate the imperious foreign kings. For alongside the Mariandynoi, Bithynians, and Gauls, the Seleucids form a foil against which Memnon, and Nymphis before him, articulated Herakleian identity, encapsulating in the interplay between Seleucus's belligerent ignorance and Chamaileon's brave arrogance the nature of Herakleian authority in the Pontic region in the years to come. On the other hand, Nymphis and Memnon reveal an important local reaction to Macedonian imperialism. Local

conjure Sophron's "Ἡρακλῆς τεοῦς κάρρων ἧς' (F59 Kassel–Austin = *GrGr* II 1.1 p. 74.21) see n. 66; for the 'Northern League', which eventually included Byzantium, Kalchedon, Tios, and Kios, see n. 70.

[2] The sixteenth book, at any rate, was written after 47 BCE, since it concludes just before Julius Caesar returned to Rome from the East (*FGrHist* 434 F1.40.4). For bibliography on Memnon and his history, see below n. 86.

[3] For Memnon's dependence on Nymphis, see below n. 46. For bibliography on Nymphis, see n. 42.

[4] Photios's epitome of Memnon contains over 11,000 words, that of Herodotus, as a point of comparison, just about 200. Photios begins his epitome of Memnon's history by reporting that he read only books nine through sixteen ('Ἀνεγνώσθη βιβλίον Μέμνονος ἱστορικὸν ἀπὸ τοῦ θ λόγου ἕως ι̅ς̅'), admitting later that he can say nothing about the first eight books nor about any books that may have followed book sixteen (τὰς δὲ πρώτας ἢ ἱστορίας καὶ τὰς μετὰ τὴν ι̅ς̅ οὔπω εἰπεῖν εἰς θέαν ἡμῶν ἀφιγμένας ἔχομεν).

[5] For the foundation of Herakleia, see Asheri 1972: 17–23; Burstein 1976: 1–22; and A. Robu 2014: 293–310.

historiography afforded individual Greeks an effective tool for endorsing particular strategies for survival and gave the community as a whole a cautious means of advancing ideologies of independence: Greek *poleis* had access to other, safer modes of resistance than open revolt.

1. Herakleides Lembos and the Uses of Local Historiography

Herakleotai were writing about Herakleia at least as far back as the late fifth century BCE.[6] By the early third century, if Nymphis is any indication, they were publishing full-fledged local histories: self-contained, historical narratives focalized by their community's territory and taking that community and its constituents as protagonists. As Memnon's activity attests, histories of Herakleia were also composed in the Roman period, but no such work can be dated to the second century BCE.[7] A similar lacuna is also observable in many other Greek communities: Greek local historiography, while flourishing in the fifth, fourth, and third centuries BCE, seems to go silent for a time thereafter. This may only be a historiographical mirage, of course, since so few of the Greek writers to whom local works are attributed can be dated with any precision. But it is worth noting that those Greek local historians who do undoubtedly belong to the second century tend to be of a particular sort, focusing on communities, often more than one, to which they do not themselves belong.

A good representative of this trend, and a writer who actually plants us firmly in the period of the Maccabean Revolt, is Herakleides Lembos.[8]

---

[6] For the various Herakleian traditions that Herodoros worked into his books on Herakles and the Argonauts, see *FGrHist* 31 FF 31, 44, 49–51, and 54–55.

[7] We know too little about the other local historians of Herakleia, Promathidas (*FGrHist* 430), Amphitheos (*FGrHist* 431), Domitios Kallistratos (*FGrHist* 433), and Timogenes (*FGrHist* 435), to say anything definitive about when they wrote. For commentary to the fragments of these works, see Jacoby 1955: 254–258, 265–267, and 283–284 and Cuypers 2016a, 2016b, 2016c, 2018. For Herakleian historiography in general, see Laqueur 1926: col. 1083–1110 at 1098–1102; Desideri 1967: 366–416; 1970: 487–537; and 1991: 7–24; and Gallotta 2009: 431–445. Very few of the surviving fragments from these histories of Herakleia explicitly treat the historical period; for the possibility that Domitios Kallistratos refers to an invasion (of Antiochus I?) of the gulf of Olbia, see the commentary to *BNJ* 433 F5 (Cuypers 2018).

[8] According to Diogenes Laertius, Herakleides, the son of Sarapion, earned the cognomen Lembos from a particular treatise he wrote called the *Lembeutikos Logos* (5.94).

An emigrant from Kallatis (a colony of Herakleia, no less, which may explain his name), Herakleides became closely associated with the court of Ptolemy VI Philometor and may even have had a hand in negotiating the crucial peace with Antiochus IV Epiphanes after Ptolemy's defeat at Pelusion in 169 BCE.[9] Like his former secretary and reader, Agatharchides of Knidos (*FGrHist* 86),[10] Herakleides himself wrote a general history of some sort, about which we know very little;[11] but he devoted much of his literary efforts to epitomizing earlier works.[12] It is among these epitomes that we find – the only one of his publications to have survived in manuscript form – his treatment of the Aristotelian *Politeiai*, that massive collection of Greek local histories that Aristotle himself composed or whose composition he oversaw in the third quarter of the fourth century BCE.[13]

Herakleides' reasons for revisiting this corpus when he did are as unclear as those of Aristotle for undertaking the project a century and a half earlier. The enduring impetus of Alexandrian antiquarianism may well have played a part, as that Aristotelian compulsion to catalogue and classify surely did for the original enterprise. But something else might also have been at stake. For Herakleides evidently published his *Politeiai* epitomes en masse, and as such, they constituted not so much a collocation of disparate Greek local histories as a cohesive and comprehensive model of the *oikoumene*. Aristotle may have had a similar aim. But while the 158 Aristotelian *Politeiai* had offered, against the backdrop of Alexander's conquest of the East, a testament to Greek authority and

---

[9] Diog. Laert. 5.94 and Souda H462 s.v. Ἡρακλείδης. See Will 1979: 316–319.
[10] *FGrHist* 86 T 2 = Phot. *Bibl.* cod. 213 p. 171a.
[11] Of the original thirty-seven books only a handful of fragments survive.
[12] Many of the works that Herakleides epitomized were biographical in nature: his six-book *Succession of Philosophers* (*Diadochai*) was a summary of Sotion's prolix treatment of the subject (Diog. Laert. 8.7), and he compiled epitomes of the *Bioi* of Satyros of Kallatis (Diog. Laert. 8.40 and 44) and of Hermippos's work on Pythagoras (*FGrHist* 1026 T5), of which some sixty-seven lines do in fact survive (*P.Oxy* 11.1367). For Herakleides' output, see in general Daebritz 1912: col. 488–491; Gallo 1975: 25–28; and the commentary to *FGrHist* 1026 T5 by J. Bollansée.
[13] That Herakleides Lembos wrote the *Politeiai*-epitomes was proven by Bloch 1940: 27–39, although the title of the transmitted work, ἐκ τῶν Ἡρακλείδου περὶ πολιτειῶν, suggests that what we are dealing with are in fact extracts from Herakleides' original text (see Polito 2001: 229–244). For a translation of and brief commentary to these extracts, see Dilts 1971. For the fragments of the Aristotelian *Politeiai* themselves, see Gigon 1987: 561–722 and Hose 2002: 15–85.

'HERAKLES IS STRONGER, SELEUCUS' 207

influence over the Mediterranean, Herakleides chose only forty Greek localities on which to focus;[14] and he pruned the original texts considerably, preferring idiosyncrasies of local custom (the behaviour of women, sexual habits, local produce, and the like) to the machinery of government.[15] To this extent, we might consider Herakleides' activity as a response, not unlike that of his contemporary, Polybius, to major shifts of power in the Mediterranean in the first half of the second century BCE. Herakleides' *symploke* would have been a reaction less to the rise of Rome, however, than to the decline of the Ptolemaic Empire, his goal less to make Aristotle's texts accessible to a new public than to rework the Aristotelian material, as the Ptolemaic Empire was fast losing its grip on old Greece, into a compendium of Greek *epikhoria* writ large.

To be sure, Herakleides' panlocal approach to Greek local historiography was not unique at Alexandria. An analogous attitude had animated the earlier work of Istros (*FGrHist* 334), for example, who wrote on Argos, Elis, and Athens, and of Staphylos of Naucratis (*FGrHist* 269), who wrote on Arcadia, Aeolia, Thessaly, Athens, and Crete, both rough contemporaries of Nymphis. Nor was it unique elsewhere in the Greek world. This is, in fact, the model of local historiography that first emerges among the Greeks.[16] Yet alongside such etic works, we tend to find emic

---

[14] Our manuscripts contain extracts from Herakleides' epitomes of the *Politeiai* of Athens, Sparta, Crete, Cyrene, Corinth, Elis, Tenedos, Paros, Keios, Samos, Cyme, Eretria, Peparethos, Lepreon, Molossia, Phasis, Amorgos, Samothrace, Magnesia, Delphi, Athamanes, Kythera, Rhegium, Corcyra, Taras, Minoa, Lokri, Chalkidike, Kephellonia, Rhodes, Ephesos, Phocaea, Kroton, Akragas, Ithaka, Aphytis, Iasos, Ikaria, Argilos, and Thespiai. Also included are treatments of four non-Greek localities, Lycia, Tyrrhenia, Lucania, and Thrace, which probably came originally from Aristotle's ancillary collection of Νόμιμα Βαρβαρικά (cf. F607 Rose[3] = F 472 Gigon = Athen. 1.23d).

[15] This is clear from a comparison of Herakleides' *Epitome* of the *Athenaion Politeia* with our surviving papyrus of the original Aristotelian text (see e.g. von Holzinger 1891).

[16] For the link between Greek local history and the early *periegeseis* of Hekataios of Miletos (*FGrHist* 1), Skylax of Karyanda (*FGrHist* 709), and Hellanikos of Lesbos (*FGrHist* 4), see Tober 2017: 479–480. We know of over 125 different Greek communities, ranging from the shores of the Black Sea to northern Africa, from Cyprus to Sicily, that produced some form of local history – there were surely others – and many of these communities produced more than one work of local history (see Orsi 1994: 149–79). Judging from Felix Jacoby's collection of fragmentary Greek historians (*FGrHist*), in fact, a Greek setting out in the Classical and Hellenistic periods to write about the past was about twice as likely to concentrate on a particular polis, island, or region than to write a war monograph, universal history, *Hellenika*, biography, or chronography. For an excellent recent appraisal of Greek local historiography, published after this chapter was submitted, see Thomas 2019. Thomas does not deal directly with the Herakleian material.

counterparts, local histories written by, and in many cases for, the locals themselves. Indeed, our evidence suggests that in the Classical and Hellenistic periods most Greek local historians wrote about their own communities and geared their narratives for local consumption.[17] At the same time that Istros and Staphylos were writing their histories, for example, the Spartan Sosibios was publishing, also from the Ptolemaic court, numerous works on his native Sparta (*FGrHist* 595).[18] But in the age of Herakleides, we find very few emic local histories of this sort, of Greek localities at any rate (for there were Jewish historians at this time writing local histories, in Greek, of their community).[19] This striking absence actually goes some way toward clarifying the nature of local historiography among the Greeks.

Communities develop in part through active self-reflection, through the communication of shared memories.[20] Such memories may be isolated moments or else a parataxis, engendered in the context, say, of civic ritual or festival, of a series of such constitutive episodes.[21] The textualization and publication of such narratives by a single community member, however, is an altogether different exercise. For while a native local historian may claim to speak as the mouthpiece of his countrymen, his

---

[17] Those Greek local historians whose provenance we can determine with certainty generally comprise two groups: on the one hand, those who wrote about a plurality of communities including, in some cases, their own – so Charon of Lampsakos (*FGrHist* 262), Hellanikos of Lesbos (*FGrHist* 4), Rhianos of Bene (*FGrHist* 265), Baton of Sinope (*FGrHist* 268), and Staphylos of Naukratis (*FGrHist* 269); on the other hand, those whose one major work of local history was devoted to their own community and who tended to enjoy in that community positions of religious or political authority. The latter group surpassed the former in number if not in fame. See Tober 2017: 474–475.
[18] For Sosibios, see Figueira 2016: 48–69.
[19] It should be emphasized that we know very little about many of the Greek local historians embraced by *FGrHist* III, the volume of Jacoby's collection devoted to fragmentary histories of *poleis* and *ethne*. But those few Greek local historians who were undoubtedly active in the second century BCE, like Zenon of Rhodes (*FGrHist* 523) and, perhaps, Antisthenes of Rhodes (*FGrHist* 508) and Leon of Samos (*FGrHist* 540), notably belonged to and wrote about autonomous *poleis*. For Jewish historians of the period, see *BNJ* 722 and 723.
[20] A helpful category for exploring the role of cultural memory in community formation is Hans-Joachim Gehrke's 'intentional history': see, in particular, Gehrke 2001: 286–313; 2003: 225–254; and 2010: 15–33.
[21] Such 'constitutive narratives' – for the term, see Bellah et al. 1985: 153 – tend to be rooted on the foundation and to feature a series of subsequent formative milestones, which are augmented and adjusted as a community evolves and in accordance with the ideology of the elite. For the related concept of a community's 'master commemorative narrative', see Zerubavel 1995: 7. For the application of this idea to Greek local historiography, see Tober 2019.

interpretation of their constitutive narrative is perforce idiosyncratic, shaped and coloured by his own experiences and aspirations. He may trim or supplement it, foreground or minimize particular events, and discount or promote certain families and individuals, in some cases even his own and himself. By emphasizing certain patterns of past behaviour, moreover, by highlighting the efficacy of some policies and the shortcomings of others, he may also endorse a course of action for the present.[22] To this extent, we may consider emic local histories as performative, inasmuch as their authors participate through their narrativization of the collective past directly in the ideation and actualization of community,[23] and parenetic or protreptic, inasmuch as they aim to persuade contemporary local audiences that their version of the collective past is authoritative and exemplary.

The performative and exhortative functions of local historiography are clearest when we have the luxury of consulting extant texts.[24] Yet even in the case of fragmentary local histories, such as those that come down to us from Classical and Hellenistic Greece,[25] we can often observe how a native historian might use his text to negotiate his own position within his community: some Greek local historians introduced themselves and their families directly into their narratives, for example, defending controversial behaviour or reminding their audience of particular acts of patriotism;[26] some offered explicit judgements on

[22] This is not to equate local historiography with political pamphleteering; there are certainly more effective ways for an individual to influence the behaviour of his community than to write its history (see Tober 2010: 420–422).
[23] For a good discussion of performativity and Greek local historiography (here, in the context of actual recitation), see Clarke 2008: 338–369; see also (with reference to modern Greek local histories), Papailias 2005: 43–92. For the performative aspects of historiography in general, see Burke 2005.
[24] Livy is a good case in point: see, for example, Chaplin 2009. For broader examinations of exemplarity in Roman literature and culture, see Hölkeskamp 1996: 301–338 and Roller 2018. For the politics of local historiography in Quattrocento Florence, to look even further ahead, see Ianziti 2012.
[25] Almost no Greek local histories survive intact from the Classical and Hellenistic periods; we have Herodotus's history of Egypt (Book II of the *Histories*) and the history of Rome written by Dionysios of Halicarnassus in the age of Augustus – both, it is worth noting, etic in form – but nothing from the four intervening centuries.
[26] See e.g. *FGrHist* 328 F67 (Philochoros), *FGrHist* 556 T3 and F56 (Philistos), and *FGrHist* 566 T3a and 3b (Timaios). The phenomenon is particularly pronounced at Rome, with the earliest Roman local historian, Fabius Pictor (*FGrHist* 809), going out of his way to foreground the exploits of the Fabii (see Bispham and Cornell 2013: 176–178). For the related tradition of memoir and autobiography that developed in the later Republic, see Marasco 2011.

individuals or events;[27] others intimated their sympathies more subtly. One of the major contributions of Felix Jacoby's work on local histories of Athens (Atthidography) was to highlight the ways in which a particular historian's political standpoint was visible in his conceptualization of the past.[28] And while Jacoby's focus on party politics and his classification of some *Atthides* as more democratic than others may oversimplify the picture,[29] there is no question that each local historian, of Athens or indeed of any Greek *polis*, shaped his community's constitutive narrative so as to reflect his own beliefs about the present and hopes for the future.[30]

As a medium through which an individual may actively participate in, even guide, his community, emic local historiography abounds. Yet it is by no means universal. Its production commonly depends not only on access to literacy but also on the degree of sovereignty of the focal community itself: a community member is most apt to write a community history, that is to say, when he believes that he has a part to play in that community meaningful enough for his particular rendition of the past to wield persuasive power. This is why in the Greek world it is not until the proliferation of prose in the early fifth century (and in many cases considerably later) that local histories emerge, why it is always the elite who write them, and why we find such textual traditions developing primarily in autonomous republics, where a plurality of individuals cooperate in the administration and governance of their community[31] and are under the impression that they have some control over their

---

[27] See *FGrHist* 328 FF69–70 (Philochoros in his *Atthis*); *FGrHist* 556 T13a (Philistos in his *Sikelika*); and *FGrHist* 566 T13 and F124d (Timaios in his *Sikelika*).

[28] He makes the point most succinctly in Jacoby 1949: 71–79 but sustains the argument in more detail in his subsequent commentaries to the individual Atthidographers in Jacoby 1954. Jacoby's points about Athenian local historians are equally applicable elsewhere; see Tober 2017: 474–476.

[29] So too the idea that 'political war was being waged' in the *Atthides* (Jacoby 1949: 76). For rebuttals to Jacoby's argument, see Harding 1977: 148–160 and P. Rhodes 1990: 73–81; but cf. McInerney 1994. For a more recent appreciation of Atthidography, see Camassa 2010: 29–52, who links the genesis of Atthidography to tensions resulting from the rise of the oligarchy at the end of the fifth century.

[30] See *FGrHist* 556 FF46–7 for indications that Philistos's account of early Sicilian history was strongly coloured by his sycophantic feelings toward the Dionysii; cf. Vanotti 1993; M. Sordi 2000: 61–76; and Pownall 2017.

[31] In the case of kingdoms (like Han Dynasty China and Nara-period Japan), on the other hand, local histories tend to emanate from the central court.

'HERAKLES IS STRONGER, SELEUCUS' 211

self-management.[32] There are of course counter-examples,[33] not to mention difficulties with the notion of autonomy to begin with.[34] But it is nevertheless rare to find a Greek historian writing about, let alone publishing a local history of, his own community during a period when it has lost its ability to self-govern or has been absorbed into a larger social entity, as was the case for many Greek communities in the second century BCE. Emic local historiography does, however, tend to flare up in moments when a community's autonomy is felt to be at risk. So Atthidography blossomed in the middle of the fourth century BCE, in the face of mounting pressure from Macedon,[35] and in the first decades of the third century, when Athens was struggling to weather Antigonid aggression.[36] In these last years of Athenian independence, both Demochares (*FGrHist* 75 T15) and Philochoros (*FGrHist* 328) were writing histories of Athens that emphasized the theme of Athenian autonomy and resistance to Macedon.[37] Demochares seems to have advanced in his narrative the same policies that he advocated daily in the assembly, the same sort of *ad hominem* attacks on Macedonians and turncoat Athenians (*FGrHist* 75 FF6–9) that characterized his orations ([Plut.], *X Orat. Vit.* 851d-f = *FGrHist* 75 T2 with T4 and 7).[38] Philochoros, for his part, did not push his

---

[32] Athenians stopped writing *Atthides* when Athens fell to Antigonos II Gonatas in the late 260s (see Jacoby 1949: 107–111). Henceforth, it is generally non-Athenians who write histories of Athens, and rarely do such texts concentrate on the recent past.

[33] Emic local histories are sometimes written about obsolete communities; see Davis 2011 and, for the case of Yizkor books written by *landsmanshaftn* about vanished Jewish communities of Eastern Europe, Kugelmass and Boyarin 1998.

[34] Several *Atthides* were composed after Chaironeia, and Philochoros was certainly working on his *Atthis* during periods in the early third century BCE when the democracy had been curtailed, nor does Atthidography suddenly reappear when Athens regains its autonomy in 220 BCE.

[35] See Jacoby 1949: 71–79.

[36] This is to say nothing of the frequency with which the Athenian *demos* during these years inscribed, primarily in the context of honorary decrees, narratives highlighting successful resistance to Macedon: see, for example, the decrees for Lykourgos in 307/6 BCE (*IG* II² 457 + 3207), Philippides in 283/2 (*IG* II³ 1 877), Demochares in 271/0 ([Plut.], *X Orat. Vit.* 851d-f), and Kallias in 270/69 (*IG* II³ 1 911, for which, see Shear 1978).

[37] As Jacoby pointed out (*FGrHist* IIIb *Text*, 248–255), Philochoros seems to have structured his Atthis around epochal dates that marked changes in Athens' hegemony and liberty; see also Costa 2007: 10–35 and Jones 2016.

[38] Jacoby categorized Demochares' Athenian history (at least twenty-one books long) as *Zeitgeschichten* and not *Horographie*; yet, while the narrative may not have begun with the *ktisis*, there is no doubt that it was focalized by the Athenian territory and took the Athenian community as its protagonist. For Demochares, see Marasco 1984 and Dmitriev 2016.

agenda in the assembly or lawcourts; yet he too was seen as a proponent of, if not participant in, the resistance movement at Athens – according to his lengthy entry in the *Souda*, in fact, Philochoros died 'at the hands of Antigonos [Gonatas] for his support of Ptolemy [II Philadelphos]', most likely as part of the purge that accompanied the king's occupation of Athens after the Chremonidean war[39] – and it was ostensibly as local historian, not as politician or general, that he fulfilled this role.

We know more about Atthidography than about local historiography in just about any other *polis*. But very few of the surviving fragments from the *Atthides* actually deal with the period after Chaironeia, none at all with the centuries that followed. In order to understand how Greek local historians treated the Macedonian kings, then, we must look outside of Athens, and a good place to turn is Herakleia. For here, too, the production of emic local historiography was closely tied to autonomy; but here, thanks to Photios's chance encounter with eight books of Memnon's history, an encounter that provides us with unparalleled access both to Memnon's narrative and to that of his primary source, Nymphis, we can begin to assess the influence of the Macedonian kings on Herakleian cultural memory and, more generally, the interface between local history and resistance in the Hellenistic world.

2. Writing Local History as an Act of Resistance: Nymphis

According to Memnon, it was not until after the Battle of Koroupedion that Nymphis came to Herakleia, perhaps for the first time – he seems to

---

[39] *Souda* s.v. Φιλόχορος (Φ441 Adler) = *FGrHist* 328 T1: Φιλόχορος... ἐτελεύτησε δὲ ἐνεδρευθεὶς ὑπὸ Ἀντιγόνου, ὅτι διεβλήθη προσκεκλικέναι τῇ Πτολεμαίου βασιλείᾳ. Philochoros evidently did not die during the war, for the *Souda* says that his *Atthis* περιέχει... τὰς Ἀθηναίων πράξεις καὶ βασιλεῖς καὶ ἄρχοντας ἕως Ἀντιόχου τοῦ τελευταίου τοῦ προσαγορευθέντος Θεοῦ†. Although he did not earn the epithet Theos until 259/8 (App. *Syr.* 65), Antiochus replaced his father as sole ruler in 262/1, the same year that Antigonos managed to seize control of Athens. And unless Philochoros had succeeded at the very instant of his death in catching his narrative up to the present moment, he was killed some time after the conclusion of the war. See Jacoby, *FGrHist* IIIb *Suppl.* Text, 222; cf. Costa 2007: 8–9. For a recent overview of the difficult chronology of the Chremonidean War, see O'Neil 2008.

have been a part of the expat community of Herakleotai occasioned by the Klearchid tyranny in the second half of the fourth century (*FGrHist* 434 F1.7.3 = 432 T3).[40] Nymphis would have been a young man at the time of his arrival, for, as Memnon tells us, he was still active in the middle of the third century, chosen in the early 240s to negotiate with a band of Gauls who were threatening Herakleia's hinterland; with a hefty bribe (5,000 gold coins to the group as a whole and an additional 200 for each leader), Nymphis managed to keep the Gauls firmly at bay (*FGrHist* 434 F1.16.3 = 432 T4).[41] That Nymphis was alive in the 240s is corroborated by our other major source for his life, the *Souda* (*FGrHist* 432 T1 = Adler N598).[42] Here we learn that Nymphis, son of Xenagoras,[43] wrote in addition to twenty-four books *On Alexander, the Diadochoi, and Epigonoi* a thirteen-book work *On Herakleia*, which stretched at least to the accession of Ptolemy III Euergetes in 246 BCE.[44]

[40] οἱ δὲ περιλειπόμενοι τῶν ἀφ' Ἡρακλείας φυγάδων, Νύμφιδος καὶ αὐτοῦ ἑνὸς ὑπάρχοντος τούτων, κάθοδον βουλεύσαντος αὐτοῖς καὶ ῥᾳδίαν εἶναι ταύτην ἐπιδεικνύντος, εἰ μηδὲν ὧν οἱ πρόγονοι ἀπεστέρηντο αὐτοὶ φανεῖεν διοχλοῦντες ἀναλήψεσθαι, ἔπεισέ τε σὺν τῷ ῥᾳστῳ. It is possible that Nymphis was raised at Herakleia and was himself exiled at a very early point in his career or else that he emigrated as a youth. More likely, however, he was born abroad, since Memnon speaks of the exiles' desires in 281 to reclaim the property of their ancestors. Perhaps he came of age in one of the Greek communities around the Black Sea, like Sinope (see *I Sinope* 1), or even at Athens, where he would have found a formidable group of Herakleotai, such as Chamaileon and an elderly Herakleides. Menander even devoted a play, *Halieis* (*PCG* 6.2 (1998), 57, no. 25 = 3.10.21–3 Kock), to the plight of Herakleote exiles; for reference to the play, which Nymphis seems to have known, see Athen. 12.72 549a-d = *FGrHist* 432 F10.
[41] διὰ ταῦτα πάλιν οἱ Γαλάται εἰς τὴν Ἡρακλεῶτιν ἔπεμψαν στράτευμα, καὶ ταύτην κατέτρεχον, μέχρις ἂν οἱ Ἡρακλεῶται διεπρεσβεύσαντο πρὸς αὐτούς. Νύμφις δὲ ἦν ὁ ἱστορικὸς ὁ κορυφαῖος τῶν πρέσβεων, ὃς τὸν μὲν στρατὸν ἐν τῷ κοινῷ χρυσοῖς πεντακισχιλίοις, τοὺς δὲ ἡγεμόνας ἰδίᾳ διακοσίοις ὑποθεραπεύσας, τῆς χώρας ἀπαναστῆναι παρεσκεύασεν. For the dating of the embassy, which occurred at some point after the accession of the Pontic King Mithridates II (*c*.250), see Beloch 1929: 214–217 and Olshausen 1978: 401.
[42] [Νύμφιδος] Ξεναγόρου, Ἡρακλεώτης ἐκ Πόντου, ἱστορικός. Περὶ Ἀλεξάνδρου καὶ τῶν Διαδόχων καὶ Ἐπιγόνων βιβλία κδ· Περὶ Ἡρακλείας βιβλία ιγ· ἔχει δὲ μέχρι τῆς καθαιρέσεως τῶν τυράννων † τὰ μετὰ τοὺς Ἐπιγόνους καὶ μέχρι τοῦ τρίτου Πτολεμαίου. For Nymphis and his output, see Laqueur 1937; Jacoby 1955: 259–265; Desideri 1967: 378–416; Gallotta 2009: 441–445; Heinemann 2010: 14–43, 196–215, and 259–265; and Billows 2016.
[43] In the spurious letters of the Herakleote Chion (dating most likely to the Roman period) we encounter a Nymphis (the historian's grandfather?) who was a friend and relative of the tyrant Klearchos (13.3=*FGrHist* 432 T2): perhaps a further indication, if the reference is authentic, of Nymphis's high status.
[44] Nymphis possibly wrote a third work on a Ptolemy (Ael. *NA*. 17.3 = *FGrHist* 432 F17: ἐν τῷ ἐνάτῳ τῶν περὶ Πτολεμαῖον λόγων λέγει Νύμφις ἐν γῇ τῇ Τρωγλοδύτιδι γίνεσθαι ἔχεις ἄμαχόν τι μέγεθος, εἰ πρὸς τοὺς ἄλλους ἔχεις ἀντικρίνοιντο· εἶναι γὰρ πηχῶν καὶ πεντεκαίδεκα. τάς γε μὴν χελώνας εἶναι τοσαύτας τὸ χελώνιον, ὡς χωρεῖν μεδίμνους Ἀττικοὺς καὶ ἐξ αὐτό). It is more likely, however, that Aelian is referring here to a section of Nymphis's general history on the Diadochoi.

Of the two histories that Nymphis wrote, the local was the more widely known, and enough references to and quotations from it remain to allow us to adumbrate its contents and contours.[45] Indeed, since Memnon based the first thirteen books of his own history very closely on that of Nymphis,[46] we actually have a very good sense of Nymphis's *On Herakleia*, especially the last five books (for Photios did not have access to Memnon's first eight books).[47] Nymphis evidently devoted Books Nine and Ten to the first native tyrants of Herakleia (364–337 BCE); Books Eleven and Twelve to the happy tenure of Dionysius and the calamitous reign and fortuitous death of Lysimachos (337–281 BCE) – it was notably the arrow of a Herakleote soldier in Seleucus's army, a certain Malakon, that did him in at the Battle of Koroupedion;[48] and Book Thirteen to the generation or so that followed Koroupedion, concluding with the donation of a Ptolemy (most likely the Euergetes to whom the *Souda* alludes) of 'five hundred *artabai* of wheat and a temple to

---

[45] The local history is cited in the scholia to Apollonius (*FGrHist* 432 FF3–5a, 8, 11–16), by Plutarch (F7), by Athenaeus (FF5b, 9–10), and by Stephanos (FF1–2). We can derive no fragments securely from Nymphis's general history of Alexander and his successors, on the other hand, unless the fragment assigned to 'the ninth of the books on Ptolemy' (*FGrHist* 432 F19) comes actually from this work (see above n. 44). It is likely, however, that it lay behind sections of Pompeius Trogus' *Historiae Philippicae* that have been preserved in Justin's *Epitome* (16.3): see Jacoby 1955: 255 and 260; Desideri 1967: 391 n.123; and Landucci Gattinoni 1992: 17–27.

[46] Not only do the first thirteen books of Memnon's history correspond very closely in content, structure, and pacing to the thirteen books of Nymphis's history, but, as is clear from the one fragment of Nymphis that survives verbatim (*FGrHist* 432 F10: a description of the tyrant Dionysius from Athenaeus's discussion of obesity (12.72 549a–d)), Memnon followed Nymphis quite closely in language and tone, as well. For Memnon's dependence on Nymphis, see Jacoby, *FGrHist* IIIb *Kommentar*, 259–261 and 269–271; Desideri 1967: 378–381 and 389–391; Janke 1963: 8–13; Heinemann 2010: 14–15, 28–43, and 96–102; and V. Davaze 2013: 58–65; but cf. Laqueur 1937: 1100–1101 and 1937: 1621–1623 on the potential influence on Memnon of Theopompos.

[47] We have only a vague sense of the shape of the first eight books: Book One clearly dealt with the pre-*ktisis* visitations of Greek heroes, like Herakles (*FGrHist* 432 F2) and the Argonauts (F4), as well with the native peoples of the region, like the Mysoi (F2) and the Mariandynoi (FF5 and 14); Book Two, which mentions the Persians (F6), probably focused on the sixth century BCE and treated the foundation of Herakleia (F6); Book Four seems to have treated the growth of the Persian Empire (F7); and by Book Six, Nymphis was narrating events from the early fifth century (F9).

[48] F 1.5.7: καὶ πίπτει ἐν τῷ πολέμῳ Λυσίμαχος παλτῷ βληθείς, ὁ δὲ βαλὼν ἀνὴρ Ἡρακλεώτης ἦν, ὄνομα Μαλάκων, ὑπὸ Σελεύκῳ ταττόμενος. πεσόντος δέ, ἡ τούτου ἀρχὴ προσχωρήσασα τῇ τοῦ Σελεύκου μέρος κατέστη. Ἀλλ' ἐνταῦθα μὲν καὶ τὸ ιβ̄ τῆς Μέμνονος ἱστορίας λήγει.

Herakles on the acropolis, built out of Prokonnesian rock' (*FGrHist* 434 F1.17.1).[49] Even though Nymphis did not complete his history until the 240s, however, he seems to have published the first twelve books considerably earlier, likely around the time of his (re)patriation.[50] If so, exile did not merely give him (as it did, say, non-local historians like Thucydides) a leisure and disengagement from local affairs conducive to industry; it also may have incited in him (as it likely did in other émigré local historians, like Philistos, Androtion, Timaios, and Douris) an anxiety about his status as a local in the first place.[51] By writing a history of Herakleia, he might claim ownership over its collective past and thereby access to a community from which he had been estranged. By ending the

---

[49] Πτολεμαῖος δὲ ὁ τῆς Αἰγύπτου βασιλεὺς εἰς ἄκρον εὐδαιμονίας ἀναβάς, λαμπροτάταις μὲν δωρεαῖς εὐεργετεῖν τὰς πόλεις προήγετο, ἔπεμψε δὲ καὶ τοῖς Ἡρακλεώταις ἀρτάβας πυροῦ πεντακοσίας, καὶ νεὼν αὐτοῖς Προκοννησίας πέτρας ἐν τῇ ἀκροπόλει Ἡρακλέος ἀνεδείματο. Photios's practice in this part of his epitome is to summarize two books at once, so Memnon's (and thus Nymphis's) original book divisions are in some cases difficult to determine. Nevertheless, since we know from the *Souda* that the local history extended to Ptolemy III, and since a Ptolemy turns up at the mid-point of Photios's summary of Books Thirteen and Fourteen, just before the abrupt transition to a potted history of Rome (see below, p. 227), this was almost certainly the event that ended the work as whole (see Desideri 1967: 390 n. 118).

[50] That Nymphis published in instalments is suggested by the *Souda*, although the text is corrupt. The lemma says that Nymphis's narrative covered events up to the dissolution of the tyranny (this probably refers to the year 281/0, when Lysimachos was killed and his puppet Herakleides of Kyme deposed, although see Billows 2016 for the possibility that it refers to the end of the Klearchid tyranny in 289/8 BCE) but also that it treated events 'after the Epigonoi and until Ptolemy III'. Either the *Souda* is confused, since it seems to give as the culmination of the work two discrete events thirty-five years apart, or else we must imagine that Nymphis himself designated two separate conclusions to his work. He would not have been the only Greek local historian to publish serially like this: see *FGrHist* 306 F3 for the two editions of Deinias's *Argolika*; and on the Roman side Livy had second thoughts about where to end the *Ab urbe condita* (see Henderson 1989: 64–84). For another interpretation of the *Souda* passage, namely that the lemma is actually designating the ending points of each of Nymphis's histories, with the local history concluding in 281 (or in 289/8) and the general history in 247/6, see Clinton 1834: 21–23; Mathisen 1978: 71; and Billows 2016. Not only does this scenario assume rather a large lacuna in the text of the *Souda*, but it also introduces problems of its own, in particular regarding the meaning of 'Epigonoi' (which Billows suggests was a flexible term; see also Primo 2009, 367–377). An initial publication date in the second quarter of the third century BCE would at any rate have allowed Apollonius to consult the work, which is what the scholiasts assert (*FGrHist* 432 T5 = F3).

[51] For Philistos, see *FGrHist* 556 T5a-d; for Androtion, see *FGrHist* 324 T14; for Timaios, see *FGrHist* 566 TT4a-e, 12, 19 and FF 34 and 124d; for Douris, see *FGrHist* 76 TT1 and 4. On the relationship between exile and historiography for Greek historians, see Momigliano 1978: 59–75 at 61 and Dillery 2007. On the importance of exile as a motivation for historiography more generally, with particular reference to Jewish historians of the Medieval age, see Yerushalmi 1982: 57–75.

first edition of his history with Lysimachos's death, moreover, he could even suggest that the resurgence of Herakleia as an independent *polis* would require not merely Malakon's arrow but also the contribution of Nymphis and the other exiles, descendants of the noble citizens who had lost their franchise as a result of the original tyranny and who would henceforth help to maintain Herakleia's autonomy and authority in the region. A generation or so later, on this reading, Nymphis issued an addendum to his history, tracking Herakleia's fortunes from Koroupedion to the 240s. We can only guess his reasons for revisiting the work at this time, but his goal now was perhaps less to prove his authority over Herakleia's constitutive narrative than to cement his role as civic leader after some thirty years of public service. It was here in the final book that Nymphis inserted himself (at least twice) into his own story,[52] each time rendering himself an upright and integral member of the Herakleote community: it was only after Nymphis and the other exiles returned, in the first place, that the *polis* was at last able to regain its ancestral nobility and *politeia*, along with its long-forgotten prosperity, mirth, and *autarkeia* (*FGrHist* 434 F1.7.3–4 = 432 T3);[53] and it was thanks to Nymphis's diplomacy that Herakleia was able to withstand the Gallic threat a generation later.

By sketching the contents, structure, and publication history of Nymphis's *On Herakleia* we can better understand not only the performativity of the text but also its parenetic functions. This is clearest in Nymphis's appraisal of the Seleucids and in his advocation, through his interpretation of the past, of a particular policy towards the kings in the future. Nymphis's attitude toward the Seleucids is embodied in his treatment of the eponymous founder of the line, who first appears at the end of Book Twelve as the liberator of Herakleia and the antithesis of

---

[52] Since Memnon clearly based the first thirteen books of his own history on that of Nymphis, it is a fair assumption that the two references he makes to Nymphis come ultimately from Nymphis himself, especially since on the second occasion that he mentions him (*FGrHist* 434 F1.16.3 = 432 T4) Memnon calls Nymphis a historian (Νύμφις δὲ ἦν ὁ ἱστορικὸς ὁ κορυφαῖος τῶν πρέσβεων).

[53] καὶ τῆς καθόδου ὃν ἐβούλευσε τρόπον γεγενημένης, οἵ τε καταχθέντες καὶ ἡ δεξαμένη πόλις ἐν ὁμοίαις ἡδοναῖς καὶ εὐφροσύναις ἀνεστρέφοντο, φιλοφρόνως τῶν ἐν τῇ πόλει τούτους δεξιωσαμένων καὶ μηδὲν τῶν εἰς αὐτάρκειαν αὐτοῖς συντελούντων παραλελοιπότων. καὶ οἱ Ἡρακλεῶται τὸν εἰρημένον τρόπον τῆς παλαιᾶς εὐγενείας τε καὶ πολιτείας ἐπελαμβάνοντο.

the oppressive Lysimachos but who returns markedly altered in the next and last book.[54] Book Thirteen began, if Photios's *Epitome* of Memnon is indeed indicative, with the news of Lysimachos's death and the consequent restoration of Herakleian independence.[55] After dismantling Lysimachos's garrison by bribing the soldiers with promises of citizenship, the Herakleotai appoint an *epimeletēs* from their own ranks and send an embassy to Seleucus – evidently, Herakleia was already recognized as Seleucus's ally, for the Bithynian king Zipoites attacked the *polis* after Koroupedion expressly because of his personal enmity with Seleucus (*FGrHist* 434 F1.6.3).[56] But the Seleucus they encounter is an unfamiliar one. Swayed by the advice of his *dioketēs* Aphrodisios, who had detected at Herakleia some hostility toward the king (*FGrHist* 434 F1.7.1),[57] Seleucus ends up threatening a visiting group of Herakleotai. This leads to Chamaileon's courageous retort, to Seleucus's anger, and finally to the breakdown of communications between *polis* and king.[58]

Chamaileon was a Herakleote, a younger contemporary of the celebrated Herakleote scholar Herakleides (Pontikos) and himself a writer of numerous works of philosophy and literary criticism, later considered of a 'Peripatetic' bent.[59] Such an output would certainly have bestowed on him in his own lifetime a celebrity that could explain his leadership of the embassy to Seleucus.[60] Yet our concern is not with the historicity

---

[54] For Nymphis's assessment of Seleucus, see Desideri 1967: esp. 406–412, and Primo 2009: 109–118.

[55] Here, we note, the death is attributed solely to a Herakleote, without any reference to Seleucus: compare the end of Book Twelve, *FGrHist* 434 F1.5.7 (ὁ δὲ βαλὼν ἀνὴρ Ἡρακλεώτης ἦν, ὄνομα Μαλάκων, ὑπὸ Σελεύκῳ ταττόμενος. πεσόντος δέ, ἡ τούτου ἀρχὴ προσχωρήσασα τῇ τοῦ Σελεύκου μέρος κατέστη) with the beginning of Book Thirteen *FGrHist* 434 F1.6.1 (Ἐν δὲ τῷ ιγ τοὺς Ἡρακλεώτας λέγει πυθομένους τὴν ἀναίρεσιν Λυσιμάχου καὶ ὡς εἴη ὁ τοῦτον ἀπεκτονὼς Ἡρακλεώτης τάς τε γνώμας ἀναρρώνυσθαι καὶ πρὸς τὸν τῆς ἐλευθερίας ἀνδραγαθίζεσθαι πόθον, ἦν δ καὶ π̄ ἔτεσιν ὑπό τε τῶν ἐμφυλίων τυράννων καὶ μετ' ἐκείνους ὑπὸ Λυσιμάχου ἀφῄρηντο).

[56] Ζιποίτης δέ, ὁ Βιθυνῶν ἐπάρχων, ἐχθρῶς ἔχων Ἡρακλεώταις πρότερον μὲν διὰ Λυσίμαχον, τότε δὲ διὰ Σέλευκον (διάφορος γὰρ ἦν ἑκατέρῳ), τὴν κατ' αὐτῶν ἐπιδρομήν, ἔργα κακώσεως ἀποδεικνύς, ἐποιεῖτο· οὐ μὴν οὐδὲ τὸ αὑτοῦ στράτευμα κακῶν ἀπαθεῖς ἔπραττον ἅπερ ἔπραττον, ἔπασχον δὲ καὶ αὐτοὶ ὧν ἔδρων οὐ κατὰ πολὺ ἀνεκτότερα.

[57] τῶν μὲν ἄλλων πόλεων ἐν ἐπαίνοις ἦν, Ἡρακλεωτῶν δὲ κατηγόρει μὴ εὐνοικῶς ἔχειν τοῖς τοῦ Σελεύκου πράγμασιν.

[58] For the text, see above n. 1.

[59] For the critic and philosopher Chamaileon, who is certainly the envoy named by Nymphis here (*pace* Wendling 1899); see Martano, Matelli, and Mirhady 2012.

[60] For the use of philosophers as ambassadors in the Hellenistic period, see Kienast 1973: col. 576–577 and Powell 2013.

of the episode: whether Herakleia did reach out to the king after Koroupedion; whether Seleucus was in fact displeased with Herakleia for some perceived intransigence; whether Chamaileon did engage in diplomacy with Seleucus; or whether, if he did, he actually uttered the words that Nymphis here assigns him. Our concern, rather, is with its narrative function in Nymphis's (and so also in Memnon's) history.[61] Seleucus's metamorphosis from redeemer of Herakleia to haughty tyrant occurs in the space between the last two books, books likely composed, as I have suggested, several decades apart. Nymphis's portrait of Seleucus would thus be a reaction less to the policy of Seleucus himself, whose life extended but briefly into the period of Herakleian resurgence, than to that of his successors, with whom Herakleia would struggle for the next fifty years.[62] By grounding Seleucid offensiveness and Herakleian audacity at the moment of Herakleia's rebirth, indeed with its first act as an independent *polis*, Nymphis could both legitimize the city's subsequent stance toward the Seleucids and distil what he took to be the essence of its future success. But what was it that Nymphis meant to communicate about the Seleucids and Herakleia in this altercation between philosopher and king?

The intent of the quip that Nymphis puts into Chamaileon's mouth, Ἡρακλῆς κάρρων, Σέλευκε, is clear enough: an assertion of local power and independence. Clear, too, is his choice to couch the taunt in metonymy. Herakles, whose exploits had featured prominently in the first book of Nymphis's history, to say nothing of Herakleian cultural memory in general, is a natural surrogate for the *polis* to whom he gave his name.[63] As we learn from Demetrios's treatise *On Style*, moreover, a tract likely dating from the same period, the best way for a Greek citizen to criticize a

---

[61] See Bittner 1998: 57–58 and Heinemann 2010: 192–194.
[62] See Desideri 1967: 407–410.
[63] See *FGrHist* 432 FF2–3, 9, and 14; see also Justin 16.3 on the foundation of Herakleia ('oraculum Delphis responderat, coloniam in Ponti regione sacram Herculi conderent'), a passage that likely derives ultimately from Nymphis (see above n. 45). For Herakles' role in Herakleian cultural memory, see Herodoros *FGrHist* 31 FF1a and 51 and Promathidas *FGrHist* 430 F3. Herakleia evidently teemed with monuments and topographical features that recalled Herakles, but the Herakleotai also peddled this image abroad, commissioning several works in various panhellenic sanctuaries – at Olympia, for example, in commemoration of their conquest over the Mariandynoi (Paus. 5.26.7) – and his image would grace Herakleian coinage from the fifth century to the Roman period (see Price 1993: pls. LVII–LVIII).

'HERAKLES IS STRONGER, SELEUCUS' 219

tyrant was through a figure of speech (5.289) – the example provided in that text, incidentally, is of a veiled barb that Demetrios of Phaleron, in the capacity of ambassador, aimed at Seleucus's former comrade Krateros after the Battle of Krannon.[64] By setting Seleucus against Herakles, finally, Chamaileon is able to query the king's authority, dissociating him from the hero with whom Seleucus had himself nurtured strong ties[65] and at the same time from the Argead house, to which Alexander and Philip had of course decidedly belonged.

Also understandable is Chamaileon's appropriation of a line from one of the *Mimes* of the fifth-century Syracusan poet, Sophron – the original was Ἡρακλῆς τεοῦς κάρρων ἦς: 'Herakles was stronger than you' (F59 Kassel–Austin).[66] Through the screen of Sophron, acknowledged as one of Plato's favourite poets and someone whose works Chamaileon and Nymphis would likely have known,[67] Chamaileon is able both to distance himself from the aggression of the sentiment and also to advance an aspect of Herakleian identity of particular significance at the time: Dorianism. For Sophron famously imbued his verse with Doric markers[68] – the phrase that Chamaileon here echoes, retained by Apollonios Dyskolos for just its use of the Doric pronoun τεοῦς (74.21), features the unmistakably Doric κάρρων (which Memnon, or perhaps Photios, helpfully glosses).[69] By placing these words in Chamaileon's mouth, then, Nymphis flaunts Herakleia's Doric roots and thereby highlights one of the things that bound it to its Greek partners in the Northern

---

[64] Demetr. *Eloc.* 289 = Dem. Phal. 183 Wehrli: Πολλάκις δὲ ἢ πρὸς τύραννον ἢ ἄλλως βίαιόν τινα διαλεγόμενοι καὶ ὀνειδίσαι ὁρμῶντες χρῄζομεν ἐξ ἀνάγκης σχήματος λόγου, ὡς Δημήτριος ὁ Φαληρεὺς πρὸς Κρατερὸν τὸν Μακεδόνα ἐπὶ χρυσῆς κλίνης καθεζόμενον μετέωρον, καὶ ἐν πορφυρᾷ χλανίδι, καὶ ὑπερηφάνως ἀποδεχόμενον τὰς πρεσβείας τῶν Ἑλλήνων, σχηματίσας εἶπεν ὀνειδιστικῶς, ὅτι 'ὑπεδεξάμεθά ποτε πρεσβεύοντας ἡμεῖς τούσδε καὶ Κρατερὸν τοῦτον': ἐν γὰρ τῷ δεικτικῷ τῷ 'τοῦτον' ἐμφαίνεται ἡ ὑπερηφανία τοῦ Κρατεροῦ πᾶσα ὠνειδισμένη ἐν σχήματι. For the reference, see Martano et al. 2012: 179.
[65] See Ogden 2017: 50–56.
[66] = *GrGr* II 1.1 p. 74.21. For the likelihood that Nymphis's Chamaileon had Sophron in mind, see K. Müller *FHG* III, 533; Kaibel 1898: 49 n.2; von Wilamowitz-Moellendorff 1900: 28; Desideri 1967: 407 n. 227; Bittner 1998: 57–58; and Heinemann 2010: 193.
[67] See Hordern 2004.   [68] Hordern 2004, 11–25.
[69] κάρρων δὲ ὁ ἰσχυρότερος παρὰ Δωριεῦσι. The word κάρρων (for which, see *Souda* K405 and K409; cf. E. *Gud.* K 301 and *E.M.* 492.38) also crops up in a similar context in Plutarch's *Life of Pyrrhus*, when the Spartan Mandrokleidas reproaches the Epeirote king in the Spartan dialect (26.11): εἰς δὲ τῶν παρόντων, ὄνομα Μανδροκλείδας, εἶπε τῇ φωνῇ λακωνίζων 'αἰ μὲν ἐσσὶ τύ γε θεός, οὐδὲν μὴ πάθωμεν οὐ γὰρ ἀδικεῦμεν αἰ δ' ἄνθρωπος, ἔσσεται καὶ τεῦ κάρρων ἄλλος'.

League.[70] Indeed, it was just after the rebuff of Chamaileon's embassy that Nymphis chose to relate Herakleia's overtures to two nearby *poleis*, Byzantium and Kalchedon (*FGrHist* 434 F1.7.2), each, like Herakleia, Doric and each nursing ties to Megara;[71] and it is the alliance that Herakleia secures with these *poleis* (supplemented by the Pontic king, Mithridates, and, later, by other powers, too) that motivates much of the action of Book Thirteen. The Herakleia that emerges resurgent from Koroupedion is an independent Doric *polis*, united with other Doric *poleis* of the region against the newcomer Macedonian kings.

As notable in the exchange between Chamaileon and Seleucus as the philosopher's calculated riposte is the king's emotional response. As Nymphis frames it, Seleucus's anger persists as a result not of Chamaileon's affront but rather of the king's inability to understand what had been said: the Doric κάρρων, the allusion to Sophron, and the import of the message itself.[72] Nymphis thus paints Seleucus as a bully and as a dunce, the antithesis of Herakles and Chamaileon alike. To be sure, we find a general disregard for philosophy elsewhere attributed to Seleucid kings: Athenaeus, for example, once cites his own work on the *Kings of Syria* about the mistreatment and murder of an Epicurean by an Antiochus (probably Sidetes VII), suggesting that the one true philosopher among the Seleucids was in fact the pretender Alexander Balas (5.47 211ad = *FGrHist* 166 F1).[73] In *2 Maccabees*, moreover, Antiochus IV Epiphanes responds with a frustration not unlike that of Seleucus when faced with a language that he cannot understand (7.21, 27, 24).[74] Such anti-intellectualism characterizes other Hellenistic kings, too, from Lysimachos to Ptolemy VIII Euergetes II, both of whom allegedly banished all philosophers from their

---

[70] For Herakleia's Doric identity, see Burstein 1976: 19–22. Well into the third century CE Herakleotai were inscribing public decrees in Doric (see Jonnes 1994: esp. nos. 1 and 3). For the Northern League, see Bevan 1902: 134–137; E. Will 1979: 138–139; C. Préaux 1978: 120–121; Saprykin 1997: 161–178; Bittner 1998: 63–69; and Gallotta 2010: 95–100.

[71] ταῦτα δὲ Ἡρακλεῶται πυθόμενοι τά τε ἄλλα παρεσκευάζοντο καὶ συμμάχους ἤθροιζον, πρός τε Μιθριδάτην τὸν Πόντου βασιλέα διαπρεσβευόμενοι καὶ πρὸς Βυζαντίους καὶ Χαλκηδονίους. See in general Hanell 1934 and Robu 2014. For Byzantium's Dorianism in particular, see Russell 2017: 188–190.

[72] The genuineness of Seleucus's reaction here, once again, is not our concern; nevertheless, it is worth noting that according to Plutarch Pyrrhos was able to understand the Spartan Mandrokleidas (see above n. 69) when he insisted that 'ἔσσεται καὶ τεῦ κάρρων ἄλλος' (*Pyrrh.* 26.11).

[73] See Braund 2000 and Ceccarelli 2011.

[74] I am grateful to Paul Kosmin for the reference.

respective kingdoms.⁷⁵ But Nymphis's depiction of Seleucus is also very much of a piece with his treatment of earlier enemies of Herakleia: the first tyrant Klearchos, for example, a former student of Plato who ostentatiously rejected his philosophical upbringing,⁷⁶ and his dullard son Satyros.⁷⁷ For Nymphis, enemies of Herakleia were enemies also of Greek learning.

In the brief exchange between Chamaileon and Seleucus, then, Nymphis is able not only to characterize Herakleia as a brave, strong, learned, and autonomous *polis*, Doric and enjoying ties to other Doric *poleis* of the Black Sea region, but also to depict Seleucus as tyrannical, irascible, ignorant, and barbaric. What is more, Seleucus' policy, for all his bravado, is ultimately bootless. Just after he fails to cow Herakleia into submission and prevent the formation of the Northern League, Seleucus gets his comeuppance: in an attempt to return to Macedon and reclaim the Macedonian throne, he is murdered by his guest, Ptolemy Keraunos (*FGrHist* 434 F1.8.2–3). The contrast with Nymphis is plain: whereas Nymphis was welcomed home by his *polis* 'with mutual joy and pleasure', his new fellow citizens embracing him hospitably and ensuring that he and his companions be well taken care of, whereas Nymphis's return had led to the re-establishment of the ancestral *politeia* at Herakleia (434 F1.7.4),⁷⁸ Seleucus's attempted *nostos* was his own ruin.⁷⁹

---

⁷⁵ For Lysimachos, see Karystios of Pergamum (Athen. 13.610e = *FHG* IV 358); for Ptolemy VIII, see Andron of Alexandria *FGrHist* 246 F1 (= Menekles of Barka *FGrHist* 270 F9 = Athen. 4.83.184b–c).

⁷⁶ The story of Klearchos's rejection of philosophy is not attributed explicitly to Nymphis, it is true, but it is mentioned by Aelian (F89 Domingo-Forasté) and in the *Souda*'s biography of Klearchos (K1714), which is almost certainly derived from Aelian. And since Aelian elsewhere (*VH* 9.13) reproduces Nymphis's description of Dionysios's corpulence (which we find also in Athenaeus: 12.72 549a–d = *FGrHist* 432 F10) and cites Nymphis directly by name (*NH* 17.3), Nymphis is very likely the original source.

⁷⁷ Memnon *FGrHist* 434 F1.2.2: τοῦτον δὲ καὶ μαθημάτων τῶν τε κατὰ φιλοσοφίαν καὶ τῶν παντὸς ἐλευθερίου ἄλλου παντελῶς ὑπάρξαι ἀπαράδεκτον, καὶ νοῦν δὲ πρὸς τὰς μιαιφονίας μόνον ὀξύρροπον ἔχοντα φιλάνθρωπον μηδὲν μηδὲ ἥμερον μήτε μαθεῖν ἐθελῆσαι μήτε φῦναι ἐπιτήδειον.

⁷⁸ οἱ δὲ περιλειπόμενοι τῶν ἀφ' Ἡρακλείας φυγάδων, Νυμφίδος καὶ αὐτοῦ ἑνὸς ὑπάρχοντος τούτων, κάθοδον βουλεύσαντος αὐτοῖς καὶ ῥᾳδίαν εἶναι ταύτην ἐπιδεικνύντος, εἰ μηδὲν ὧν οἱ πρόγονοι ἀπεστέρηντο αὐτοὶ φανεῖεν διοχλοῦντες ἀναλήψεσθαι, ἔπεισέ τε σὺν τῷ ῥᾴστῳ· καὶ τῆς καθόδου ὃν ἐβούλευσε τρόπον γεγενημένης, οἵ τε καταχθέντες καὶ ἡ δεξαμένη πόλις ἐν ὁμοίαις ἡδοναῖς καὶ εὐφροσύναις ἀνεστρέφοντο, φιλοφρόνως τῶν ἐν τῇ πόλει τούτους δεξιωσαμένων καὶ μηδὲν τῶν εἰς αὐτάρκειαν αὐτοῖς συντελούντων παραλελοιπότων. καὶ οἱ Ἡρακλεῶται τὸν εἰρημένον τρόπον τῆς παλαιᾶς εὐγενείας τε καὶ πολιτείας ἐπελαμβάνοντο.

⁷⁹ For an illuminating treatment of the passage, which brings out the theme of *pothos*, see Kosmin 2014: 80–82; cf. Primo 2009a: 109–117 for the idea that Nymphis is here offering a sympathetic portrait of Seleucus and even reflecting Seleucid court tradition.

The altercation between Chamaileon and Seleucus serves also as an *aition* for future interaction between Herakleia and the Seleucid kings. According to Nymphis, Herakleia's first act after Seleucus's murder was to assist his murderer, Keraunos, who found himself at loggerheads with Antigonos Gonatas (*FGrHist* 434 F1.8.4–6). And although the alliance with Keraunos was short lived – he was himself murdered gruesomely by the Gauls in 279 – the successive Seleucid kings, whose explicit aim, we are told, was 'to put an end to the democracies of the region' (11.4),[80] quickly emerge in Book Thirteen as Herakleia's primary antagonists.[81] Antiochus's first act after taking power, in fact, is to send his general Patrokles over the Taurus Mountains to lay claim to his father's territory (*FGrHist* 434 F1.9.1); when Antiochus later attacks King Nikomedes of Bithynia, Herakleia sends thirteen triremes in his defence (*FGrHist* 434 F1.9.3; 10.2); and when, later still, Byzantium finds itself at war with an Antiochus (probably the Younger), Herakleia dispatches a larger fleet in support of its ally (*FGrHist* 434 F1.15.1). In every case, the Seleucids flounder in the face of Herakleia's resolute bravery, as had Seleucus before Chamaileon.

Yet Nymphis is also careful to emphasize that against the individual Seleucid kings the Herakleotai never actually engage in combat. Rather than fight Patrokles' troops in 281, for example, they manage to convince his lieutenant, Hermogenes, to withdraw (*FGrHist* 434 F1.9.1); when they confront Antiochus on behalf of Nikomedes, meanwhile, they avoid battle and return 'without achieving anything' (10.2);[82] and when, finally, they join the Byzantines some time later against Antiochus II, they ensure that 'the war not proceed beyond threats' (15.1).[83] The Herakleotai do sometimes take up arms in Book Thirteen – aside from the naval battle between Keraunos and Antigonos after Koroupedion, they clash with the Bithynian king Zipoites over Thynian Thrace in 279 BCE (1.9.5), fight alongside Nikomedes in his bid for power in Bithynia

---

[80] τῶν γὰρ βασιλέων τὴν τῶν πόλεων δημοκρατίαν ἀφελεῖν σπουδαζόντων, αὐτοὶ [Γαλάται] μᾶλλον ταύτην ἐβεβαίουν, ἀντικαθιστάμενοι τοῖς ἐπιτιθεμένοις.
[81] See Desideri 1967: 407.
[82] ἐπὶ χρόνον δέ τινα ἀντικαταστάντες ἀλλήλοις, οὐδέτεροι μάχης ἦρξαν, ἀλλ' ἄπρακτοι διελύθησαν.
[83] Βυζαντίους δὲ Ἀντιόχου πολεμοῦντος, τριήρεσι συνεμάχησαν μ̄ οἱ Ἡρακλεῶται, καὶ τὸν πόλεμον παρεσκεύασαν μέχρις ἀπειλῶν προκόψαι.

the following year (1.11.5), and help the Bithynians, after Nikomedes' death, stave off Zieles' attacks (1.14.2-3) – but such acts of Herakleian aggression are rare, and never are they aimed against the Seleucid kings. Far more frequently, Herakleia resists hostile powers by following Chamaileon's lead, through cautious defiance and forceful words. In many cases, however, Herakleotai prefer to bolster these words with perquisites. It is by coin that the Herakleotai dismantle Herakleides' garrison after Lysimachos's death, persuading his soldiers to defect by offering to match their current salaries (6.2); it is almost certainly by similar ruse that they effect Hermogenes' withdrawal (9.3); it is with the help of a 'great deal of money' that they recover their former possessions of Kieros and Tios (9.4), through a gift of 4,000 gold coins that they help their ally Byzantium repel the Gauls (11.1), and through a generous donation of grain that they keep them from Amisos (16.2); and when, finally, the Gauls arrived at Herakleia's doorstep, it is with a large sum of money that Nymphis convinces them to leave (16.2). Nymphis concludes his history with one last exchange of gifts, this time with Herakleia as the recipient: Ptolemy's donation of grain and a new temple to Herakles on the acropolis, a fulfilment of Chamaileon's prophecy to Seleucus and a fitting validation of Herakleia's autonomy and strength (17).

In Book Thirteen, Nymphis thus offers both an explanation for Herakleia's enmity with the Seleucids and a key to its success. Survival as an independent *polis* depends, he suggests, on resistance, but on a resistance characterized less by aggression than by defence, diplomacy, and preparedness.[84] It was through such a policy that Chamaileon, that Nymphis himself, had helped Herakleia withstand the Seleucid advance in the first half of the third century, and it would presumably be along a similar path that Herakleia could maintain its independence in the years to come. Little could Nymphis predict, however, how differently Herakleia would fare without the Seleucids as adversaries. When Memnon repossessed Nymphis's narrative and extended it for another three books and

---

[84] We see evidence of Herakleia's diplomacy elsewhere in Nymphis's narrative, for example in Herakleia's arbitration during the so-called 'Monopoly War' between Byzantium and Kallatis and Istria (*FGrHist* 434 F1.13: see Avram 2003: 1187–1188 and 1211–1212, and Gabrielsen 2011a: 223–226). See also Just. 16.3 regarding Herakleian preference for diplomacy over war in the late fifth century BCE.

two centuries, he showed just how difficult it was to heed Nymphis's call for measured resistance in the face of Roman might.[85]

3. Greek Local History in the Shadow of Rome: Memnon

We know much less about Memnon than about Nymphis.[86] He was undoubtedly Greek[87] and probably Herakleote.[88] The praise that he continually heaps on Herakleia and its citizens,[89] along with his defence of the city's actions during the Mithridatic Wars, in any case gives us a good idea of his intended audience.[90] He lived at some point after the

---

[85] It is sometimes suggested that Memnon did not rely on Nymphis directly but rather on an intermediary, Domitios Kallistratos (*FGrHist* 433), who had himself appropriated Nymphis's narrative and augmented it to include the Mithridatic Wars (Jacoby 1955: 270–271 and 278; Desideri 1970: 494–496; Ameling 1995: 374–375; Heinemann 2010: 216 and 265–268; and Davaze 2013: 58–68; cf. Laqueur 1926: col. 1101). The evidence for this position is slim (see Yarrow 2006: 144, n.19). Even if we agree with Desideri 1970: 494 that the original author of the Mithridatic Wars account must himself have been an eyewitness to the events, there is no reason to deny Memnon himself this privilege: Memnon's obvious reliance on Nymphis for the early part of Herakleia's history should not perforce deprive him of any initiative of his own.

[86] Biographical details would have been offered, if at all, in the preface, a part of Memnon's work to which Photios did not have access (*FGrHist* 434 T1). For commentary on Memnon's history, see Jacoby 1955: 267–283; Janke 1963; Keaveny and Madden 2016; Heinemann 2010; and Davaze 2013. See also Bittner 1998: 162–213; Yarrow 2006: 109–110, 138–145, and 355–357; Arslan 2007 and 2011, and Gallotta 2014.

[87] The *Bibliotheke* comprises summaries and reviews of Greek texts only. Memnon describes the besieger of Herakleia, M. Aurelius Cotta, moreover, as speaking before the Senate τῇ πατρίῳ γλώττῃ (*FGrHist* 434 F1.39.3) and the temple on the Roman Capitoline as dedicated to Zeus (18.10), and he tellingly deems βάρβαροι several groups of non-Greeks (*FGrHist* 434 F1.11.2, 11.5, 24.4, 29.9, 30.2); see Janke 1963: 7 and Dueck 2006: 45.

[88] He evidently knew the region well (*FGrHist* 434 F1.20.1, 37.7, 28.6, 34.2). He is less precise, however, with his geography of the west (see F1.21, for example, where the Marsi, Paeligni, and Marrucini are described as living in Libya on the borders of Gades). For Memnon's conflation of Italians and Romans, see Yarrow 2006: 141–142.

[89] It is a Herakleote who kills Lysimachos (*FGrHist* 434 F1.5.7); the Herakleian army that fights most bravely in the war against the Bithynian Zipoites (9.5) and in the Bithynian civil war (14.2); and the Herakleian navy that excels in the battle between Keraunos and Antigonos (8.5–6). In the later books, when he was not relying on Nymphis, Memnon commends Herakleia: for its actions in the Social War (21), for its defeat of the Rhodian navy (34.7), for its repelling of two difficult sieges in the early second century (19.2–3 and 20), for its ability to withstand the difficult Roman siege for two years, succumbing only after a betrayal from within (34), and for its marvelous works of art (35.8).

[90] He maintains that the polis had tried to remain neutral but was compelled to provide supplies to Mithridates (*FGrHist* 434 1.27.5), that the murder of the Roman δημοσιῶναι was really the fault of only one very rash citizen (27.6), and that the polis had opened its doors to the Pontic garrison only through betrayal (29.3–5).

death of the Herakleote politician Brithagoras in 47 BCE, for this is the last event that Photios mentions in the *Epitome* (*FGrHist* 434 F1.40.4).[91] And while Photios is not explicit that the sixteenth book was the last Memnon wrote, some of Memnon's terminology (which has been preserved by Photios) suggest that he was roughly contemporary with the events that conclude Book Sixteen and that Brithagoras's death did indeed mark the conclusion of the history as a whole.[92] Like Nymphis before him, then, Memnon would have been writing local history during a period when the Herakleote community was keenly aware of the fragility of its autonomy. Yet Memnon would have had little reason for optimism: because of its support for Mithridates, Herakleia had been sacked, looted, and depopulated by the Romans in the late 70s BCE (*FGrHist* 434 F1.35.5); and despite the initiative of Brithagoras and his colleagues, it would never recover. Under Caesar, the Romans founded a *colonia* at Herakleia, and Mark Antony later assigned the Greek part of the *polis* to none other than Adiatorix, son of the Galatian tetrarch Domnekleios (Strab. 12.3.6).[93] Memnon was thus writing about and for a Herakleia markedly different from that of Nymphis.

Book Fourteen, the first that Memnon undertook without Nymphis's blueprint, actually says very little about Herakleia itself. Herakleotai first appear only about half way through the book, when they send an embassy in 191–90 BCE to Romans, in the region to deal with Antiochus III, and

---

[91] As K. Müller noted, Memnon is completely absent from the scholia to Apollonius, which do allude to Promathidas, Nymphis, and Domitios Kallistratos (Müller 1849: 525; see Jacoby 1955: 172 n. 6).

[92] For Photios's lexicon, see Yarrow 2006: 356–357 and Davaze 2013: 65–67. It has been suggested that Memnon's history originally filled twenty-four volumes, with only the middle octad available to Photios (see e.g. Vogt 1902: 717; Desideri 1967: 373–374 and 2007: 46). But Photios, ambiguous though he may be, suggests nothing of the sort; he seems simply not to have known whether or not the sixteenth book was the last. It is true that had Memnon lived to experience the brief rule of Adiatorix and see Herakleia fully incorporated into the province *Bithynia et Pontos*, we would expect him to have said so (and so to have said so in a subsequent book). But Memnon may well have published his history between 47 and the Battle of Actium (this is the opinion of Laqueur 1937: col. 1098; cf. Jacoby 1955: 172, n.6). Of course, Memnon may also have been interrupted (like Thucydides, Philochoros, and Livy) by his death.

[93] According to Strabo, Adiatorix ended up slaughtering the Romans, allegedly on the orders of Mark Antony, and as a consequence was marched in Octavian's triumph after Actium and killed (cf. 12.3.35; see Janke 1963: 128; see also Magie 1950: 415).

manage to procure friendship from the Senate (*FGrHist* 434 F1.18.6);[94] Memnon thereafter seems interested in Herakleia only insofar as it interacted with Rome.[95] He mentions envoys that the *polis* subsequently sent to P. Cornelius Scipio Africanus to confirm the earlier agreement (18.7); Herakleia's attempt to broker peace between the Romans and Antiochus through Scipio and his brother – Memnon even claims to quote verbatim a letter that Africanus wrote to the *polis* (18.8); and the defensive and offensive alliance that Herakleia formalized with Rome after the Battle of Magnesia in 189, which was inscribed on two bronze tablets and set up prominently in each city (1.18.10).[96] Book Fifteen takes a similar tack, considering Herakleia primarily to set the scene for its eventual confrontation with Rome. The book apparently began with two sieges that Herakleia successfully withstood in the early second century, that of the Bithynian King Prousias I, whose leg the defending Herakleotai shattered with a stone (1.19.2–3),[97] and that of the Gauls, two thirds of whom were surprised and massacred by a Herakleote sally (1.20),[98] that serve to foreshadow Herakleia's ultimate capitulation to Rome a century later. Next, he treats Herakleia's support for Rome during the Social War (F1.21), a gesture that will be unreciprocated when Herakleia finds itself embroiled in Mithridates' revolt.[99] The rest of Book Fifteen, however,

[94] ἀναλαβὼν δὲ γράφει, ὅπως Ἡρακλεῶται διαπρεσβευσάμενοι πρὸς τοὺς τῶν Ῥωμαίων στρατηγοὺς ἐπὶ τὴν Ἀσίαν διαβεβηκότας, ἀσμένως τε ἀπεδέχθησαν καὶ ἐπιστολῆς φιλοφρονουμένοι ἔτυχον, Ποπλίου † Αἰμιλίου ταύτην ἀποστείλαντος, ἐν ᾗ φιλίαν τε πρὸς αὐτοὺς τῆς συγκλήτου βουλῆς ὑπισχνεῖτο, καὶ τὰ ἄλλα προνοίας τε καὶ ἐπιμελείας, ἐπειδάν τινος αὐτῶν δέοιντο μηδεμιᾶς ὑστερεῖσθαι. On the identity of Photios's otherwise unknown P. Aemilius, see Davaze 2013: 421–423.

[95] We are accessing Memnon, it is true, through Photios, who had his own distinct set of interests (see e.g. Treadgold 1980 and Mendels 1986). Nevertheless, given Photios's detailed approach to the earlier books of Memnon, which clearly interested him less than the Mithridatic Wars, we would expect him to mention local affairs, however briefly, if Memnon had recorded them.

[96] ἡ δὲ τῶν Ἡρακλεωτῶν πόλις πρὸς τοὺς ἐκπεμπομένους παρὰ τῶν Ῥωμαίων τῶν στρατηγῶν διαδόχους τὰ αὐτά τε διεπρεσβεύετο, καὶ ταῖς ὁμοίαις ἀντεδεξιοῦντο εὐνοίαις καὶ φιλοφρονήσεσι. καὶ τέλος συνθῆκαι προῆλθον Ῥωμαίοις τε καὶ Ἡρακλεώταις, μὴ φίλους εἶναι μόνον ἀλλὰ καὶ συμμάχους ἀλλήλοις, καθ᾽ ὧν τε καὶ ὑπὲρ ὧν δεηθεῖεν ἑκάτεροι. καὶ χαλκοῖ πίνακες δύο τὰς ὁμολογίας ἴσους καὶ ὁμοίας ἔφερον, ὧν ὁ μὲν παρὰ Ῥωμαίοις ἐν τῷ κατὰ τὸ Καπιτώλιον ἱερῷ τοῦ Διὸς καθηλώθη, ὁ δὲ κατὰ τὴν Ἡράκλειαν καὶ αὐτὸς ἐν τῷ τοῦ Διὸς ἱερῷ.

[97] For the date, probably in the early 180s BCE, see Janke 1963: 31–35; Bittner 1998: 84 with n. 510; and Dmitriev 2007.

[98] For the date, see Jacoby 1955: 136–138 and Dmitriev 2007: 134.

[99] According to Livy, Herakleia also supported Rome in its war against Perseus (42.56.6).

details the outbreak of hostilities between Rome and Mithridates, with Herakleia cropping up only rarely and by way of apology.[100] This emphasis on Rome is prefigured by the potted Roman history which commences Book Fourteen.[101] The digression serves not only to caulk the temporal gap between Ptolemy's benefaction in the 240s BCE (the event that concluded the previous book)[102] and Herakleia's next entrance in the narrative just before the Battle of Magnesia,[103] but also to compare and contrast the newcomer Rome with the other protagonists of Memnon's narrative. Like Herakleia, on the one hand, Rome was a self-styled colony whose early history was marked by struggles first with indigenous tribes and then with various aggressive outsiders, including the Gauls (1.18.1) and the Diadochoi (1.18.1). Prompted by sage advice from Alexander the Great, however – the Macedonian king had allegedly urged them to conquer whomever they could but to yield to the more powerful (1.18.2)[104] – the Romans embarked on a course far different from that of Herakleia. Like the Seleucids, on the other hand, Rome found itself suddenly endowed with significant power in the Black Sea region; but rather than threaten and then alienate the Herakleotai, as had Seleucus to Chamaileon, the Romans received the first Herakleian embassies kindly, and goodwill continued for the next century.

In Nymphis's history, we recall, it did not take long for Seleucus, whose defeat of Lysimachos had liberated Herakleia from years of oppression, to pass from tyrannicide to tyrant of the *polis* in his own right. So too in Memnon's history does Rome, in driving the hostile

---

[100] Memnon reminds his readers that the Herakleotai had not always supported Mithridates: they saved some Chian captives from Pontic ships, for example, and restored them to their homeland (23.2); and they provided Mithridates with triremes only after two distinguished citizens, Silenos and Satyros, had been taken hostage (27.5).

[101] See n. 49 above for a discussion of Memnon's book divisions.

[102] For the argument that this lacuna was already part of Memnon's narrative and not a consequence of Photios's epitomization, see Laqueur 1937: col. 1099–1101 and Desideri 1967: 377 n. 50 and 1970, 488. n.3 (contra Jacoby 1955: *Text*, 270 and *Noten*, 172–173 nn. 25–26).

[103] We would perhaps expect Memnon's digression to have ended at the start of the Syrian War, the event that first brought Rome into contact with Herakleia. Memnon's choice to extend his account of Roman history to Pydna may reflect the nature of the source on which he was relying (see Desideri 1970: 494 and 2007, 48).

[104] ὅπως τε ἐπὶ τὴν Ἀσίαν Ἀλεξάνδρῳ διαβαίνοντι, καὶ γράψαντι ἢ κρατεῖν, ἐὰν ἄρχειν δύνωνται, ἢ τοῖς κρείττοσιν ὑπείκειν, στέφανον χρυσοῦν ἀπὸ ἱκανῶν ταλάντων Ῥωμαῖοι ἐξέπεμψαν·

Antiochus from Europe, eventually take his place as Herakleides' prime antagonist. Angered that the Herakleotai had provided Mithridates with supplies and ships, the Romans send *publicani* (*dēmosiōnai*) into the city to demand contributions, and the Herakleotai view their mandates and flagrant disregard for local custom as the beginning of slavery. Yet, rather than assert Herakleian authority with jingoism and a *bon mot*, as had Nymphis's Chamaileon, or with a well-placed bribe, Nymphis's preferred method, Memnon's disgruntled citizens succumb to a hotheaded demagogue, fall upon their Roman guests, and massacre them to a man (1.27.5–6).[105] What is more, thanks to the machinations of a certain prominent Herakleote named Lamachos, they soon (*c*.73 BCE) even welcome into their midst a Pontic garrison of 4,000 soldiers (1.29.3–4). The Romans retaliate and besiege Herakleia, and when they succeed in storming the *polis* two years later they reduce the population significantly and loot many of its treasures (1.34–5). Among the works of art that the proconsul of Bithynia and Pontus, M. Aurelius Cotta, plundered was an exquisite statue of Herakles, replete with golden club, quiver, and lion skin (*FGrHist* 434 F1.35.7–8).[106] Herakles may have been stronger than Seleucus, but he falls to Rome.

For Memnon, as for Nymphis, the preservation of Herakleia's autonomy did not depend on aggression and militancy: Herakleia's decision to

---

[105] καὶ ἀπὸ ταύτης τῆς πράξεως (ὅπερ καὶ Ἀρχέλαος ἐμηχανᾶτο) τὴν Ῥωμαίων ἀπέχθειαν ὁ Ἡρακλεώτης δῆμος ἐκτήσατο· δημοσιωνίας δὲ τῶν Ῥωμαίων ἐν ταῖς ἄλλαις πόλεσι καθιστώντων, καὶ τὴν Ἡράκλειαν διὰ τὴν εἰρημένην αἰτίαν ταύταις ὑπέβαλλον. οἱ δὲ δημοσιῶναι πρὸς τὴν πόλιν ἀφικόμενοι παρὰ τὰ ἔθη τῆς πολιτείας καὶ ἀργύριον ἀπαιτοῦντες τοὺς πολίτας ἐλύπουν, ἀρχήν τινα δουλείας τοῦτο νομίζοντας. οἱ δὲ διαπρεσβεύσασθαι δέον πρὸς τὴν σύγκλητον ὥστε τῆς δημοσιωνίας ἀπολυθῆναι, ἀναπεισθέντες ὑπό τινος θρασυτάτου τῶν ἐν τῇ πόλει, τοὺς τελώνας ἀφανεῖς ἐποίησαν, ὡς καὶ τὸν θάνατον αὐτῶν ἀγνοεῖσθαι.

[106] χρήματα γοῦν διερευνώμενος οὐδὲ τῶν ἐν ἱεροῖς ἐφείδετο, ἀλλὰ τούς τε ἀνδριάντας καὶ τὰ ἀγάλματα ἐκίνει, πολλὰ καὶ καλὰ ὄντα. καὶ δὴ καὶ τὸν Ἡρακλέα τὸν ἐκ τῆς ἀγορᾶς ἀνῄρει, καὶ σκευὴν αὐτοῦ τὴν ἀπὸ τῆς πυραμίδος, πολυτελείας καὶ μεγέθους καὶ δὴ καὶ ῥυθμοῦ καὶ χάριτος καὶ τέχνης οὐδενὸς τῶν ἐπαινουμένων ἀπολειπομένην· ἦν δὲ ῥόπαλον σφυρήλατον ἀπέφθου χρυσοῦ πεποιημένον, κατὰ δὲ αὐτοῦ λεοντῆ μεγάλη ἐκέχυτο, καὶ γωρυτὸς τῆς αὐτῆς μὲν ὕλης, βελῶν δὲ γέμων καὶ τόξου. πολλὰ δὲ καὶ ἄλλα καλὰ καὶ θαυμαστὰ ἀναθήματα ἔκ τε τῶν ἱερῶν καὶ τῆς πόλεως ἀφελών, ταῖς ναυσὶν ἐγκατέθετο. καὶ τὸ τελευταῖον πῦρ ἐνεῖναι τοῖς στρατιώταις κελεύσας τῇ πόλει, κατὰ πολλὰ ταύτην ὑπέπρησε μέρη. That the statue of Herakles Cotta looted had stood beside a pyramid perhaps suggests that it was part of the temple complex dedicated by Ptolemy nearly two centuries earlier. According to Photios, however, the stolen statue of Herakles had stood in the agora, Ptolemy's temple to Herakles on the acropolis (*FGrHist* 434 F1.17; for the identification of the temple, see Hoepfner 1966: 25). There may well have been multiple monuments to Herakles at Herakleia, but it is also possible that Photios has erred here.

'HERAKLES IS STRONGER, SELEUCUS' 229

take violent, preemptive action against Rome was its downfall. Successful resistance depended rather on diplomacy, and on a diplomacy, more to the point, backed by financial security.[107] Herakleia had understood this, Memnon suggests, until Mithridates' revolt.[108] Caught as it was between Mithridates and Rome, however, the Herakleotai could no longer act on Alexander's alleged advice to the Romans: yielding to one power meant active resistance against the other. Memnon underscores Herakleia's error by juxtaposing its fate to that of two other Black Sea communities, Prousias and Nikaia. Both *poleis*, like Herakleia, were colonies that enjoyed putative ties to Herakles and the Argonauts; both, however, had submitted without a fight to Rome and were as a consequence spared (1.28.7–11).[109]

While Nymphis had told the story of Herakleia's triumph as an autonomous *polis*, Memnon framed his narrative as a tragedy. The siege does not conclude Memnon's history, it is true; Memnon goes on to record the *aristeia* of a certain captive Herakleote named Thrasymedes, whose histrionics persuaded the Senate to punish Cotta and release the Herakleote prisoners (*FGrHist* 434 F1.39.2–3) and who subsequently succeeded in assembling some eight thousand new settlers to revive the *polis* (F1.40.2). Yet, liberated though the Herakleotai may have been as individuals, the community of Herakleia itself was no longer free.[110] Some years later, Memnon tells us, Thrasymedes' compatriot Brithagoras ingratiated himself with Julius Caesar and spent the next dozen years entreating him to recognize Herakleia's autonomy

---

[107] At the beginning of Book Fifteen, the Herakleotai manage to overcome the Gallic siege because they, and not the Gauls, are so well supplied (20.2); and Herakleia is able to withstand the Roman siege for so long because it is able to benefit from support of its colonies and allies, falling only when Triarius succeeded in blocking the port (34.5).

[108] It even went out of its way to negotiate peace between Rome and Antiochus III (18.8–9), an episode that Memnon neatly counterpoises to Herakleia's earlier arbitration between Byzantium and Kallatis in Book Thirteen (see above n. 84). Herakleia's first reaction to Mithridates' revolt, moreover, was to maintain its neutrality, explaining to emissaries from Rome and Mithridates that support of either side was impossible (*FGrHist* 434 F1.26.2).

[109] On Photios's confusion between Prusias *ad mare* (formerly Kios) and Prusias *ad Hypium* (formerly Kieros) see Janke 1963: 93.

[110] *FGrHist* 434 F1.40.3: Βριθαγόρας δέ, ἤδη τῆς πόλεως αὐξομένης, ἐλπίδας ἐποιήσατο πρὸς ἐλευθερίαν τὸν δῆμον ἀνενεγκεῖν. It had evidently not yet been recognized as a *civitas libera* (see Jones 1971: 162 and 423 n. 27).

(F1.40.3-4).[111] But he succumbed to old age and exhaustion before accomplishing his goal, the lamentation that his death induced among the Herakleotai, the last scene of Book Sixteen, serving as Herakleia's own swan song (40.4).[112]

Emic Greek local historiography does not completely disappear after the rise of Rome; but what began in the fifth century as an expression of autonomy and *autarkeia*, what became in the hands of Nymphis and his contemporaries a powerful tool of local resistance, emerges on the other side of the crises of the second century as an exercise in nostalgia.[113] Even through his pessimism, however, Memnon does not completely forgo the theme of Herakleian resistance: the ships carrying Cotta's looted Herakleian treasures, he reports, were destroyed as they made their way to Rome, some sunk by the weight of their own load, others driven by winds into the shallows, and much of the cargo (including, perhaps, the statue of Herakles itself) slipped decidedly from Roman hands (1.36).[114]

---

[111] Janke 1963: 128 may be right that Photios should have written twelve months rather than twelve years.

[112] Βριθαγόρας... οὐ μὴν ἐξ ἐφόδου γε λαβεῖν τὴν ἐλευθερίαν ἠδυνήθη, ἅτε δὴ οὐκ ἐν τῇ Ῥώμῃ ἀλλ᾽ ἐφ᾽ ἕτερα τοῦ Γαίου περιτρέχοντος. οὐκ ἀφίστατο μέντοι γε Βριθαγόρας, ἀλλὰ περὶ πᾶσαν τὴν οἰκουμένην αὐτός τε καὶ Πρόπυλος συμπεριαγόμενος τῷ Καίσαρι ἐβλέπετο παρ᾽ αὐτοῦ, ὡς ἐπισημειούμενον τὸν αὐτοκράτορα τῆς λιπαρήσεως αὐτὸν ἀποδέχεσθαι. δωδεκαετίας δὲ τὴν παρεδρίαν διαμετρούσης, καὶ περὶ τῆς εἰς Ῥώμην ἐπανόδου τοῦ Καίσαρος διανοουμένου, ὑπό τε τοῦ γήρους καὶ τῶν συνεχῶν πόνων κατατρυχωθεὶς Βριθαγόρας τελευτᾷ, μέγα πένθος τῇ πατρίδι καταλιπών. The timing of Brithagoras's death adds to the tragedy: he would have been successful, Memnon suggests, had he lived to accompany Caesar back to Rome (Caesar was evidently unable to grant Brithagoras's request while he was abroad).

[113] See above n. 33 for local histories of extinct communities.

[114] τῶν δὲ νεῶν, αἳ τὰ τῆς πόλεως λάφυρα ἦγον, αἱ μὲν κατάφορτοι γενόμεναι μικρὸν ἄποθεν τῆς γῆς διελύθησαν, αἱ δὲ ἀπαρκτίου πνεύσαντος ἐξεβράσθησαν εἰς τὰ τενάγη, καὶ πολλὰ τῶν ἀγωγίμων ἀπεβάλοντο. On the theme of divine retribution in Memnon, see Dueck 2006: 58.

9
Central Asian Challenges to Seleucid Authority
Synchronism, Correlation, and Causation as Historiographical Devices in Justin's *Epitome* of Trogus

Rachel Mairs

1. Introduction

As scholars of Hellenistic Central Asia are accustomed to bemoan, there are few chronological anchors in Graeco-Bactrian history. The few we do have are offered by Justin, in his epitome of the lost *Philippic Histories* of the universal historian Pompeius Trogus:[1] a flimsy enough source, but then Bactrian historians are used to making the best of a bad lot. Justin or Trogus – I shall return to the ambiguity of authorship below – presents a veritable age of rebellions in the 240s BCE. As the Seleucid Dynasty descended into brother-against-brother warfare, in Justin's representation, rebels against Seleucid authority were not pursued (41.4: *huius defectionis inpunitatem illis duorum fratrum regum, Seleuci et Antiochi, discordia dedit, qui dum inuicem eripere sibi regnum uolunt, persequi defectores omiserunt*). How Justin sets up his next vignette is significant. At the same time (*eodem tempore*), he states, Theodotus (i.e. Diodotos) 'governor of the thousand cities of Bactria' revolted and assumed the title of king. Following his example, 'all the peoples of the East' forsook the

---

[1] See, most recently, Borgna 2018.

Macedonians. The chain of correlation – and causation – continues. At that same time (*eo tempore*), Arsaces invaded Parthia and set himself up as king, having heard that Seleucus (II) was being defeated by the Gauls (although he does not mention it, in alliance with Antiochus Hierax). In Justin's and/or Trogus' view, four spheres of threat to Seleucid control in the mid-third century BCE are linked: the war between Seleucus II and Antiochus Hierax; the independence of Bactria; the independence of Parthia; and the presence of Gallic armies in Asia Minor.

In a later Parthian-Bactrian synchronism, Justin does not posit the same causal relationship between simultaneous events, but does emphasize the perfect storm created by their co-occurrence.[2] Almost at the same time (41.6: *eodem fere tempore*) as Mithridates I of Parthia ascended the throne, Eucratides became king of Bactria. Eucratides weathered conflicts with the Sogdians, Drangians, and Indians, surviving a siege by an Indo-Greek king, Demetrius, against overwhelming numerical superiority. The Graeco-Bactrian state had, however, been fatally weakened by this, and was defeated by Parthia. Eucratides was murdered by his own son and co-regent. Mithridates, in contrast, was strengthened by victory in war against the Medes and Elymaeans at around the same time as his war against Bactria. Justin makes an implied connection to the earlier Bactrian-Parthian synchronism by mentioning Mithridates' ancestor, Arsaces.

Chapter 41 of Justin's epitome of Trogus, then, offers us two explicit points of historical synchronism in Central Asian history: the independence of Parthia and Bactria from the Seleucids in the 240s BCE, and the rise of two kings with very different fates in the late 170s BCE. If we include the brief treatment of the affairs after the death of Alexander with which the chapter opens, we have in fact three such synchronisms, where multiple revolts and wars occurred simultaneously. Justin's presentation of these three historical moments invites us to consider the distinction between correlation and causation in simultaneous revolts against Seleucid authority. My concern in the present discussion is, however, not primarily historical, but historiographical. As well as the historical connections which we can trace between revolts in different regions – in

---

[2] Mairs 2014: 151–156.

terms of inspiration, reaction to common forms of oppression, or simply opportunism – simultaneity also offers a powerful rhetorical strategy in presenting events, one which plays into our construction of broader narratives of Seleucid rise and decline. Justin's historical correlations act as a narrative and heuristic device, one which he has in common with many contemporary and more recent historians.

2. Historical Synchronisms

David Hackett Fischer's still-salutary dissection of 'historians' fallacies' offers (at least) two reasons to tread carefully in our approach to Justin's synchronisms. One should not mistake correlation for cause, and one should not fall prey to the 'fallacy of indiscriminate pluralism' in listing numerous potential contributing factors to an end result without providing some assessment of their relative weight.[3] Justin arguably does both; but it is also evident that he uses synchronism as a rhetorical strategy.

Synchronisms are a recurring trope in the epitome of the *Philippic Histories*.[4] Whether this fondness for the device comes from Trogus or Justin is open to debate.[5] My own inclination is to give more credit to Trogus as author than has tended to be the case (in line, for example, with the approach of Yarrow).[6] Like Bartlett, I see Justin as the preserver of 'a fragmented picture of Trogus' worldview', retaining much in the way of philosophical stance and rhetorical structure from the original.[7] For the sake of strict source accuracy I shall nevertheless refer to 'Justin'.

Justin uses the device of synchronism to achieve several different effects. Synchronisms of distant events, such as the fall of Athens, death of Darius II and exile of Dionysius I of Syracuse in 404 BCE, reinforce the claim to universality of the *Philippic Histories*.[8] Here is an historian with a comprehensive knowledge of the polities and politics of the

---

[3] Fischer 1971: 167–169, 175–177.
[4] Noted, for example, in the commentary of Yardley and Heckel 1997: 27.
[5] On Trogus' versus Justin's language use, see Yardley 2003; and on Trogus' sources, Richter 1987.
[6] Yarrow 2006.   [7] Bartlett 2014: 279.   [8] 5.8.7; Alonso-Nuñez 1992: 84.

Mediterranean world, capable of providing a broad historical perspective. Synchronisms can be employed with teleological intent, as, for example, in the juxtaposition of the rise to power of Seleucus and Sandrocottus (i.e. Chandragupta), who would late come into conflict with one another.[9] In his description of the breakaway of Bactria and Parthia from Seleucid control, Justin, by-the-by, gives the Roman consular date and mentions that this was during the First Punic War. There is no direct connection between Roman and Seleucid affairs at this time, but Justin provides a chronological anchor with which his (Roman, Latin-literate) audience will have been more familiar, and presages the later rise to domination of Rome over the Seleucid Empire and other Hellenistic kingdoms.

As Denis Feeney has discussed, our modern concept of historical events as dates, numbers in a fixed, universal framework, has little in common with the perspective and priorities of most ancient historians, who construct their historical framework by connecting significant events and people. 'The Romans' time horizons are not plotted out with numbered milestones in a series but dotted with clusters of people in significant relationships with each other through memorable events'.[10] Synchronism is an invaluable orientation device in a world with multiple competing systems for reckoning time, and where time is for the most part reckoned by people (consulships, regnal years), not by absolute dates (although see Kosmin on the Seleucid Era system[11]). In the age of Augustus, the time when Trogus was composing his history, universal histories which synchronized events across large distances flourished, because the diverse histories of regions had come together in an 'unprecedented involvement of times and places' under Roman rule.[12] Here we find the teleological and chronological anchoring device of synchronism especially salient; another argument, incidentally, for viewing synchronisms as a device retained from Trogus' original history, not as an innovation of Justin. But historians seldom draw synchronisms for purely utilitarian purposes, divorced from historical resonance. Although not necessarily identified explicitly with one another, synchronism and causality are not entirely separate concepts. The choice

---

[9] 15.4.20–21; Alonso-Nuñez 1992: 84.   [10] Feeney 2007: 16.   [11] Kosmin 2018.
[12] Feeney 2007: 64–65.

of people and events to synchronize is not a neutral one, and 'Justin' chooses to see his synchronized events not just as contemporaneous, but as thematically connected in some way. Whether they are historically connected, in a causal relationship with each other or with subsequent events, is a slightly different matter. The crucial question, in Feeney's analysis, is 'what actually makes synchronism not just technically useful or contingently convenient or thought-provokingly piquant, but historically or ideologically significant'?[13]

The Introduction to this volume advocated a globalizing approach to the study of revolt and resistance in the Hellenistic world. It argued that, for the modern historian, 'global comparison is possible without historical connection' but also that one might employ a more emic perspective to trace substantive connections between individual episodes of revolt. Mediated through the historical perspective of Trogus or Justin, challenges to Seleucid authority do indeed synchronize, producing discrete moments of revolt. As well as a rhetorical device, these synchronisms are an artefact of annalistic record-keeping as a source for historians. The question remains as to whether these have a deeper significance.

Before examining the historical as well as historiographical value of synchronizing moments in Hellenistic history as Justin does, I should like to look at some historical contexts where multiple revolts against a central imperial authority in diverse places and cultures *have* had direct relationships with one another. The most instructive case is the British Empire in the nineteenth and twentieth centuries. As Elleke Boehmer has discussed – following on from the observations of those, such as Frantz Fanon, who were themselves involved in cross-national oppositions to imperialism – anti-imperial and nationalist movements 'found inspirational solidarity and instructive models in *one another's* work and experience' (emphasis in original).[14] Irish Nationalism is a good example. An Irish brigade fought on the side of the Boers against the British during the Boer War. Sinn Féin and the Swadeshi movement in India took inspiration from one another in their ideologies of self-reliance. The Nationalist slogan 'England's difficulty is Ireland's opportunity' found new resonance during the First World War, with the Easter

[13] Feeney 2007: 21.   [14] Boehmer 2002: 2.

Rising of 1916.[15] Nineteenth-century Irish and Egyptian Nationalism serve as resonant comparanda for the Egyptian writer Bahaa Taher in his 2007 historical novel *Sunset Oasis* (*Wāḥat al-Ghurūb*). In present-day Northern Ireland, with perverse logic, Palestinian and Israeli flags have been co-opted as symbols of Irish Nationalism and Ulster Unionism.[16] In Boehmer's analysis of Irish, Indian, and South African oppositions to British imperialism at the turn of the nineteenth-twentieth centuries, these movements are more than analogous: there was 'a distinct and enabling perception of correspondence *at the time*' (emphasis in original).[17] In a still clearer case of events spurring contemporaneous opposition in distant regions, Seema Alavi examines the repercussions of the exile of Indian Muslim intellectuals in the aftermath of the Indian Rebellion of 1857, and the role of trans-imperial networks in the mid-nineteenth century 'age of revolts'.[18] A rebellion against British imperialism created a 'Muslim cosmopolitanism' which aimed to transcend national and (British and Ottoman) imperial boundaries.

These same issues are of salience to the Seleucid context. To what extent did actors in simultaneous revolts against Seleucid authority in different regions of the empire (Bactria, Judea, Parthia) conceive of themselves as participants in a greater game of opposition to Seleucid rule? What was the ethnic component to such revolts, and was there any sense of cross-ethnic solidarity against Greek authority? Modern collaboration and synchronization of revolt has been facilitated by communications superior to those of the Hellenistic world. Does simultaneity of revolt imply communication, and of what nature and degree? In the absence of direct communication, how would distant revolt have been felt locally?

3. Three Moments of Bactrian Revolt I: The Settler Revolts (320s BCE)

Let me ground some of these hypothetical questions more firmly in the Central Asian context. As I have already noted, Justin presents three

---

[15] For the preceding examples, see Boehmer 2002: 25–33.
[16] Respectively, McDonald 2002; Humphries 2014; Dizard 2014.
[17] Boehmer 2002: 11.   [18] Alavi 2015: 16–22.

points in Graeco-Bactrian history where unrest corresponds to unrest elsewhere in the Seleucid orbit. The first is the clearest-cut case of connected, mutually inspired revolt across great distances in the Hellenistic world: the years following the death of Alexander the Great in 323 BCE. The settler revolts in Bactria in fact spanned two discrete moments of revolt: the growing Greek and Macedonian unrest at Alexander's continued march into India, and the Lamian War and wars among the Successors following his death.

The Bactrian settler revolts are described in grim and sometimes emotive detail in the literary sources. Alexander's policy of settlement had been carried out in a hasty and not always efficient manner.[19] Aside from the problems resulting from the unresolved issue of local opposition, the practice of settling those troops no longer fit for active service had more to do with the pragmatic operation of a field army than the successful foundation of a settlement. They were jettisoned as a liability to the army, and there is nothing to suggest that this would not make them a liability to a city. Although the sources give little information, discontent had clearly been brewing among the Greek settlers for some time. They had reason to resent Alexander's decision to settle them in Bactria-Sogdiana, a region in which their numbers had suffered attrition from adverse climatic conditions and the guerrilla tactics used by Spitamenes and other Central Asian opponents. In addition, some of the mercenaries used to settle the region may have been chosen specifically because they had formed part of an anti-Macedonian Army in Greece:[20] a good way of getting rid of troublesome forces, but surely a very poor one of forming a stable settlement in a hostile country.[21]

The first rebellion came in 325, with the news that Alexander had been wounded in India. He was widely believed to be dead and the settlers thus felt safe to revolt (Diodorus Siculus 17.99.5–6). In Curtius' view, the motivation was a desire for exodus, not independence and the Greeks 'compelled the barbarians to also join in the revolt' (9.7.2: *barbaros quoque in societatem defectionis impulerant*). One Athenodorus assumed the title of king. According to Curtius (9.7.3), this was 'not so much out

---

[19] Mairs and Fischer-Bovet 2021.   [20] Holt 1988: 72–73.
[21] On the background and causes of the revolts, see Iliakis 2013.

of desire for power, than of returning home' (*non tam imperii cupidine, quam in patriam revertendi*). The revolt disintegrated into an internal dispute. Athenodorus occupied the citadel of Bactra, but was then assassinated at a banquet by a Bactrian named Boxus, at the instigation of Biton, a rival Greek. Biton, according to Curtius (9.7.11), did in the end manage to escape both retribution from the Greek settlers and Bactria itself, taking with him an unspecified number of Greeks.

The role of Bactrians in the first revolt provides an important reminder that we cannot consider the Greek community in social isolation from its Bactrian neighbours. Angelos Chaniotis cites the (rare) attested incidents of co-operation between foreign garrisons and local citizens in Hellenistic cities, against the power which had established the garrison, and argues that 'such a co-operation presupposes intensive interaction between the foreign soldiers and the inhabitants of the garrisoned settlement'.[22] The garrison at Bactra was the centre of such co-operation in the first settler revolt: Bactrians and Greeks feasted together and conspired together. We might take or leave Curtius' contention that the Bactrians were 'forced' to be a part of the revolt. The inter-ethnic character of the first revolt may in fact serve as an example of the kind of socio-economic, cross-ethnic solidarity examined by Christelle Fischer-Bovet in her dissection of Hellenistic revolts.[23]

The first revolt, although it declined into internecine squabbling, was a serious comment upon the settlement of Bactria and the situation which it had produced. The genesis of the second revolt, in 323, followed a, by now, familiar pattern of discontent, hesitation, and opportunism.[24] Pausing only to make sure that Alexander was really dead this time, the Greeks took counsel together, elected a man named Philon as their general and raised a force of 20,000 infantry and 3,000 cavalry. A Macedonian expeditionary force was dispatched under Peithon to suppress them. Diodorus claims that Peithon intended to treat the Bactrian Greeks with clemency and win them over to form an alliance which would see him made ruler of the Upper Satrapies. Perdiccas suspected that this was what Peithon was plotting and gave him orders

---

[22] Chaniotis 2002: 105; see also John Ma's reply 2002, especially 119 on billeting.
[23] Fischer-Bovet 2015.   [24] Diodorus 18.7.1.

to kill them instead. After some hesitation on the part of Peithon, the Macedonian troops took matters into their own hands and massacred the rebellious Greek settler army.

There is reason to doubt that this dramatic cause-and-effect chain of conspiracy and bloodbath transpired quite as Diodorus would have us believe. Although paranoia on Perdiccas' part would be quite understandable, given the contemporary political situation, the massacre of 23,000 settlers seems a little extreme, not to mention detrimental to effective Graeco-Macedonian control over the Upper Satrapies. Diodorus plays up a neat Macedonian-versus-Greek conflict which may have been considerably more complex in reality.

It is important to view the Bactrian settler revolts in their wider Hellenistic context. The period before and after the death of Alexander was marked by widespread unrest on the part of Greeks and non-Greeks alike. Alexander did not fully consolidate his grip on large areas, such as Sogdiana and India. After his death, Alexander's successors fought among themselves, moving large forces of mercenaries about the former Achaemenid Empire in the process; Atrosokes in north-western Media and Chandragupta in India were able to take advantage of the lack of secure centralized control and seize territory; in Greece itself, the Lamian War erupted.[25] Yet this extended period of disruption did not lead to the complete collapse of Graeco-Macedonian authority. (I do not treat early Seleucid policy in Central Asia here, for which, see Kosmin, and Mairs.[26]) These episodes of simultaneous unrest in multiple regions, involving actors of multiple ethnicities and differing relationships to Graeco-Bactrian authority, were made possible because of the same political circumstances.

4. Three Moments of Bactrian Revolt II: Diodotus and Arsaces (240s BCE)

Justin (41.4) notes the simultaneity of Graeco-Bactrian and Parthian autonomy from the Seleucids in the mid-third century BCE, but his

---

[25] On the latter conjunction, as treated in Diodorus, see Walsh 2009.
[26] Kosmin 2014 and Mairs and Fischer-Bovet 2021.

neat presentation masks a more complicated reality. There was no sudden declaration of Graeco-Bactrian independence, the kind of overt and deliberate assault on Seleucid authority that might have provoked a clampdown. A clampdown of a sort did come, but not for several decades. The Diodotids, the father and son dynasty under whom Bactria achieved effective independence from the Seleucids, struck coins of the Seleucids for a long time before they struck coins under their own name.[27] Bactrian independence was a long-term process. Parthian independence, in contrast, took place over a short period, and involved an outright declaration of autonomy from the Seleucids (by Andragoras) and a military conquest (the defeat of Andragoras by Arsaces).

As I have already discussed, Justin juxtaposes Parthian and Bactrian independence with contemporary Seleucid Dynastic feuds, and the instability caused by the incursion of Gauls into Anatolia. What he does not directly mention is the Third Syrian War (246–241 BCE), the wider geopolitical context for the civil war between the brothers Seleucus II and Antiochus Hierax.[28] At a time when Seleucid forces were divided between different allegiances and theatres of war, keeping attention in the west, regions in the east of the empire, such as Parthia and Bactria, were not subject to such direct imposition of Seleucid authority. The relationship between simultaneous revolts in Bactria and Parthia was a causal one, in the sense that both were made possible by a common atmosphere of weakened Seleucid authority.

The question of what constituted rebellion against Seleucid authority was contested at the time. After some decades of Graeco-Bactrian independence, Antiochos III conducted the first concerted attempt by a Seleucid ruler to assert direct authority in the East in some time.[29] Antiochos' blitzkrieg anabasis in the East, with military successes and impositions of vassal status not followed by lasting and effective control, recalls that of Alexander in the region. The primary target was Parthia, but Antiochus went much further east. He besieged the city of Bactra, the Graeco-Bactrian capital, from 208–206 BCE.[30] The current king of Bactria

---

[27] On the timing of Diodotid independence, see Holt 1999; Wengehofer 2018.
[28] Chrubasil 2016: 72–82; Coşkun 2018.
[29] On Seleucid-Parthian relations over the long(u)e(r) durée, see Strootman 2018.
[30] On what follows see Polybius 11.34 and Mairs 2014: 148–150.

was Euthydemos, who was not a member of the Diodotid Dynasty which had originally established autonomy from the Seleucids several decades earlier. The appeals which Euthydemos made to end the siege of Bactra play on the common Hellenicity of the Graeco-Bactrian and Seleucid kings. Teleas, an envoy sent by Antiochus to negotiate an end to the siege, was a Magnesian, and Euthydemos too claimed Magnesian descent. This is typical of regions elsewhere in the Hellenistic world, such as Egypt, where a Greek regional identity was maintained over many generations. Euthydemos and Teleas also appeal to a common barbarian threat – as we shall see, not entirely convincingly. Euthydemos' first move, however, was to portray himself, not as a rebel against Seleucid authority but, in a roundabout way, a loyalist: 'he alleged that it was unjust for Antiochos to demand his removal from power, since he himself had not rebelled against the king. Rather, when others had revolted, he had destroyed their descendants and thus gained possession of the Bactrian throne'.[31] He had overthrown the Diodotids, the actual rebels. Euthydemos' logic is the kind that can only work if the target wants it to work. Behind the negotiations and statements of common purpose, what this discussion is really about is giving Antiochus a way to save face. As in earlier periods, a Bactrian client state as a buffer against external threats, was much more useful to the Seleucids than an integrated province, over which it would be difficult to maintain control. There was a further imperative to end the siege: 'if Antiochos did not make these concessions, neither of them would be safe: not far away were great numbers of nomads who not only posed a danger to them both but also threatened to barbarize the whole area if they attacked'.[32]

Euthydemos' rhetoric of civilized Greeks banding together against barbarian nomadic hordes presents, deliberately, an inaccurate picture of what relations between the Greek-ruled kingdom of Bactria and mobile populations actually were.[33] In one of the very few Greek documentary texts from Bactria, we find a reference to Scythians, who are apparently being used as mercenaries.[34] Archaeological field survey, too, reveals the integration and interdependence of settled agriculture and the

[31] Polybius 11.34, 6; trans. Holt 1999.   [32] Polybius 11.34, 6; trans. Holt 1999.
[33] Mairs 2014: 146–176.   [34] Clarysse and Thompson 2007; Mairs 2014: 149–159.

pastoral economy in Bactria. It is hard to tell who, if anyone, believed in the fiction of this Greek versus barbarian dichotomy – Justin, Antiochus, Teleas, Euthydemos. Graeco-Bactrian rebellion against the Seleucids, whatever the true ethnic, linguistic, and cultural picture in the region, was presented in formal discourse as a rebellion of Greeks, not indigenous populations. Indigenous threat, in turn, to the Graeco-Bactrian kingdom was presented as a matter of external barbarians. What was happening inside the Graeco-Bactrian state was undoubtedly more complex, as the earlier example of co-operation between Greek settler and Bactrians indicates.

But let us return to Polybius' account of the siege of Bactra. The accommodation reached is, indeed, one between Greek kings. As well as Euthydemos' appeals to common Hellenicity on a more general level, the meeting between Euthydemos and his son Demetrios and Antiochus is presented as an alliance between Hellenistic kings. As with Seleucus' campaigns in the region a century earlier, however, what this is really about is neutralizing the threat in the East, and equipping the army for success in the west. Antiochus provisions his troops, and leaves with Euthydemos' war elephants.[35] The conclusion to the gradual Bactrian secession of the 240s is a definitive moment of diplomatic compromise between two kings several decades later.

5. Three Moments of Bactrian Revolt III: Eucratides and Mithridates (170s BCE)

My final moment of Bactrian revolt is the one which coincides most closely with the 'Big Events' considered by Erich Gruen and Anne-Emmanuelle Veïsse in the opening chapters of this volume. It is not a revolt by Bactria, but one affecting Bactria. By the period of the Maccabean and Theban revolts, it cannot be argued that Central Asia was of much concern to the Seleucids. More important threats and relationships were with Judea, Rome, and Parthia, which I do not consider here. Around the turn of the third-second centuries, the

[35] Kosmin 2014: 35–37.

Greek kingdom of Bactria began to expand across the Hindu Kush and into north-western India. This was made possible, in part, by the new relationship between the Seleucid and Graeco-Bactrian kingdoms established at Bactra in 206 BCE. Justin's third synchromism comes some decades after this, in around 171 BCE, and marks the end of this period of Graeco-Bactrian growth and military success, with the rise to power, at the same period, of Mithridates in Parthia and Eucratides in Bactria.

Historical and archaeological evidence for the period of Graeco-Bactrian expansion into India in the early second century BCE is still more scant than it is for the kingdom of Bactria itself.[36] As new kingdoms were established in India by Bactrian kings and their generals, the kingdom of Bactria itself came under threat from a combination of internal dynastic strife, war with Parthia, and incoming nomad groups from the north.[37] Justin's presentation of the collapse of the Graeco-Bactrian kingdom in the reign of Eucratides is strikingly similar to his presentation of how this kingdom had itself been a factor in earlier threats to the Seleucids. We find, in fact, the same range of factors at work: an external, state-level enemy (Parthia), 'barbarians' (Gauls, Central Asian nomads), and an internal enemy (Antiochus Hierax, Demetrius, Eucratides' son). As with earlier periods of instability, it cannot be said that the relationship between these was a directly causal one, but the coincidence of more than one threat to the Graeco-Bactrian state created circumstances where each separate force was aided by the division of Graeco-Bactrian military might among multiple enemies.

Given our reliance on Justin as one of the very few historical sources on the period of Indo-Greek expansion and Graeco-Bactrian collapse, his use – once again – of synchronism as a narrative device, and his crafting of a narrative with such parallels with his own previous accounts of threats to the Seleucids, one might reasonably ask whether we are in a position to examine this episode of revolt as a historical event at all. Reading this episode in its wider context within Books 41 and 42 of the *Epitome*, we can see that, rather than events in Bactria and India, Justin's

---

[36] On the archaeological evidence, see Olivieri 2021, and on the Indo-Greeks in Indian sources, Kubica 2021.
[37] Mairs 2013.

principle concern is Parthia. The historiographical, narrative purpose of his description of Eucratides in Bactria is to introduce another synchronism, and to contrast the dramatic rise of Mithridates with the fall of Eucratides.

6. Conclusions

There was no direct connection between Bactria and other regions of the Hellenistic world, such as Judea and the Thebaid, which revolted against Seleucid or Ptolemaic authority, and political events in one cannot be said to have influenced the other. What Central Asia has to offer to this book's comparative study of resistance to the Hellenistic kingdoms is a little different: a chance to examine Seleucid responses to drives for regional autonomy; a case study where secessionist states made direct appeals to common Hellenicity with the Seleucids; and an opportunity to question what simultaneity in revolt against Seleucid rule in different areas of the empire means.

The successful establishment and maintenance of Graeco-Bactrian autonomy was dependent on Seleucid weakness, or the concentration of Seleucid attention elsewhere. In this respect, we can indeed draw a causal link between simultaneous rebellions in different parts of the empire, especially in the reign of Seleucus II.[38] The Seleucid Army could not be everywhere at once. Rebellions may not have been inspired by others – the Greek kings of Bactria, for example, never depicted themselves as indigenous rebels against Greek Seleucid authority – but they benefitted from the ability of other challenges to the Seleucids to help them succeed. In the absence of mass communication on a modern scale, it is nevertheless clear that a distant revolt would have been felt on a local level. Such events as the depletion of a Seleucid garrison or simply a lack of Seleucid response to the growing autonomy of local dynasts will have, in their own way, contributed to an empire-wide atmosphere of instability and common revolt.

---

[38] Strootman 2018.

But Seleucid weakness or preoccupation was not the only reason for Graeco-Bactrian autonomy. The old scholarly narrative of inevitable and terminal Seleucid decline is increasingly being revised to put greater emphasis on Seleucid strengths.[39] In many ways, the Seleucids pursued a deliberate policy of cutting their losses in the Far East: they aimed to establish defensible boundaries.[40] Some areas, such as Arachosia and India, were jettisoned entirely, in exchange for peace in the region, and elephants to support the Seleucid war effort in areas where they did need and intend to face a military challenge – notably Syria and Egypt. Seleucid policy to Bactria changed between the late fourth and late third centuries BC. Bactria was initially consolidated as part of the empire. Later, during and after Antiochos III's siege of Bactria, the policy of neutralization of threat and maximization of income and military equipment was also pursued here.

Justin's synchronisms invite us to consider the distinction between correlation and causation in simultaneous revolts against Seleucid authority. As Erich Gruen has noted in a recent volume on revolt and resistance in the ancient world, 'the search for pattern in revolutions can too often undervalue the diverse motives of insurgents and overlook the part played by chance in history. Sometimes a revolt is just a revolt'.[41] As well as the historical connections which we can trace between revolts in different regions – in terms of inspiration, reaction to common forms of oppression, or simply opportunism – simultaneity also offers a powerful rhetoric strategy in presenting events, one which plays into our construction of broader narratives of Seleucid rise and decline.

---

[39] See, for example, Coşkun and Engels 2019.
[40] Kosmin 2014: 31–76.
[41] Gruen 2016: 37.

Bibliography

Aalders, Gerhard Jean Daniel. 1965. Review of *The King Is Dead: Studies in the Near Eastern Resistance to Hellenism, 334–31 B.C.*, by Samuel Kennedy Eddy. *Mnemosyne* 18: 322–326.

Abercrombie, Nicholas, Stephen Hill, and Bryan S. Turner. 1980. *The Dominant Ideology Thesis*. London: Allen & Unwin.

Abercrombie, Nicholas, Stephen Hill, and Bryan S. Turner, eds. 1990. *Dominant Ideologies*. London: Unwin Hyman.

Agut-Labordère, Damien. 2013. '"L'argent est un sortilège": penser la richesse en Égypte ancienne à travers la sagesse du Insinger (VIème siècle av. J.-C. – Ier siècle ap. J.-C.)'. In *Richesse et sociétés*, edited by Catherine Baroin and Cécile Michel, 53–65. Paris: De Boccard.

Agut-Labordère, Damien and Juan Carlos Moreno Garcia. 2016. *L'Égypte des pharaons: de Narmer à Dioclétien, 3150 av. J.C.- 284 apr. J.-C.* Paris: Belin.

Aitken, James K. 2004. Review of *Judentum und Hellenismus*, by Martin Hengel. *Journal of Biblical Literature* 123: 331–341.

Alavi, Seema. 2015. *Muslim Cosmopolitanism in the Age of Empire*. Cambridge, MA: Harvard University Press.

Allam, Schafik. 1991. 'Egyptian Law Courts in Pharaonic and Hellenistic Times'. *The Journal of Egyptian Archaeology* 77: 109–127.

Alonso-Nuñez, José Miguel. 1992. *La Historia Universal de Pompeyo Trogo. Coordenadas espaciales y temporales*. Madrid: Ediciones Clásicas.

Alston, Richard. 2002. *The City in Roman and Byzantine Egypt*. London: Routledge.

Ameling, Walter. 1995. 'Domitius Kallistratos, FGrHist 433'. *Hermes* 123: 373–376.

Ameling, Walter. 2012. 'Seleukidische Religionspolitik in Koile-Syrien und Phönizien nach der neuen Inschrift von Maresha'. In *Die Septuaginta—Entstehung, Sprache, Geschichte*, edited by Siegfried Kreuzer, Martin Meiser, and Marcus Sigismund, 337–59. Tübingen: Mohr Siebeck.

Aperghis, Gerassimos George. 2004. *The Seleukid Royal Economy: The Finances and Financial Administration of the Seleukid Empire*. Cambridge: Cambridge University Press.

Aperghis, Gerassimos George. 2011. 'Antiochus IV and His Jewish Subjects: Political, Cultural and Religious Interaction'. In *Seleucid Dissolution: The Sinking of the Anchor*, edited by Kyle Erickson and Gillian Ramsey, 67–83. Wiesbaden: Harrassowitz.

Archibald, Zofia H. 2007. 'Contacts between the Ptolemaic Kingdom and the Black Sea in the Early Hellenistic Age'. In *The Black Sea in Antiquity: Regional and Interregional Economic Exchanges*, edited by Vincent Gabrielsen and John Lund, 253–271. Aarhus: Aarhus University Press.

Arlt, Carolin. 2011. 'Scribal Offices and Scribal Families in Ptolemaic Thebes'. In *Perspectives on Ptolemaic Thebes: Occasional Proceedings of the Theban Workshop*, edited by Peter F. Dorman and Betsy M. Bryan, 17–34. Chicago: Oriental Institute of the University of Chicago.

Armoni, C. 2013. *Das Archiv der Taricheuten Amenneus und Onnophris aus Tanis* (P. Tarich). Paderborn.

Armoni, C., and A. Jördens. 2018. 'Der König und die Rebellen. Vom Umgang der Ptolemäer mit strittigen Eigentumsfragen im Gefolge von Bürgerkriegen', *Chiron* 48: 77–106.

Arnold, Dieter. 1999. *Temples of the Last Pharaohs*. Oxford: Oxford University Press.

Arslan, Murat, ed. 2007. *Memnon: Herakleia Pontike Tarihi (Περὶ Ἡρακλείας)*. Istanbul: Odin Yayıncılık.

Arslan, Murat. 2011. 'Küçük Asya Yerel Historiograflarına bir Örnek: Herakleia Pontike'li Memnon ve Eseri'. *OLBA* 19: 383–405.

Asheri, David. 1972. *Über die Frühgeschichte von Herakleia Pontike*. Forschungen an der Nordküste Kleinasiens 1. Vienna: Böhlau.

Asheri, David. 1983. *Fra ellenismo e iranismo. Studi sulla società e cultura di Xanthos nella età achemenide*. Bologna: Pàtron.

Assefa, D. 2007. *L'Apocalypse des Animaux (1 Hen 85–90): une propagande militaire? Approches narrative, historico-critique, perspectives théologiques*. Leiden: Brill.

Atkinson, Kenneth. 2016. *A History of the Hasmonean State: Josephus and Beyond*. London: Bloomsbury.

Avram, Alexandre. 2003. 'Antiochos II Théos, Ptolémée II Philadelphe et la mer Noire'. *Comptes rendus des séances de l'Académie des Inscriptions et Belles-Lettres* 3: 1181–1213.

Avram, Alexandru, and Gocha R. Tsetskhladze. 2014. 'A New Attalid Letter from Pessinus'. *Zeitschrift für Papyrologie und Epigraphik* 191: 151–181.

Azoulay, Vincent. 2014. 'Repenser le politique en Grèce ancienne'. *Annales. Histoire, Sciences Sociales* 69: 605–626.

Babota, Vasile. 2014. *The Institution of the Hasmonean High Priesthood*. Leiden: Brill.

Bagnall, Roger S. 1997. 'Decolonizing Ptolemaic Egypt'. In *Hellenistic Constructs: Essays in Culture, History, and Historiography*, edited by Paul Cartledge, Peter Garnsey, and Erich S. Gruen, 225–241. Berkeley: University of California Press.

Bagnall, Roger S. 2011. *Everyday Writing in the Graeco-Roman East*. Berkeley: University of California Press.

Baker, Patrick. 2001. 'La vallée du Méandre au IIe siècle: relations entre les cités et institutions militaires'. In *Les cités d'Asie Mineure occidentale au IIe siècle a.C.*, edited by Alain Bresson and Raymond Descat, 61–75. Bordeaux: Ausonius.

Baker, Patrick, and Gaétan Thériault. 2005. 'Les Lyciens, Xanthos et Rome dans la première moitié du 1er s. a. C'. *Revue des études grecques* 118: 329–366.

Barbantani, Silvia. 2014. '"Attica in Syria": Persian War Reenactments and Reassessments of the Greek-Asian Relationship: A Literary Point of View'. *Erga-Logoi* 2: 21–91.

Barguet, Paul. 1962. *Le temple d'Amon-Rê à Karnak. Essai d'exégèse*. Cairo: Institut Français d'Archéologie Orientale.

BIBLIOGRAPHY 249

Bar-Kochva, Bezalel. 1976. *The Seleucid Army. Organization and Tactics in the Great Campaigns.* Cambridge: Cambridge University Press.

Bar-Kochva, Bezalel. 1989. *Judas Maccabaeus: The Jewish Struggle against the Seleucids.* Cambridge: Cambridge University Press.

Barth, Fredrik. 1969. *Ethnic Groups and Boundaries: The Social Organization of Culture Difference.* Bergen; London: Universitetsforlaget; Allen & Unwin.

Bartlett, Brett. 2014. 'Justin's Epitome: The Unlikely Adaptation of Trogus' World History'. *Histos* 8: 246–283.

Bayly, Christopher A. 1988. *Indian Society and the Making of the British Empire.* New Cambridge History of India, 2.1. Cambridge: Cambridge University Press.

Bayoumi, Abbas and Octave Guéraud. 1947. 'Un nouvel exemplaire du décret de Canope'. *Annales du service des antiquités de l'Égypte* 46: 373–382.

Beaulieu, Paul-Alain. 1993. 'The Historical Background of the Uruk Prophecy'. In *The Tablet and the Scroll: Near Eastern Studies in Honor of William W. Hallo*, edited by Mark E. Cohen, David C. Snell, and David B. Weisberg, 41–52. Bethesda, MD: CDL Press.

Beaulieu, Paul-Alain. 2017. *A History of Babylon, 2200 BC-AD 75.* Chichester: Wiley-Blackwell.

Beck, Hans and Peter Funke, eds. 2015. *Federalism in Greek Antiquity*, Cambridge: Cambridge University Press.

Behrwald, Ralf. 2000. *Der lykische Bund: Untersuchungen zu Geschichte und Verfassung.* Bonn: Habelt.

Behrwald, Ralf. 2015. 'The Lykian League'. In *Federalism in Greek Antiquity*, edited by Hans Beck and Peter Funke, 403–418. Cambridge: Cambridge University Press.

Bellah, Robert N., Richard Madsen, William N. Sullivan, Ann Swidler, and Steven M. Tipton, eds. 1985. *Habits of the Heart: Individualism and Commitment in American Life.* Berkeley: University of California Press.

Beloch, Karl Julius. 1929. *Griechische Geschichte.* 2nd ed. Vol. 4.2. Berlin: W. de Gruyter.

Bencivenni, Alice. 2011. '"Massima considerazione": forma dell'ordine e immagini del potere nella corrispondenza di Seleuco IV'. *Zeitschrift für Papyrologie und Epigraphik* 176: 139–153.

Benda-Weber, Isabella. 2005. *Lykier und Karer: zwei autochthone Ethnien Kleinasiens zwischen Orient und Okzident.* Bonn: R. Habelt.

Bengtson, Hermann. 1960. *Griechische Geschichte von den Anfängen bis in die römische Kaiserzeit.* 2nd ed. Handbuch der Altertumswissenschaft, 3.4. Munich: Beck.

Berlin, Andrea. 2016. 'Not So Fast: Ceramic Conservatism and Change at Sardis in the Early Hellenistic Period'. In *Traditions and Innovations. Tracking the Development of Pottery from the Late Classical to the Early Imperial Periods*, edited by S. Japp and P. Kögler, 351–358. Vienna: Phoibos Verlag.

Berlin, Andrea. 2019. 'The Archaeology of a Changing City'. In Berlin and Kosmin, 2019, 50–67.

Berlin, Andrea, and Paul J. Kosmin. 2019. 'A New View of Sardis'. In Berlin and Kosmin, 2019, 235–240.

Berlin, Andrea, and Paul J. Kosmin, eds. 2019. *Spear-Won Land: Sardis from the King's Peace to the Peace of Apamea.* Madison: University of Wisconsin Press.

Bernhardt, J. C. 2017. *Die jüdische Revolution: Untersuchungen zu Ursachen, Verlauf und Folgen der hasmonäischen Erhebung.* KLIO. Beiträge zur Alten Geschichte. Beihefte, neue Folge, Band 22. Berlin: De Gruyter.

Berthelot, Katell. 2009. '4QTestimonia as a Polemic against the Prophetic Claims of John Hyrcanus'. In *Prophecy after the Prophets? The Contribution of the Dead Sea Scrolls to the Understanding of Biblical and Extra-Biblical Prophecy,* edited by Kristin de Troyer and Armin Lange, 99–116. Leuven: Peeters.

Berthelot, Katell. 2014. 'Judas Maccabeus' Wars Against Judaea's Neighbours in 1 Maccabees 5: A Reassessment of the Evidence'. *Electrum* 21: 73–85.

Berthelot, Katell. 2018. *In Search of the Promised Land? The Hasmonean Dynasty Between Biblical Models and Hellenistic Diplomacy.* Göttingen: Vandenhoeck and Ruprecht.

Besançon-Pisa-Roma (= Institut des sciences et techniques de l'Antiquité, Besançon; École français de Rome; Scuola normale superiore, Pisa) 1983. *Modes de contacts et processus de transformation dans les sociétés anciennes: actes du colloque de Cortone, 24-30 mai 1981.* Pisa: Scuola normale superiore; Rome: École française de Rome, 1983.

Bevan, Edwyn Robert. 1902. *The House of Seleucus.* 2 vols. London: Edward Arnold.

Bhabha, Homi K. 1985. 'Sly Civility'. *October* 34: 71–80.

Bickerman, Elias J. 1935. 'La charte séleucide de Jérusalem'. *Revue des Études Juives* 100: 4–35.

Bickerman, Elias J. 1937. *Der Gott der Makkabäer: Untersuchungen über Sinn und Ursprung der makkabäischen Erhebung.* Berlin: Schocken Verlag.

Bickerman, Elias J. 1946. 'Une proclamation séleucide relative au temple de Jérusalem'. *Syria* 25: 67–85.

Bickerman, Elias J. 1979. *The God of the Maccabees: Studies on the Meaning and Origin of the Maccabean Revolt.* Translated by Horst R. Moehring. Leiden: Brill.

Bickerman, Elias J. 1980. 'Héliodore au temple de Jérusalem'. In *Studies in Jewish and Christian History,* by Elias J. Bickerman, 2:159–191. Leiden: Brill.

Bickerman, Elias J. 2007. 'The Seleucid Charter for Jerusalem'. In *Studies in Jewish and Christian History: A New Edition in English Including The God of the Maccabees,* by Elias J. Bickerman, edited by Amram Tropper, 1:315–356. Leiden: Brill.

Billows, Richard A. 1995. *Kings and Colonists: Aspects of Macedonian Imperialism.* Leiden: Brill.

Billows, Richard A. 2016. 'Nymphis (432)'. In *Brill's New Jacoby Online,* edited by Ian Worthington. Leiden: Brill.

Bingen, Jean. 2007 [1970]. 'Greeks and Egyptians According to *PSI* V 502'. In *Hellenistic Egypt: Monarchy, Society, Economy, Culture,* by Jean Bingen, edited by Roger S. Bagnall, 229–239. Berkeley: University of California Press.

Birk, Ralph. 2016. 'Genormt? Zur überregionalen Normierung von priesterlichen Epitheta in der Ptolemäerzeit'. In *Ägyptologische Tempeltagung: ägyptische Tempel zwischen Normierung und Individualität,* edited by Martina Ullmann, 17–35. Wiesbaden: Harrassowitz.

BIBLIOGRAPHY 251

Birk, Ralph. 2020. *Türöffner des Himmels: prosopographische Studien zur thebanischen Hohepriesterschaft der Ptolemäerzeit*. Wiesbaden: Harrassowitz.

Bispham, Edward H., and Timothy J. Cornell. 2013. 'Q. Fabius Pictor: Introduction'. In *The Fragments of the Roman Historians*, edited by Timothy J. Cornell, 1: 160–178. Oxford: Oxford University Press.

Bittner, Angela. 1998. *Gesellschaft und Wirtschaft in Herakleia Pontike: eine Polis zwischen Tyrannis und Selbstverwaltung*. Bonn: Habelt.

Blasius, Andreas, and Bernd Ulrich Schipper, eds. 2002. *Apokalyptik und Ägypten: eine kritische Analyse der relevanten Texte aus dem griechisch-römischen Ägypten*. Leuven: Peeters.

Bloch, Herbert. 1940. 'Herakleides Lembos and His *Epitome* of Aristotle's *Politeiai*'. *Transactions of the American Philological Association* 71: 27–39.

Blümel, Wolfgang. 1994. 'Über die chronologische und geographische Verteilung einheimischer Personennamen in griechischen Inschriften aus Karien'. In *La decifrazione del Cario*, edited by Maria Eliana Giannotta and Roberto Gusmani, 65–86. Rome: Consiglio Nazionale delle Ricerche.

Bochi, Patricia A. 1999. 'Death by Drama: The Ritual of Damnatio Memoriae in Ancient Egypt'. *Göttinger Miszellen* 171: 73–88.

Boehmer, Elleke. 2002. *Empire, the National, and the Postcolonial, 1890–1920: Resistance in Interaction*. Oxford: Oxford University Press.

Boffo, Laura. 1988. 'Epigrafi di città greche: un'espressione di storiografia locale'. In *Studi di storia e storiografia antiche per Emilio Gabba*, edited by Laura Boffo, 9–48. Pavia: New Press.

Boffo, Laura. 2007. 'I centri religiosi d'Asia Minore all'epoca della conquista romana'. In *Tra Oriente e Occidente. Indigeni, Greci e Romani in Asia Minore*, edited by Gianpaolo Urso, 105–128. Pisa: ETS.

Boiy, Tom. 2004. *Late Achaemenid and Hellenistic Babylon*. Leuven: Peeters.

Boiy, Tom, and Peter Franz Mittag. 2011. 'Die lokalen Eliten in Babylonien'. In *Lokale Eliten und hellenistische Könige: zwischen Kooperation und Konfrontation*, edited by Boris Dreyer and Peter Franz Mittag, 105–131. Berlin: Verlag Antike.

Borchhardt, Jürgen. 2003. 'Lykische Inschriften im archäologischen Kontext'. In *Licia e Lidia prima dell'ellenizzazione*, edited by Mauro Giorgieri, Mirjo Salvini, Marie-Claude Trémouille, and Pietro Vannicelli, 37–67. Rome: Consiglio Nazionale delle Ricerche.

Borgna, Alice. 2018. *Ripensare la storia universale Giustino e l'Epitome delle Storie Filippiche di Pompeo Trogo*. Spudasmata, Band 176. Hildesheim: Georg Olms Verlag.

Bosworth, A. B. 2002. *The Legacy of Alexander: Politics, Warfare, and Propaganda under the Successors*. Oxford: Oxford University Press.

Bousquet, Jean. 1992. 'Les inscriptions gréco-lyciennes'. In *Fouilles de Xanthos IX*, edited by Henri Metzger. Paris: Klincksieck.

Bousquet, Jean, and Philippe Gauthier. 1994. 'Inscriptions du Létôon de Xanthos'. *Revue des études grecques* 107: 319–361.

Bracke, Hilde. 1993. 'Pisidia in Hellenistic Times (334-25 B.C.)'. In *Sagalassos I: First General Report on the Survey (1986–1989) and Excavations (1990–1991)*, edited by Marc Waelkens, 15–36. Leuven: Leuven University Press.

Bradley, Keith R. 1983. 'Slave Kingdoms and Slave Rebellions in Ancient Sicily'. *Historical Reflections/Réflexions Historiques* 10: 435-451.
Brand, Peter J. 2001. 'Repairs Ancient and Modern in the Great Hypostyle Hall at Karnak'. *Bulletin of the American Research Center in Egypt* 180: 1-6.
Braund, David. 2000. 'Athenaeus, On the Kings of Syria'. In *Athenaeus and His World: Reading Greek Culture in the Roman Empire*, edited by David Braund and John Wilkins, 514-522. Exeter: University of Exeter Press.
Braun-Holzinger, Eva, and Eckart Frahm. 1999. 'Liebling des Marduk – König der Blasphemie: große babylonische Herrscher in der Sicht der Babylonier und in der Sicht anderer Völker'. In *Babylon: Focus mesopotamischer Geschichte, Wiege früher Gelehrsamkeit, Mythos in der Moderne*, edited by Johannes Renger, 131-156. Saarbrücken: SDV.
Bresson, Alain. 1998. 'Rhodes, Cnide et les Lyciens au début du IIe siècle av. J.-C'. *Revue des études anciennes* 100: 65-88.
Bresson, Alain. 1999. 'Rhodes and Lycia in Hellenistic Times'. In *Hellenistic Rhodes: Politics, Culture, and Society*, edited by Vincent Gabrielsen, 98-131. Aarhus: Aarhus University Press.
Bresson, Alain. 2007a. 'Les Cariens ou La mauvaise conscience du barbare'. In *Tra Oriente e Occidente. Indigeni, Greci e Romani in Asia Minore*, edited by Gianpaolo Urso, 209-228. Pisa: ETS.
Bresson, Alain. 2007b. 'Unity, Diversity and Conflict in Hellenistic Lykia'. In *Regionalism in Hellenistic and Roman Asia Minor*, edited by Hugh Elton and Gary L. Reger, 73-79. Bordeaux: Ausonius.
Briant, Pierre. 1976. '"Brigandage," dissidence et conquête en Asie achéménide et hellénistique'. *Dialogues d'histoire ancienne* 2: 163-258.
Briant, Pierre. 1996. *Histoire de l'Empire perse: de Cyrus à Alexandre*. Paris: Fayard.
Briant, Pierre. 1999. 'Colonizzazione ellenistica e popolazione locale'. In *I Greci*, edited by Salvatore Settis, 2: 309-333. Torino: Einaudi.
Briant, Pierre. 2002. *From Cyrus to Alexander: A History of the Persian Empire*. Translated by Peter T. Daniels. Winona Lake, IN: Eisenbrauns.
Briant, Pierre. 2006. 'L'Asie Mineure en transition'. In *La transition entre l'empire achéménide et les royaumes hellénistiques (vers 350-300 av. J.-C.)*, edited by Pierre Briant and Francis Joannès, 309-351. Paris: De Boccard.
Briant, Pierre, Patrice Brun, and Ender Varınlıoğlu. 2001. 'Une inscription inédite de Carie et la guerre d'Aristonicos'. In *Les cités d'Asie Mineure occidentale au IIe siècle a.C.*, edited by Alain Bresson and Raymond Descat, 241-259. Bordeaux: Ausonius.
Bringmann, Klaus, and Hans von Steuben, eds. 1995. *Schenkungen hellenistischer Herrscher an griechische Städte und Heiligtümer*. Vol. 1. Berlin: Akademie Verlag.
Brixhe, Claude. 1993. 'Le grec en Carie et en Lycie au IVe siècle'. In *La Koiné grecque antique*, edited by Claude Brixhe, 59-82. Nancy: Presses Universitaires de Nancy.
Brixhe, Claude. 2002. 'Interactions between Greek and Phrygian under the Roman Empire'. In *Bilingualism in Ancient Society: Language Contact and the Written Text*, edited by James N. Adams, Mark Janse, and Simon Swain, 246-266. Oxford: Oxford University Press.

BIBLIOGRAPHY 253

Brixhe, Claude. 2004. 'Nouvelle chronologie anatolienne et date d'élaboration des alphabets grec et phrygien'. *Comptes rendus des séances de l'Académie des Inscriptions et Belles-Lettres* 148: 271–289.

Brixhe, Claude. 2010. 'Linguistic Diversity in Asia Minor during the Empire: Koine and Non-Greek Languages'. In *A Companion to the Ancient Greek Language*, edited by Egbert J. Bakker, 228–252. Oxford: Wiley-Blackwell.

Brixhe, Claude. 2013. 'The Personal Onomastics of Roman Phrygia'. In *Roman Phrygia: Culture and Society*, edited by Peter Thonemann, 55–69. Cambridge: Cambridge University Press.

Brooke, George J. 1998. 'Parabiblical Prophetic Narratives'. In *The Dead Sea Scrolls after Fifty Years: A Comprehensive Assessment*, edited by Peter W. Flint and James C. VanderKam, 1: 271–301. Leiden: Brill.

Brosius, Maria. 1996. *Women in Ancient Persia, 559–331 BC*. Oxford: Clarendon Press.

Bryan, David. 1995. *Cosmos, Chaos, and the Kosher Mentality*. Sheffield: Sheffield Academic Press.

Bryce, Trevor R. 1983a. 'Political Unity in Lycia during the "Dynastic" Period'. *Journal of Near Eastern Studies* 42: 31–42.

Bryce, Trevor R. 1983b. 'The Arrival of the Goddess Leto in Lycia'. *Historia* 32: 1–13.

Bryce, Trevor R. 1986. *The Lycians: A Study of Lycian History and Civilisation to the Conquest of Alexander the Great*. Copenhagen: Museum Tusculanum Press.

Burke, Peter. 2005. 'Performing History: The Importance of Occasions'. *Rethinking History* 9: 35–52.

Burstein, Stanley M. 1976. *Outpost of Hellenism: The Emergence of Heraclea on the Black Sea*. Berkeley: University of California Press.

Burstein, Stanley Mayer. 1985. *The Hellenistic Age from the Battle of Ipsos to the Death of Kleopatra VII*. Cambridge: Cambridge University Press.

Camassa, Giorgio. 2010. 'L'attidografia nella storia degli studi'. In *Storie di Atene, storia dei Greci. Studi e ricerche di attidografia*, edited by Cinzia Bearzot and Franca Landucci, 29–51. Milan: Vita e Pensiero.

Canepa, Matthew P. 2018. *The Iranian Expanse : Transforming Royal Identity through Architecture, Landscape, and the Built Environment, 550 BCE-642 CE*. Berkeley, CA: University of California Press.

Capart, Jean. 1947. 'Troisième rapport sommaire sur les fouilles de la fondation Egyptologique Reine Elisabeth à El Kab: Novembre 1945 à Février 1946'. *Annales du service des antiquités de l'Égypte* 46: 337–355.

Capdetrey, Laurent. 2007. *Le pouvoir séleucide. Territoire, administration, finances d'un royaume hellénistique, 312–129 avant J.-C*. Rennes: Presses Universitaires de Rennes.

Capdetrey, Laurent. 2012. 'Le roi, le satrape et le *koinon*: la question du pouvoir en Carie à la fin du IVe s. a. C'. In *Stephanèphoros: de l'économie antique à l'Asie Mineure*, edited by Koray Konuk, 229–248. Bordeaux: Ausonius.

Carr, David M. 2005. *Writing on the Tablet of the Heart: Origins of Scripture and Literature*. Oxford: Oxford University Press.

Carstens, Anne Marie. 2009. 'Tomb Cult and Tomb Architecture in Karia from the Late Archaic to the Hellenistic Period'. In *Die Karer und die Anderen*, edited by Frank Rumscheid, 377–395. Bonn: Habelt.

Cavalier, Laurence, and Jacques des Courtils. 2013. 'Empreinte lagide au Létôon de Xanthos?' In *Euploia: la Lycie et la Carie antiques. Dynamiques des territoires, échanges et identités*, edited by Patrice Brun and Laurence Cavalier, 143–152. Bordeaux: Ausonius.

Cavigneaux, Antoine. 2005. 'Shulgi, Nabonide, et les Grecs'. In *'An Experienced Scribe Who Neglects Nothing': Ancient Near Eastern Studies in Honor of Jacob Klein*, edited by Yitzhak Sefati, Pinhas Artzi, Chaim Cohen, Barry L. Eichler, and Victor Avigdor Hurowitz, 63–72. Bethesda, MD: CDL Press.

Ceccarelli, Paola. 2011. 'Kings, Philosophers and Drunkards: Athenaeus' Information on the Seleucids'. In *Seleucid Dissolution: The Sinking of the Anchor*, edited by Kyle Erickson and Gillian Ramsey, 189–207. Wiesbaden: Harrassowitz.

Cenival, Françoise de. 1972. *Les associations religieuses en Égypte d'après les documents démotiques*. Cairo: Institut Français d'Archéologie Orientale.

Černý, Jaroslav, ed. 1976. *Coptic Etymological Dictionary*. Cambridge: Cambridge University Press.

Certeau, Michel de. 1986. *Heterologies: Discourse on the Other*. Translated by Brian Massumi. Minneapolis: University of Minnesota Press.

Chakrabarty, Dipesh. 2008. *Provincializing Europe: Postcolonial Thought and Historical Difference*. New ed. Princeton: Princeton University Press.

Chaniotis, Angelos. 1988. *Historie und Historiker in den griechischen Inschriften: epigraphische Beiträge zur griechischen Historiographie*. Stuttgart: Steiner.

Chaniotis, Angelos. 2002. 'Foreign Soldiers - Native Girls? Constructing and Crossing Boundaries in Hellenistic Cities with Foreign Garrisons'. In *Army and Power in the Ancient World*, edited by Angelos Chaniotis and Pierre Ducrey, 99–113. Stuttgart: Steiner.

Chaniotis, Angelos. 2005. *War in the Hellenistic World: A Social and Cultural History*. Oxford: Blackwell.

Chaplin, Jane D. 2000. *Livy's Exemplary History*. Oxford: Oxford University Press.

Chatzopoulos, Miltiades V. 1996. *Macedonian Institutions under the Kings*. 2 vols. Athens: Kentron Hellēnikēs kai Rōmaïkēs Archaiotētos.

Chaufray, Marie-Pierre, and Wolfgang Wegner. 2016. 'Two Early Ptolemaic Documents from Pathyris'. In *Sapientia Felicitas: Festschrift für Günter Vittmann zu seinem 64. Geburtstag am 29. Februar 2016*, edited by Sandra L. Lippert, Maren Schentuleit, and Martin A. Stadler, 23–49. CENiM 14. Montpellier: Université Paul Valéry.

Chevrier, Henri. 1929. 'Rapport sur les travaux de Karnak'. *Annales du Service des Antiquités de l'Egypte* 29, 133–149.

Christensen, Thorolf. 2003. 'P. Haun. inv. 407 and Cleruchs in the Edfu Nome'. In *Edfu: An Egyptian Provincial Capital in the Ptolemaic Period*, edited by Willy Clarysse and Katelijn Vandorpe, 9–16. Brussels: Koninklijke Vlaamse Academie van België voor Wetenschappen en Kunsten.

Chrubasik, Boris. 2016. *Kings and Usurpers in the Seleukid Empire: The Men who would be King*. (Oxford scholarship online.) Oxford: Oxford University Press.
Clancier, Philippe. 2007. 'La Babylonie hellénistique: aperçu d'histoire politique et culturelle'. *Topoi. Orient—Occident* 15: 21-74.
Clancier, Philippe. 2009. *Les bibliothèques en Babylonie dans la deuxième moitié du Ier millénaire av. J.-C*. Münster: Ugarit-Verlag.
Clancier, Philippe 2012. 'Les compétences judiciaires des temples babyloniens à l'époque hellénistique et parthe'. In *Transferts culturels et droits dans le monde grec et hellénistique*, edited by Bernard Legras, 255-268. Paris: Publications de la Sorbonne.
Clancier, Philippe. 2014. 'Antiochos IV dans les sources babyloniennes'. In *Le projet politique d'Antiochos IV*, edited by Christophe Feyel and Laetitia Graslin-Thomé, 415-438. Nancy: Association pour la Diffusion de la Recherche sur l'Antiquité.
Clancier, Philippe. 2017. 'The Polis of Babylon: An Historiographical Approach'. In *Hellenism and the Local Communities of the Eastern Mediterranean: 400 BCE-250 CE*, edited by Boris Chrubasik and Daniel King, 53-81. Oxford: Oxford University Press.
Clancier, Philippe, and Julien Monerie. 2014. 'Les sanctuaires babyloniens à l'époque hellénistique: évolution d'un relais de pouvoir'. *Topoi. Orient—Occident* 19: 181-237.
Clarke, Katherine. 2008. *Making Time for the Past: Local History and the Polis*. Oxford: Oxford University Press.
Clarysse, Willy. 1978. 'Notes de prosopographie thébaine 7. Hurgonaphor et Chaonnophris, les derniers pharaons indigènes'. *Chronique d'Égypte* 53: 243-253.
Clarysse, Willy. 1995a. 'Gli ultimi faraoni'. *Communicazioni. Instituto Papirologico G. Vitelli* 1: 3-18.
Clarysse, Willy. 1995b. 'Greeks in Ptolemaic Thebes'. In *Hundred-Gated Thebes: Acts of a Colloquium on Thebes and the Theban Area in the Graeco-Roman Period*, edited by Sven P. Vleeming, 1-19. Leiden: E. J. Brill.
Clarysse, Willy. 2000. 'Ptolémées et Temples'. In *Le décret de Memphis. Colloque de la Fondation Singer-Polignac à l'occasion de la célébration du bicentenaire de la découverte de la Pierre de Rosette*, edited by Dominique Valbelle and Jean Leclant, 41-65. Paris: De Boccard.
Clarysse, Willy. 2003. 'The Archive of the Praktor Milon'. In *Edfu: An Egyptian Provincial Capital in the Ptolemaic Period*, edited by Willy Clarysse and Katelijn Vandorpe, 17-27. Brussels: Koninklijke Vlaamse Academie van België voor Wetenschappen en Kunsten.
Clarysse, Willy. 2004. 'The great revolt of the Egyptians (205-186 B.C.)', http://www.lib.berkeley.edu/sites/default/files/files/TheGreatRevoltoftheEgyptians.pdf.
Clarysse, Willy, and Dorothy J. Thompson. 2007. 'Two Greek Texts on Skin from Hellenistic Bactria'. *Zeitschrift für Papyrologie und Epigraphik* 159: 273-279.
Claytor, W. Graham. 2014. 'Mechanics of Empire: The Karanis Register and the Writing Offices of Roman Egypt'. Ph.D., Ann Arbor: University of Michigan.
Clinton, Henry Fynes. 1834. *Fasti Hellenici: The Civil and Literary Chronology of Greece, from the Earliest Accounts to the Death of Augustus*. Vol. 3. Oxford: Oxford University Press.

Cohen, Getzel. 1995. *The Hellenistic Settlements in Europe, the Islands, and Asia Minor*. Berkeley: University of California Press.

Collins, Adela Yarbro. 1986. 'Introduction: Early Christian Apocalypticism'. In *Early Christian Apocalypticism: Genre and Social Setting*, edited by Adela Yarbro Collins, 1–11. *Semeia* 36. Atlanta: Society of Biblical Literature.

Collins, John J. 1977. *The Apocalyptic Vision of the Book of Daniel*. Missoula, MT: Scholars Press.

Collins, John J. 1979. 'Introduction: Towards the Morphology of a Genre'. In *Apocalypse: The Morphology of a Genre*, edited by John J. Collins, 1–19. *Semeia* 14. Missoula, MT: Society of Biblical Literature.

Collins, John J. 2002. 'Temporality and Politics in Jewish Apocalyptic Literature'. In *Apocalyptic in History and Tradition*, edited by Christopher Rowland and John Barton, 26–43. London: Sheffield Academic Press.

Collins, John J. 2015. *Apocalypse, Prophecy, and Pseudepigraphy: On Jewish Apocalyptic Literature*. Grand Rapids, MI: William B. Eerdmans.

Collins, John J. 2016. 'Temple or Taxes? What Sparked the Maccabean Revolt?' In *Revolt and Resistance in the Ancient Classical World and the Near East: In the Crucible of Empire*, edited by John J. Collins and Joseph G. Manning, 189–201. Leiden: Brill.

Collins, John J., and Joseph G. Manning, eds. 2016. *Revolt and Resistance in the Ancient Classical World and the Near East: In the Crucible of Empire*. Leiden: Brill.

Colvin, Stephen. 2004. 'Names in Hellenistic and Roman Lycia'. In *The Greco-Roman East: Politics, Culture, Society*, edited by Stephen Colvin, 44–48. Yale Classical Studies 31. Cambridge: Cambridge University Press.

Corsten, Thomas. 2007. 'The Foundation of Laodikeia on the Lykos: An Example of Hellenistic City Foundations in Asia Minor'. In *Regionalism in Hellenistic and Roman Asia Minor*, edited by Hugh Elton and Gary L. Reger, 131–136. Bordeaux: Ausonius.

Corsten, Thomas. 2013. 'Termessos in Pisidien und die Gründung griechischer Städte in "Nord-Lykien"'. In *Euploia: la Lycie et la Carie antiques. Dynamiques des territoires, échanges et identités*, edited by Patrice Brun and Laurence Cavalier, 77–84. Bordeaux: Ausonius.

Coşkun, Altay. 2011. 'Die Stratios-Mission des Jahres 167 v.Chr., ein später Einschub in den Polybios-Text (30,2,6) und die dynastische Erbfolge der späteren Attaliden', *Historia* 60: 94–114.

Coşkun, Altay. 2014. 'Latène-Artefakte im hellenistischen Kleinasien: ein problematisches Kriterium für die Bestimmung der ethnischen Identität(en) der Galater'. *IstMitt* 64, 129–162.

Coşkun, Altay. 2018. 'The War of Brothers, the Third Syrian War, and the Battle of Ankyra (246-241 BC): a Reappraisal'. In *The Seleukid Empire 281–222 BC: War within the Family*, 197–252, edited by Kyle Erickson. Swansea: The Classical Press of Wales.

Coşkun, Altay. 2019. 'Epilogue: Rome, the Seleukid East and the Disintegration of the Largest of the Successor Kingdoms in the 2nd Century BC'. In Coşkun and Engels, 2019, 457–480.

BIBLIOGRAPHY 257

Coşkun, Altay, and David Engels, eds. 2019. *Rome and the Seleukid East: Selected Papers from Seleukid Study Day V, Brussels, 21–23 August 2015*. (Collection Latomus.) Brussels: Latomus.

Costa, Virgilio, ed. 2007. *Filocoro di Atene. I. Testimonianze e frammenti dell'Atthis*. 2nd ed. Tivoli: Tored.

Cotton, Hannah M., and Michael Wörrle. 2007. 'Seleukos IV to Heliodorus: A New Dossier of Royal Correspondence from Israel'. *Zeitschrift für Papyrologie und Epigraphik* 159: 191–205.

Coulon, Laurent. 2008. 'La nécropole osirienne de Karnak sous les Ptolémées'. In *'Et maintenant ce ne sont plus que des villages': Thèbes et sa région aux époques hellénistique, romaine et byzantine*, edited by Alain Delattre and Paul Heilporn, 17–31. Brussels: Association égyptologique Reine Élisabeth.

Coulon, Laurent. 2010. 'Le culte osirien au Ier millénaire av. J.-C. Une mise en perspective(s)'. In *Le culte d'Osiris au Ier millénaire av. J.-C. Découvertes et travaux récents*, edited by Laurent Coulon, 1–19. Cairo: Institut Français d'Archéologie Orientale.

Coulon, Laurent. 2011. 'Les inscriptions des catacombes osiriennes d'Oxyrhynchos. Témoignages du culte osirien sous les règnes de Ptolémée VI et Ptolémée VIII'. In *Ägypten zwischen innerem Zwist und äusserem Druck: die Zeit Ptolemaios' VI. Bis VIII.*, edited by Andrea Jördens and Joachim Friedrich Quack, 77–91. Wiesbaden: Harrassowitz.

Courtils, Jacques des. 2001. 'L'archéologie du peuple lycien'. In *Origines gentium*, edited by Valérie Fromentin and Sophie Gotteland, 123–133. Bordeaux: Ausonius.

Courtils, Jacques des. 2003. 'Xanthos en Lycie : nouvelles données sur la romanisation d'une ancienne cité indigène'. *Revue des études grecques* 116: 1–16.

Crum, Walter Ewing, ed. 1939. *A Coptic Dictionary*. Oxford: Clarendon Press.

Curty, Olivier. 1995. *Les parentés légendaires entre cités grecques*. Geneva.

Curty, Olivier. 2005. 'Un usage fort controversé : la parenté dans le langage diplomatique de l'époque hellénistique', *Ancient Society* 35: 101–117.

Cuypers, Martine. 2016a. 'Amphitheos (?) of Herakleia (431)'. In *Brill's New Jacoby Online*, edited by Ian Worthington. Leiden: Brill.

Cuypers, Martine. 2016b. 'Promathidas of Herakleia (430)'. In *Brill's New Jacoby Online*, edited by Ian Worthington. Leiden: Brill.

Cuypers, Martine. 2016c. 'Timogenes of Miletos (435)'. In *Brill's New Jacoby Online*, edited by Ian Worthington. Leiden: Brill.

Cuypers, Martine. 2018. 'Domitius Kallistratos (433)'. In *Brill's New Jacoby Online*, edited by Ian Worthington. Leiden: Brill.

Da Riva, Rocío. 2008. *The Neo-Babylonian Royal Inscriptions: An Introduction*. Münster: Ugarit-Verlag.

Da Riva, Rocío. 2017. 'The Figure of Nabopolassar in Late Achaemenid and Hellenistic Historiographic Tradition: BM 34793 and CUA 90'. *Journal of Near Eastern Studies* 76: 75–92.

Dąbrowa, Edward. 2010. *The Hasmoneans and Their State: A Study in History, Ideology, and the Institutions*. Electrum 16. Kraków: Jagiellonian University Press.

Daebritz, Rudolf. 1912. 'Herakleides Lembos'. In *Paulys Real-Encyclopädie der Classischen Altertumswissenschaft*, edited by Wilhelm Kroll, 15: 488-491. Stuttgart: J. B. Metzlersche Verlagsbuchhandlung.

Dandamaev, Muhammad. 1993. 'Xerxes and the Esagila Temple in Babylon'. *Bulletin of the Asia Institute* 7: 41-45.

Darbyshire, Gareth, Stephen Mitchell, and Levent Vardar. 2000. 'The Galatian Settlement in Asia Minor'. *Anatolian Studies* 50: 75-98.

Davaze, Virginie. 2013. 'Memnon, historien d'Héraclée du Pont. Commentaire historique'. Ph.D., Le Mans: Université du Maine.

Davis, Rochelle A. 2011. *Palestinian Village Histories: Geographies of the Displaced*. Stanford: Stanford University Press.

De Breucker, Geert. 2015. 'Heroes and Sinners: Babylonian Kings in Cuneiform Historiography of the Persian and Hellenistic Periods'. In *Political Memory in and after the Persian Empire*, edited by Jason M. Silverman and Caroline Waerzeggers, 75-94. Atlanta: SBL Press.

De Giorgi, Andrea. 2011. 'Hellenistic Founders, Roman Builders: Anazarbos in Cilicia'. In *Hellenismus in der Kilikia Pedias*, edited by Adolf Hoffmann, Richard Posamentir, and Mustafa Hamdi Sayar, 121-138. Istanbul: Ege Yayınları.

Debord, Pierre. 1982. *Aspects sociaux et économiques de la vie religieuse dans l'Anatolie gréco-romaine*. Leiden: Brill.

Debord, Pierre. 1985. 'La Lydie du nord-est'. *Revue des études anciennes* 87: 345-358.

Debord, Pierre. 1999. *L'Asie Mineure au Ive siècle (412-323 a.C.). Pouvoirs et jeux politiques*. Bordeaux: Ausonius.

Debord, Pierre. 2001. 'Sur quelques Zeus cariens : religion et politique'. *Studi ellenistici* 13: 19-37.

Debord, Pierre. 2003. 'Cité grecque - village carien : des usages du mot "koinon"'. *Studi ellenistici* 15: 115-180.

Debord, Pierre. 2005. 'Côte/intérieur : les acculturations de la Carie'. *La Parola del Passato* 60: 357-378.

Debord, Pierre. 2009. 'Peut-on définir un panthéon carien?' In *Die Karer und die Anderen*, edited by Frank Rumscheid, 251-265. Bonn: Habelt.

Debord, Pierre, and Ender Varınlıoğlu, eds. 2001. *Les hautes terres de Carie*. Bordeaux: Ausonius.

Depauw, Mark. 2003. 'Elkab and Edfu: A Survey of Local Textual Sources from the Later Periods'. In *Edfu: An Egyptian Provincial Capital in the Ptolemaic Period*, edited by Willy Clarysse and Katelijn Vandorpe, 29-43. Brussels: Koninklijke Vlaamse Academie van België voor Wetenschappen en Kunsten.

Depauw, Mark. 2006. 'Egyptianizing the Chancellery During the Great Theban Revolt (205-186 BC): A New Study of Limestone Tablet Cairo 38258'. *Studien zur Altägyptischen Kultur* 34: 97-105.

Derchain, Philippe. 1995. 'La justice à la porte d'Évergète'. In *Systeme und Programme der ägyptischen Tempeldekoration. 3. Ägyptologische Tempeltagung*, edited by Dieter Kurth, 1-12. Wiesbaden: Harrassowitz.

Desideri, Paolo. 1967. 'Studi di storiografia eracleota I'. *Studi classici e orientali* 16: 366-416.

Desideri, Paolo. 1970. 'Studi di storiografia eracleota II: la guerra con Antioco il Grande'. *Studi classici e orientali* 19/20: 487–537.

Desideri, Paolo. 1991. 'Cultura eracleota: da Erodoro a Eraclide Pontico'. In *Pontica I. Recherches sur l'histoire du Pont dans l'antiquité*, edited by Bernard Rémy, 7–24. Saint-Etienne: Université Jean Monnet.

Desideri, Paolo. 2007. 'I Romani visti dall'Asia: riflessioni sulla sezione romana della *Storia di Eraclea* di Memnone'. In *Tra Oriente e Occidente. Indigeni, Greci e Romani in Asia Minore*, edited by Gianpaolo Urso, 45–59. Pisa: ETS.

Dignas, Beate. 2003. 'Urban Centres, Rural Centres, Religious Centres in the Greek East: Worlds Apart?' In *Religion und Region: Götter und Kulte aus dem östlichen Mittelmeerraum*, edited by Elmar Schwertheim and Engelbert Winter, 77–91. Bonn: Habelt.

Dillery, John. 2005. 'Greek Sacred History'. *American Journal of Philology* 126: 505–526.

Dillery, John. 2007. 'Exile: The Making of the Greek Historian'. In *Writing Exile: The Discourse of Displacement in Greco-Roman Antiquity and Beyond*, edited by Jan Felix Gaertner, 51–70. Leiden: Brill.

Dillery, John. 2013. 'Berossos' Narrative of Nabopolassar and Nebuchadnezzar II from Josephus'. In *The World of Berossos*, edited by Johannes Haubold, Giovanni B. Lanfranchi, Robert Rollinger, and John Steele, 75–96. Wiesbaden: Harrassowitz.

Dillery, John. 2015. *Clio's Other Sons: Berossus and Manetho, with an Afterword on Demetrius*. Ann Arbor: University of Michigan Press.

Dilts, Mervin R., ed. 1971. *Heraclidis Lembi Excerpta politiarum*. Durham, N.C.: Duke University.

Dimant, Devorah. 1981. 'Jerusalem and the Temple According to the Animal Apocalypse (1 Enoch 85–90) in the Light of the Ideology of the Dead Sea Sect'. *Shnaton: An Annual for Biblical and Ancient Near Eastern Studies* 5–6: 177–193.

Dimant, Devorah. 2001. *Qumrân Cave 4. Volume 21: Parabiblical Texts, Part 4: Pseudo-Prophetic Texts*. Oxford: Clarendon Press.

DiTommaso, Lorenzo. 2007. 'Apocalypses and Apocalypticism in Antiquity (Part I)'. *Currents in Biblical Research* 5: 235–286.

Dizard, Wilson. 2014. 'Northern Ireland Hears an Echo of Itself in Israeli-Palestinian Conflict'. *Al Jazeera America*, 31 July 2014. http://america.aljazeera.com/articles/2014/7/31/palestine-israelireland.html.

Dmitriev, Sviatoslav V. 2007. 'Memnon on the Siege of Heraclea Pontica by Prusias I and the War between the Kingdoms of Bithynia and Pergamum'. *The Journal of Hellenic Studies* 127: 133–138.

Dmitriev, Sviatoslav V. 2011. *The Greek Slogan of Freedom and Early Roman Politics in Greece*. Oxford: Oxford University Press.

Dmitriev, Sviatoslav V. 2016. 'Demochares (75)'. In *Brill's New Jacoby Online*, edited by Ian Worthington. Leiden: Brill.

Donker van Heel, Koenraad, ed. 1990. *The Legal Manual of Hermopolis*. Leiden: Papyrologisch Institut.

Doran, Robert. 1999. 'Independence or Co-Existence: The Responses of 1 and 2 Maccabees to Seleucid Hegemony'. *Society of Biblical Literature Seminar Papers* 38: 94–103.

Doran, Robert. 2011. 'The Persecution of Judeans by Antiochus IV: The Significance of "Ancestral Laws"'. In *The 'Other' in Second Temple Judaism: Essays in Honor of John J. Collins*, edited by Daniel C. Harlow, Karina Martin Hogan, Matthew Goff, and Joel S. Kaminsky, 423–433. Grand Rapids, MI: William B. Eerdmans.

Doran, Robert. 2012. *2 Maccabees: A Critical Commentary*, edited by Harold W. Attridge. Minneapolis: Fortress Press.

Drews, Robert. 1975. 'The Babylonian Chronicles and Berossus'. *Iraq* 37: 39–55.

Dreyer, Boris. 2011. 'How to Become a "Relative" of the King: Careers and Hierarchy at the Court of Antiochus III'. *American Journal of Philology* 132: 45–57.

Dreyer, Boris, and Engelmann, H. 2003. *Die Inschriften von Metropolis*, vol. 1: *Die Dekrete für Apollonios: Städtische Politik unter den Attaliden und im Konflikt zwischen Aristonikos und Rom*. Bonn: Habelt.

Droysen, Johann Gustav. 1877. *Geschichte des Hellenismus*. 3 vols. Gotha: F. A. Perthes.

Dueck, Daniela. 2006. 'Memnon of Herakleia on Rome and the Romans'. In *Rome and the Black Sea Region*, edited by Tønnes Bekker-Nielsen, 43–61. Aarhus: Aarhus University Press.

Eckhardt, Benedikt. 2015. 'Achaemenid Religious Policy after the Seleucid Decline: Case Studies in Political Memory and Near Eastern Dynastic Representation'. In *Political Memory in and after the Persian Empire*, edited by Jason M. Silverman and Caroline Waerzeggers, 269–298. Atlanta: SBL Press.

Eckhardt, Benedikt. 2018. 'Die "hellenistische Krise" und der Makkabäeraufstand in der neueren Diskussion'. *Theologische Literaturzeitung* 143 (2018) 10: 983–998.

Eddy, Samuel Kennedy. 1958. 'Oriental Religious Resistance to Hellenism'. Ph.D., Ann Arbor: University of Michigan.

Eddy, Samuel Kennedy. 1961. *The King Is Dead: Studies in the Near Eastern Resistance to Hellenism, 334–31 B.C.* Lincoln: University of Nebraska Press.

El-Aguizy, Ola. 1988. 'A Ptolemaic Judicial Document from Ḥwt-nsw'. *Bulletin de l'Institut français d'archéologie orientale* 88: 51–62.

el-Masri, Yahya, Hartwig Altenmüller, and Heinz-Josef Thissen. 2012. *Das Synodaldekret von Alexandria aus dem Jahre 243 v. Chr.* Hamburg: Buske.

Eldamaty, Mamdouh Mohamed, ed. 2005. *Ein ptolemäisches Priesterdekret aus dem Jahr 186 v. Chr.: eine neue Version von Philensis II in Kairo*. Munich: Saur.

Ellis, Maria deJong. 1989. 'Observations on Mesopotamian Oracles and Prophetic Texts: Literary and Historiographical Considerations'. *Journal of Cuneiform Studies* 41: 127–186.

Ellis-Evans, Aneurin. 2019. *The Kingdom of Priam. Lesbos and the Troad between Anatolia and the Aegean*. Oxford.

Elton, Hugh, and Gary L. Reger, eds. 2007. *Regionalism in Hellenistic and Roman Asia Minor*. Bordeaux: Ausonius.

Engels, David. 2013. 'A New Fratarakā Chronology'. *Latomus* 72: 28–80.

Engels, David. 2017. *Benefactors, Kings, Rulers: Studies on the Seleukid Empire between East and West*. Leuven: Peeters.

Engels, David. 2019. 'Mais où sont donc passés les soldats babyloniens? La place des contingents "indigènes" dans l'armée séleucide'. In *Rome and the Seleukid East*.

Select Papers from Seleukid Study Day V, Brussels, 21–23 Aug. 2015, edited by A. Coşkun and D. Engels, 403–433. Brussels.
Erman, Adolf, and Hermann Grapow, eds. 1926. Wörterbuch der ägyptische Sprache. 5 vols. Leipzig: J. C. Hinrichs.
Eshel, Hanan. 2008. The Dead Sea Scrolls and the Hasmonean State. Grand Rapids, MI: William B. Eerdmans.
Farid, Adel. 2005. 'Zwei demotische Privatbriefe'. Zeitschrift für Ägyptische Sprache 132: 1–11.
Faucher, Thomas, and Catharine Lorber. 2010. 'Bronze Coinage of Ptolemaic Egypt in the Second Century BC'. American Journal of Numismatics 22: 35–80.
Faucher, Thomas, Andrew Meadow, and Catharine Lorber. 2017. Egyptian Hoards I. The Ptolemies, Bibliothèque d'étude 168. Cairo.
Feeney, Denis C. 2007. Caesar's Calendar: Ancient Time and the Beginnings of History. Berkeley: University of California Press.
Felber, Heinz. 2002. 'Die Demotische Chronik'. In Apokalyptik und Ägypten: eine kritische Analyse der relevanten Texte aus dem griechisch-römischen Ägypten, edited by Andreas Blasius and Bernd Ulrich Schipper, 65–111. Leuven: Peeters.
Ferrary, Jean-Louis. 2001. 'Rome et les cités grecques d'Asie Mineure au IIe siècle'. In Les cités d'Asie Mineure occidentale au IIe siècle a.C., edited by Alain Bresson and Raymond Descat, 93–106. Bordeaux: Ausonius.
Feyel, Christophe, and Graslin-Thomé, Laetitia, eds. 2014. Le projet politique d'Antiochos IV (Journées d'études franco-allemandes, Nancy 17–19 juin 2013). Nancy: Association pour la diffusion de la recherche sur l'Antiquité.
Feyel, Christophe, and Graslin-Thomé, Laetitia, eds. 2017. Antiochos III et l'Orient. Actes de la rencontre franco-allemande tenue à Nancy du 6 au 8 juin 2016. Paris: Association pour la diffusion de la recherche sur l'Antiquité.
Figueira, Thomas J. 2007. 'Spartan Constitutions and the Enduring Image of the Spartan Ethos'. In Hē symvolē tēs archaias Spartēs stēn politikē skepsē kai praktikē = The Contribution of Ancient Sparta to Political Thought and Practice, edited by Paul Cartledge, Nikos Birgalias, and Kostas Bourazelis, 143–158. Athens: Alexandreia.
Figueira, Thomas J. 2016. 'Politeia and Lakonika in Spartan Historiography'. In Myth, Text, and History at Sparta, edited by T. J. Figueira, 7–104. Piscataway, NJ: Gorgias Press.
Fischer, David Hackett. 1971. Historians' Fallacies: Toward a Logic of Historical Thought. London: Routledge & Kegan Paul.
Fischer, Thomas. 1980. Seleukiden und Makkabäer: Beiträge zur Seleukidengeschichte und zu den politischen Ereignissen Judäa während der 1. Hälfte des 2. Jahrhunderts v. Chr. Bochum: Studienverlag N. Brockmeyer.
Fischer-Bovet, Christelle. 2014. Army and Society in Ptolemaic Egypt. Cambridge: Cambridge University Press.
Fischer-Bovet, Christelle. 2015a. 'A challenge to the concept of decline for understanding Hellenistic Egypt. From Polybius to the twenty-first century', Topoi 20/1, 2015: 209–237.

Fischer-Bovet, Christelle. 2015b. 'Social Unrest and Ethnic Coexistence in Ptolemaic Egypt and the Seleucid Empire'. *Past & Present* 229: 3-45.

Fischer-Bovet, Christelle. 2016a. 'A Challenge to the Concept of Decline for Understanding Hellenistic Egypt: From Polybius to the Twenty-First Century'. *Topoi. Orient—Occident* 20: 209-237.

Fischer-Bovet, Christelle. 2016b. 'Toward a Translocal Elite Culture in the Ptolemaic Empire'. In *Cosmopolitanism and Empire: Universal Rulers, Local Elites, and Cultural Integration in the Ancient Near East and Mediterranean*, edited by Myles Lavan, Richard E. Payne, and John Weisweiler, 103-128. Oxford: Oxford University Press.

Frei, Peter. 1993. 'Solymer, Milyer, Termilen, Lykier: ethnische und politische Einheiten auf der lykischen Halbinsel'. In *Akten des II. Internationalen Lykien-Symposions*, edited by Jürgen Borchhardt and Gerhard Dobesch, 1: 87-97. Vienna: Österreichische Akademie der Wissenschaften.

Frei, Peter, and Christian Marek. 1997. 'Die karisch-griechische Bilingue von Kaunos: eine zweisprachige Staatsurkunde des 4. Jh.s v. Chr'. *Kadmos* 36: 1-89.

Frei, Peter, and Christian Marek. 2000. 'Neues zu den karischen Inschriften von Kaunos'. *Kadmos* 39: 83-132.

Funck, Bernd. 1996. 'Konig Perserfreund: die Seleukiden in der Sicht ihrer Nachbar: (Beobachtungen zu einigen ptolemaischen Zeugnissen des 4. und 3. Jh.s v. Chr.)' in *Hellenismus : Beiträge zur Erforschung von Akkulturation und politischer Ordnung in den Staaten des hellenistischen Zeitalters: Akten des Internationalen Hellenismus-Kolloquiums, 9. - 14. März 1994 in Berlin*, ed. B. Funck, 95-215. Tübingen: Mohr Siebeck.

Gabrielsen, Vincent. 2011a. 'Profitable Partnerships: Monopolies, Traders, Kings, and Cities'. In *The Economies of Hellenistic Societies, Third to First Centuries BC*, edited by Zosia H. Archibald, John Kenyon Davies, and Vincent Gabrielsen, 216-250. Oxford: Oxford University Press.

Gabrielsen, Vincent. 2011b. 'The Chrysaoreis of Caria'. In *Labraunda and Karia*, edited by Lars Karlsson and Susanne Carlsson, 331-353. Uppsala: Uppsala Universitet.

Gallo, Italo, ed. 1975. *Frammenti biografici da papiri. I. La biografia politica*. Rome: Edizioni dell'Ateneo.

Gallo, Paolo. 1987. 'Some Demotic Architectural Terms'. In *Aspects of Demotic Lexicography*, edited by Sven P. Vleeming, 35-39. Leuven: Peeters.

Gallotta, Stefania. 2009. 'Introduzione ai *Pontika*'. In *Tradizione e trasmissione degli storici greci frammentari*, edited by Eugenio Lanzillotta, Virgilio Costa, and Gabriella Ottone, 431-445. Tivoli: Tored.

Gallotta, Stefania. 2010. 'Appunti per una storia della lega del Nord'. In *Incontri e conflitti. Ripensando la colonizzazione greca*, edited by Francesca Gazzano and Luigi Santi Amantini, 95-100. Rome: L'Erma di Bretschneider.

Gallotta, Stefania. 2014. 'Appunti su Memnone di Eraclea'. *Erga-Logoi* 2: 65-77.

Gauger, Jörg-Dieter. 1977. *Beiträge zur jüdischen Apologetik: Untersuchungen zur Authentizität von Urkunden bei Flavius Josephus und im 1. Makkabäerbuch*. Cologne: P. Hanstein.

BIBLIOGRAPHY 263

Gauger, Jörg-Dieter. 1990. 'Überlegungen zum Programma Antiochos' III. für den Tempel und die Stadt Jerusalem (Jos. Ant. Jud. 12,145-146) und zum Problem jüdischer Listen'. *Hermes* 118: 150-164.

Gehrke, Hans-Joachim. 2001. 'Myth, History and Collective Identity: Uses of the Past in Ancient Greece and Beyond'. In *The Historian's Craft in the Age of Herodotus*, edited by Nino Luraghi, 286-313. Oxford: Oxford University Press.

Gehrke, Hans-Joachim. 2003. 'Bürgerliches Selbstverständnis und Polisidentität im Hellenismus'. In *Sinn (in) der Antike: Orientierungssysteme, Leitbilder und Wertkonzepte im Altertum*, edited by Karl-Joachim Hölkeskamp, 225-254. Mainz: Von Zabern.

Gehrke, Hans-Joachim. 2010. 'Greek Representations of the Past'. In *Intentional History: Spinning Time in Ancient Greece*, edited by Lin Foxhall, Hans-Joachim Gehrke, and Nino Luraghi, 15-33. Stuttgart: Steiner.

Geller, Markham J. 1991. 'New Information on Antiochus IV from Babylonian Astronomical Diaries'. *Bulletin of the School of Oriental and African Studies* 54: 1-4.

George, Andrew R. 2005. 'The Tower of Babel: Archaeology, History and Cuneiform Texts'. *Archiv für Orientforschung* 51: 75-95.

George, Andrew R. 2010. 'Xerxes and the Tower of Babel'. In *The World of Achaemenid Persia: History, Art and Society in Iran and the Ancient Near East*, edited by John Custis and St John Simpson, 472-480. London: I. B. Tauris.

Gera, Dov. 1987. 'Ptolemy Son of Thraseas and the Fifth Syrian War'. *Ancient Society* 18: 63-73.

Gera, Dov. 1998. *Judaea and Mediterranean Politics, 219 to 161 B.C.E.* Leiden: Brill.

Gera, Dov. 2009. 'Olympiodoros, Heliodoros and the Temples of Koilē Syria and Phoinikē'. *Zeitschrift für Papyrologie und Epigraphik* 169: 125-155.

Gera, Dov. 2014. 'The Seleucid Road towards the Religious Persecution of the Jews'. In *La mémoire des persécutions. Autour des livres des Maccabées*, edited by Marie-Françoise Baslez and Olivier Munnich, 21-57. Leuven: Peeters.

Giddens, Anthony. 1981. *A Contemporary Critique of Historical Materialism*. Berkeley: University of California Press.

Gigon, O., ed. 1987. *Aristotelis opera III. Librorum deperditorum fragmenta*. Berlin: De Gruyter.

Giorgieri, Mauro, Mirjo Salvini, Marie-Claude Trémouille, and Pietro Vannicelli, eds. 2003. *Licia e Lidia prima dell'ellenizzazione*. Rome: Consiglio Nazionale delle Ricerche.

Girardin, M. Forthcoming. 'Religion et fiscalité en Judée hellénistique et romaine'. In *Religion et fiscalité de l'Antiquité à nos jours*, edited by M.-C. Marcellesi and A.-V. Pont. Paris: Presses Universitaires Paris-Sorbonne.

Glassner, Jean-Jacques. 2005. *Mesopotamian Chronicles*, edited by Benjamin Foster. Leiden: Brill.

Goldstein, Jonathan A., ed. 1976. *I Maccabees: A New Translation, with Introduction and Commentary*. 1st ed. Garden City, N.Y.: Doubleday.

Goldstein, Jonathan A., ed. 1983. *II Maccabees: A New Translation, with Introduction and Commentary*. 1st ed. Garden City, N.Y.: Doubleday.

Goldstein, Jonathan A. 1988. 'The Historical Setting of the Uruk Prophecy'. *Journal of Near Eastern Studies* 47: 43-46.
Goldstein, Jonathan A. 1989. 'The Hasmonean Revolt and the Hasmonean Dynasty'. In *The Cambridge History of Judaism*, edited by William D. Davies and Louis Finkelstein, 2: 292-351. Cambridge: Cambridge University Press.
Goodblatt, David M. 1987. 'Josephus on Parthian Babylonia (Antiquities XVIII, 310-379)'. *Journal of the American Oriental Society* 107: 605-622.
Goodblatt, David M. 2006. *Elements of Ancient Jewish Nationalism*. New York: Cambridge University Press.
Gorre, Gilles. 2009a. 'La place des scribes des temples dans l'administration lagide du troisième siècle'. In *Egyptian Archives*, edited by Patrizia Piacentini and Christian Orsenigo, 127-142. Milan: Cisalpino.
Gorre, Gilles. 2009b. *Les relations du clergé égyptien et des Lagides d'après les sources privées*. Leuven: Peeters.
Gorre, Gilles. 2012. 'Les monnaies lagides et les papyrus démotiques'. In *Les monnaies des fouilles du Centre d'études alexandrines. Les monnayages de bronze à Alexandrie de la conquête d'Alexandre à l'Égypte moderne*, edited by Olivier Picard, 109-124. Alexandria: Centre d'Études Alexandrines.
Gorre, Gilles. 2014. 'La monnaie de bronze lagide et les temples égyptiens. La diffusion de la monnaie de bronze en Thébaïde au IIIe siècle av. J.-C'. *Annales. Histoire, Sciences Sociales* 69: 91-113.
Gorre, Gilles, and Sylvie Honigman. 2013. 'Kings, Taxes and High Priests: Comparing the Ptolemaic and Seleukid Policies'. In *Egitto dai Faraoni agli Arabi*, edited by Silvia Bussi, 105-119. Pisa: Fabrizio Serra.
Gorre, Gilles, and Sylvie Honigman. 2014. 'La politique d'Antiochos IV à Jérusalem à la lumière des relations entre rois et temples aux époques perse et hellénistique'. In *Le projet politique d'Antiochos IV*, edited by Christophe Feyel and Laetitia Graslin-Thomé, 301-338. Nancy: Association pour la Diffusion de la Recherche sur l'Antiquité.
Gorre, Gilles, and Catharine Lorber. 2020. 'The Survival of the Silver Standard after the Grand Mutation'. In *Money Rules! The Monetary Economy of Egypt, from Persians until the beginning of Islam*, edited by T. Faucher, 149-170. IFAO, Cairo.
Goudriaan, Koen. 1988. *Ethnicity in Ptolemaic Egypt*. Amsterdam: Gieben.
Grabbe, Lester L. 2002. 'The Jews and Hellenization: Hengel and His Critics'. In *Second Temple Studies III: Studies in Politics, Class and Material Culture*, edited by Philip R. Davies and John M. Halligan, 52-66. Sheffield: Sheffield Academic.
Grabowski, Tomasz. 2008. 'Ptolemy's Military and Political Operations in Greece in 314-308 BC'. *Electrum* 14: 33-46.
Grabowski, Tomasz. 2013. 'Ptolemaic Foundations in Asia Minor and the Aegean as the Lagids' Political Tool'. In *Colonization in the Ancient World*, edited by Edward Dąbrowa, 57-76. *Electrum* 20. Kraków: Jagiellonian University Press.
Grabowski, Tomasz. 2014. 'The Cult of the Ptolemies in the Aegean in the 3rd Century BC'. *Electrum* 21: 21-41.
Grainger, John D. 2009. *The Cities of Pamphylia*. Oxford: Oxbow Books.

Granerød, Gard. 2013. '"By the Favour of Ahuramazda I Am King": On the Promulgation of a Persian Propaganda Text among Babylonians and Judaeans'. *Journal for the Study of Judaism* 44: 455-480.

Grayson, Albert Kirk. 1975a. *Assyrian and Babylonian Chronicles*. Locust Valley, N.Y.: J. J. Augustin.

Grayson, Albert Kirk. 1975b. *Babylonian Historical-Literary Texts*. Toronto: University of Toronto Press.

Green, Peter. 1961. 'The First Sicilian Slave War'. *Past & Present* 20: 10-29.

Grenfell, Bernard P., and Arthur S. Hunt. 1900-1901. *The Amherst papyri: being an account of the Greek papyri in the collection of Lord Amherst of Hackney*. 2 vols. London: Frowde.

Griffiths, John Gwyn. 1979. 'Egyptian Nationalism in the Edfu Temple Texts'. In *Glimpses of Ancient Egypt: Studies in Honour of H. W. Fairman*, edited by John Ruffle, Gaballa A. Gaballa, and Kenneth A. Kitchen, 174-179. Warminster: Aris & Phillips.

Gruen, Erich S. 1984. *The Hellenistic World and the Coming of Rome*. 2 vols. Berkeley: University of California Press.

Gruen, Erich S. 1993. 'Hellenism and Persecution: Antiochus IV and the Jews'. In *Hellenistic History and Culture*, edited by Peter Green, 238-164. Berkeley: University of California Press.

Gruen, Erich S. 1998. *Heritage and Hellenism: The Reinvention of Jewish Tradition*. Berkeley: University of California Press.

Gruen, Erich S. 1999. 'Seleucid Royal Ideology'. *Society of Biblical Literature Seminar Papers* 38: 24-53.

Gruen, Erich S. 2010. 'Hellenism and Judaism: Fluid Boundaries'. In *Follow the Wise: Studies in Jewish History and Culture in Honor of Lee I. Levine*, edited by Zeev Weiss, Oded Irshai, Jodi Magness, and Seth Schwartz, 53-70. Winona Lake, IN: Eisenbrauns.

Gruen, Erich S. 2016. 'When Is a Revolt Not a Revolt? A Case for Contingency'. In *Revolt and Resistance in the Ancient Classical World and the Near East: In the Crucible of Empire*, edited by John J. Collins and Joseph G. Manning, 10-37. Leiden: Brill.

Guha, Ranajit. 1983. 'The Prose of Counter-Insurgency'. In *Subaltern Studies: Writings on South Asian History and Society*, edited by Ranajit Guha, 2: 1-42. Delhi: Oxford University Press.

Habicht, Christian. 1958. 'Die herrschende Gesellschaft in den hellenistischen Monarchien'. *Vierteljahrschrift für Sozial- und Wirtschaftsgeschichte* 45: 1-16.

Hadas, Moses. 1964. Review of *The King Is Dead: Studies in the Near Eastern Resistance to Hellenism, 334-31 B.C.*, by Samuel Kennedy Eddy. *American Journal of Philology* 85: 204-206.

Hadot, Jean. 1970. Review of *The King Is Dead: Studies in the Near Eastern Resistance to Hellenism, 334-31 B.C.*, by Samuel Kennedy Eddy. *Revue de l'histoire des religions* 178: 80-83.

Halbwachs, M. 1925. *Les cadres sociaux de la mémoire*. Paris.

Halbwachs, M. 1950. *La mémoire collective*. Paris [English translation by F. J. Ditter Jr. and V. Yazdi Ditter, with introduction by M. Douglas, *The Collective Memory*. New York 1980].

Hall, Jonathan M. 1997. *Ethnic Identity in Greek Antiquity*. Cambridge: Cambridge University Press.

Hall, Jonathan M. 2002. *Hellenicity: Between Ethnicity and Culture*. Chicago: University of Chicago Press.

Hall, Jonathan M. 2015. 'Federalism and Ethnicity'. In *Federalism in Greek Antiquity*, edited by Hans Beck and Peter Funke, 30–48. Cambridge: Cambridge University Press.

Hallmannsecker, M. 2020. "The Ionian Koinon and the Koinon of the 13 Cities at Sardis", *Chiron*, 50: 1–27.

Hanell, Krister. 1934. *Megarische Studien*. Lund: Lindstedt.

Hannestad, Lise. 1996. '"This Contributes in No Small Way to One's Reputation": The Bithynian Kings and Greek Culture'. In *Aspects of Hellenistic Kingship*, edited by Per Bilde, Troels Engberg-Pedersen, Lise Hannestad, and Jan Zahle, 67–98. Aarhus: Aarhus University Press.

Harding, Phillip E. 1977. 'Atthis and Politeia'. *Historia* 26: 148–160.

Haring, B. J. J. 2003. 'Egyptian Text Denominatives'. In *Writing in a Workmen's Village: Scribal Practice in Ramesside Deir el-Medina*, edited by Koenraad Donker van Heel and B. J. J. Haring, 85–123. Leiden: Nederlands Instituut voor het Nabije Oosten.

Haubold, Johannes. 2013. *Greece and Mesopotamia: Dialogues in Literature*. Cambridge: Cambridge University Press.

Haubold, Johannes. 2016. 'Hellenism, Cosmopolitanism, and the Role of Babylonian Elites in the Seleucid Empire'. In *Cosmopolitanism and Empire: Universal Rulers, Local Elites, and Cultural Integration in the Ancient Near East and Mediterranean*, edited by Myles Lavan, Richard E. Payne, and John Weisweiler, 89–102. Oxford: Oxford University Press.

Haubold, Johannes. 2017. 'Converging Perspectives on Antiochus III'. In *Hellenism and the Local Communities of the Eastern Mediterranean: 400 BCE–250 CE*, edited by Boris Chrubasik and Daniel King, 111–130. Oxford: Oxford University Press.

Haubold, Johannes. 2019. 'History and Historiography in the Early Parthian Diaries'. In *Keeping Watch in Babylon: The Astronomical Diaries in Context*, edited by Johannes Haubold, John Steele, and Kathryn Stevens, 269–293. Leiden: Brill.

Haubold, Johannes, Giovanni B. Lanfranchi, Robert Rollinger, and John Steele, eds. 2013. *The World of Berossos*. Wiesbaden: Harrassowitz.

Haubold, Johannes, John Steele, and Kathryn Stevens, eds. 2019. *Keeping Watch in Babylon: The Astronomical Diaries in Context*. Leiden: Brill.

Haynes, Douglas E., and Gyan Prakash. 1992. *Contesting power: resistance and everyday social relations in South Asia*. Berkeley: University of California Press.

Hazzard, Richard A., and Stephen M. Huston. 2015. 'The Surge in Prices under Ptolemies IV and V'. *Chronique d'Égypte* 90: 105–120.

Heinemann, Uwe. 2010. *Stadtgeschichte im Hellenismus: die lokalhistoriographischen Vorgänger und Vorlagen Memnons von Herakleia*. Munich: Utz.

Held, Winfried. 2013. 'Heiligtümer und lokale Identität auf der karischen Chersones'. In *Euploia: la Lycie et la Carie antiques. Dynamiques des territoires, échanges et identités*, edited by Patrice Brun and Laurence Cavalier, 93-100. Bordeaux: Ausonius.

Hellholm, David, ed. 1983. *Apocalypticism in the Mediterranean World and the Near East*. Tübingen: Mohr Siebeck.

Hellström, Pontus. 2009. 'Sacred Architecture and Karian Identity'. In *Die Karer und die Anderen*, edited by Frank Rumscheid, 267-290. Bonn: Habelt.

Henderson, John. 1989. 'Livy and the Invention of History'. In *History as Text: The Writing of Ancient History*, edited by Averil Cameron, 64-85. London: Duckworth.

Hengel, Martin. 1974. *Judaism and Hellenism: Studies in Their Encounter in Palestine during the Early Hellenistic Period*. Translated by John Bowden. Philadelphia: Fortress Press.

Henry, Olivier. 2009. *Tombes de Carie. Architecture funéraire et culture carienne, Vie-Iie s. av. J.-C.* Rennes: Presses Universitaires de Rennes.

Henry, Olivier, ed. 2013a. *4th Century Karia: Defining a Karian Identity under the Hekatomnids*. Istanbul: Institut Français d'Études Anatoliennes Georges Dumézil.

Henry, Olivier. 2013b. 'Tombes cariennes, tombes lyciennes: un processus analogue de pétrification architecturale?' In *Euploia: la Lycie et la Carie antiques. Dynamiques des territoires, échanges et identités*, edited by Patrice Brun and Laurence Cavalier, 257-268. Bordeaux: Ausonius.

Henten, Jan Willem van. 2001. 'The Honorary Decree for Simon the Maccabee (1 Macc 14:25-49) in Its Hellenistic Context'. In *Hellenism in the Land of Israel*, edited by John J. Collins and Gregory E. Sterling, 116-145. Notre Dame: University of Notre Dame.

Henze, Matthias. 2009. '4Qapocryphon of Jeremiah C and 4Qpseudo-Ezekiel: Two 'Historical' Apocalypses'. In *Prophecy after the Prophets? The Contribution of the Dead Sea Scrolls to the Understanding of Biblical and Extra-Biblical Prophecy*, edited by Kristin de Troyer and Armin Lange, 25-41. Leuven: Peeters.

Hill, George Francis. 1897. *Catalogue of the Greek Coins of Lycia, Pamphylia, and Pisidia*. London: British Museum: Department of Coins and Medals.

Himmelfarb, Martha. 2002. 'The Book of the Watchers and the Priests of Jerusalem'. *Henoch* 24: 131-135.

Himmelfarb, Martha. 2007. 'Temple and Priests in the Book of the Watchers, the Animal Apocalypse and the Apocalypse of Weeks'. In *The Early Enoch Literature*, edited by Gabriele Boccaccini and John J. Collins, 219-236. Leiden: Brill.

Himmelfarb, Martha. 2013. *Between Temple and Torah: Essays on Priests, Scribes, and Visionaries in the Second Temple Period and Beyond*. Tübingen: Mohr Siebeck.

Hoepfner, Wolfram. 1966. *Herakleia Pontike-Ereğli: eine baugeschichtliche Untersuchung*. Vienna: Böhlau.

Hölbl, Günther. 2001. *A History of the Ptolemaic Empire*. Translated by Tina Saavedra. London: Routledge.

Hölkeskamp, Karl-Joachim. 1996. '*Exempla* und *mos maiorum*: Überlegungen zum kollektiven Gedächtnis der Nobilität'. In *Vergangenheit und Lebenswelt: soziale*

Kommunikation, Traditionsbildung und historisches Bewusstsein, edited by Hans-Joachim Gehrke and Astrid Möller, 301–338. Tübingen: Narr.

Holt, Frank Lee. 1988. *Alexander the Great and Bactria: The Formation of a Greek Frontier in Central Asia*. Leiden: E. J. Brill.

Holt, Frank Lee. 1999. *Thundering Zeus: The Making of Hellenistic Bactria*. Berkeley: University of California Press.

Von Holzinger, C. 1891. 'Aristoteles' athenische Politie und die Heraklidischen Excerpte', *Philologus* 50 (1891): 436–446.

Honigman, Sylvie. 2007. 'Permanence des stratégies culturelles grecques à l'œuvre dans les rencontres inter-ethniques, de l'époque archaïque à l'époque hellénistique'. In *Identités ethniques dans le monde grec antique*, edited by Jean-Marc Luce, 125–140. *Pallas* 73. Toulouse: Presses Universitaires du Mirail.

Honigman, Sylvie. 2014a. *Tales of High Priests and Taxes: The Books of the Maccabees and the Judean Rebellion against Antiochos IV*. Berkeley: University of California Press.

Honigman, Sylvie. 2014b. 'The Religious Persecution as a Narrative Elaboration of a Military Suppression'. In *La mémoire des persécutions. Autour des livres des Maccabées*, edited by Marie-Françoise Baslez and Olivier Munnich, 59–76. Leuven: Peeters.

Honigman, Sylvie. 2020. 'Early Judean Apocalyptic Literature, between Resistance Literature and Literate Hermeneutics'. In *Judaea in the Long Third Century BCE: The Transition between the Persian and Hellenistic Periods*, edited by Sylvie Honigman, Oded Lipschits, and Christophe Nihan. Winona Lake, IN: Eisenbrauns.

Honigman, Sylvie, and Anne-Emmanuelle Veïsse. 2021. 'Regional Revolts in the Seleucid and Ptolemaic Empires'. In *Comparing the Ptolemaic and Seleucid Empires: Integration, Communication, and Resistance*, edited by Christelle Fischer-Bovet and Sitta von Reden, 301–328. Cambridge: Cambridge University Press.

Hordern, James H., ed. 2004. *Sophron's Mimes: Text, Translation, and Commentary*. Oxford: Oxford University Press.

Horsley, Richard A. 2005. 'Politics of Cultural Production in Second Temple Judea: Historical Context and Political-Religious Relations of the Scribes Who Produced 1 Enoch, Sirach, and Daniel'. In *Conflicted Boundaries in Wisdom and Apocalypticism*, edited by Benjamin G. Wright and Lawrence M. Wills, 123–145. Atlanta: Society of Biblical Literature.

Horsley, Richard A., ed. 2008. *In the Shadow of Empire: Reclaiming the Bible as a History of Faithful Resistance*. Louisville and London: Westminster John Knox Press.

Horsley, Richard A. 2010. *Revolt of the Scribes: Resistance and Apocalyptic Origins*. Minneapolis: Fortress Press.

Horsley, Richard A., and Patrick A. Tiller. 2002. 'Ben Sira and the Sociology of the Second Temple'. In *Second Temple Studies III: Studies in Politics, Class and Material Culture*, edited by Philip R. Davies and John M. Halligan, 74–107. Sheffield: Sheffield Academic.

Hose, Martin, ed. 2002. *Aristoteles: die historischen Fragmente.* Aristoteles Werke in deutscher Übersetzung, 20/3. Berlin: Akademie Verlag.

Hoz, María Paz de. 1999. *Die lydischen Kulte im Lichte der griechischen Inschriften.* Bonn: Habelt.

Hudson, Stephanie E. 2014. 'Ostraca Varia: Unpublished Deir el-Medina Ramesside Administrative Ostraca from the Ashmolean Museum, Oxford'. *Journal of the American Research Center in Egypt* 50: 79–94.

Humphries, Conor. 2014. 'Northern Ireland's Protestants and Catholics Adopt Israeli, Palestinian Flags as Symbols'. *Haaretz,* 4 September 2014. http://www.haaretz.com/world-news/1.614110.

Hunger, Hermann, and Stephen A. Kaufman. 1975. 'A New Akkadian Prophecy Text'. *Journal of the American Oriental Society* 95: 371–375.

Huss, Werner. 1994. *Der makedonische König und die ägyptischen Priester: Studien zur Geschichte des ptolemaiischen Ägypten.* Stuttgart: Steiner.

Ianziti, Gary. 2012. *Writing History in Renaissance Italy: Leonardo Bruni and the Uses of the Past.* Cambridge, MA: Harvard University Press.

Iliakis, Michael. 2013. 'Greek Mercenary Revolts in Bactria: A Re-Appraisal'. *Historia* 62: 182–195.

Isager, Signe. 1998. 'The Pride of Halikarnassos: *editio princeps* of an Inscription from Salmakis'. *Zeitschrift für Papyrologie und Epigraphik* 123: 1–23.

Jacoby, Felix. 1949. *Atthis: The Local Chronicles of Ancient Athens.* Oxford: Clarendon Press.

Jacoby, Felix, ed. 1954. *Die Fragmente der Griechischen Historiker.* Vol. 3b (Supplement). Leiden: E. J. Brill.

Jacoby, Felix, ed. 1955. *Die Fragmente der Griechischen Historiker.* Vol. 3b. Leiden: E. J. Brill.

Janke, Manfred. 1963. 'Historische Untersuchungen zu Memnon von Herakleia: Kap. 18-40, FgrHist Nr. 434'. Würzburg: Julius-Maximilians-Universität.

Jennings, Justin. 2011. *Globalizations and the Ancient World.* Cambridge: Cambridge University Press.

Johnson, Janet H. 1983. 'The Demotic Chronicle as a Statement of a Theory of Kingship'. *Journal of the Society for the Study of Egyptian Antiquities* 13: 61–76.

Johnson, Janet H. 1984. 'Is the Demotic Chronicle an Anti-Greek Tract?' In *Grammata demotika: Festschrift für Erich Lüddeckens zum 15. Juni 1983,* edited by Heinz-Josef Thissen and Karl-Theodor Zauzich, 107–124. Würzburg: Zauzich.

Johstono, P. 2017. 'Rumor, Rage, and Reversal: Tragic Patterns in Polybius' Account of Agathocles at Alexandria', *AHB* 31: 1–20.

Jones, A. H. M. 1971. *The Cities of the Eastern Roman Provinces.* 2nd ed. Oxford: Clarendon Press.

Jones, Christopher P. 1999. *Kinship Diplomacy in the Ancient World.* Cambridge, MA: Harvard University Press.

Jones, Christopher P. 2009. 'The Inscription from Tel Maresha for Olympiodoros'. *Zeitschrift für Papyrologie und Epigraphik* 171: 100–104.

Jones, Nicholas F. 2016. 'Philochoros of Athens (328)'. In *Brill's New Jacoby Online,* edited by Ian Worthington. Leiden: Brill.

Jones, Siân. 1997. *The Archaeology of Ethnicity: Constructing Identities in the Past and Present*. London: Routledge.
Jonnes, Lloyd, ed. 1994. *The Inscriptions of Heraclea Pontica*. Bonn: Habelt.
Jursa, Michael. 2007. 'Die Söhne Kudurrus und die Herkunft der neubabylonischen Dynastie'. *Revue d'assyriologie et d'archéologie orientale* 101: 125–136.
Kaibel, Georg. 1898. *Die Prolegomena Περὶ Κωμῳδίας*. Berlin: Weidmann.
Kearsley, Rosalinde A. 1994. 'The Milyas and the Attalids: A Decree of the City of Olbasa and a New Royal Letter of the Second Century B.C'. *Anatolian Studies* 44: 47–57.
Keaveney, Arthur, and John A. Madden. 2016. 'Memnon (434)'. In *Brill's New Jacoby Online*, edited by Ian Worthington. Leiden: Brill.
Keen, Antony G. 1998. *Dynastic Lycia: A Political History of the Lycians and Their Relations with Foreign Powers, c. 545–362 B.C*. Leiden: Brill.
Keen, Antony G. 2002. 'The Poleis of the Southern Anatolian Coast (Lycia, Pamphlyia, Pesidia) and Their Civic Identity: The 'Interface' between the Hellenic and the Barbarian Polis'. In *Greek Settlements in the Eastern Mediterranean and the Black Sea*, edited by Gocha R. Tsetskhladze and Anthony M. Snodgrass, 27–40. Oxford: Archaeopress.
Kelp, Ute. 2015. *Grabdenkmal und lokale Identität: ein Bild der Landschaft Phrygien in der römischen Kaiserzeit*. Bonn: Habelt.
Kerkeslager, Allen. 1998. 'The Apology of the Potter: A Translation of the *Potter's Oracle*'. In *Jerusalem Studies in Egyptology*, edited by Irene Shirun-Grumach, 67–79. *Ägypten und Altes Testament* 40. Wiesbaden: Harrassowitz.
Kienast, Dietmar. 1973. 'Presbeia'. In *Paulys Real-Encyclopädie der Classischen Altertumswissenschaft*, edited by Konrat Ziegler, 13 (Suppl.): 499–628. Munich: Alfred Druckenmüller Verlag.
Kistler, E. 2009. *Funktionalisierte Keltenbilder. Die Indienstnahme der Kelten zur Vermittlung von Normen und Werten in der hellenistischen Welt*. Frankfurt am Main.
Klotz, David. 2009. 'The Statue of the *dioikêtês* Harchebi/Archibios, Nelson Atkins Museum of Art 47-12'. *Bulletin de l'Institut français d'archéologie orientale* 109: 281–310.
Knibb, M. A. 2009. 'The Exile in the Literature of the Intertestamental Period'. In *Essays on the Book of Enoch and Other Early Jewish Texts and Traditions*, 191–212. Leiden: Brill. Reprint from *Heythrop Journal* 17 (1976): 253–272.
Knoepfler, Denis. 2010. 'Épigraphie et histoire des cités grecques'. *Annuaire du Collège de France* 109: 691–715.
Koenen, Ludwig. 1959. 'Θεοίσιν ἐχθρός: ein einheimischer Gegenkönig in Ägypten (132/1a)'. *Chronique d'Égypte* 34: 103–119.
Koenen, Ludwig. 1968. 'Die Prophezeiungen des "Töpfers"'. *Zeitschrift für Papyrologie und Epigraphik* 2: 178–209.
Koenen, Ludwig. 1970. 'The Prophecies of a Potter: A Prophecy of World Renewal Becomes an Apocalypse'. In *Proceedings of the Twelfth International Congress of Papyrology*, edited by Deborah H. Samuel, 249–254. Toronto: A. M. Hakkert.

BIBLIOGRAPHY 271

Koenen, Ludwig. 2002. 'Die Apologie des Töpfers an König Amenophis oder das Töpferorakel'. In *Apokalyptik und Ägypten: eine kritische Analyse der relevanten Texte aus dem griechisch-römischen Ägypten*, edited by Andreas Blasius and Bernd Ulrich Schipper, 139–187. Leuven: Peeters.

Koenen, Ludwig, and Andreas Blasius. 2002. 'Die Apologie des Töpfers an König Amenophis oder das Töpferorakel'. In *Apokalyptik und Ägypten. Eine kritische Analyse der relevanten Texte aus dem griechisch-römischen Ägypten*, edited by Andreas Blasius and Bernd U. Schipper, 139-87. Leuven: Peeters.

Kolb, Frank. 2000. 'Von der Burg zur Polis: Akkulturation in einer kleinasiatischen Provinz'. Jahrbuch des Historischen Kollegs, 39–83.

Kolb, Frank. 2003. 'Aspekte der Akkulturation in Lykien in archaischer und klassischer Zeit'. In *Licia e Lidia prima dell'ellenizzazione*, edited by Mauro Giorgieri, Mirjo Salvini, Marie-Claude Trémouille, and Pietro Vannicelli, 207–237. Rome: Consiglio Nazionale delle Ricerche.

Kolb, Frank. 2007. 'Akkulturation in der lykischen "Provinz" unter römischer Herrschaft'. In *Tra Oriente e Occidente. Indigeni, Greci e Romani in Asia Minore*, edited by Gianpaolo Urso, 271–291. Pisa: ETS.

Kolb, Frank. 2010. 'Die Einführung der Polis in Zentrallykien: Modernisierung und Traditionalismus der politischen und gesellschaftlichen Strukturen'. In *Società indigene e cultura greco-romana*, edited by Elvira Migliario, Lucio Troiani, and Giuseppe Zecchini, 77–93. Rome: L'Erma di Bretschneider.

Kolb, Frank. 2013. 'Le pouvoir politique et son cadre architectural en Lycie antique'. In *Euploia: la Lycie et la Carie antiques. Dynamiques des territoires, échanges et identités*, edited by Patrice Brun and Laurence Cavalier, 113–126. Bordeaux: Ausonius.

Kooij, Arie van der. 2012. 'The Claim of Maccabean Leadership and the Use of Scripture'. In *Jewish Identity and Politics Between the Maccabees and Bar Kokhba: Groups, Normativity, and Rituals*, edited by Benedikt Eckhardt, 29–49. Leiden: Brill.

Kosmetatou, Elizabeth. 1997. 'Pisidia and the Hellenistic Kings from 323 to 133 BC'. *Ancient Society* 28: 5–67.

Kosmetatou, Elizabeth. 2005. 'Macedonians in Pisidia'. *Historia* 54: 216–221.

Kosmetatou, Elizabeth, and Marc Waelkens. 1997. 'The "Macedonian" Shields of Sagalassos'. In *Sagalassos IV: Report on the Survey and Excavation Campaigns of 1994 and 1995*, edited by Marc Waelkens and Jeroen Poblome, 277–291. Leuven: Leuven University Press.

Kosmin, Paul J. 2014. *The Land of the Elephant Kings: Space, Territory, and Ideology in the Seleucid Empire*. Cambridge, MA: Harvard University Press.

Kosmin, Paul J. 2016. 'Indigenous Revolts in 2 Maccabees: The Persian Version'. *Classical Philology* 111: 32–53.

Kosmin, Paul J. 2018. *Time and Its Adversaries in the Seleucid Empire*. Cambridge, MA: Belknap Press of Harvard University Press.

Kraeling, C. H. 1964. Review of *The King Is Dead: Studies in the Near Eastern Resistance to Hellenism, 334–31 B.C.*, by Samuel Kennedy Eddy. *Journal of the American Oriental Society* 84: 431–433.

Kubica, Olga. 2021. 'Reading the Milindapañha: Indian historical sources and the Greeks in Bactria'. In *The Graeco-Bactrian and Indo-Greek World*, 430–445, edited by Rachel Mairs. Abingdon: Routledge.

Kugelmass, Jack, and Jonathan Boyarin, eds. 1998. *From a Ruined Garden: The Memorial Books of Polish Jewry*. 2nd ed. Bloomington: Indiana University Press.

Kuhrt, Amélie. 1987. 'Berossus' *Babyloniaka* and Seleucid Rule in Babylon'. In *Hellenism in the East: The Interaction of Greek and Non-Greek Civilizations from Syria to Central Asia after Alexander*, edited by Amélie Kuhrt and Susan M. Sherwin-White, 32–56. London: Duckworth.

Kuhrt, Amélie. 1988a. 'Babylonia from Cyrus to Xerxes'. In *The Cambridge Ancient History. Volume IV: Persia, Greece and the Western Mediterranean, c. 525 to 479 B.C.*, edited by John Boardman, N. G. L. Hammond, David M. Lewis, and Martin Ostwald, 2nd ed., 112–138. Cambridge: Cambridge University Press.

Kuhrt, Amélie. 1988b. 'The Achaemenid Empire: A Babylonian Perspective'. *Proceedings of the Cambridge Philological Society* 34: 60–76.

Kuhrt, Amélie. 1990. 'Alexander and Babylon'. In *Achaemenid History V: The Roots of European Tradition*, edited by Heleen Sancisi-Weerdenburg and Jan Willem Drijvers, 121–130. Leiden: Nederlands Instituut voor het Nabije Oosten.

Kuhrt, Amélie. 1996. 'The Seleucid Kings and Babylonia: New Perspectives on the Seleucid Realm in the East'. In *Aspects of Hellenistic Kingship*, edited by Per Bilde, Troels Engberg-Pedersen, Lise Hannestad, and Jan Zahle, 41–54. Aarhus: Aarhus University Press.

Kuhrt, Amélie. 2002. '"Greeks" and "Greece" in Mesopotamian and Persian Perspectives: Twenty-First J. L. Myres Memorial Lecture.' Oxford. Leopard's Head Press.

Kuhrt, Amélie. 2014. 'Reassessing the Reign of Xerxes in the Light of New Evidence'. In *Extraction and Control: Studies in Honor of Matthew W. Stolper*, edited by Michael Kozuh, Wouter Henkelman, Charles E. Jones, and Christopher Woods, 163–169. Chicago: Oriental Institute of the University of Chicago.

Kuhrt, Amélie, and Susan Sherwin-White. 1987. 'Xerxes' Destruction of Babylonian Temples'. In *Achaemenid History II: The Greek Sources*, edited by Heleen Sancisi-Weerdenburg and Amélie Kuhrt, 69–78. Leiden: Nederlands Instituut voor het Nabije Oosten.

Kuhrt, Amélie, and Susan Sherwin-White. 1991. 'Aspects of Seleucid Royal Ideology: The Cylinder of Antiochus I from Borsippa'. *The Journal of Hellenic Studies* 111: 71–86.

Lambert, Wilfred G. 1978. *The Background of Jewish Apocalyptic*. London: The Athlone Press.

Lanciers, Eddy. 2014. 'The Development of the Greek Dynastic Cult under Ptolemy V'. *Archiv für Papyrusforschung und verwandte Gebiete* 60: 373–383.

Landucci Gattinoni, Franca. 1992. *Lisimaco di Tracia. Un sovrano nella prospettiva del primo ellenismo*. Milan: Jaca Book.

Lanfranchi, Giovanni B. 2013. '*Babyloniaca*, Book 3: Assyrians, Babylonians and Persians'. In *The World of Berossos*, edited by Johannes Haubold, Giovanni B. Lanfranchi, Robert Rollinger, and John Steele, 61–74. Wiesbaden: Harrassowitz.

Lang, Philippa. 2016. 'Manetho (609)'. In *Brill's New Jacoby Online*, edited by Ian Worthington. Leiden: Brill.

Laqueur, Richard. 1926. 'Lokalchronik'. In *Paulys Real-Encyclopädie der Classischen Altertumswissenschaft*, edited by Wilhelm Kroll, 25:1083–1110. Stuttgart: J. B. Metzlersche Verlagsbuchhandlung.

Laqueur, Richard. 1937. 'Nymphis'. In *Paulys Real-Encyclopädie der Classischen Altertumswissenschaft*, edited by Wilhelm Kroll, 34:1609–1623. Stuttgart: J. B. Metzlersche Verlagsbuchhandlung.

Laroche, Emmanuel. 1976. 'Lyciens et Termiles'. *Revue archéologique* 15–19.

Lauffray, Jean, Ramadan M. Saad, and Serge Sauneron. 1970. 'Rapport sur les travaux de Karnak: activités du Centre franco-égyptien en 1968-1969'. *Kêmi* 20: 57–99.

Laumonier, Alfred. 1958. *Les cultes indigènes en Carie*. Paris: De Boccard.

Lavan, Myles, Richard Payne and John Weiswiler, 'Cosmopolitan Politics'. In *Cosmopolitanism and Empire: Universal Rulers, Local Elites, and Cultural Integration in the Ancient Near East and Mediterranean*, edited by Myles Lavan, Richard E. Payne, and John Weisweiler, 1–28. Oxford: Oxford University Press.

Le Rider, Georges. 1999. 'Les ressources financières de Séleucos IV (187–175) et le paiement de l'indemnité aux Romains'. In *Études d'histoire monétaire et financière du monde grec: écrits 1958-1998*, by Georges Le Rider, edited by Eleni Papaefthymiou, François de Callataÿ, and François Queyrel, 3:1265–1279. Athens: Société Hellénique de Numismatique.

Le Roy, Christian. 1987. 'Araméen, lycien et grec: pluralité des langues et pluralité des cultures'. In *Hethitica VIII. Acta Anatolica E. Laroche oblata*, edited by René Lebrun, 263–266. Louvain: Peeters.

Le Roy, Christian. 1991. 'Le développement monumental du Létôon de Xanthos'. *Revue archéologique* 341–352.

Le Roy, Christian. 2004a. 'Dieux anatoliens et dieux grecs en Lycie'. In *Les cultes locaux dans les mondes grec et romain*, edited by Guy Labarre, 263–274. Lyon: Université Lumière-Lyon.

Le Roy, Christian. 2004b. 'Lieux de mémoire en Lycie'. *Cahiers du Centre Gustave-Gl otz* 15: 7–15.

Levick, Barbara. 2013. 'In the Phrygian Mode: A Region Seen from Without'. In *Roman Phrygia: Culture and Society*, edited by Peter Thonemann, 41–54. Cambridge: Cambridge University Press.

Levine, Lee I. 1998. *Judaism and Hellenism in Antiquity: Conflict or Confluence?* Seattle: University of Washington Press.

Lieberman, Samuel. 1962. Review of *The King Is Dead: Studies in the Near Eastern Resistance to Hellenism, 334–31 B.C.*, by Samuel Kennedy Eddy. *Classical World* 56: 76.

Limme, Luc. 2008. 'Elkab, 1937-2007: Seventy Years of Belgian Archaeological Research'. *British Museum Studies in Ancient Egypt and Sudan* 9: 15–50.

Lippert, Sandra Luisa. 2004. *Ein demotisches juristisches Lehrbuch: Untersuchungen zu Papyrus Berlin P 23757 rto*. Wiesbaden: Harrassowitz.

López-Sánchez, F., and T. Ñaco del Hoyo, eds. 2018. *War, Warlords, and Interstate Relations in the Ancient Mediterranean*. Leiden and Boston.

Lorber, Catharine. 2000. 'Large Ptolemaic bronzes in third-century hoards', *AJN* 12: 67–92.

Luce, Jean-Marc. 2007. 'Introduction'. In *Identités ethniques dans le monde grec antique*, edited by Jean-Marc Luce, 11–23. *Pallas* 73. Toulouse: Presses Universitaires du Mirail.

Ludlow, Francis, and Joseph G. Manning. 2016. 'Revolts under the Ptolemies: A Paleoclimatological Perspective'. In *Revolt and Resistance in the Ancient Classical World and the Near East: In the Crucible of Empire*, edited by John J. Collins and Joseph G. Manning, 154–171. Leiden: Brill.

Ma, John. 2000a. *Antiochus III and the Cities of Western Asia Minor*. Oxford: Oxford University Press.

Ma, John. 2000b. 'Seleukids and Speech-Acts: Performative Utterances, Legitimacy and Negotiation in the World of the Maccabees'. *Scripta Classica Israelica* 19: 71–112.

Ma, John. 2002. '"Oversexed, Overpaid and Over Here": A Response to Angelos Chaniotis'. In *Army and Power in the Ancient World*, edited by Angelos Chaniotis and Pierre Ducrey, 115–122. Stuttgart: Steiner.

Ma, John. 2012. 'Relire les *Institutions des séleucides* de Bikerman'. In *Rome, a City and Its Empire in Perspective: The Impact of the Roman World Through Fergus Millar's Research = Rome, une cité impériale en jeu. L'impact du monde romain selon Fergus Millar*, edited by Stéphane Benoist, 59–84. Leiden: Brill.

Ma, John. 2013a. *Statues and Cities: Honorific Portraits and Civic Identity in the Hellenistic World*. Oxford: Oxford University Press.

Ma, John. 2013b. 'Re-Examining Hanukkah'. *Marginalia* July 2013.

Ma, John. 2019. 'The Restoration of the Temple in Jerusalem by the Seleukid State: 2 Macc 11:16–38'. In *Seleukeia: Studies in Seleucid History, Archaeology and Numismatics in Honor of Getzel M. Cohen*, edited by Roland Oetjen and Francis X. Ryan: 38–80. Berlin: De Gruyter.

Madreiter, Irene. 2016. 'Antiochos the Great and the Robe of Nebuchadnezzar: Intercultural Transfer between Orientalism and Hellenocentrism'. In *Cross-Cultural Studies in Near Eastern History and Literature*, edited by Saana Svärd and Robert Rollinger, 111–136. Münster: Ugarit-Verlag.

Magie, David. 1950. *Roman Rule in Asia Minor to the End of the Third Century after Christ*. 2 vols. Princeton: Princeton University Press.

Mairs, Rachel. 2013. 'Waiting for the Barbarians: The "Fall" of Greek Bactria'. *Parthica* 15: 9–30.

Mairs, Rachel. 2014. *The Hellenistic Far East: Archaeology, Language, and Identity in Greek Central Asia*. Berkeley: University of California Press.

Mairs, Rachel, ed. 2020. *The Graeco-Bactrian and Indo-Greek World*. London: Routledge.

Mairs, Rachel, and Christelle Fischer-Bovet. 2021. 'Reassessing Hellenistic Settlement Policies'. In *Comparing the Ptolemaic and Seleucid Empires: Integration, Communication, and Resistance*, edited by Christelle Fischer-Bovet and Sitta von Reden, 48–85. Cambridge: Cambridge University Press.

Malkin, Irad, ed. 2001. *Ancient Perceptions of Greek Ethnicity*. Cambridge, MA: Harvard University Press.

Malkin, Irad, and Christel Müller. 2012. 'Vingt ans d'ethnicité: bilan historiographique et application du concept aux études anciennes'. In *Mobilités grecques. Mouvements, réseaux, contacts en Méditerranée de l'époque archaïque à l'époque hellénistique*, edited by Laurent Capdetrey and Julien Zurbach, 24–37. Bordeaux: Ausonius.

Manning, Joseph G. 1997. *The Hauswaldt Papyri: A Third Century B.C. Family Dossier from Edfu*. Sommerhausen: Gisela Zauzich.

Manning, Joseph G. 1999. 'The Auction of Pharaoh'. In *Gold of Praise: Studies on Ancient Egypt in Honor of Edward F. Wente*, edited by Emily Teeter and John A. Larson, 277–284. Chicago: Oriental Institute of the University of Chicago.

Manning, Joseph G. 2003a. 'Edfu as a Central Place in Ptolemaic History'. In *Edfu: An Egyptian Provincial Capital in the Ptolemaic Period*, edited by Willy Clarysse and Katelijn Vandorpe, 61–73. Brussels: Koninklijke Vlaamse Academie van België voor Wetenschappen en Kunsten.

Manning, Joseph G. 2003b. *Land and Power in Ptolemaic Egypt: The Structure of Land Tenure*. Cambridge: Cambridge University Press.

Manning, Joseph G., Francis Ludlow, Alexander R. Stine, William R. Boos, Michael Sigl, and Jennifer R. Marlon. 2017. 'Volcanic Suppression of Nile Summer Flooding Triggers Revolt and Constrains Interstate Conflict in Ancient Egypt'. *Nature Communications* 8 (1): 900.

Marasco, Gabriele. 1984. *Democare di Leuconoe. Politica e cultura in Atene fra IV e III sec. A.C.* Florence: Università degli Studi di Firenze.

Marasco, Gabriele, ed. 2011. *Political Autobiographies and Memoirs in Antiquity*. Leiden: Brill.

Marchesi, Gianni. 2010. 'The Sumerian King List and the Early History of Mesopotamia'. In *Ana turri gimilli. Studi dedicati al Padre Werner R. Mayer, S. J., da amici e allievi*, edited by Maria Giovanna Biga and Mario Liverani, 231–248. Rome: Università di Roma La Sapienza.

Marek, Christian. 2003. *Pontus et Bithynia: die römischen Provinzen im Norden Kleinasiens*. Mainz: Von Zabern.

Marek, Christian. 2006. *Die Inschriften von Kaunos*. Munich: Beck.

Marek, Christian. 2009. 'Hellenisation and Romanisation in Pontos-Bithynia: An Overview'. In *Mithridates VI and the Pontic Kingdom*, edited by Jakob Munk Højte, 35–46. Aarhus: Aarhus University Press.

Marek, Christian. 2013. 'Political Institutions and the Lykian and Karian Language in the Process of Hellenization between the Achaemenids and the Early Diadochi'. In *Shifting Social Imaginaries in the Hellenistic Period: Narrations, Practices, and Images*, edited by Eftychia Stavrianopoulou, 233–251. Leiden: Brill.

Marek, Christian. 2015. 'Zum Charakter der Hekatomnidenherrschaft im Kleinasien des 4. Jh. v. Chr'. In *Zwischen Satrapen und Dynasten: Kleinasien im 4. Jahrhundert v. Chr*, edited by Engelbert Winter and Klaus Zimmermann, 1–20. Bonn: Habelt.

Marks, John H. 1963. Review of *The King Is Dead: Studies in the Near Eastern Resistance to Hellenism, 334-31 B.C.*, by Samuel Kennedy Eddy. *Journal of Biblical Literature* 82: 462.

Martano, Andrea, Elisabetta Matelli, and David C. Mirhady, eds. 2012. *Praxiphanes of Mytilene and Chamaeleon of Heraclea: Text, Translation, and Discussion*. New Brunswick: Transaction Publishers.

Masséglia, Jane. 2013. 'Phrygians in Relief: Trends in Self-Representation'. In *Roman Phrygia: Culture and Society*, edited by Peter Thonemann, 95-123. Cambridge: Cambridge University Press.

Mathisen, Ralph Whitney. 1978. 'The Activities of Antigonos Gonatas 280-277 B.C. and Memnon of Herakleia, Concerning Herakleia'. *The Ancient W orld* 1: 71-74.

Matthey, Philippe. 2011. 'Récits grecs et égyptiens à propos de Nectanébo II: une réflexion sur l'historiographie égyptienne'. In *L'oiseau et le poisson. Cohabitations religieuses dans les mondes grec et romain*, edited by Nicole Belayche and Jean-Daniel Dubois, 303-328. Paris: PUPS.

Matthey, Philippe. 2012. 'Pharaon, magicien et filou: Nectanébo II entre l'histoire et la légende'. Ph.D., Université de Genève.

McDonald, Henry. 2002. 'Rebel with a Confused Cause'. *Observer*, 19 May 2002.

McDowell, Andrea Griet. 1990. *Jurisdiction in the Workmen's Community of Deir el-Medîna*. Leiden: Nederlands Instituut voor het Nabije Oosten.

McGing, Brian C. 1997. 'Revolt Egyptian Style: Internal Opposition to Ptolemaic Rule'. *Archiv für Papyrusforschung und verwandte Gebiete* 43: 273-314.

McGing, Brian C. 2003. 'Subjection and Resistance: To the Death of Mithradates'. In *A Companion to the Hellenistic World*, edited by Andrew Erskine, 71-89. Oxford: Blackwell.

McGing, Brian C. 2006. Review of *Les 'révoltes égyptiennes'. Recherches sur les troubles intérieurs en Égypte du règne de Ptolémée III Evergète à la conquête romaine*, by Anne-Emmanuelle Veïsse. *Archiv für Papyrusforschung und verwandte Gebiete* 52: 58-63.

McGing, Brian C. 2012. 'Revolt in Ptolemaic Egypt: Nationalism Revisited'. In *Actes du 26e Congrès international de papyrologie*, edited by Paul Schubert, 509-516. Geneva: Droz.

McGing, Brian C. 2016. 'Revolting Subjects: Empires and Insurrection, Ancient and Modern'. In *Revolt and Resistance in the Ancient Classical World and the Near East: In the Crucible of Empire*, edited by John J. Collins and Joseph G. Manning, 141-153. Leiden: Brill.

McInerney, Jeremy. 1994. 'Politicizing the Past: The *Atthis* of Kleidemos'. *Classical Antiquity* 13: 17-37.

McInerney, Jeremy, ed. 2014. *A Companion to Ethnicity in the Ancient Mediterranean*. Chichester: Wiley-Blackwell.

McKenzie, Judith. 2003. 'Glimpsing Alexandria from Archaeological Evidence'. *Journal of Roman Archaeology* 16: 35-61.

McKenzie, Judith. 2007. *The Architecture of Alexandria and Egypt, c. 300 B.C. to A.D. 700*. New Haven: Yale University Press.

BIBLIOGRAPHY 277

Mehl, A. 1999. 'Zwischen West und Ost / Jenseits von West und Ost. Das Reich der Seleukiden'. In *Zwischen West und Ost. Studien zur Geschichte des Seleukidenreichs*, edited by K. Brodersen, 9–43. Hamburg.

Mehl, Andreas. 2003. 'Gedanken zur "herrschenden Gesellschaft" und zu den Untertanen im Seleukidenreich'. *Historia: Zeitschrift für Alte Geschichte* 52: 147–160.

Mendels, Doron. 1986. 'Greek and Roman History in the *Bibliotheca* of Photius: A Note'. *Byzantion* 56: 196–206.

Mermelstein, A. 2014. *Creation, Covenant and the Beginnings of Judaism: Reconceiving Historical Time in the Second Temple Period*. SBL Suppl. 168. Leiden; Boston: Brill.

Metcalfe, Michael John. 2005. 'Reaffirming Regional Identity: Cohesive Institutions and Local Interactions in Ionia 386-129 BC'. Ph.D., University College London.

Mileta, Christian. 1998. 'Eumenes III und die Sklaven: neue Überlegungen zum Charakter des Aristonikosaufstandes'. *Klio* 80: 47–65.

Milik, József Tadeusz, ed. 1976. *The Books of Enoch: Aramaic Fragments of Qumrân Cave 4*. Oxford: Clarendon Press.

Mitchell, Stephen. 1991. 'The Hellenization of Pisidia'. *Mediterranean Archaeology* 4: 119–145.

Mitchell, Stephen. 1992. 'Hellenismus in Pisidien'. In *Forschungen in Pisidien*, edited by Elmar Schwertheim, 1–27. Bonn: Habelt.

Mitchell, Stephen. 1993. *Anatolia: Land, Men, and Gods in Asia Minor*. 2 vols. Oxford: Clarendon Press.

Mitchell, Stephen. 2003. 'The Galatians: Representation and Reality'. In *A Companion to the Hellenistic World*, edited by A. Erskine, 280–292. Oxford.

Mitchell, Stephen. 2005. 'Olive cultivation in the economy of Roman Asia Minor'. In *Patterns in the Economy of Roman Asia Minor*, edited by S. Mitchell and C. Katsari, 83–113. Swansea.

Mitchell, Stephen. 2018. 'Disspelling Seleukid Phantoms: Macedonians in Western Asia Minor from Alexander to the Attalids'. In *The Seleukid Empire, 281–222 BC. War within the Family*, edited by K. Erickson, 11–35. Swansea.

Mitchell, Stephen. 2019. 'Makedonen überall. Die makedonische Landnahme in Kleinasien'. In *Panegyrikoi Logoi. Festschrift für Johannes Nollé zum 65. Geburtstag*, edited by Nollé, M., Rothenhöfer, P. M., Schmied-Kowarzik, G., Schwarz, H., and von Mosch, H. C., 331–352. Bonn.

Mittag, Peter Franz. 2006. *Antiochos IV. Epiphanes: eine politische Biographie*. Berlin: Akademie Verlag.

Modes de contacts et processus de transformation dans les sociétés anciennes. Actes du colloque de Cortone (24–30 mai 1981). 1983. Collection de l'École Française de Rome 67. Pisa, Rome: Scuola Normale Superiore; École Française de Rome.

Momigliano, Arnaldo. 1978. 'The Historians of the Classical World and Their Audiences: Some Suggestions'. *Annali della Scuola Normale Superiore di Pisa* 8: 59–75.

Momigliano, Arnaldo. 1994. 'Daniel and the Greek Theory of Imperial Succession'. In *Essays on Ancient and Modern Judaism*, by Arnaldo Momigliano, edited by

Silvia Berti, translated by Maura Masella-Gayley, 29–35. Chicago: University of Chicago Press.

Monerie, Julien. 2017. *L'économie de la Babylonie à l'époque hellénistique (Ivème–IIème siècle avant J.C.)*. Berlin: De Gruyter.

Monson, Andrew. 2012. *From the Ptolemies to the Romans. Political and Economic Change in Egypt*. Cambridge.

Morgan, Catherine A. 2003. *Early Greek States beyond the Polis*. London: Routledge.

Morgan, Jacques de, Urbain Bouriant, Georges Legrain, Gustave Jéquier, and Alexandre Barsanti. 1895. *Catalogue des monuments et inscriptions de l'Égypte antique. II. Kom Ombos*. Vienna: Holzhausen.

Moyer, Ian S. 2011a. 'Court, Chora, and Culture in Late Ptolemaic Egypt'. *American Journal of Philology* 132: 15–44.

Moyer, Ian S. 2011b. *Egypt and the Limits of Hellenism*. Cambridge: Cambridge University Press.

Moyer, Ian S. 2011c. 'Finding a Middle Ground: Culture and Politics in the Ptolemaic Thebaid'. In *Perspectives on Ptolemaic Thebes: Occasional Proceedings of the Theban Workshop*, edited by Peter F. Dorman and Betsy M. Bryan, 115–145. Chicago: Oriental Institute of the University of Chicago.

Moyn, Samuel, and Andrew Sartori, eds. 2013. *Global Intellectual History*. New York: Columbia University Press.

Mueller, Katja. 2006. *Settlements of the Ptolemies: City Foundations and New Settlement in the Hellenistic World*. Leuven: Peeters.

Müller, Christel. 2014. 'Introduction: la fin de l'ethnicité?' *Dialogues d'histoire ancienne. Supplément* 10: 15–33.

Müller, Christel, and Francis Prost. 2013. 'Un décret du koinon des Ioniens trouvé à Claros'. *Chiron* 43: 93–126.

Müller, Karl, ed. 1849. *Fragmenta historicorum graecorum*. Vol. 3. Paris: A. Firmin Didot.

Müller, Karlheinz. 1973. 'Die Ansätze der Apokalyptik'. In *Literatur und Religion des Frühjudentums: eine Einführung*, edited by Johann Maier and Josef Schreiner, 31–42. Würzburg: Echter Verlag.

Müller, Wilhelm Max. 1920. *Egyptological Researches*. Vol. 3. Washington, D.C.: Carnegie Institution of Washington.

Nafissi, Massimo. 2015. 'Königliche Ansprüche der Hekatomniden: das neue Monument für die Basileis Kariens aus Iasos'. In *Zwischen Satrapen und Dynasten: Kleinasien im 4. Jahrhundert v. Chr*, edited by Engelbert Winter and Klaus Zimmermann, 21–48. Bonn: Habelt.

Nespoulous-Phalippou, Alexandra, ed. 2015. *Ptolémée Épiphane, Aristonikos et les prêtres d'Égypte. Le Décret de Memphis (182 a.C.). Édition commentée des stèles Caire RT 2/3/25/7 et JE 44901. CENiM* 12. Montpellier: Université Paul Valéry.

Neujahr, Matthew. 2005. 'When Darius Defeated Alexander: Composition and Redaction in the Dynastic Prophecy'. *Journal of Near Eastern Studies* 64: 101–107.

Neujahr, Matthew. 2012. *Predicting the Past in the Ancient Near East: Mantic Historiography in Ancient Mesopotamia, Judah, and the Mediterranean World*. Providence: SBL Press.

BIBLIOGRAPHY 279

Nickelsburg, George W. E. 2001. *1 Enoch 1: A Commentary on the Book of 1 Enoch, Chapters 1–36, 81–108*, edited by Klaus Baltzer. Minneapolis: Fortress Press.

Nielsen, John P. 2015. '"I Overwhelmed the King of Elam": Remembering Nebuchadnezzar I in Persian Babylonia'. In *Political Memory in and after the Persian Empire*, edited by Jason M. Silverman, and Caroline Waerzeggers, 53–74. Atlanta: SBL Press.

Nielsen, John P. 2018. *The Reign of Nebuchadnezzar I in History and Historical Memory*. Abingdon, Oxon: Routledge.

Nihan, Christophe. 2009. 'Apocalypses juives'. In *Introduction à l'Ancien Testament*, edited by Thomas Römer, Jean-Daniel Macchi, and Christophe Nihan, 661–693. Geneva: Labor et Fides.

Nihan, Christophe. 2010. 'The Emergence of the Pentateuch as "Torah"'. *Religion Compass* 4: 353–364.

Nims, Charles F. 1938. 'Notes on University of Michigan Demotic Papyri from Philadelphia'. *The Journal of Egyptian Archaeology* 24: 73–82.

Nodet, Etienne. 2005. *La crise maccabéenne. Historiographie juive et traditions bibliques*. Paris: Cerf.

Oberleitner, Wolfgang. 1981. 'Ein hellenistischer Galaterfries aus Ephesos'. *Jahrbuch der Kunsthistorischen Sammlungen in Wien* 77: 57–104.

Oelsner, Joachim. 1986. *Materialien zur Babylonischen Gesellschaft und Kultur in hellenistischer Zeit*. Budapest: Eötvös University.

Oelsner, Joachim. 2003. 'Cuneiform Archives in Hellenistic Babylonia: Aspects of Content and Form'. In *Ancient Archives and Archival Traditions: Concepts of Record-Keeping in the Ancient World*, edited by Maria Brosius, 284–301. Oxford: Oxford University Press.

Ogden, Daniel. 2017. *The Legend of Seleucus: Kingship, Narrative and Mythmaking in the Ancient World*. Cambridge: Cambridge University Press.

Olivier, J., and B. Redon. 2020. 'Reconsidérer la politique monétaire des Lagides à la lumière des sources numismatique. Frappes et trésors monétaires aux IIIe et IIe s. av. J.-C. (env. 294-116)'. In *Money Rules ! The Monetary Economy of Egypt, from Persians until the beginning of Islam*, 107–139, edited by T. Faucher. Le Caire: IFAO.

Olivieri, Luca M. 2021. 'Gandhāra and North-Western India'. In *The Graeco-Bactrian and Indo-Greek World*, 386–416, edited by Rachel Mairs. Abingdon: Routledge.

Olshausen, Eckart. 1978. 'Pontos'. In *Paulys Real-Encyclopädie der Classischen Altertumswissenschaft*, edited by Hans Gärtner, 15 (Suppl.): 396–442. Munich: Alfred Druckenmüller Verlag.

Olson, Daniel C. 2004. *Enoch: A New Translation. The Ethiopic Book of Enoch, or 1 Enoch, Translated with Annotations and Cross-References by Daniel C. Olson, in Consultation with Melkesedek Workeneh*. North Richland Hills, TX: BIBAL Press.

Olson, Daniel C. 2013. *A New Reading of the Animal Apocalypse of 1 Enoch: 'All Nations Shall Be Blessed'*. Leiden: Brill.

O'Neil, James L. 2008. 'A Re-Examination of the Chremonidean War'. In *Ptolemy II Philadelphus and His World*, edited by Paul McKechnie and Philippe Guillaume, 65–90. Leiden: Brill.

O'Neil, James L. 2012. 'The Native Revolt against the Ptolemies (206-185 BC): Achievements and Limitations', *CdE* 87: 133-149.

Orsi, D. P. 1994. 'La storiografia locale'. In *Lo spazio letterario della Grecia antica*, edited by G. Cambiano, L. Canfora, and D. Lanza, 149-79. Rome: Salerno.

Papailias, Penelope. 2005. *Genres of Recollection: Archival Poetics and Modern Greece*. New York: Palgrave Macmillan.

Pedersen, Poul. 2013. 'The 4th Century BC "Ionian Renaissance" and Karian Identity'. In *4th Century Karia: Defining a Karian Identity under the Hekatomnids*, edited by Olivier Henry, 33-64. Istanbul: Institut Français d'Études Anatoliennes Georges Dumézil.

Peremans, Willy. 1978. 'Les révolutions égyptiennes sous les Lagides'. In *Das ptolemäische Ägypten*, edited by Herwig Maehler and Volker Michael Strocka, 39-50. Mainz: Von Zabern.

Pestman, Pieter Willem. 1995a. 'A Family Archive Which Changes History: The Archive of an Anonym'. In *Hundred-Gated Thebes: Acts of a Colloquium on Thebes and the Theban Area in the Graeco-Roman Period*, edited by Sven P. Vleeming, 91-100. Leiden: E. J. Brill.

Pestman, Pieter Willem. 1995b. 'Haronnophris and Chaonnophris: Two Indigenous Pharaohs in Ptolemaic Egypt (205-186 B.C.)'. In *Hundred-Gated Thebes: Acts of a Colloquium on Thebes and the Theban Area in the Graeco-Roman Period*, edited by Sven P. Vleeming, 101-137. Leiden: E. J. Brill.

Pfeiffer, Stefan. 2004. *Das Dekret von Kanopos (238 v. Chr.): Kommentar und historische Auswertung eines dreisprachigen Synodaldekretes der ägyptischen Priester zu Ehren Ptolemaios' III. und seiner Familie*. Munich: Saur.

Picard, Olivier, and Thomas Faucher. 2012. 'La grande mutation des bronzes lagides: l'adoption d'une comptabilité décimale'. In *Les monnaies des fouilles du Centre d'études alexandrines. Les monnayages de bronze à Alexandrie de la conquête d'Alexandre à l'Égypte moderne*, edited by Olivier Picard, 60-108. Alexandria: Centre d'Études Alexandrines.

Piras, Daniela. 2009. 'Der archäologische Kontext karischer Sprachdenkmäler und seine Bedeutung für die kulturelle Identität Kariens'. In *Die Karer und die Anderen*, edited by Frank Rumscheid, 229-250. Bonn: Habelt.

Piras, Daniela. 2010. 'La nuova autoconsapevolezza dei Cari in età ellenistica: cause e modalità espressive alla luce dell'evidenza delle necropoli'. *Bollettino di archeologia online* 1: 16-25.

Pirngruber, Reinhard. 2012. 'The Impact of Empire on Market Prices in Babylon in the Late Achaemenid and Seleucid Periods, ca. 400 - 140 B.C'. Ph.D., Amsterdam: Vrije Universiteit.

Pirngruber, Reinhard. 2013. 'The Historical Sections of the Astronomical Diaries in Context: Developments in a Late Babylonian Scientific Text Corpus'. *Iraq* 75: 197-210.

Pirngruber, Reinhard. 2017. *The Economy of Late Achaemenid and Seleucid Babylonia*. Cambridge: Cambridge University Press.

Plischke, Sonja. 2014. *Die Seleukiden und Iran: die seleukidische Herrschaftspolitik in den östlichen Satrapien*. Wiesbaden: Harrassowitz.

BIBLIOGRAPHY 281

Polito, M. 2001. *Dagli scritti di Eraclide sulle costituzioni. Un commento storico.* Naples: Arte tipografica.

Pollock, Sheldon I. 2006a. 'Power and Culture beyond Ideology and Identity'. In *Margins of Writing, Origins of Cultures*, edited by Seth L. Sanders, 277–287. Chicago: Oriental Institute of the University of Chicago.

Pollock, Sheldon I. 2006b. *The Language of the Gods in the World of Men: Sanskrit, Culture, and Power in Premodern India.* Berkeley: University of California Press.

Portier-Young, Anathea. 2011. *Apocalypse against Empire: Theologies of Resistance in Early Judaism.* Grand Rapids, MI: William B. Eerdmans.

Potter, David. 2007. 'The Identities of Lykia'. In *Regionalism in Hellenistic and Roman Asia Minor*, edited by Hugh Elton and Gary L. Reger, 81–88. Bordeaux: Ausonius.

Potts, Daniel T. 2016. *The Archaeology of Elam: Formation and Transformation of an Ancient Iranian State.* 2nd ed. Cambridge: Cambridge University Press.

Pouilloux, Jean. 1965. Review of *The King Is Dead: Studies in the Near Eastern Resistance to Hellenism, 334–31 B.C.*, by Samuel Kennedy Eddy. *L'Antiquité Classique* 34: 330–332.

Powell, Jonathan G. F. 2013. 'The Embassy of the Three Philosophers to Rome in 155 BC'. In *Hellenistic Oratory: Continuity and Change*, edited by Christos Kremmydas and Kathryn Tempest, 219–248. Oxford: Oxford University Press.

Pownall, Frances. 2017. 'The Horse and the Stag: Philistus' View of Tyrants'. In *Ancient Historiography on War and Empire*, edited by Timothy Howe, Sabine Müller, and Richard Stoneman, 62–78. Oxford: Oxbow Books.

Préaux, Claire. 1936. 'Esquisse d'une histoire des révolutions égyptiennes sous les Lagides'. *Chronique d'Égypte* 11: 522–552.

Préaux, Claire. 1978. *Le monde hellénistique. La Grèce et l'Orient de la mort d'Alexandre à la conquête romaine de la Grèce (323–146 av. J.-C.).* 2 vols. Paris: Presses Universitaires de France.

Preys, René. 2015. 'La royauté lagide et le culte d'Osiris d'après les portes monumentales de Karnak'. In *Documents de théologies thébaines tardives (D3T 3)*, edited by Christophe Thiers, 159–215. *CENiM* 13. Montpellier: Université Paul Valéry.

Price, Martin Jessop. 1993. *The British Museum. Part 1: The Black Sea.* Sylloge nummorum Graecorum 9. London: British Museum.

Primo, Andrea. 2009. 'Il termine ἐπίγονοι nella storiografia sull'ellenismo'. *Klio* 91: 367–377.

Primo, Andrea. 2009a. *La storiografia sui seleucidi: da Megastene a Eusebio di Cesarea.* Pisa: Fabrizio Serra.

Prost, Francis. 2007. 'Identité des peuples, identité des cités: l'exemple lycien'. In *Identités ethniques dans le monde grec antique*, edited by Jean-Marc Luce, 99–113. *Pallas* 73. Toulouse: Presses Universitaires du Mirail.

Prost, Francis. 2013. 'Retour au Mausolée et au Monument des Néréides: identités ethniques et frontières culturelles en Lycie et en Carie'. In *Euploia: la Lycie et la Carie antiques. Dynamiques des territoires, échanges et identités*, edited by Patrice Brun and Laurence Cavalier, 175–188. Bordeaux: Ausonius.

Quack, Joachim Friedrich. 1991. 'Über die mit ʿnḫ gebildeten Namenstypen und die Vokalisation einiger Verbalformen'. *Göttinger Miszellen* 123: 91–100.

Quaegebeur, J. 1993. 'La justice à la porte des temples et le toponyme Premit'. In *Individu, société et spiritualité dans l'Égypte pharaonique et copte*, edited by Christian Cannuyer and Jean-Marie Kruchten, 201–220. Athens: Association Montoise d'Egyptologie.

Queyrel, François. 2005. *L'autel de Pergame. Images et pouvoir en Grèce d'Asie*. Paris: Picard.

Quirke, Stephen, and Carol Andrews. 1988. *The Rosetta Stone: Facsimile Drawing*. London: British Museum.

Rajak, Tessa. 1996. 'Hasmonean Kingship and the Invention of Tradition'. In *Aspects of Hellenistic Kingship*, edited by Per Bilde, Troels Engberg-Pedersen, Lise Hannestad, and Jan Zahle, 99–105. Aarhus: Aarhus University Press.

Ratté, Christopher. 2009. 'The Carians and the Lydians'. In *Die Karer und die Anderen*, edited by Frank Rumscheid, 135–147. Bonn: Habelt.

Recklinghausen, Daniel von. 2011. 'Les deux décrets synodaux de Ptolémée V à Philae'. *Égypte. Afrique & Orient* 61: 43–56.

Recklinghausen, Daniel von. 2018. *Die Philensis-Dekrete: Untersuchungen über zwei Synodaldekrete aus der Zeit Ptolemaios' V. und ihre geschichtliche und religiöse Bedeutung*. Wiesbaden: Harrassowitz.

Redon, B. 2018. 'La prise en main du désert oriental par les Lagides: nouvelles données archéologiques'. In *Le désert oriental d'Egypte durant la période gréco-romaine: bilans archéologiques*, Collège de France, Paris. https://books.openedition.org/cdf/4932

Reed, Annette Yoshiko. 2004. 'Heavenly Ascent, Angelic Descent, and the Transmission of Knowledge in 1 Enoch 6-16'. In *Heavenly Realms and Earthly Realities in Late Antique Religions*, edited by Raʿanan S. Boustan and Annette Yoshiko Reed, 47–66. Cambridge: Cambridge University Press.

Rees, B. R. 1964. Review of *The King Is Dead: Studies in the Near Eastern Resistance to Hellenism, 334–31 B.C.*, by Samuel Kennedy Eddy. *The Journal of Egyptian Archaeology* 50: 196–197.

Reger, Gary L. 2007. 'Karia: A Case Study'. In *Regionalism in Hellenistic and Roman Asia Minor*, edited by Hugh Elton and Gary L. Reger, 89–96. Bordeaux: Ausonius.

Regev, Eyal. 2013. *The Hasmoneans: Ideology, Archaeology, Identity*. Göttingen: Vandenhoeck & Ruprecht.

Reynolds, Frances. 1999. 'Stellar Representations of Tiamat and Qingu in a Learned Calendar Text'. In *Languages and Cultures in Contact: At the Crossroads of Civilizations in the Syro-Mesopotamian Realm*, edited by Karel van Lerberghe and Gabriela Voet, 369–378. Leuven: Peeters.

Reynolds, Frances. 2019. *A Babylon calendar treatise: scholars and invaders in the late first millennium BC*. Oxford: Oxford University Press.

Rheidt, Klaus. 2008. 'Aizanoi in hellenistischer Zeit'. In *Neue Funde und Forschungen in Phrygien*, edited by Elmar Schwertheim and Engelbert Winter, 107–122. Bonn: Habelt.

Rhodes, Peter J. 1990. 'The Atthidographers'. In *Purposes of History: Studies in Greek Historiography from the 4th to the 2nd Centuries B.C.*, edited by Herman Verdin, Guido Schepens, and Els de Keyser, 73–81. Leuven: Catholic University Press.

Richter, Heinz-Dietmar. 1987. *Untersuchungen zur hellenistischen Historiographie: die Vorlage des Pompeius Trogus für die Darstellung der nachalexandrinischen hellenistischen Geschichte (Iust. 13–40)*. Frankfurt am Main: Peter Lang.

Rigsby, Kent J. 1996. *Asylia: Territorial Inviolability in the Hellenistic World*. Berkeley: University of California Press.

Ritner, Robert K. 1993. *The Mechanics of Ancient Egyptian Magical Practice*. Chicago: Oriental Institute of the University of Chicago.

Rivault, Joy. 2016. 'L'acculturation de la vie religieuse en Carie. Cultes et représentations associés aux épiclèses des Zeus'. Ph.D., Université Bordeaux Montaigne.

Robert, Jeanne, and Louis Robert. 1983. *Fouilles d'Amyzon en Carie*. Paris: Commission des Fouilles et Missions Archéologiques au Ministère des Relations Extérieures.

Robert, Louis. 1962. *Villes d'Asie Mineure. Études de géographie ancienne*. 2nd ed. Paris: De Boccard.

Robert, Louis. 1963. *Noms indigènes dans l'Asie Mineure gréco-romaine*. Paris: Adrien-Maisonneuve.

Robert, Louis, and Jeanne Robert. 1989. *Claros I. Décrets hellénistiques*. Paris: Éditions Recherche sur les Civilisations.

Robson, Eleanor. 2017. 'The Socio-Economics of Cuneiform Scholarship after the "End of Archives": Views from Borsippa and Uruk'. In *At the Dawn of History: Ancient Near Eastern Studies in Honour of J. N. Postgate*, edited by Yağmur Heffron, Adam Stone, and Martin Worthington, 455–470. Winona Lake, IN: Eisenbrauns.

Robson, Eleanor. 2018. 'Do Not Disperse Collection! Motivations and Strategies for Protecting Cuneiform Scholarship in the First Millennium BCE'. In *Sharing and Hiding Religious Knowledge in Early Judaism, Christianity, and Islam*, edited by Mladen Popović, Lautaro Roig Lanzillotta, and Clare Wilde, 8–45. Berlin: De Gruyter.

Robson, Eleanor. 2019. 'Who Wrote the Babylonian Astronomical Diaries?' In *Keeping Watch in Babylon: The Astronomical Diaries in Context*, edited by Johannes Haubold, John Steele, and Kathryn Stevens, 120–153. Leiden: Brill.

Robu, Adrian. 2014. *Mégare et les établissements mégariens de Sicile, de la Propontide et du Pont-Euxin. Histoire et institutions*. Bern: Lang.

Rochberg, Francesca. 2011. 'Observing and Describing the World through Divination and Astronomy'. In *The Oxford Handbook of Cuneiform Culture*, edited by Karen Radner and Eleanor Robson, 618–636. Oxford: Oxford University Press.

Roller, Duane W. 2016. 'Dionysios, On India (717)'. In *Brill's New Jacoby Online*, edited by Ian Worthington. Leiden: Brill.

Roller, L. E. 1999. *In Search for the Mother: The Cult of Anatolian Cybele*. Berkeley.

Roller, Matthew B. 2018. *Models from the Past in Roman Culture: A World of Exempla*. Cambridge: Cambridge University Press.

Rollinger, Robert. 1993. *Herodots babylonischer Logos: eine kritische Untersuchung der Glaubwürdigkeitsdiskussion an Hand ausgewählter Beispiele. Historische Parallelüberlieferung, Argumentationen, archäologischer Befund, Konsequenzen für eine Geschichte Babylons in persischer Zeit*. Innsbruck: Verlag des Instituts für Sprachwissenschaft der Universität Innsbruck.

Rollinger, Robert. 2013. 'Berossos and the Monuments: City Walls, Sanctuaries, Palaces and the Hanging Garden'. In *The World of Berossos*, edited by Johannes Haubold, Giovanni B. Lanfranchi, Robert Rollinger, and John Steele, 137–162. Wiesbaden: Harrassowitz.

Rollinger, Robert. 2014. 'Von Kyros bis Xerxes: Babylon in persischer Zeit und die Frage der Bewertung des herodoteischen Geschichtswerkes – eine Nachlese'. In *Babylonien und seine Nachbarn in neu- und spätbabylonischer Zeit*, edited by Manfred Krebernik and Hans Neumann, 147–194. Münster: Ugarit-Verlag.

Rollinger, Robert. 2017. 'Assyria in Classical Sources'. In *A Companion to Assyria*, edited by Eckart Frahm, 570–582. Chichester: Wiley-Blackwell.

Rollinger, Robert, and Reinhold Bichler. 2005. 'Die Hängenden Gärten zu Ninive – Die Lösung eines Rätsels?' In *Von Sumer bis Homer: Festschrift für Manfred Schretter zum 60. Geburtstag am 25. Februar 2004*, edited by Robert Rollinger, 153–217. Münster: Ugarit-Verlag.

Rostovtzeff, Michael Ivanovitch. 1941. *The Social and Economic History of the Hellenistic World*. 3 vols. Oxford: Clarendon Press.

Rousset, Denis. 2010. *Fouilles de Xanthos X. De Lycie en Cabalide: la convention entre les Lyciens et Termessos près d'Oinoanda*. Geneva: Droz.

Ruby, Pascal. 2006. 'Peuples, fictions? Ethnicité, identité ethnique et sociétés anciennes'. *Revue des études anciennes* 108: 25–60.

Ruggieri, Vincenzo. 2009. 'The Carians in the Byzantine Period'. In *Die Karer und die Anderen*, edited by Frank Rumscheid, 207–218. Bonn: Habelt.

Rumscheid, Frank, ed. 2009. *Die Karer und die Anderen*. Bonn: Habelt.

Russell, Thomas James. 2017. *Byzantium and the Bosporus: A Historical Study, from the Seventh Century BC until the Foundation of Constantinople*. Oxford: Oxford University Press.

Sachs, Abraham Joseph, and Hermann Hunger, eds. 1988. *Astronomical Diaries and Related Texts from Babylonia. Volume 1: Diaries from 652 B.C. to 262 B.C.* Vienna: Verlag der Österreichischen Akademie der Wissenschaften.

Sachs, Abraham Joseph, and Hermann Hunger, eds. 1989. *Astronomical Diaries and Related Texts from Babylonia. Volume 2: Diaries from 261 B.C. to 165 B.C.* Vienna: Verlag der Österreichischen Akademie der Wissenschaften.

Sachs, Abraham Joseph, and Hermann Hunger, eds. 1996. *Astronomical Diaries and Related Texts from Babylonia. Volume 3: Diaries from 164 B.C. to 62 B.C.* Vienna: Verlag der Österreichischen Akademie der Wissenschaften.

Salmeri, Giovanni. 2000. 'Regioni, popoli e lingue epicorie d'Asia Minore ne la *Geografia* di Strabone'. In *Strabone e l'Asia Minore*, edited by Anna Maria Biraschi and Giovanni Salmeri, 157–188. Naples: Edizioni Scientifiche Italiane.

BIBLIOGRAPHY 285

Salmeri, Giovanni. 2003. 'Processes of Hellenization in Cilicia'. *Olba* 8: 265–293.
Saprykin, Sergei Yurievich. 1997. *Heracleia Pontica and Tauric Chersonesus before Roman Domination: VI-I Centuries B.C.* Amsterdam: Hakkert.
Sartre, Maurice. 2003. *L'Anatolie hellénistique: de l'Égée au Caucase (334–31 av. J.-C.)*. Paris: Colin.
Sartre, Maurice. 2010. 'Sociétés indigènes et culture gréco-romaine: institutions et pratiques politiques dans la Syrie gréco-romaine'. In *Società indigene e cultura greco-romana*, edited by Elvira Migliario, Lucio Troiani, and Giuseppe Zecchini, 105–116. Rome: L'Erma di Bretschneider.
Sauneron, Serge. 1954. 'La justice à la porte des temples (à propos du nom égyptien des propylées)'. *Bulletin de l'Institut français d'archéologie orientale* 54: 117–127.
Sauneron, Serge. 1957. 'Un cinquième exemplaire du décret de Canope: la stèle de Boubastis'. *Bulletin de l'Institut français d'archéologie orientale* 56: 67–75.
Savalli-Lestrade, Ivana. 2001. 'Les Attalides et les cités grecques d'Asie Mineure au IIe siècle a.C'. In *Les cités d'Asie Mineure occidentale au IIe siècle a.C.*, edited by Alain Bresson and Raymond Descat, 77–91. Bordeaux: Ausonius.
Sayar, Mustafa Hamdi. 2007. 'Historical Development of Urbanization in Cilicia in Hellenistic and Roman Periods'. In *Tra Oriente e Occidente. Indigeni, Greci e Romani in Asia Minore*, edited by Gianpaolo Urso, 247–257. Pisa: ETS.
Scholten, Joseph. 2007. 'Building Hellenistic Bithynia'. In *Regionalism in Hellenistic and Roman Asia Minor*, edited by Hugh Elton and Gary L. Reger, 17–24. Bordeaux: Ausonius.
Schuler, Carl. 1966. Review of *The King Is Dead: Studies in the Near Eastern Resistance to Hellenism, 334–31 B.C.*, by Samuel Kennedy Eddy. *Classical Philology* 61: 203–204.
Schuol, Monika. 2000. *Die Charakene: ein mesopotamisches Königreich in hellenistisch-parthischer Zeit*. Stuttgart: Steiner.
Schürer, Emil. 1973. *The History of the Jewish People in the Age of Jesus Christ (175 B.C.-A.D. 135)*, edited by Géza Vermès and Fergus Millar. Rev. ed. Vol. 1. Edinburgh: Clark.
Schürr, Diether. 2013. 'Über den Gebrauch der Schrift in Lykien: Dynasten, Familienväter und Poeten'. In *Euploia: la Lycie et la Carie antiques. Dynamiques des territoires, échanges et identités*, edited by Patrice Brun and Laurence Cavalier, 29–40. Bordeaux: Ausonius.
Schwartz, Daniel R. 2008. *2 Maccabees*. Berlin: Walter de Gruyter.
Schwartz, Seth. 1991. 'Israel and the Nations Roundabout: 1 Maccabees and the Hasmonean Expansion'. *Journal of Jewish Studies* 42: 16–38.
Schwartz, Seth. 2001. *Imperialism and Jewish Society, 200 B.C.E. to 640 C.E.* Princeton: Princeton University Press.
Schweyer, Anne-Valérie. 1996. 'Le pays lycien: une étude de géographie historique aux époques classique et hellénistique'. *Revue archéologique*, 3–68.
Schweyer, Anne-Valérie. 2002. *Les Lyciens et la mort. Une étude d'histoire sociale*. Istanbul: Institut Français d'Études Anatoliennes d'Istanbul.
Scott, James C. 1985. *Weapons of the Weak: Everyday Forms of Peasant Resistance*. New Haven: Yale University Press.

Scott, James C. 1990. *Domination and the Arts of Resistance: Hidden Transcripts.* New Haven: Yale University Press.
Scurlock, JoAnn. 2006. 'Whose Truth and Whose Justice? The Uruk and Other Late Akkadian Prophecies Re-Revisited'. In *Orientalism, Assyriology and the Bible,* edited by Steven W. Holloway, 447-465. Sheffield: Sheffield Phoenix Press.
Seeman, Chris. 2013. *Rome and Judea in Transition: Hasmonean Relations with the Roman Republic and the Evolution of the High Priesthood.* New York: Peter Lang.
Seidl, Ursula. 1999. 'Ein Monument Darius' I. aus Babylon'. *Zeitschrift für Assyriologie und Vorderasiatische Archäologie* 89: 101-114.
Sethe, Kurt. 1904. *Urkunden des ägyptischen Altertums* II. *Hieroglyphische Urkunden der griechisch-römischen Zeit.* Leipzig.
Sethe, Kurt. 1917. 'Die historische Bedeutung des 2. Philä-Dekrets aus der Zeit des Ptolemaios Epiphanes'. *Zeitschrift für Ägyptische Sprache* 53: 35-49.
Sethe, Kurt, ed. 1977. *Hieroglyphische Urkunden der griechisch-römischen Zeit.* Reprint. 3 vols. Milan: Cisalpino-La Goliardica.
Shayegan, M. Rahim. 2011. *Arsacids and Sasanians: Political Ideology in Post-Hellenistic and Late Antique Persia.* Cambridge: Cambridge University Press.
Shear, T. Leslie. 1978. *Kallias of Sphettos and the Revolt of Athens in 286 B.C. Hesperia* Supplement 17. Princeton: American School of Classical Studies at Athens.
Sherwin-White, Susan M. 1987. 'Seleucid Babylonia: A Case-Study for the Installation and Development of Greek Rule'. In *Hellenism in the East: The Interaction of Greek and Non-Greek Civilizations from Syria to Central Asia after Alexander,* edited by Amélie Kuhrt and Susan M. Sherwin-White, 1-31. London: Duckworth.
Sherwin-White, Susan M., and Amélie Kuhrt. 1993. *From Samarkhand to Sardis: A New Approach to the Seleucid Empire.* Berkeley: University of California Press.
Sievers, Joseph. 1990. *The Hasmoneans and Their Supporters: From Mattathias to the Death of John Hyrcanus I.* Atlanta: Scholars Press.
Silverman, Jason M. 2012. *Persepolis and Jerusalem: Iranian Influence on the Apocalyptic Hermeneutic.* New York: T & T Clark International.
Silverman, Jason M., and Caroline Waerzeggers. 2015. 'Assessing Persian Kingship in the Near East: An Introduction'. In *Political Memory in and after the Persian Empire,* edited by Jason M. Silverman and Caroline Waerzeggers, 1-6. Atlanta: SBL Press.
Simpson, R. S. 1996. *Demotic Grammar in the Ptolemaic Sacerdotal Decrees.* Oxford: Griffith Institute, Ashmolean Museum.
Smith, Anthony D. 1981. *The Ethnic Revival.* Cambridge: Cambridge University Press.
Smith, Jonathan Z. 1971. 'Native Cults in the Hellenistic Period'. *History of Religions* 11: 236-249.
Smith, Jonathan Z. 1978. *Map Is Not Territory: Studies in the History of Religions.* Leiden: Brill.
Smith, Jonathan Z. 1982. *Imagining Religion: From Babylon to Jonestown.* Chicago: University of Chicago Press.

BIBLIOGRAPHY 287

Smith, Jonathan Z. 2003. 'Here, There, and Anywhere'. In *Prayer, Magic, and the Stars in the Ancient and Late Antique World*, edited by Scott Noegel, Joel Walker, and Brannon Wheeler, 21-36. University Park: Pennsylvania State University Press.

Sordi, Marta. 2000. 'L'Europa di Filisto'. In *Studi sull'Europa antica*, edited by Marta Sordi, 61-76. Alessandria: Edizioni dell'Orso.

Spek, Robert J. van der. 1993. 'New Evidence on Seleucid Land Policy'. In *De agricultura: in memoriam Pieter Willem De Neeve (1945-1990)*, edited by Heleen Sancisi-Weerdenburg, Robert J. van der Spek, Hans C. Teitler, and Herman T. Wallinga, 61-77. Amsterdam: J. C. Gieben.

Spek, Robert J. van der. 2003. 'Darius III, Alexander the Great and Babylonian Scholarship'. In *A Persian Perspective: Essays in Memory of Heleen Sancisi-Weerdenburg*, edited by Wouter Henkelman and Amélie Kuhrt, 289-346. Leiden: Nederlands Instituut voor het Nabije Oosten.

Spek, Robert J. van der, Finkel, L. and Pirngruber, R. Forthcoming. *Babylonian Chronographic Texts from the Hellenistic Period*. Atlanta: SBL Press.

Spek, Robert J. van der, and Ronald Wallenfels. 2014. 'Copy of Record of Entitlement and Exemptions to Formerly Royal Lands'. In *Cuneiform Texts in the Metropolitan Museum of Art. Volume 4: The Ebabbar Temple Archive and Other Texts from the Fourth to the First Millennium B.C.*, edited by Ira Spar and Michael Jursa, 213-227. New York: Metropolitan Museum of Art.

Spencer, Patricia. 1984. *The Egyptian Temple: A Lexicographical Study*. London: Kegan Paul.

Spiegelberg, Wilhelm. 1912. 'Zwei Kalksteinplatten mit demotischen Texten'. *Zeitschrift für Ägyptische Sprache* 50: 32-36.

Spiegelberg, Wilhelm, ed. 1914. *Die sogenannte Demotische Chronik des Pap. 215 der Bibliothèque Nationale zu Paris*. Leipzig: J. C. Hinrichs.

Steele, John. 2011. 'Astronomy and Culture in Late Babylonian Uruk'. *Proceedings of the International Astronomical Society* 7 (S278): 331-341.

Steinkeller, Piotr. 2003. 'An Ur III Manuscript of the Sumerian King List'. In *Literatur, Politik und Recht in Mesopotamien: Festschrift für Claus Wilcke*, edited by Walther Sallaberger, Konrad Volk, and Annette Zgoll, 267-292. Wiesbaden: Harrassowitz.

Sterling, Gregory E. 1992. *Historiography and Self-Definition: Josephos, Luke-Acts, and Apologetic Historiography*. Leiden: E. J. Brill.

Stevens, Kathryn. 2014. 'The Antiochus Cylinder, Babylonian Scholarship and Seleucid Imperial Ideology', *Journal of Hellenic Studies* 134: 66-88.

Stevens, Kathryn. 2016. 'Empire Begins at Home: Local Elites and Imperial Ideologies in Hellenistic Greece and Babylonia'. In *Cosmopolitanism and Empire: Universal Rulers, Local Elites, and Cultural Integration in the Ancient Near East and Mediterranean*, edited by Myles Lavan, Richard E. Payne, and John Weisweiler, 65-88. Oxford: Oxford University Press.

Stevens, Kathryn. 2019. *Between Greece and Babylonia: Hellenistic Intellectual History in Cross-Cultural Perspective*. Cambridge: Cambridge University Press.

Stökl, Jonathan. 2013. 'Nebuchadnezzar: History, Memory, and Myth-Making in the Persian Period'. In *Remembering Biblical Figures in the Late Persian and Early*

Hellenistic Periods: Social Memory and Imagination, edited by Diana V. Edelman and Ehud Ben Zvi, 257–269. Oxford: Oxford University Press.

Strobel, Karl. 1991. 'Die Galater im hellenistischen Kleinasien: historische Aspekte einer keltischen Staatenbildung'. In *Hellenistische Studien: Gedenkschrift für Hermann Bengtson*, edited by Jakob Seibert, 101–134. Munich: Editio Maris.

Strobel, Karl. 1994. 'Keltensieg und Galatersieger: die Funktionalisierung eines historischen Phänomens als politischer Mythos der hellenistischen Welt'. In *Forschungen in Galatien*, edited by Elmar Schwertheim, 67–96. Bonn: Habelt.

Strobel, Karl. 1996. *Die Galater: Geschichte und Eigenart der keltischen Staatenbildung auf dem Boden des hellenistischen Kleinasien*. Berlin: Akademie Verlag.

Strobel, Karl. 2002. 'State Formation by the Galatians of Asia Minor: Politico-Historical and Cultural Processes in Hellenistic Central Anatolia'. *Anatolica* 28: 1–46.

Strobel, Karl. 2009. 'The Galatians in the Roman Empire: Historical Tradition and Ethnic Identity in Hellenistic and Roman Asia Minor'. In *Ethnic Constructs in Antiquity: The Role of Power and Tradition*, edited by Ton Derks and Nico Roymans, 117–144. Amsterdam: Amsterdam University Press.

Strootman, Rolf. 2014. *Courts and Elites in the Hellenistic Empires: The Near East after the Achaemenids, c. 330 to 30 BCE*. Edinburgh: Edinburgh University Press.

Strootman, Rolf. 2017. 'Imperial Persianism: Seleukids, Arsakids and *Fratarakā*'. In *Persianism in Antiquity*, edited by Rolf Strootman and Miguel John Versluys, 177–200. Stuttgart: Steiner.

Strootman, Rolf. 2018. 'The Coming of the Parthians: Crisis and resilience in the reign of Seleukos II'. In *The Seleukid Empire, 281–222 BC. War within the Family*, edited by Kyle Erickson, 151–171. Swansea: Classical Press of Wales.

Talloen, Peter. 2015. *Cult in Pisidia: Religious Practice in Southwestern Asia Minor from Alexander the Great to the Rise of Christianity*. Turnhout: Brepols.

Tarn, W. W., and G. T. Griffith. 1952. *Hellenistic Civilisation*. 3rd ed. London: Edward Arnold.

Taylor, Michael J. 2014. 'Sacred Plunder and the Seleucid Near East'. *Greece and Rome* 61: 222–241.

Tcherikover, Victor. 1959. *Hellenistic Civilization and the Jews*. Translated by Shimon Applebaum. New York: Atheneum.

Thiers, Christophe. 2009. *La stèle de Ptolémée VIII Évergète II à Héracléion*. Oxford: Oxford Centre for Maritime Archaeology.

Thomas, Rosalind. 2019. *Polis Histories: Collective Memories and the Greek World*. Cambridge: Cambridge University Press.

Thompson, Dorothy J. *Memphis under the Ptolemies*. 2nd ed. Princeton: Princeton University Press.

Thompson, Edward P. 1971. 'The Moral Economy of the English Crowd in the Eighteenth Century'. *Past & Present* 50: 76–136.

Thompson, Herbert. 1934. *A Family Archive from Siut, from Papyri in the British Museum, Including an Account of a Trial before the Laocritae in the Year B.C. 170*. Oxford: Oxford University Press.

Thonemann, Peter. 2013a. 'Alexander, Priene, and Naulochon'. In *Epigraphical Approaches to the Post-Classical Polis: Fourth Century BC to Second Century AD*, edited by Paraskevi Martzavou and Nikolaos Papazarkadas, 23–36. Oxford: Oxford University Press.

Thonemann, Peter. 2013b. 'Phrygia: An Anarchist History, 950 BC–AD 100'. In *Roman Phrygia: Culture and Society*, edited by Peter Thonemann, 1–40. Cambridge: Cambridge University Press.

Tietz, Werner. 2009. 'Karer und Lykier: politische und kulturelle Beziehungen im 5./4. Jh. v. Chr'. In *Die Karer und die Anderen*, edited by Frank Rumscheid, 163–172. Bonn: Habelt.

Tietze, Christian, Eva R. Lange, and Klaus Hallof. 2005. 'Ein neues Exemplar des Kanopus-Dekrets aus Bubastis'. *Archiv für Papyrusforschung und verwandte Gebiete* 51: 1–29.

Tiller, Patrick A. 1993. *A Commentary on the Animal Apocalypse of I Enoch*. Atlanta: Scholars Press.

Tober, Daniel. 2010. '*Politeiai* and Spartan Local History'. *Historia* 59: 412–431.

Tober, Daniel. 2017. 'Greek Local Historiography and Its Audiences'. *Classical Quarterly* 67: 460–484.

Tober, Daniel. 2019. 'Greek Local History and the Shape of the Past'. In *Historiographies of Identity Vol. 1: Historiographies as Reflection about Community: Ancient and Christian Models*, edited by Walter Pohl and Veronika Wieser. Turnhout: Brepols.

Treadgold, Warren. 1980. *The Nature of the Bibliotheca of Photius*. Washington, D.C.: Dumbarton Oaks.

Trotter, J. R. 2017. '2 Maccabees 10:1–8: Who Wrote It and Where Does It Belong?' *JBL* 136/1: 117–130.

Troxell, Hyla A. 1982. *The Coinage of the Lycian League*. New York: American Numismatic Society.

Tsetskhladze, G. R., ed. 2018: *Pessinus and Its Regional Setting*, vol. 1, Leuven.

Tuplin, Christopher. 2008. 'The Seleucids and Their Achaemenid Predecessors: A Persian Inheritance?' In *Ancient Greece and Ancient Iran: Cross-Cultural Encounters*, edited by Seyed Mohammad Reza Darbandi and Antigoni Zournatzi, 109–136. Athens: National Hellenic Research Foundation; Hellenic National Commission for UNESCO; Cultural Center of the Embassy of the Islamic Republic of Iran.

Uggetti, Lorenzo. Forthcoming. 'Les archives bilingues de Totoès et de Tatéhathyris'. Ph.D., Paris Sciences et Lettres.

Van Bremen, Riet. 2004. 'Leon Son of Chrysaor and the Religious Identity of Stratonikeia in Caria'. In *The Greco-Roman East: Politics, Culture, Society*, edited by Stephen Colvin, 207–244. Yale Classical Studies 31. Cambridge: Cambridge University Press.

Van De Mieroop, Marc. 1999. 'Literature and Political Discourse in Ancient Mesopotamia: Sargon II of Assyria and Sargon of Agade'. In *Munuscula Mesopotamica: Festschrift für Johannes Renger*, edited by Barbara Böck, Eva Cancik-Kirschbaum, and Thomas Richter, 327–339. Münster: Ugarit-Verlag.

VanderKam, James C. 2004. *From Joshua to Caiaphas: High Priests after the Exile*. Minneapolis: Fortress Press.

VanderKam, James C. 2010. 'The Book of Enoch and the Qumran Scrolls'. In *The Oxford Handbook of the Dead Sea Scrolls*, edited by Timothy H. Lim and John J. Collins, 254–277. Oxford: Oxford University Press.

Vandorpe, Katelijn. 1995. 'City of Many a Gate, Harbour for Many a Rebel: Historical and Topographical Outline of Greco-Roman Thebes'. In *Hundred-Gated Thebes: Acts of a Colloquium on Thebes and the Theban Area in the Graeco-Roman Period*, edited by Sven P. Vleeming, 203–239. Leiden: E. J. Brill.

Vandorpe, Katelijn. 2000. 'The Ptolemaic Epigraphe or Harvest Tax (*shemu*)'. *Archiv für Papyrusforschung und verwandte Gebiete* 46: 169–232.

Vandorpe, Katelijn. 2005. 'Agriculture, Temples and Tax Law in Ptolemaic Egypt', *CRIPEL* 25: 165–171.

Vandorpe, Katelijn. 2007. 'Agriculture, Temples and Tax Law in Ptolemaic Egypt'. *Cahier de recherches de l'Institut de papyrologie et d'egyptologie de Lille* 25: 165–171.

Vandorpe, Katelijn. 2011. 'A Successful, but Fragile Biculturalism: The Hellenization Process in the Upper-Egyptian Town of Pathyris under Ptolemy VI and VIII'. In *Ägypten zwischen innerem Zwist und äusserem Druck: die Zeit Ptolemaios' VI. bis VIII.*, edited by Andrea Jördens and Joachim Friedrich Quack, 292–308. Wiesbaden: Harrassowitz.

Vandorpe, Katelijn. 2014. 'The Ptolemaic Army in Upper Egypt (2nd-1st centuries B.C.)'. In *L'armée en Égypte aux époques perse, ptolémaïque et romaine*, edited by Anne-Emmanuelle Veïsse and Stéphanie Wackenier, 105–135. Geneva: Droz.

Vanhaverbeke, Hannelore, and Marc Waelkens. 2005. 'If You Can't Beat Them, Join Them? The Hellenization of Pisidia'. *Mediterranean Archaeology* 18: 49–65.

Vanhaverbeke, Hannelore, et al. 2010. 'Pisidian' culture? The Classical-Hellenistic site at Düzen Tepe near Sagalassus (southwest Turkey)'. *Anatolian Studies* 60: 105–128.

Vanotti, Gabriella. 1993. 'L'archaiologhìa siciliana di Filisto'. *Hesperìa. Studi sulla grecità di Occidente* 3: 115–135.

Veïsse, Anne-Emmanuelle. 2004. *Les 'révoltes égyptiennes'. Recherches sur les troubles intérieurs en Égypte du règne de Ptolémée III Évergète à la conquête romaine*. Leuven: Peeters.

Veïsse, Anne-Emmanuelle. 2009. 'L'expression "ennemi des dieux": *theosin echthros*'. In *Faces of Hellenism: Studies in the History of the Eastern Mediterranean, 4th Century B.C.-5th Century A.D.*, edited by Peter van Nuffelen, 169–177. Leuven: Peeters.

Veïsse, Anne-Emmanuelle. 2011. 'L' "ennemi des dieux" Harsièsis'. In *Ägypten zwischen innerem Zwist und äusserem Druck: die Zeit Ptolemaios' VI. bis VIII.*, edited by Andrea Jördens and Joachim Friedrich Quack, 92–102. Wiesbaden: Harrassowitz.

Veïsse, Anne-Emmanuelle. 2013. 'Retour sur les révoltes égyptiennes'. In *Villes et campagnes aux rives de la Méditerranée ancienne. Hommages à Georges Tate,* edited by Gérard Charpentier and Vincent Puech, 507–516. *Topoi. Orient—Occident*, Suppl. 12. Paris: De Boccard.

Veïsse, Anne-Emmanuelle. 2016. 'Polybe, les Lagides et les Rebelles'. *Cahiers Du Centre Gustave-Glotz* 27: 199–213.

Veïsse, Anne-Emmanuelle. 2019. 'Violences extrêmes en milieu urbain: Alexandrie, 203 av. nè (Polybe, XV, 25–33)'. In *Violences et cruautés en Égypte depuis la Préhistoire jusqu'au Moyen-Age. La violence, un outil rhétorique?*, edited by A. Zaouache. Cairo: Institut Français d'Archéologie Orientale.

Veïsse, Anne-Emmanuelle. Forthcoming. 'De la Grande Révolte thébaine aux événements de 88 : un siècle de séparatisme thébain ?'. In *The Thebaid in Times of Crisis*, edited by R. Birk and L. Coulon. Bibliothèque d'Etude, Le Caire.

Verlinde, A. 2010. 'Monumental Architecture in Hellenistic and Julio-Claudian Pessinus', *BaBesch* 85: 111–139.

Verlinde, A. 2015. 'The Pessinuntine Sanctuary of the Mother of the Gods in light of the excavated Roman temple: fact, fiction and feasibility', *Latomus* 74: 30–72.

Virgilio, Biagio. 1981. ,Il „Templo Stato „ di Pessinunte fra Pergamo e Roma nel II-I secolo A.C. (C. B. Welles, Royal Corr., 55-61). Pisa: Giardini.

Visscher, Marijn. 2019. 'Royal Presence in the Astronomical Diaries'. In *Keeping Watch in Babylon: The Astronomical Diaries in Context*, edited by Johannes Haubold, John Steele, and Kathryn Stevens, 237–268. Leiden: Brill.

Vitale, Marco. 2012. *Eparchie und Koinon in Kleinasien von der ausgehenden Republik bis ins 3. Jh. n. Chr.* Bonn: Habelt.

Vittmann, Günter. 2005. '"Feinde" in den ptolemäischen Synodaldekreten'. In *Feinde und Aufrührer: Konzepte von Gegnerschaft in ägyptischen Texten besonders des Mittleren Reiches*, edited by Heinz Felber, 198–219. Leipzig: Verlag der Sächsischen Akademie der Wissenschaften zu Leipzig.

Vittmann, Günther, ed. 1998. *Der demotische Papyrus Rylands 9.* 2 vols. Wiesbaden: Harrassowitz.

Vogt, Martin. 1902. 'Die griechischen Lokalhistoriker'. *Jahrbücher für classische Philologie* Suppl. 27: 699–786.

Waelkens, Marc, ed. 1993. *Sagalassos I: First General Report on the Survey (1986–1989) and Excavations (1990–1991).* Leuven: Leuven University Press.

Waelkens, Marc. 2004. 'Ein Blick von der Ferne: Seleukiden und Attaliden in Pisidien'. *Istanbuler Mitteilungen* 54: 435–471.

Waelkens, Marc. 2013. 'Euploia: Exchange and Identity in Ancient Caria and Lycia. Concluding Remarks'. In *Euploia: la Lycie et la Carie antiques. Dynamiques des territoires, échanges et identités*, edited by Patrice Brun and Laurence Cavalier, 385–438. Bordeaux: Ausonius.

Waelkens, Marc, Jeroen Poblome, and Kim Vyncke. 2011. 'Indigenous versus Greek Identity in Hellenistic Pisidia: Myth or Reality?' In *Hellenes and Non-Hellenes/Beyond Identity in the Hellenistic East*, edited by Martina Dalla Riva and Helga Di Guiseppe, 19–54. *Bollettino di archeologia online*, Edizione speziale 1.

Waelkens, Marc and Lutgarde Vanderput. 2007. 'Regionalism in Hellenistic and Roman Pisidia'. In *Regionalism in Hellenistic and Roman Asia Minor*, edited by Hugh Elton and Gary L. Reger, 97–105. Bordeaux: Ausonius.

Waerzeggers, Caroline. 2003. 'The Babylonian Revolts Against Xerxes and the "End of Archives"'. *Archiv für Orientforschung* 50: 150-173.
Waerzeggers, Caroline. 2012. 'The Babylonian Chronicles: Classification and Provenance'. *Journal of Near Eastern Studies* 71: 285-298.
Waerzeggers, Caroline. 2015. 'Babylonian Kingship in the Persian Period: Performance and Reception'. In *Exile and Return: The Babylonian Context*, edited by Jonathan Stökl and Caroline Waerzeggers, 181-222. Berlin: De Gruyter.
Walbank, F. W. 1970. *A Historical Commentary on Polybius*. 3 vols. Oxford: Clarendon Press.
Walsh, John. 2009. 'Historical Method and a Chronological Problem in Diodorus, Book 1'. In *Alexander and His Successors: Essays from the Antipodes*, edited by Pat Wheatley and Robert Hannah, 72-87. Claremont: Regina.
Wartelle, André. 1965. Review of *The King Is Dead: Studies in the Near Eastern Resistance to Hellenism, 334-31 B.C.*, by Samuel Kennedy Eddy. *Bulletin de l'Association Guillaume Budé* 1: 273-275.
Weber, Max. 1958. *From Max Weber: Essays in Sociology*. Translated by Hans H. Gerth and Charles W. Mills. New York: Oxford University Press.
Weitzman, Steven. 2004. 'Plotting Antiochus's Persecution'. *Journal of Biblical Literature* 123: 219-234.
Weitzman, Steven. 2008. 'On the Political Relevance of Antiquity: A Response to David Goodblatt's *Elements of Ancient Jewish Nationalism*'. *Jewish Social Studies* 14: 165-172.
Welles, Charles Bradford. 1934. *Royal Correspondence in the Hellenistic Period: A Study in Greek Epigraphy*. New Haven: Yale University Press.
Wendling, Emil. 1899. 'Chamaileon 1'. In *Paulys Real-Encyclopädie der Classischen Altertumswissenschaft*, edited by Georg Wissowa, 6: 2103-2104. Stuttgart: J. B. Metzlersche Verlagsbuchhandlung.
Wenghofer, Richard. 2018. 'Rethinking the Relationship between Hellenistic Baktria and the Seleukid Empire'. In *The Seleukid Empire 281-222 BC: War within the Family*, edited by Kyle Erickson, 151-171. Swansea: The Classical Press of Wales.
Whitmarsh, Tim. 2010. 'Thinking Local'. In *Local Knowledge and Microidentities in the Imperial Greek World*, edited by Tim Whitmarsh, 1-16. Cambridge: Cambridge University Press.
Wiesehöfer, Josef. 1994. *Die 'dunklen Jahrhunderte' der Persis: Untersuchungen zu Geschichte und Kultur von Fārs in frühhellenistischer Zeit (330-140 v. Chr.)*. Munich: Beck.
Wilamowitz-Moellendorff, Ulrich von. 1900. *Die Textgeschichte der griechischen Lyriker*. Berlin: Weidmann.
Wilcke, Claus. 2001. 'Gestaltetes Altertum in antiker Gegenwart: Königslisten und Historiographie des älteren Mesopotamien'. In *Die Gegenwart des Altertums: Formen und Funktionen des Altertumsbezugs in den Hochkulturen der Alten Welt*, edited by Dieter Kuhn and Helga Stahl, 93-116. Heidelberg: Forum.
Wilker, Julia. 2011. 'Von Aufstandsführern zur lokalen Elite: der Aufstieg der Makkabäer'. In *Lokale Eliten und hellenistische Könige: zwischen Kooperation*

und Konfrontation, edited by Boris Dreyer and Peter Franz Mittag, 219-256. Berlin: Verlag Antike.

Will, Édouard. 1979. *Histoire politique du monde hellénistique: 323-30 av. J.-C.* 2nd ed. 2 vols. Nancy: Presses Universitaires de Nancy.

Will, Édouard. 1985. 'Pour une anthropologie coloniale du monde hellénistique'. In *The Craft of the Ancient Historian: Essays in Honor of Chester G. Starr*, edited by John W. Eadie and Josiah Ober, 273-301. Lanham, MD: University Press of America.

Will, Édouard, and Claude Orrieux. 1986. *Ioudaïsmos-hellènismos. Essai sur le judaïsme judéen à l'époque hellénistique.* Nancy: Presses Universitaires de Nancy.

Wilson, Penelope. 1997. *A Ptolemaic Lexicon: A Lexicographical Study of the Texts in the Temple of Edfu.* Leuven: Peeters.

Winnicki, Jan Krzysztof 1991. 'Der zweite syrische Krieg im Lichte des demotischen Karnak-Ostrakons und der griechischen Papyri des Zenon-Archivs'. *The Journal of Juristic Papyrology* 21: 87-104.

Winnicki, Jan Krzysztof. 2001. 'Die letzten Ereignisse des vierten syrischen Krieges: eine Neudeutung des Raphiadekrets'. *The Journal of Juristic Papyrology* 31: 133-145.

Winter, Engelbert, and Klaus Zimmermann, eds. 2015. *Zwischen Satrapen und Dynasten: Kleinasien im 4. Jahrhundert v. Chr.* Bonn: Habelt.

Wise, Michael O. 2003. 'Dating the Teacher of Righteousness and the Floruit of His Movement'. *Journal of Biblical Literature* 122: 53-87.

Wise, Michael O. 2010. 'The Origins and History of the Teacher's Movement'. In *The Oxford Handbook of the Dead Sea Scrolls*, edited by Timothy H. Lim and John J. Collins, 92-122. Oxford: Oxford University Press.

Wörrle, Michael. 1977. 'Epigraphische Forschungen zur Geschichte Lykiens I'. *Chiron* 7: 43-66.

Wörrle, Michael. 1978. 'Epigraphische Forschungen zur Geschichte Lykiens II: Ptolemaios II und Telmessos'. *Chiron* 8: 201-246.

Wörrle, Michael. 1991. 'Epigraphische Forschungen zur Geschichte Lykiens IV: drei griechische Inschriften aus Limyra'. *Chiron* 21: 203-239.

Wright, Benjamin G. 2015. *The Letter of Aristeas: 'Aristeas to Philocrates' or 'On the Translation of the Law of the Jews'.* Berlin: De Gruyter.

Yardley, John. 2003. *Justin and Pompeius Trogus: A Study of the Language of Justin's Epitome of Trogus.* Toronto: University of Toronto Press.

Yardley, John, and Waldemar Heckel, eds. 1997. *Epitome of the Philippic History of Pompeius Trogus.* Vol. 1. Oxford: Clarendon Press.

Yarrow, Liv Mariah. 2006. *Historiography at the End of the Republic: Provincial Perspectives on Roman Rule.* Oxford: Oxford University Press.

Yerushalmi, Yosef Hayim. 1982. *Zakhor: Jewish History and Jewish Memory.* Seattle: University of Washington Press.

Yoshiko Reed, A. 2004. 'Heavenly Ascent, Angelic Descent, and the Transmission of Knowledge in 1 Enoch 1-16'. In *Heavenly Realms and Earthly Realities in Late Antique Religions*, edited by R. S. Boustan and A. Yoshiko Reed, 47-66. Cambridge: Cambridge University Press.

Yoyotte, Jean. 1963. 'L'égypte ancienne et les origines de l'antijudaïsme' *Revue de l'histoire des religions* 163: 133-143.

Zawadzki, Stefan. 1995. 'The Circumstances of Darius II's Accession in the Light of BM 54557 as against Ctesias' Account'. *Jaarbericht Ex Oriente Lux* 34: 45-49.

Zerubavel, Yael. 1995. *Recovered Roots: Collective Memory and the Making of Israeli National Tradition*. Chicago: University of Chicago Press.

Zimmermann, Martin. 1992. *Untersuchungen zur historischen Landeskunde Zentrallykiens*. Bonn: Habelt.

Zivie-Coche, Christiane. 2008. 'Late Period Temples'. In *UCLA Encyclopedia of Egyptology*, edited by Willeke Wendrich. Los Angeles: University of California.

Index

Abydos 58, 60, 65–66
Achaean League 13, 199
Achaemenid Empire 117, 239
   cultural memory of 3, 4, 18–19, 28, 79–85, 93–94, 103–104
Ada, Queen of Caria 187
Adam 132, 143
Administration 7, 39, 71, 73, 81–82, 108, 109, 168, 187, 195, 197, 199, 201, 210
   linguistic biases 165, 167–168, 182
   within revolting indigenous regimes 61–64
Aelian 122, 213, 221
Agatharchides of Cnidus 206
Agathocles, Ptolemaic courtier 60, 160
Akitu, Babylonian festival 101
Akkadian 96, 100–101, 106, 116
   biases of Akkadian texts 88, 98
   in relation to Jewish literature 97, 103, 131
Alcimus, High Priest of Jerusalem 49–50, 130, 137
Alexander I Balas 51–52, 220
Alexander III of Macedon 18, 27, 34, 81–82, 104–105, 122, 186–187, 189, 191, 214, 219, 227, 229, 232, 237, 239–240
Alexandria 14, 23, 60, 61, 97, 153, 160, 161, 166, 206–207, 221
Alexandrianism, literary and intellectual movement 23, 206–207
Amon 158–159
   ideological significance 66, 163
   priests of 62, 66–67, 70–71
Anachoresis 155–156
Animal Apocalypse, the 127–128, 131, 134–147
   date of composition 128

Antigonus I Monophthalmus 113
Antigonus II Gonatas 211, 212, 222, 224
Antiochus and Sin Temple Chronicle 119
Antiochus, Bactria, and India Chronicle 119
Antiochus Hierax 232, 240, 243
Antiochus I 101, 116, 119, 189, 205
Antiochus II 108, 222
Antiochus III 16, 86, 91, 111, 154, 225, 229
   imperial policies 33–36, 39, 40, 78–79, 101, 108, 123, 242
Antiochus IV 13, 51, 123, 151, 154, 158, 170, 206
   as promoter of Hellenism 113, 120–121, 128–131
   interventions in Babylon 19, 28, 86–87, 91, 93, 107–113, 114, 122
   interventions in Judea 16–17, 20, 28, 33, 41–42, 47–48, 50, 55, 96, 103, 125, 128, 136, 140–145, 147, 220
Antiochus V 47, 48, 50, 81, 111
Antiochus VI 53
Antiochus VII 220
Antiquarianism 23, 206
Anu, cult at Uruk 115, 116–117
Apocalypse of Weeks 127
Apocalypticism
   development as literary genre 3, 8, 15, 20–21, 28, 125–128, 134, 139, 142, 145, 146
   in the Book of Daniel 21, 78, 125
Apollo 183, 197
Apollonios Dyskolos 219
Apollonius, Ptolemaic courtier 155, 157
Appian of Alexandria 113, 114, 122
Aramaic 19, 89, 98, 125, 127, 134, 146

296 INDEX

Archaicism 17, 25, 64, 101, 172
Architecture
   cultural adaptation and imitation
      through 177, 182, 185–186,
      187–188, 198, 201, 202
Aristonikos Revolt 193–194
Aristotle 206–207
Arsaces I of Parthia 232, 240
Artapanus, Judeo-Hellenistic
   author 57
Artaxerxes I 84
Artaxerxes IV 104
Artaxias I of Armenia 25
Artemis 197
Asia Minor 14, 22, 39, 177–203, 232
Asia, Roman Province 199
Ashurbanipal 166
Assyria 5, 15, 45, 115
   cultural memories of in Babylon 18, 82–83, 85–87, 92
Astronomical Book, of the Dead Sea
   Scrolls 125, 127
Astronomical Diaries, the 19, 81
   content and biases 86, 89–91, 100–101, 110
Asylia 157
Athenaeus 214, 220–221
Athens 191, 207, 210–213, 233
Attalids, dynasty 99, 190–191, 194
Attalus II of Pergamon 190
Atthidography 210–212

Babylon 14, 18–20, 25, 28, 47, 77–94, 95–124
   establishment as *polis* 82, 108
   stability and violence under Seleucid
      rule 81–82, 97, 99–102
Babyloniaca, of Berossus 83, 86
Babylon Stele, of Nabonidus 80
Bacchides, Seleucid courtier 50
Bactria 231–232, 234, 236–245
Bagnall, Roger 155–156
Barbarians
   as structural category in Greek
      thought 191–192, 194, 241–243

Battle for the Armor of Inaros 62
Behistun Inscription 80, 170
Benefaction
   language of 39, 85
   monarchic 34–36, 48, 51, 154, 167, 227
Berenice II 153
Berossus 8, 81, 83–88, 94, 118
Beth-zur, Battle of 136
Bickerman, Elias 4, 34, 37, 44
Bithynia 183, 189, 222, 225, 228
British Empire
   as unit of comparison 235–236
Book of Daniel 8, 18, 19, 43, 77–79, 94, 99, 103, 105, 106, 125, 126, 127
   date of composition 78, 125, 127
Book of the Watchers 127
Borsippa Cylinder 19, 89, 108, 118
Byzantium 204, 220, 222, 223, 229

Cairo 38258, Demotic document 61
Canopus Decree 21, 153, 161, 163, 165, 166, 168
Caria 22, 27, 180, 183–186, 189, 192–193, 195–198, 199
   ethnic self-consciousness 179, 182, 186–188, 201
Cartouche
   in Ptolemaic self-representations 65, 161, 167
Ceramics
   as sign of cultural
      transformation 177, 187
Chaironea, Battle of 211–212
Chakrabarty, Dipesh 10–11
Chaldeans 84, 86
Chaonnophris 17, 57, 58, 59–67, 149, 159, 163
   question of identification with
      Haronnophris 17, 59, 65
Charter of Jerusalem, the 16–17, 34
China
   as unit of comparison 210
Chronicles
   as literary form 101, 132

INDEX   297

Chronicles, Babylonian 19, 81, 87, 108, 109, 111, 116–120
  biases 97, 100–102, 106–107
  in comparison to Greek historiography 118
Chronicles, Book of 132
Chrysaorians 196, 199
Cilicia 28, 181, 184
Climate studies
  as partial explanation for the Great Thebaid Revolt 95, 152
Coele-Syria and Phoenicia 37–39, 40, 42, 60
Collaboration 4, 7
  as mechanism for subversion 96, 126
  effect on indigenous institutions 86, 158
Comets
  as eschatological marker 110–111
Comparativism v, 3, 5, 7, 149, 244
  methodology and application 12–13, 29, 173
Consensus
  in relation to legitimacy 10, 150
Constructivism 6
  theory of identity construction 177–178
Coptite Nome 58, 63
Corupedium, Battle of 203, 212, 214, 216, 217, 218, 220, 222
Cosmopolitanism 236
  in relation to Hellenism 15, 26–27
  terminology and application v, 24
Cotta, M. Aurelius 228–230
Ctesias of Cnidus 78, 81, 83, 85
Culture 177, 187, 188, 192
  as factor influencing revolt v, 4, 5, 22–23, 44, 112–113, 120, 123, 151
  definition and terminology 6–7, 9–10, 12, 24, 27, 150
  role of non-elites 153
Cybele 183
Cyclicalism, of historical time 139, 145
  in contrast to helicalism 140
Cyrus I 103
Cyrus II 84
  as new Nebuchadnezzar 80

Daphne, games of Antiochus IV 112
Darius I 18, 80–81, 84, 85, 170, 180
Darius II Ochus 84, 233
Darius III 104–106
David, King
  ideological importance in the Maccabean Revolt 45–46
Dead Sea Scrolls 50, 125, 127, 146
Decolonization
  discursive elements 162, 173, 179
Defacement
  as act of resistance 21, 161–170
Demetrius of Phaleron 219
Denderah 71
Decree of Memphis of 196 BCE 60, 61, 68, 69, 153, 155
Decree of Memphis of 182 BCE 61, 68
Decrees, Sacerdotal
  defacement as form of protest 161–170
  logic and form as texts 159
Delta Revolt, of Egypt 60–61, 68, 69
Demetrius I, Seleucid King 49–51
Demetrius II, Seleucid King 53, 86
Demonetization
  influence on Great Thebaid Revolt 70
Demotic Chronicle 4, 21, 28, 106, 150, 151
Demotic Egyptian 57, 59, 60, 64, 66, 70, 103, 153, 155, 162, 166, 171
  biases as source 61–64, 98, 165, 167–168
Deuteronomy 139
Diodorus Siculus 91, 113, 122, 154, 237–239
Diodotus I of Bactria 23
Diodotus Tryphon 14, 52–53
Dionysius of Halicarnassus 189, 192, 209
Dionysius Petosarapis 14, 154, 170
Divination
  as form of political commentary 101, 110, 127
Domestica Seditio, earliest indigenous revolt against the Ptolemies 169
Doran, Robert 13

Dorianism, form of Greek localism 23, 219, 220
Dream of Nectanebo, the 151
Droysen, J. G. 6
Dynastic Prophecy 19, 103, 106–107

Eclipses
　in the Astronomical Diaries 110
Economics 77, 88, 121, 150, 160, 179
　as cause of revolt 2, 7–11, 17, 24, 38, 92–93, 95–96, 110, 112, 123, 126, 148–149, 151–154, 156, 161, 173, 194, 238
Eddy, Samuel K. 3–5, 7, 8, 19, 82, 95, 97, 121, 173
Edfu, Temple of Horus at 28, 58, 71, 72, 163, 164, 165
Elam 113
　in the cultural memory of Babylon 19, 86–93, 103
Elijah, Prophet 134, 144
Elites 25, 28, 79, 80, 158, 180, 182, 185, 188
　displacement of as cause for unrest 7, 14, 81–82, 83, 114, 120, 121, 123
　over-emphasis on 10, 88–91, 98, 152, 172
Elkab, in Egypt 161–166, 168
Enoch, Book of 20, 125, 127–128, 131–147
Enochic Judaism 126
Epichoric Literature 152
　of the Greek *polis* 26, 203–230
Epistates 63
Epistolographos 62
Esagila, Temple of 100–101, 109, 111, 113, 117, 120, 123
Eschatology 8, 15, 20, 28, 127, 132, 138, 140, 143
　relation to apocalypticism 126
Ethnicity and Ethnic Identity
　manifestations and representations 13, 21–23, 26, 29, 80, 93, 100–101, 119, 131, 151, 173, 181–189, 189–194, 194–202, 219–220, 236, 238, 239, 242
　terminology and applications 5–9, 24–25, 148, 158, 173, 177–179

Eucratides I of Bactria 23, 232, 242–244
Eumenes II of Pergamon 184, 190, 192
Eumenes III of Pergamon 193
Euthydemus of Bactria 26, 240–242

Fabius Pictor 209
Fayyum, Region of Egypt 69, 155, 158, 159, 171
Feeney, Denis 234–235
Festivals 33, 101, 129, 165–166, 208
　as mechanism for popular criticism 153
Fifth Syrian War 17, 33, 34, 60
First Maccabees 20–21, 25, 43, 50, 112, 135–138, 141–146
　attitude of author towards Greeks and Romans 44–47, 51, 52–54, 56, 128–131, 145–146
　date of composition 145
　in comparison to Second Maccabees 41, 49, 141
First Philae Decree 153
Fischer-Bovet, Christelle 13, 68, 238
Frataraka 5, 15, 25
Friend of the King, *Philos* 51, 53
Functionalism
　as form of cultural analysis 9–10

Galatians 47, 187, 190, 191–192, 202, 225
Gerousia, of Jerusalem 34
Globalism v, 24, 28, 29
　impact 78, 200
　terminology and applications 12–16, 27, 235
Gramsci, Antonio 8
Great Theban Revolt
　attitudes toward the Ptolemies 69, 149–151
　chronology 58–61, 157–158, 164
　comparison with Maccabean Revolt 72–73
　stakes and causes 11–12, 14, 17, 25, 68–72, 95
　state-building in 61–64, 68, 172
Greek Language 89, 98, 155
　as identity marker 6, 182–183, 219–220

INDEX 299

Gudea 123
Guha, Ranajit 155
Gymnasion 42, 128, 130, 188

Habicht, Christian 7
Halicarnassus 189
Hanean 104, 105
  pejorative term for Greeks and Macedonians in Babylon 101
Hanging Gardens of Babylon 85–86
Hanukkah 33, 129
Haronnophris 17, 57–59, 60, 61–70, 149–150, 159, 163, 164, 172
  question of origins 58, 64
Harsiesis 150–151, 163
  historicity 57, 151
Hasidim 141
Hasmonaeans 34–56, 78, 129, 134, 200
  ideas about legitimacy 20, 25, 26, 53, 130–131, 142–143, 145, 146, 147, 179
  relationship with the Seleucids 53, 55–56, 68
Hecatomnids, Dynasty of Caria 182, 195, 196
Hecateus of Miletus 207
Hellenism
  as cause for revolt 1–3, 6–8, 13, 20, 21, 44, 128–131, 146
  as imperial policy of Antiochus IV 44, 112–113
  as set of norms promoted by Greco-Macedonians 13–15, 26, 191, 192
  effect of local customs and norms on 12, 27, 192–193, 198
Hellenismos 128, 146
  as term of legitimacy in Maccabees 130–131
Hellanicus of Mytilene 207, 208
Hengel, Martin 44
Herakleia Pontica 22–23, 203–230
Herakleides Lembos 23, 205–208, 213
Herakles 22, 203, 205, 214, 215, 218–220, 223, 228, 229, 230
  in Seleucid representations 219
Hermopolis Legal Code 168

Herodotus 78, 81, 85, 122, 180, 189, 209
Hieroglyphics 98, 155, 166
  as component of multilingual decrees 153, 162, 165, 167
Historiography, Greco-Roman
  as source for Mesopotamian events 113–114, 121–122
  universal history 16, 23, 231–245
Historiography, Local
  as form of identity negotiation 26, 208–210
  as mode of evaluation and criticism 22–23, 212–230
  comparison of Greek and Near Eastern forms 113–114, 118
Historiography, Mesopotamian 77–94, 95–124
  as mode of criticism 8, 80–81, 82–86, 101, 103
Historiography, of Judea 131, 140, 144
Horus 58, 64–65, 150, 164
Hybridisation 179, 181–188
Hypomnematographos 62
Hyspaosines of Characene 89

Identity 23, 118, 139, 171, 180, 181, 183, 186–188, 189–191, 194, 195–202, 204, 219, 220, 241
  as historical process of differentiation 177–179
  concepts and terminology 9, 12, 14, 22, 148–149
Imperialism 12, 18, 28–29, 39–40, 51–52, 96, 235–236, 244–245
  linguistic forms 6, 89, 182–183
  local and global perspectives on 13–15, 121, 204
  promotion of common norms see Hellenism
India 232, 235–237, 239, 243, 245
Isis
  as contested symbol of Egyptian monarchy 65–66, 163
Israel 45–46, 53, 79, 93, 132, 137, 138, 140, 145, 236

Iudaismos 21
  as term of legitimacy in Maccabees 128–131, 139

Jacoby, Felix 207, 208, 210, 211
Japan, as unit of comparison 210
Jason, High Priest of Jerusalem 42, 109, 128, 130, 142, 143, 144, 147
Jason of Cyrene 28, 129, 137
Jeremiah 143–144
Jerusalem 13, 33, 37, 39, 40, 41, 43, 49, 54, 78, 105, 106, 109, 112, 113, 128–129, 130, 132, 134, 138, 139
  administrative status under the Seleucids 17, 34–35, 38, 42, 51, 79, 141
John Hyrcanus 134–135, 145, 146–147
Jonathan Maccabee 17, 50–53, 55, 56, 130
Josephus 33–34, 35, 36, 43, 112, 138, 146
  authenticity of letters 34
Judah Maccabee 33, 44–46, 47, 48, 49–50, 52, 55–56, 128, 133, 134–138, 141
  as object of memory 129, 130–131, 142, 144, 146, 147
  fashioning as biblical hero 46, 143
Judea 1, 14, 16–17, 18, 19, 20–21, 23, 26, 28, 33, 35, 38, 40–45, 50, 52–53, 55, 68, 73, 77, 94, 95, 97, 103, 112, 121, 125–127, 129, 131, 138, 140, 141, 142, 144–146, 178, 179, 195, 200, 236, 242, 244
Juniper Garden Chronicle 119
Justin, Roman historian 23, 169, 214, 218, 231–245
  evaluation as historical source 231, 233, 234

Karnak 58, 64, 65, 67, 161–163, 165, 166, 168
Kings, Book of 131, 132
Kingship
  Hellenistic 15, 26, 60, 77, 154, 173–174
  in a Babylonian cultural context 19–20, 28, 83, 84, 97, 99, 104, 115, 121
  in relation to ideas of legitimacy 2–3, 8, 14, 18, 20, 25, 107, 140, 143, 146, 150, 153, 163–164, 170
  retrospective ideology in the Great Thebaid Revolt 64–65
Koinon 167, 187, 195–199
Krannon, Battle of 219
Kuhrt, Amélie 97, 101, 122

Labashi-Marduk 84
Labraunda, Sanctuary of Zeus 180, 184, 196
Lamian War 237, 239
Language
  as a form of resistance 64–65, 149–150, 219, 220
  in relation to identity 6, 182–183, 186, 192, 201
Laokritai 168
Legitimacy 9–10, 14, 80–86, 100, 119, 123, 187
  in a Jewish context 21, 53, 129–130, 142–144, 147
  in an Egyptian context 18, 65, 68, 150, 159, 161, 167, 172
Lehman Text 108
Letter of Aristeas 34
Leviticus 139
Literacy 129, 210
  in Ptolemaic Egypt 152, 169, 172
Livy 41, 112, 209, 215, 225, 226
Localism 91–92, 118–121, 149–151, 157–160, 170, 185–187, 195–202, 204, 207–211, 244
  concepts and terminology 15, 22–29, 121
  stress and decline of its Greek form 22–23, 205, 230
Lycia 184, 185, 188, 190
  ethnic self-consciousness 179, 180, 181, 182–183, 186–187, 190, 195, 197–199, 201–202

Lycopolis 60, 64, 68
Lycopolite Nome 59, 68
Lydia 181, 186, 187, 193, 194, 201
Lysias, Seleucid courtier 47–48
Lysimachus 203, 214–217, 220, 223, 224, 227

Ma, John 13
Maʿat
  concept of order and legitimacy in Egypt 150, 153
Maccabean Revolt 1, 15, 20–21, 33–56, 95–96, 125, 128, 131, 132, 133–134, 136–137, 138–147
  comparison with Great Thebaid Revolt 18, 72–73
  in relation to Hellenism 26, 44, 46, 112–113
  role of internecine conflict 42, 50, 56
  stakes and causes 44–47, 55–56
Macedonians
  as colonists 113, 119, 180–181, 194, 195, 229
  demographic impact 181, 187–188
  portrayal in literature 101, 103–107, 119, 133, 167–168, 211–212, 239
Maeonia 183
Manetho 8, 118
Manning, Joseph 5, 14, 70
Marcus Antonius 225
Marduk 80, 88–92, 104
Marxism 9, 10, 150
Materialism 9, 148, 149
Mattathias Maccabee 46, 141
McGing, Brian 5, 60, 148, 149, 152, 155, 159, 169, 171
Megasthenes, Seleucid courtier 78, 81
Memnon of Heraclea Pontica 23, 203–205, 212–219, 223–230
Memory, Collective
  as factor in the evaluation of foreign rulers 18–19, 77–79, 82–94, 142, 167
  as factor limiting the malleability of the past 18, 94
  concepts and terminology 78

local histories as constitutive and reflective of 208–212, 215
  pluralism of 20–21, 78, 128, 142–143, 144, 147
Menander 213
Menelaus, High Priest of Jerusalem 42, 50, 128
  treatment in Maccabees 130, 138, 142–144, 147
Milik, Józef Tadeusz 125, 134–135
Mithridates I of Parthia 232, 243
Mithridates VI of Pontus 224–229
Mithridatic Wars 189, 203, 224, 226
Momigliano, Arnaldo 78
Monumentalism
  in relation to cultural memory 164, 197–198, 201
Moyn, Samuel 12–13, 27
Multiculturalism
  relationship of Greek colonists and indigenous populations 113, 181, 236–239
  relationship of Hellenism to Judaism 21, 26, 44, 128–131
Multilingualism 7, 89, 98, 167, 169, 182–183

Nabonidus 80, 83, 84, 103
Nabopolassar 83, 87, 115
Nabu, Temple of 119
Nationalism
  in relation to Egypt 68–69, 148–149, 151–152, 158, 161–162, 171
  in relation to Judea 43–47, 52–56
  in relation to Mesopotamia 85, 95
  terminology and applications 5–6, 24–25, 151
Naucratis 61
Nebuchadnezzar I 90
Nebuchadnezzar II 79–82, 87, 115
  as model for later rulers 79–82, 88, 91, 101, 116, 123
  Jewish reception of 93
Nectanebo I 106, 162, 166
Neo-Babylonian Empire 18, 81, 83–85, 87, 115–116, 131

Nicanor, Seleucid courtier 39, 44, 49, 137
Noah, biblical figure 132, 143
Non-elites
  in relation to ideologies of revolt 153
Northern League, of Doric Greek *poleis* 23, 203–204, 220, 221
Nubia 61, 64
Nymphis of Heraclea Pontica 23, 204–205, 207, 212–225, 227–230

Olympia, location in Greece 218
Olympiodorus, Seleucid courtier 38–39
Omens 19, 110–111, 120
Onias III, High Priest of Jerusalem 36, 128, 130, 138, 141–143
Opis, Battle of 80
Oracle of the Potter 4, 21, 97, 103, 105, 150–152
Osiris
  as paradigm of Egyptian kingship 65–66, 150
  in relation to Ptolemaic ideologies 65
Otherness
  as discursive strategy 178–179, 188–194, 200

Parthia 14, 89, 91–92, 97, 110, 232, 234, 236, 239–240, 242–244
Pathyris 58, 62, 63, 67, 164
Peithon, Macedonian general 238–239
Pelusion, Battle of 206
Pentateuch 127
Perdiccas, Macedonian general 238–239
Pergamon, Great Altar of 191
Pericles of Limyra 180, 186
Persian Verse Account 80
Persica, of Ctesias 83
Persis 15, 25, 93
Pestman, P. W. 58, 59, 164
Petition of Petiese 62
Pharaoh 21, 25, 107, 151, 153–154, 157, 167–168, 173
  use as title in the Great Thebaid Revolt 17–18, 57–70, 149–150, 163, 172
Philetairos of Pergamon 183
Philochorus of Athens 211–212, 225
Philopoemen of Achaea 26
Photios, Byzantine compiler 204, 212, 214, 215, 217, 219, 224, 225, 226, 227, 228, 229, 230
Piracy 190
Pisidia 22, 179–186, 188–191, 195, 199, 201
Plato 219, 221
Pliny the Elder 113–114, 122
Poliadization 123, 185–186
Politai
  at Babylon 19, 107–113
Polis 26, 82, 108, 128, 130, 167, 207–212, 220–221, 223
  regional variations 185, 197
Pollock, Sheldon 9–10, 150
Polybius 15, 99, 112–113, 242
  concept of *symploke* 13, 207
  interpretation of Egyptian revolts 68–69, 153, 154, 161
Pompeius Trogus 23, 214, 231–235
Pontus 183, 189, 228
Prophecy
  as form of criticism 103–107, 137, 150–151
  in relation to apocalyptic literature 127
Prophecy of the Lamb 151
Prousias I of Bithynia 226–229
Ptah
  ideological significance under the Ptolemies 66–67, 163
Ptolemaeus, Seleucid courtier 34, 42
Ptolemaic Dynasty
  representations 65–66, 132, 146, 150–151, 153–154, 163, 207
Ptolemaic Empire
  administrative policies 7, 14, 70–72, 95, 148, 155–156, 165, 168–169, 170–172, 187, 195–197, 199

INDEX 303

integration of priesthoods into administrative framework 4, 71, 96, 152, 158, 159, 166
internal and external problems at the time of the Great Thebaid Revolt 13, 17-18, 60
Ptolemy Ceraunus 221, 222, 224
Ptolemy I 4, 34
Ptolemy II 34, 66
Ptolemy III 66, 67, 153, 167, 168, 213, 215
Ptolemy IV 58, 60, 65, 66, 153
taxation policies 69-70
Ptolemy V 58, 60-61, 63, 64, 69, 160
epithets 65-66
Ptolemy VI 23, 63, 154, 166, 206
Ptolemy VIII 63, 154, 220
Ptolemy IX 72
Ptolemy X 72
Publicani 228
Public Space
as location for criticism 159-170, 172-174
Pydna, Battle of 227

Qumran 125, 127, 134, 138, 146

Raphia Decree 153
Regionalism 177-202, 219-220
Religion
in relation to social and economic causes of revolt 1-2, 152
perseverance of indigenous forms 183, 186, 200
Reš, temple of Uruk 116
Resistance Literature 97, 103-107, 121, 134, 136, 140, 147, 212-224, 230
concept and applications 3, 20, 25, 125-128
Revolt
ancient terminologies 155
concepts and terminologies 1-16, 24-29, 44, 55, 148-149, 151-152, 161, 189
in relation to Egyptian concepts of statehood 18, 68

Revolt, Egyptian of 88 BCE 72, 163
Rhetoric 22, 192, 233, 235, 241, 245
relation to causes of indigenous revolt 95-96
Rhodes 195, 197, 199, 207, 208
Rome 15, 23, 41, 44, 50, 106, 111, 193, 194, 198, 204, 207, 209, 215, 226-230, 234, 242
Rostovtzeff, Michael 2, 171
Royal Cult 159
Ruin of Esagila Chronicle 119-120

Sargon of Akkad 117
Sartori, Andrew 12-13, 27
Scott, James 126
Scribes, Egyptian 61-63, 67, 70, 71, 72
Scylax of Caryanda 207
Sebennytos 60, 61, 71
Second Maccabees 20-21, 25, 28, 37, 39, 40-43, 45-49, 112, 128-131, 135-138, 146-147, 220
in relation to First Maccabees 41, 49, 141
Scipio Africanus, P. Cornelius 226
Second Philae Decree 57, 61, 62
Second Temple 142
Seleucia-on-the-Tigris 89, 91-92, 93, 102, 111, 113-114, 118, 119
Seleucid Empire
characterization in literature 18-19, 46-47, 78, 82-86, 101, 114-115, 119, 132-133, 141-142, 144-146, 216-224, 232, 239-245
fiscal and administrative structures in Judea 33-38, 41
in relation to local elites 1, 4, 5, 15-16, 26, 51-52, 55, 68, 96, 121-124, 204
policies and stability in Mesopotamia 91-94, 96-102
Seleucus I 22, 26, 203, 221
policies and reputation in Mesopotamia 113-120
Seleucus III 100

Seleucus IV 17, 36, 38, 50
Semiramis 85
Sennacherib 45, 84, 85
Septuagint 46
Seth, Egyptian deity
   in relation to Ptolemaic
      ideologies 150–151
Seven Wonders 80
Sherwin-White, Susan 97, 105
Sibylline Oracles 106
Simon Maccabee 52–55, 130, 137
   policies in relation to Seleucid
      power 17, 53–56
Slavery 34, 43
   role of slaves in revolt 193
Smith, Jonathan Z. 2, 8
Sogdiana 237–239
Solomon, biblical figure 46
Sparta 13, 207, 208, 219
Spitamenes of Sogdia 237
State-building 25, 57–58
   as element of the Great Thebaid
      Revolt 61–68
   role of Greeks in indigenous
      projects 13–14, 51–52, 70
Statehood 1, 36, 159, 161, 167, 172
   theories and their application to the
      ancient world 5
Stephanus of Byzantium 61, 214
Strabo 61, 113, 122, 154, 193, 225
Stratonicea 194, 196, 197
Subartu 116–117
Succession of Empires 83
   origins of concept 78
Suda, Byzantine encyclopedia 212–215, 219, 221
Šulgi Chronicle 117
Šulgi, Ur III King 116–117
   as avatar for Seleucus I 118, 124
Sumerian King List 99
Suzerainty 22, 33, 43, 53, 55–56
Symploke 13, 23, 207
Synchronism 23, 231–245
Syncretism 6
Syngeneia 193, 200

Syngraphophylax 170–172
Synods, Priestly 166
Syntaxis 42, 69, 70, 71

Tachos 106
Tacitus 111
Tanis 71
Taxation 34–35, 37–39, 42, 51–52, 54, 62, 69, 104, 108, 119, 144, 154, 163
   as potential cause for revolt 70–71, 148, 152, 155
Temple of Jerusalem 34–39, 45–48, 56, 126, 128–132, 138–139, 140, 141–147
   despoilment by Antiochus IV 41, 43, 141, 143, 145
Temples, Babylonian institution 79, 88, 98, 100, 101, 115, 116–118, 122, 123
   in relation to Seleucid power 19, 96, 106–107, 108–110, 112–113, 119–122
Temples, Egyptian institution 21, 62–63, 67, 151, 153, 156–169
   in relation to Ptolemaic power 17, 60, 69–72, 148, 152, 154
Thebaid 14, 16, 17, 23, 68–73, 166, 244
   increasing Ptolemaic presence 70–71
Thebes, in Egypt 58, 65, 163, 166, 170
   role in Great Thebaid Revolt 60–61, 66, 67, 71, 163, 172
Third Syrian War 240
Thompson, E. P. 148–149, 156
Thucydides 215, 225
Tiamat 90
Treaty of Apamea 41, 79, 192, 195
Tribute 34, 41, 42, 43, 53, 128, 154

Universalism 9–15, 24, 27, 152, 167, 173, 233–236
   in relation to Egyptian views on
      monarchy 68
Ur 116–118
Urbanization
   as vector of cultural and political
      change 113–118, 184–187
Uruk 7, 12, 19, 82, 83, 114–118, 121, 123

Uruk Prophecy 114, 115, 117
Usurpation 20, 80, 91, 105, 129–130, 144
 in relation to Ptolemaic power 68, 150
 in relation to Seleucid power 50, 52, 53, 68

Vandorpe, K. 70
Violence
 in relation to conflict over culture and identity 113, 121, 189–194

Weber, Max 9, 150

Xanthos 182, 184, 186, 189
Xerxes I 18, 80–81, 84, 85, 122, 170
Xerxes II 84

Zazakku, Babylonian official 109–110, 113
Zenon archive 155